Raise Happy Children...
Raise Them Saints!

By

Mary Ann Budnik

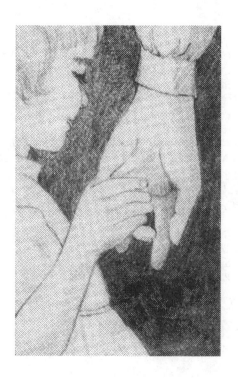

R.B. Media, Inc.

Springfield, IL

IMPRIMATUR: Most Reverend George J. Lucas
             Bishop of Springfield in Illinois
             June 26, 2002

The Imprimatur is a declaration that a book or pamphlet is considered to be free
from doctrinal or moral error.

First Edition: October 6, 2002

For additional copies of *Raise Happy Children Through A Happier Marriage,* or
for copies of Mary Ann Budnik's other books, *Raise Happy Children...Raise Them
Saints!, Raise Happy Children...Teach Them Virtues!, You Can Become A Saint!,
You Can Become A Saint! Workbook* and *Looking For Peace? Try Confession!*
and her *Why Suffer?* booklet contact:

R.B. Media, Inc.
154 Doral
Springfield, IL 62704
Phone: (217) 546-5261 Fax: (217) 546-0558
Website: www.rbmediainc.com
E-mail: MABudnik@worldnet.att.net

Library of Congress catalog card number: 2001117921
R.B. Media, Inc.: ISBN 0-9700021-3-0

This book is dedicated to my husband, Bob, who sacrificed himself, his time, and, all of his financial resources to raise our daughters saints. The final outcome now depends on their free will.

When other men were involved with sports and hobbies, Bob was teaching Mary Kate, Marianne, and Mary Terese their catechism in the evening after listening to them, playing with them, and reading them stories.

When offered a promotion that would advance his career but would necessitate relocation to another country, he instead took a lesser position. He felt it was more important that his daughters attend The Willows Academy, in the Chicago suburbs, where they would be taught the faith and morals of the Catholic Church. He choose the formation of their souls over his own career advancement.

When other men grew wealthy through financial investments, he invested all of his funds in private school tuition for his daughters, paying the equivalent of college tuition from kindergarten on.

Now that his daughters are raised, rather than relaxing and enjoying the "good life," Bob continues to give of himself, his time, and his complete financial support to bring my books and tapes to you. Any good that comes from these apostolates is the fruit of his sacrifice, not my words.

Acknowledgements

This book would not be possible if not for the help of:

- My husband, Bob, who sacrificed himself in countless ways so that this book could now be in your hands.

- My daughters, Mary Kate Stangel, Marianne Budnik, and Mary Terese Wills who permitted me to use them as examples, sometimes not too flattering, to make a point. They also acted as editors and advisers.

- Reverend Michael Giesler, STD, of the Prelature of the Holy Cross and Opus Dei who acted as my chief editor, theologian and coach.

- Reverend Edward J. Thein, Pastor of Holy Family Parish in Marietta, Georgia for permitting me to quote his homily notes.

- Frank J. O'Connell who provided the illustration for "Additional Helps" and Giedre Vaitys who provided the illustrations of the little girls. Giedre's illustrations were originally used in *Family Future Digest.*

- My copy editors, Nancy and Jim Hanlon, Carol Kelly, and Mary Kate Budnik Stangel. Their input and editing skills added the polish.

- Much gratitude goes to Kim Redington who gave me many of the resources listed in Appendix A and Carol Kelly for her extensive research on the Harry Potter books. Her research is detailed in Appendix C. Carol went from a devotee of Harry Potter to a staunch critic of the series. Appreciation is also extended to Lucy Retzenthaler of Ohio and Carol Carobi of Floria who also supplied me with valuable material on the Potter books.

- Mr. Thomas Monaghan for permitting me to interview him in Michigan.

- Dr. & Mrs. Peter Popovich for allowing me to interview them in regard to their experience with home schooling.

- Roseanna Hatke for permitting me to quote her teaching material.

- Katie Brown for allowing me to quote her paper on the "Effects of Music."

- Dr. David Isaacs of the University of Navarre in Pamplona, Spain, for permitting me to quote extensively his course material on family.

- Dick and Lou Prince who audiotaped Dr. Isaacs' course, "Parents and Their Adolescent Children," for us in Spain.

- Other resource material that I was permitted to use freely.

- Brother Francis Mary Kalvelage, F.I. for allowing me to use the material on the parents of saints that I previously wrote for his books.

- Scepter Publishers, Inc. for allowing me to quote many of their publications.

- My grandchildren (l-r) Michael, Matthew and Margaret Mary Stangel who are my cover children. They and their younger sisters and cousins are on my back cover. Top picture (l-r) Elizabeth, Michael, Matthew holding Kathryn and Margaret Mary Stangel. Bottom picture (l-r) Emma, Isabel and Noelle Wills.

- My readers who suggested this book, then sent audio tapes, videos, books and prayers. The latter kept me writing!

In writing this book I found inclusive language awkward. For this reason I use the tradition meaning of he/him as including men and women, boys and girls.

Table Of Contents

Study the parenting techniques of the parents of St. Thérèse, St. Padre Pio, St. Escrivá, St. Maximilian Kolbe, St. Thomas More, St. Jeanne-Francoise de Chantel and Alice of Montar. (All of Alice's children are either beatified or canonized.) See how their techniques contrasted with the example of the parents of the visionaries of La Salette, who were never canonized. Learn the formula for raising your children saints.

The character of a child is strongly influenced by faith. Learn how the Catholic faith/the lack of the faith changed the similar lives of billionaires Tom Monaghan, the founder of Domino's Pizza and Ted Turner, the founder of CNN.

There are numerous saintly families in the Church. Yours can be one too! Learn how to begin to raise your child a saint before birth. Discover the importance of naming a child. Find out fun ways to teach the faith pre-school through high school years and beyond. Study how to teach your children the importance of the Bible, the guardian angels, the lives of the saints, prayer, and Holy Mass. Tips are given on how to teach your child the value of self-sacrifice, to differentiate between "wants" and "needs."

CHAPTER 4
THE SACRAMENTS HELP CHILDREN TO GROW HOLY!

Using the example of the saints and the parents of saints, explore the importance of the seven sacraments. Why is Baptism necessary? When should a baby be baptized? What is the responsibility of godparents? At what age should a child make his First Confession? What should the child know? What age should a child make his First Communion? Learn how to develop love for the Eucharist in your children. Explore the gifts of the Holy Spirit, fruits of the Holy Spirit and how these gifts influence your childrens' daily lives in the Sacrament of Confirmation. Discover how to prepare your children for the Sacrament of Matrimony. Learn how to guide your children in their choice of a future spouse. The power of the priesthood is explored in Holy Orders. Tips are given as to how to encourage vocations in your family using the examples of the parents of saints. The Sacrament of the Sick is explained.

CHAPTER 5
WHICH METHOD OF EDUCATION IS BEST FOR YOUR CHILD?

Parents are the primary educators of their children. Learn why the saints and parents of saints put such effort into the education of their children. Learn how to select the right school or educational method by considering the pros and cons of educational choices: public, Catholic, private Catholic and home schooling. What are the rights and specific duties of parents in the matter of schooling? Consider the problems of the overprogrammed child. Discover the impact of negative outside influences on your children: computer, TV, radio, reading material, movies, music, food allergies. Study how to teach your children to live the spiritual and corporal works of mercy. Put together a reading program for your children that will teach virtues and goodness.

INTRODUCTION

Want to be happy? Strive to become holy.   Want happy children? Raise them to become saints. This is the theme of this second book in the *Raise Happy Children* series. For those who may not understand exactly what holiness is, John Paul II defines it in his Apostolic Letter, *Novo Millennio Ineunte*, as *the living reflection of the face of Christ.*

How does one become holy? We become holy through the infusion of God's life into our souls. We call this "grace." It is *grace that He [God] imparts to the soul [that]...make[s] it really, intrinsically pleasing and holy in His sight. The necessary condition for obtaining the infusion of that divine gift is faith, not a bare speculative faith, but a practical faith which through the love of God effects the observance of the commandments and the performance of other good works.*[1]

This is the type of faith *Raise Happy Children...Raise Them Saints!* will help you to instill in your children. Not only does the happiness of your children rely on their growing in sanctity but the re-evangelization of the world depends on the quality of their faith...not when they become adults but right now! Did you realize that it was children who brought the Catholic faith to Ethiopia? According to Church historian, H. Daniel-Rops, Frumentius and another unnamed child, both Christians, were traveling in a caravan with their parents. When the caravan was attacked, all were massacred except these two children.

---

[1] *The New Testament* [Confraternity of Christian Doctrine] (NY: Benziger Brothers, Inc. 1960. Footnote on p. 419.

Taken to Ethiopia, they were raised at court. They spoke *so persuasively about their faith that the king himself...desired to become a Christian.*[2] When Frumentius became an adult, he was consecrated a bishop by St. Athanasius, then returned to Ethiopia around 350 to established the Church in that country. Daniel-Rops further notes, *[i]t was he who founded the Church whose ancient traditions are one of the most direct links we possess between modern Christianity and the faith of the primitive Church.*[3] The spiritual formation you give to your children can have a similar or even greater impact.

It was a child who was responsible for the selection of the great St. Ambrose as bishop of Milan. At the time of his selection, Ambrose was a layman and not as yet <u>even</u> baptized. But he did have a reputation for justice and integrity. When the Catholic and Arian bishops met to select a bishop for Milan there arose such a bitter struggle that Ambrose, the governor, was called upon to resolve the conflict before it turned into a riot. Suddenly, a child's voice rang from the crowd surrounding the basilica, *Let Ambrose be our bishop!* The crowd picked up his cry. With public pressure mounting, the warring bishops selected him over his protests. It was this same St. Ambrose that brought St. Augustine to his senses and back into the Catholic Church. And speaking about St. Augustine, it was again a child who gave him the final push to convert. Augustine, tormented by the pull of grace to convert and the seductive pull of the world, was sitting in his garden one day. Sobbing over his struggle to convert he suddenly heard the voice of a child in the next garden chanting over and over, *"Go and read, Go and read." He leapt to his feet and open St. Paul; the pages fell open to Chapter XIII of Paul's Epistle to the Romans;* **"Let us pass our time honorably, as by the light of day, not in reveling and drunkenness, not in lust and wantonness, not in quarrels and rivalries. Rather, arm yourselves with the Lord Jesus Christ; spend no more thought on nature and nature's appetite"** *(Rom. 13, 13-14). The book fell from his hands...He was at peace in his soul. At last*

---

[2] H. Daniel-Rops, *The Church Of Apostles And Martyrs* (NY: E. P. Dutton & Co. Inc., 1960) p. 498.

[3] *Ibid.*

he understood.[4]

St. Martin of Tours, again living in the 300's, was responsible for the conversion of rural Europe. He was but a child when he converted to Christianity. His parents were pagans. While he longed to consecrate his life to Christ, his father forced him to join the Roman army when he was fourteen. One day while he was serving in France he encountered a shivering beggar without a coat. Martin took his military cloak and with his sword cut it in two to share with the beggar. That night Christ appeared to him holding the other half of his cloak. The next day Martin asked for and was granted a military discharge. He spent the rest of his life evangelizing Western Europe to the point that he is considered *the first of the great confessors of the West, and her [the Church] liturgy awards him a place equal to that of the Apostles...More than 4,000 parish churches in France are still dedicated to him...and 485 villages or townships bear his name.*[5]

Your influence, not only through personal example but also by exercising your duty as the primary educator of your children in the faith and morals of the Catholic Church, is beyond measure. St. Basil, who lived in the fourth century, was one of the great Fathers of the Eastern Church. He was the grandson of a martyr. His wealthy family, given the choice of renouncing their faith or abandoning their wealth and possessions, left their wealth to flee the persecution of Diocletian. His brothers are Sts. Gregory of Nyssa and Peter of Sebaste. The sacrifices of his family created a family tree of sanctity! St. Escrivá, the founder of the Prelature Opus Dei, was likewise influenced by the piety and good example of his parents and relatives. His grandmother, Constancia, always had a rosary in her hands. He learned from her example that *all our efforts must be based on unceasing prayer.*[6] What a powerful influence just these two families have had on the world! The holiness of your family can also positively impact the world. Give your children your example of piety, faithfulness, reverence,

---

[4] H. Daniel-Rops, *The Church In The Dark Ages* (New York: E.P. Dutton & Co., Inc., 1959) p. 12.

[5] *The Church Of Apostles And Martyrs, Op. Cit.*, p. 501.

[6] Andrés Vázquez de Prada, *The Founder of Opus Dei, The Life of Josemaría Escrivá* , Vol. 1 (Princeton: Scepter, 2001) p. 37.

religious zeal for souls and your daily struggle to practice the various virtues. Let them see you try and fail then try again. This is how you teach them perseverance in the spiritual life. When your prayer becomes dry or an effort let your children see your constancy in this spiritual struggle. Your effort, more than your spiritual successes will help to propel them along the path of holiness. A woman told Bl. Francis Xavier Seelos (1819-1867), a German immigrant to the U.S., that she couldn't understand a word of his homily but his effort to try to preach in English spiritually moved her more than any words.

On the other hand, giving bad example can destroy the faith of your children and others, as well as change the course of history. In **Raise Happy Children Through A Happier Marriage**, I discussed how once Constantine came to power, the persecution against Christians ceased in the Roman Empire. Unfortunately, this happy state of affairs did not last for long. His nephew, Julian, a Christian from birth, although wanting to become a priest when he was sixteen years old, was surrounded by bad example. One of his close teachers changed his religion four times. Next he fell under the evil influence of an apostate bishop who had become an Arian. To make matters even worse, fellow Christians murdered his parents to prevent his father from becoming the Roman Emperor. Following these murders, Julian and his half-brother, Gallus, were exiled. Is it any wonder that when he escaped from exile, then rose to power as emperor he rejected Christianity, made neo-paganism the religion of the realm, and is known in history as Julian the Apostate for his persecution of Christians? Likewise look at the disorder, as well as the suffering, that Luther, Henry VIII, the French Revolutionaries, and Hitler afflicted on the world by their lack of fidelity to Christ and the Catholic Church. Consider the dysfunctional families that surround us today. It is usually the lack or loss of faith in one or more family members that caused the destruction of the family bringing unhappiness and suffering to all the members. Consider the moral epidemic of abortion and contraception that destroys millions of lives annually. To put this into better perspective, the number of babies aborted every two days matches the number of lives lost in the terrorist attack

September 11, 2001. This horror can only flourish in families and in societies that have lost their faith in God.

St. Augustine discovered, then taught, that *Christianity [was] the most comforting of religions for man's soul, and the most satisfying for his mind, but it was also, in the order of things on this earth, the answer to everything.*[7] That is precisely why he wrote his spiritual classic, **The City of God.** Augustine learned from his rebellion against God that happiness could only be acquired through union with God. Furthermore, he wrote that government is to complement and be consistent with the ideals of our spiritual destiny. So much for separation between God and state! When governments honor the laws of God there is peace, prosperity, and happiness for their citizens. St. Henry and St. Louis, two powerful kings, became saints by uniting their kingdoms and their own souls to God.

But governments are made up of people. Our morality and ethical standards, or the lack of them, personally influence our government for the good or for evil. Therefore, when a government violates the law of God, it brings a plague of sufferings down upon its citizens. In the **Old Testament** the Prophet Baruch enlightens the Israelites as to the cause of their sufferings and captivity: ***Justice is with the Lord, our God; and we today are flushed with shame...[We] have sinned in the Lord's sight and disobeyed Him. We have neither heeded the voice of the Lord, our God, nor followed the precepts which the Lord set before us...[E]ach one of us went off after the devices of his own wicked heart, served other gods, and did evil in the sight of the Lord, Our God*** (*Baruch* 1: 16, 22). A stubborn people, he had to further exhort them: ***You were sold to the nations...because you angered God...Fear not, my children; call out to God! He who brought this upon you will remember you. As your hearts have been disposed to stray from God, turn now...to seek Him; For He who has brought disaster upon you will, in saving you, bring you back enduring joy*** (*Baruch* 4:6, 27-29).

In the **New Testament** St. Paul takes up where Baruch left off:

---

[7] *The Church In The Dark Ages, Op. Cit.*, p. 42.

The wrath of God is being revealed from heaven against all ungodliness and wickedness of those men who in wickedness hold back the truth of God...In fact, whatever can be known about God is clear to them; He Himself made it so. Since the creation of the world...God's eternal power and divinity, have become visible, recognized through the things He has made. Therefore these men are inexcusable. They certainly had knowledge of God, yet they did not glorify Him as God or give Him thanks...In consequence, God delivered them up in their lusts, to unclean practices; they engaged in the mutual degradation of their bodies, these men who exchanged the truth of God for a lie and worshiped and served the creature rather than the Creator...And as they have resolved against possessing the knowledge of God, God has given them up to a reprobate sense, so that they do what is not fitting, being filled with all iniquity, malice, immorality, avarice, wickedness; being full of envy, murder, contention, deceit, malignity; being whisperers, detractors, hateful to God, irreverent, proud, haughty, plotters of evil; disobedient to parents, foolish, dissolute, without affection, without fidelity, without mercy...And not only do they do these things, but they applaud others doing them (**Romans** 1:18-25, 28-32). Wow, see all the suffering that evolves when one refuses to follow God's universal call to holiness?

In our own age, Pope John Paul II repeatedly urges us to seek God if we value happiness. Likewise he, along with Mother Teresa and Mother Angelica warned us what would happen if we failed to convert. The terrorist attacks that disrupted our lives, our economy and our standard of living is the fruit of our violence against the unborn. Contrast the economic prosperity, standard of living, freedom from fear, and the moral climate prior to the legalization of abortion and widespread contraception use to the world we live in now. Need I say more? Blessed Henry Suso, a German Dominican, was privileged to receive this interlocution from Divine Wisdom. In it, God explained to St. Henry how we mortals search for happiness in all the wrong places, avoiding joy out of fear. *They [we] are stricken with spiritual blindness;*

the satisfaction which they [we] so madly strive for, thinking to find pleasure and happiness therein, always evades them. Before one delight comes to them, ten sorrows overtake them, and the more they follow their concupiscences the farther away from satisfying peace do they run.

It is indeed true that irreligious hearts are fated for fear and terror. Even the short-lived joy that is allotted to them is bitter because they acquire it with difficulty, are uneasy while enjoying it, and rancorous when deprived of it.

The world is full of faithlessness, duplicity and inconstancy; so-called friendship is broken when selfish desires have been fulfilled. This, in short, is what it all amounts to: no human heart ever yet found true and lasting love, happiness, or peace in creatures.[8]

Rather than suffering and sorrow, St. Paul promises **to all...called to holiness, grace and peace from God our Father and the Lord Jesus Christ** (**Romans** 1:7). You have the ability to restore your life and your country to greatness and happiness through your own and your children's quest to grow holy...to become saints.

Why have I brought happiness, holiness and government together? The present and future happiness of your children begins with their unity with God but it also depends on their ability to evangelize and positively influence the culture in which they live, the schools that they attend, their future professions, their marriages/families and ultimately the government of their country.

A vibrant, living faith, that fills one's soul with grace, leaves its "footprints" of peace, joy and happiness everywhere...even in a culture's sculpture. Daniel-Rops, notes that after Constantine, the first Christian Roman Emperor, sculpture even changed: *[I]t is interesting to note a change of expression as compared with preceding ages. Whereas so many earlier statues show faces with care-worn, tired features and drooping mouths, those of the fourth century display an extraordinary sweetness and serenity of*

[8] Bl. Henry Suso, *The Exemplar, Vol. Two,* Sr. M. Ann Edward, O.P., OSA, (Dubuque: The Priory Press, Tran. 1962).

expression.[9]

On the other hand, without God unhappiness permeates every aspect of society. Daniel-Rops gives the following description of the fall of the Roman Empire: *Among ordinary people, the consciousness of an impending threat was expressed in a general feeling of unease...[P]roof that "things were going badly" was afforded by the obvious state of economic disequilibrium, whose consequences were felt by even the most humble of citizens...The monetary crisis had become chronic; inflation, the black market, devaluation—all the symptoms of a sick regime were there...[T]he Romans themselves were working less and less...[The] State was there...with its crushing system of taxation...According to St. John Chrysostom, many fathers could be seen selling their daughters, in order to discharge their debts...No one could work or travel without the permission of some inspector or other...[A]ll human values had collapsed. Morality now existed only in a few places, which were like islands, surrounded by waves of sludge and scandal... Debauchery, depopulation and general dishonesty were everywhere; it was useless to insist on higher standards. As for creative values, they followed the same downward curve of decadence.* There was *excess and vulgarity* in the arts.[10] Astrology, the occult with its emphasis on the practice of magic [Harry Potter isn't anything new], and the spread of the Eastern religions likewise played a part in the destruction of the Empire. Then he observes: *Everything that comprises human grandeur falls apart when the human personality is mortally stricken.*[11]

It was at this point that Christianity stepped in to give the world not only new direction but also hope. By infusing into the decadent culture *the Way, the Truth, and the Life* anchored to faith, grace and the practice of virtues, our great Western civilization was created.

Tragically, our great Western civilization is now suffering from the same spiritual cancer as the Roman Empire. Its demise began with the Protestant Revolt. As Fr. John Hardon, S.J., observed,

---

[9] *The Church Of Apostles And Martyrs, Op. Cit.*, p. 537.

[10] *Ibid.,* p. 550-553.

[11] *Ibid.,* p. 553.

the virtue of faith is lost when an article of faith or morality is rejected. This loss of faith spreads out over the world like an epidemic, silently and quietly eating away at the souls of mankind until the symptoms break forth as they did in the Roman Empire, the French Revolution, Nazism, Communism, and in our secular culture. The growth of Protestantism and other religions depends on the loss of faith of Catholics. It is the loss of faith that separates a soul from the truth deposited within the Catholic Church. It's so common, but still shocking, to be introduced to "former" Catholics or hear from Protestants that their parents or grandparents were Catholics. Sadly, these people do not realize that they are destroying not only their culture but their own personal happiness by abandoning the Bride of Christ. Those who want to mold the world for their own self-interests acutely realize that the fastest way to destroy a culture is to destroy the Catholic faith of its people. We have seen this in Catholic countries destroyed by communism or secularism. Mexican Archbishop Javier Lozano Barragan, points to a report written in 1969 for President Richard Nixon by Nelson A. Rockefeller as one such example. In this shocking report Rockefeller maintains that since Vatican II *"the Catholic Church is no longer a trustworthy ally of the United States and the guarantee of social stability in the [South American] continent." The reported insisted on "the need to replace Catholics with other Christians in Latin American," by "supporting Christian [Protestant] fundamentalist groups, and churches such as Moon and Hare Krishna."*[12] Why would Rockefeller attack the Catholic Church so strongly? Without the acceptance of the whole, complete truth, morality and ethics become relative. Anything and everything becomes acceptable. And so unhappiness grows, lives are destroyed, families fall apart then government easily falls into the hands of the corrupt and the depraved.

Our second U.S. President, John Adams, a Protestant and one of the founders of the United States, attended Sunday Mass out of curiosity while a member of the Continental Congress in Philadelphia. He was so awe struck by our liturgy that he was puzzled by the success of the Protestant Revolt.

---

[12] Zenit August 1, 2001.

Just as Christianity supplanted the decadence of the Roman Empire with Western civilization, by instilling a deep, vibrant, living Catholic faith within the souls of your children you will supplant the decadence of your culture with a renewed, re-energized Christianity that will influence government, art, theatre, literature but most of all the hearts of everyone they touch. Not only will statues begin smiling again, but so will you and your children. John Paul II notes: *Sometimes when we look at the young, with the problems and weaknesses that characterize them in contemporary society, we tend to be pessimistic. The Jubilee of Young People, however, changed that, telling us that young people, whatever their possible ambiguities, have a profound longing for those genuine values which find their fullness in Christ. Is not Christ the secret of true freedom and profound joy of heart? Is not Christ the supreme friend and the teacher of all genuine friendship? If Christ is presented to young people as He really is, they experience Him as an answer that is convincing and they can accept His message, even when it is demanding and bears the mark of the cross. For this reason, in response to their enthusiasm, I did not hesitate to ask them to make a radical choice of faith and life and present them with a stupendous task: to become "morning watchmen" at the dawn of the new millennium.*[13]

By virtue of your children's Baptism they are called to be holy...to be saints. It is your responsibility to train them, then lead them along the path of holiness. Doesn't look too promising from your viewpoint? Consider this analogy that struck me as I read an explanation for fall color in a brochure. The writer asks the question, *Why do the tree leaves change colors?...Actually, all the colors you see in fall are present in the leaves throughout the entire year. The green chlorophyll masks the red, yellow and orange. When autumn occurs, a waterproof tissue layer forms within each leaf; this cuts the flow of water and nutrients causing the leaf cells to die. When this happens, the green chlorophyll disintegrates to reveal the wonderful fiery colors within.* The effects of original sin likewise mask the powerful spiritual potential your children receive in the graces of Baptism. It's through the

---

[13] John Paul II, *Novo Millennio Ineunte*, #9.

scorching heat of life, the torrent of sorrows, the sunshine of graces obtained through the reception of the sacraments and their prayer life that enriches, energizes and brings growth to the hidden graces of Baptism within your children's souls. Just as the death of the leaves bring out their breathtaking beauty, when your children stand before God at the moment of death He will disclose either the beauty of their soul or its lost potential.

John Paul II reiterates that the *gift of holiness is offered to all the baptized. But the gift in turn becomes a task, which must shape the whole of Christian life:* **"This is the will of God, your sanctification"** *(1 Thes.* 4:3*). It is a duty which concerns not only certain Christians: "All the Christian faithful, of whatever state or rank, are called to the fullness of the Christian life and to the perfection of charity."...It implies the conviction that, since Baptism is a true entry into the holiness of God through incorporation into Christ and the indwelling of His Spirit, it would be a contradiction to settle for a life of mediocrity, marked by a minimalist ethic and a shallow religiosity. To ask catechumens: "Do you wish to receive Baptism?" means at the same time to ask them: "Do you wish to become holy?" It means to set before them the radical nature of the Sermon on the Mount:* **"Be perfect as your heavenly Father is perfect"** *(Matt.* 5:48*).*

As the Council itself explained, this ideal of perfection must not be misunderstood as if it involved some kind of extraordinary existence, possible only for a few "uncommon heroes" of holiness. The ways of holiness are many, according to the vocation of each individual. I thank the Lord that in these years He has enabled me to beatify and canonize a large number of Christians, and among them many lay people who attained holiness in the most ordinary circumstances of life. The time has come to repropose wholeheartedly to everyone this <u>high standard of ordinary Christian living:</u> *the whole life of the Christian community and of Christian families must lead in this direction. It is also clear, however, that the paths to holiness are personal and call for a genuine "training in holiness."*[14] This training is the responsibility of you and your spouse, not the Catholic school.

---

[14] *Ibid.,* #30-31.

Think your children are too strong-willed and obstinate to become saints? Some of the greatest saints had the same characteristics but with prayer and formation they turned around. We will discuss St. Thérèse's sister, Léonie, in Chapter 1. For now consider the following description of the great St. Augustine: *As a boy he was uncouth, undisciplined, and had little taste for serious studies. His intelligence, which was much above the average, persuaded him that it was quite pointless to make more than the minimum effort, and his hot blood would suffer no restraints...[N]o one could do anything with him.*[15] God's grace is freely available. The only thing lacking in your child is his will, his drive, his perseverance. Will and drive can be trained and perseverance taught.

Is the health of your children too fragile to strive for holiness? Few great saints actually had robust health. In fact, most of the saints suffered from ill health. H. Daniel Rops names some saints who accomplished great things despite poor health such as St. Paul, St. Bernard, St. Ignatius, and St. Augustine. Augustine was plagued with chronic insomnia, asthma and bronchitis. Other people who became saints despite poor health are St. Escrivá, St. Catherine of Siena, St. Thérèse, St. Maximilian Kolbe and St. Teresa of Avila. It is possible to achieve spiritual greatness with a sick body!

Yes, even teens have the capacity to become saints if guided properly. John Paul II told youth gathered in Rome: *For a long time, salt was...used to preserve food. As the salt of the earth, you are called to preserve the faith, which you have received, and to pass it on, intact to others. Your generation is being challenged in a special way to keep safe the deposit of faith.*

Discover your Christian roots, learn about the Church's history, deepen your knowledge of the spiritual heritage that has been passed on to you, follow in the footsteps of the witnesses and teachers who have gone before you! Only by staying faithful to God's commandments, to the Covenant which Christ sealed with His blood poured out on the Cross will you be the apostles and witnesses of the new millennium...

---

[15] *The Church In The Dark Ages, Op. Cit.,* p. 5.

Dear young people, do not be content with anything less than the highest ideals!...If you have an ardent desire for the Lord you will steer clear of the mediocrity and conformism so widespread in our society...Let the Gospel be the measure and guide of life's decisions and plans! Then you will be missionaries in all that you do and say, and wherever you work and live you will be signs of God's love, credible witnesses to the loving presence of Jesus Christ. Never forget: "No one lights a lamp and then puts it under a bushel" (Matt. 5:15)!

Just as salt gives flavor to food and light illumines the darkness, so too holiness gives full meaning to life and makes it reflect God's glory. How many saints, especially young saints, can we count in the Church's history! In their love for God their heroic virtues shone before the world, and so they became models of life which the Church has held up for imitation by all. Let us remember only a few of them: Agnes of Rome, Andrew of Phu Yen, Pedro Calugsod, Josephine Bakhita, Thérèse of Lisieux, Pier Giorgio Frassati, Marcel Callo, Francisco Castello Aleu or again Kateri Tekakwitha, the young Iroquois called the "Lily of the Mohawks". Through the intercession of this great host of witnesses, may God make you too, dear young people, the saints of the third millennium![16]

The steps toward holiness are really quite simple. Bl. Angela Maria Truszkowska (1825-1800) began by making visits to the Blessed Sacrament and helping the poor while still a child. Once she hit the teens, she made the commitment to be the first person to arrive for early morning Mass. She attended socials and balls but her path to sanctity finally led her to found the Felician Sisters. High-spirited Bl. Philippa De Chantemilian (1412-1451) lost her devout mother when she was fifteen. She loved to dress fashionably. Although she enjoyed attending parties, she left them early so she could visit the Blessed Sacrament. Over time she gave up her beautiful clothes, vowing to live a simple life of lay celibacy. She devoted her time to prayer and to caring for the poor and sick.

Give your children the example of the saints as well as your

---

[16] Zenit, August 3, 2001.

own example. Several readers told me charming anecdotes about their children. One mom in Wichita, Kansas related how she overheard her eleven-year-old daughter telling a friend, *my mom does everything for the honor and glory of God.* In Springfield, Illinois, a convert from Buddhism, Deena Bell, told me that her five-year-old daughter, Mona, asks, *Mom, when are you going to become a saint?* Her mother responds by saying, *Monica, I'm trying everyday.* Tom Gustafson, also of Springfield, told me how his four-year-old asked, *you're best buddies with God, aren't you, Dad?* These parents, by striving for sanctity are teaching their children the purpose of life. Remember, you have to train your children to be saints. One does not inherit sanctity!

Be aware that you will meet with contradictions, negative outside pressures, and the forces of anti-Catholicism but so did all the saints. As St. Escrivá reminded people, there is *no day without a cross!* There will even be days when it seems that there is not even a minute without a cross. But on those days take heart because you are following in the bloody footsteps of Christ.

Remember, the early Christians were victorious despite the persecution and obstacles they endured. Don't let "being different" deter you from doing what God expects of you. With the grace of God and perseverance you will be victorious. But Jesus warns us, **Whoever puts his hand to the plow but keeps looking back is unfit for the reign of God** (*Luke* 9:62). Once you begin, you must persevere. What scandal you give your children should you become discouraged and give up!

Daniel-Rops reflects: *Societies in decline are invariably fascinated by their deadliest enemies and, whether they know it or not, are influenced by them.*[17] Catholicism is the deadly enemy of our dying, humanistic society. Instill a vibrant, living faith in your children now then watch them change the world for God!

Mary Ann Budnik, October 6, 2002
The Canonization of Josemaría Escrivá

---

[17]*The Church Of Apostles And Martyrs, Op. Cit.,* p. 561.

CHAPTER 1

THE DOS AND DON'TS OF PARENTING

"The saints are like a group of trees, each bearing different fruit, but watered from the same source. The practices of one saint differ from those of another, but it is the same spirit that works in all of them."   St. John

The Cure of Ars, St. John Vianney believed that *if a child goes to hell because of the neglect of his parents to teach him his faith, you can be sure the parents will follow.* If this is true, then surely the converse is also true, as we see in the example of the <u>parents</u> of saints. But before we begin, let's briefly consider the importance of God's grace in this great adventure to raise our children saints.

Fr. Peter-Thomas Rohrbach, O.C.D. reminds us: *According to Catholic theology, habitual grace is a created gift of God which inheres in the soul and makes man, to some degree, a participator in the Divine Nature. The person possessing grace, therefore, has been raised to a new plane of existence on which he lives and operates. There is, within him, a new source of life—in act, a new kind of life—and it has been popularly explained by saying that there is as much difference between a man who possesses grace and one who does not as there is between a man and an animal.*

The saint lives this life of grace completely, to an eminent and heroic degree, allowing it to become the source of strength for his spiritual activities and the final motivation for them. Thus, the saint's biographer is confronted with the added difficulty of studying two lives—the human life and the life of grace—in order to arrive at a full understanding of the complete person. The problem is compounded by the fact that, in the saint, there is no cleavage, no dichotomy, between these two lives. The saint does not operate sometimes under the force of his human nature, and at other times under the impulse of grace; rather, these two lives are fused into one so that, while remaining a complete human being, the saint is continually operating under the influence of divine grace. In observing a saint, then, we are witnessing God's activity in the human soul. And this is what intrigues us and inspires us—we watch someone like us struggling through our poor human clay until he emerges to touch the stars, to see God, to live with Him. We are observing, as the old peasant said of the Cure of Ars, "God in a man."[1]

In my previous books, I explained how each of us is given a specific mission in life by God that only we can perform. Only we have the ability and are given the graces to perform this "specific mission." This mission is a component of our call to become saints in the place, profession, and circumstances in which God has placed us. Hans Urs Von Balthasar explains how we are to become saints along an individualized path: *The mission which each individual receives contains within itself the form of sanctity which has been granted to him and is required of him. In following that mission he fulfils his appropriate capacity for sanctity. This sanctity is essentially social, something outside the arbitrary disposition of any individual. For each Christian God has an Idea which fixes his place within the membership of the Church; this Idea is unique and personal, embodying for each his appropriate sanctity. There is no danger that it will not prove high enough or broad enough in any instance. Indeed, it is so sublime, so intimately bound to divine infinity that it is perfectly achieved by no one except Mary. The*

[1] Peter-Thomas Rohrbach, O.C.D., *The Search for St. Therese* (Garden City, NY: Hanover House, 1961) pp. 25-26.

Christian's supreme aim is to transform his life into this Idea...[2]

The Venerable Martins

Let's study how saintly parents raised their children to be holy...to become saints. We will begin with the Martin family who gave us St. Thérèse of the Child Jesus. St. Thérèse achieved the exalted position of Doctor of the Church by drawing on the spiritual formation she received from her parents, Louis and Zélie Guérin Martin, and her elder sisters, Pauline and Marie, following her mother's death. As proof that *God gave me [Thérèse] a father and a mother more worthy of Heaven than of earth,* her parents have been declared Venerable. But even before the Church recognized their holiness, a pilgrim scratched on their gravestones in pencil: *Thank you, dear Christian parents, for giving us a saint to look after us.* While their youngest daughter, Thérèse is canonized, if you read the biographies of her four sisters, they likewise were very holy women.

Her Mother[3]

Zélie Marie Guérin, the mother of St. Thérèse, was the second of three children. The eldest in her family was her sister, Marie-Louise, and the youngest was her brother, Isidore. The Guérin family tree was one of staunch faithfulness to the Catholic faith even in times of cruel persecution. (We will explore this later in Chapter 3.) Although raised in a devout Catholic family, Zélie's young life was not easy: *My childhood and youth were shrouded in sadness; our mother...did not know how to treat me, so...I suffered deeply.* Still, the faith and pious practices taught in her home led both her and her sister, Marie-Louise, to seek religious vocations. Her sister, at the age of twenty-nine, was accepted by the Visitation convent at Le Mans. Upon entering she told the superior, *I have come here to be a saint!* Although

---

[2] Han Urs von Balthasar, translated by Donald Nicholl, *Therese of Lisieux, The Story of a Mission* (New York: Sheed and Ward, 1954) pp. xii-xiii.

[3] Mary Ann Budnik, "Heroic Parents—Models For Our Times," *St. Therese—Doctor of the Little Way* (New Bedford: Friars of the Immaculate, 1997) pp. 35-44.

separated by miles, the two sisters kept closely in touch through frequent letters. When Pauline and Marie Martin went away to school, they were enrolled in the Visitation Convent School so that their aunt could closely supervise their activities and friendships, keeping their mother informed of all details.

Isidore, high-spirited and spoiled by his mother, worried his two sisters. He began studies to become a doctor but dropped out to become a pharmacist. His plans to marry a wealthy girl worried Zélie who valued the quality of virtues over money for his future spouse. Fortunately he eventually married a young woman who not only was virtuous but also wealthy. He eventually took over his father-in-law's thriving pharmacy business, became a leading citizen of Lisieux, and a devout Catholic. It was to Isidore and his wife, Celine, that the widowed Louis Martin turned for help in raising his daughters, hence the move of the Martin family from Alençon to Lisieux following Zélie's death. Later, Isidore's daughter, Marie, joined the same convent of Carmelites as her Martin cousins.

Living in an age of strong anti-clericalism and anti-Catholicism, Isidore knew the importance of Catholic schools in educating youth in the faith. He purchased a building and helped to fund a school for girls along with financially supporting a boys' school run by the Salesians. At the urging of his niece, Celine Martin, he took over the local Catholic newspaper, *Le Normand,* directing it, writing long apologetic articles for it and supporting it financially. He understood the power of the press in molding opinion. The Carmel, where his nieces and daughter were cloistered, struggled financially. It was to him that they turned when they had no money for food. He donated thousand of dollars in francs, over and above his regular contributions to keep the Carmel financially viable. It was he also who paid for the printing of his niece Thérèse Martin's autobiography, **Story of a Soul.** By preserving the letters of his sister and nieces, Isidore gives us a deep insight into the Martin family.

A Dilemma: A Religious Vocation Or Marriage?

When Zélie Guérin asked for permission to enter the Daughters of Charity, at the age of eighteen or nineteen-years-old, the superior told her God did not will her to become a religious. Disappointed, she prayed: *Lord, since, unlike my sister, I am not worthy to be your bride, I will enter the married state in order to fulfill Your holy will.* God answered her prayer by sending her Louis Martin for her husband.

While Zélie waited for God to arrange her marriage she prayed to Our Lady for direction as to her uncertain future. December 8th, 1851, she received her answer in the form of an interior locution: *See to the making of Pont d'Alencon lace.* She immediately entered a lace-making school, quickly mastering the intricate art in order to begin her business, which proved a successful and lucrative career. It was here also that she met her future mother-in-law, Marie-Anne Martin, who immediately decided that Zélie would be the perfect wife for her son Louis. Later in life, her daughter, Celine, described Zélie as a woman who *had a superior intelligence and extraordinary energy. Nothing was too difficult for her.* Another daughter, Pauline, agreed: *My mother was abnegation personified; she had an extraordinary energy.*[4]

Her Father

Louis Martin, Thérèse's father, was one of five children. His father, like Zélie's, was a soldier, not only of France but also of Christ. But again, we will discuss this later in Chapter 3.

Louis, besides being a handsome man, was well read, witty and cultured. He enjoyed gardening, hunting, fishing, socializing, singing and traveling. His love of traveling took him as far as Constantinople. Even during his leisurely pursuits he thought of others. His fishing catch went to the convent of Poor Clares to supplement their meager diet. But before all else, he put God and prayer. He purchased a piece of property that was to become his retreat called Le Pavilion. It was there

---

[4] *The Search for St. Thérèse, Op. Cit.,* p. 45.

in the tower where he could read and pray or putter in the garden that surrounded the building.

Gifted with artistic skills, he decided upon a clock and watch-making career. While apprenticed in Strasbourg, he saved the son of his father's friend from drowning but was unable to bring this lax Catholic family back to the faith. He felt they were *pursuing their earthly way without casting a thought to what awaits them at the end.*

Louis sought to enter the monastery of the Great St. Bernard but the Prior told him to first learn Latin and then re-apply. After a year and a half of unsuccessful private tutoring in Latin (120 lessons), Louis resumed his career as a clock and watchmaker and later as a jeweler. This time he studied his craft in Paris. While in Paris, Louis was approached to join a "philanthropic club" that turned out to be a branch of freemasonry. Louis, indignant over the deception of his friends, refused to join. Another time a group of his friends decided to have a séance. At first he refused to take part because of the demonic element involved. He finally agreed to be a passive spectator, all the while praying that if the demonic was involved the attempt would fail, which it did.

Louis had a reputation of doing everything with patience, order, neatness, and precision. His tedious and precise work he did well, offering it to God. Proof of his skillfulness is in the fact that his watches still ran long after his death. Although absorbed by his profession, he set strict priorities, God first and everything else in the proper order. On Sundays, his shop was closed in order to keep holy the Sabbath. Despite the fact that it was the custom of the country people to come to town on Sunday to shop, he refused to buy or sell on Sunday although this cost him business. After his marriage, when his growing family brought increased financial concerns, he continued to strictly observe Sunday as a day of prayer and rest. Friends suggested that he keep a side door open if he wanted to keep the appearance that he was closed.   Louis refused by saying, *I would rather have the blessings of God [rather than money].* His wife, Zélie, believed that Louis' eventual prosperity was linked to his strict observance of Sunday: *I can only attribute the easy circumstances he enjoys to a special blessing, the reward of his faithful observance of Sunday...All those, perfect or imperfect, who faithfully observe the Lord's Day, succeed in their undertakings and in the end, by one means or another, become rich.*   In justice, he paid his bills and salaries promptly.   He never lived beyond his means.

Louis Martin was also a volunteer fireman, who not only saved a woman's life but on another occasion, his parish church from completely burning down. A strong swimmer, he saved several people from drowning. During the Franco-Prussian War he was a military scout in the woods near Alençon. When forced to house German soldiers, he was firm with them. When one stole an item from his shop, he wrestled with him and ejected him from the shop. Next he reported him to his commander. When he found that the soldier was going to be shot, he asked for his life to be spared. He was also the founder of the Catholic Club in town. His life was certainly well-rounded.

Mr. Martin, not bothered by human respect, always tipped his hat when passing a church, and would kneel down in the street when the Blessed Sacrament passed by in procession. During one such procession, he even removed the hat of a man who sneered as the monstrance processed down the street. Likewise, it was Louis who made sure that anyone dying in the neighborhood had a priest present to give the last sacraments.

In describing her father, Celine Martin notes: *When I want to imagine St. Joseph, I think of my father. His heart had an exceptional tenderness towards us, and he lived for us.*[5]   Abbe Dumaine insists, *He was esteemed by everybody; he was a perfect, honest man.* His daughter, Celine, agrees: *My father had an admirable charity for his neighbor, and he never said the least unkind thing about anyone. He excused everybody's faults and never permitted us to criticize anybody. He had a profound veneration for all priests. It was said of him that he was a saint.*[6] Pope Benedict XV called Louis *a true model of a Christian parent.*[7]

[5] Fr. Stephane-Joseph Piat, OFM, *The Story of a Family* (Rockford:Tan,1994),p. 45.
[6] *Ibid.*, p. 47.   [7] *Ibid.*, p. 55.

For Thérèse, who lost her mother at the age of four, her father became the center of her world. *Thérèse loved him, almost idolized him...her relationship to him taught her that obedience and love are indivisible, because they are ultimately one. Through her father's authority she comes to understand what God's authority means. She looks towards her father; her father looks towards God, and so she learns to look to God.*[8]

The Marriage Made By Heaven

Crossing the bridge of Saint Leonard, Zélie passed a distinguished looking young man. Glancing at him, she heard interiorly: *This is he whom I have prepared for you.* Introduced shortly thereafter, the couple was married three months later on July 13th, 1858. Louis was thirty-five and Zélie was twenty-seven years old. It was definitely a love-match.

When Zélie visited her brother in Lisieux she wrote to her husband: *My Dear Louis...I feel just like the fish you take out of water; they are no longer in their element and must perish...I am with you all day in spirit, and say to myself: "Now he is doing such and such a thing." I long to be with you, Louis dear. I love you with all my heart and I feel my affection doubled by being deprived of your company. I could not live apart from you...I embrace you as I love you. The little girls wish me to tell you that they are enjoying themselves at Lisieux and send you a big hug.*[9]

While on a business trip, Louis wrote to Zélie: *Dearest, I cannot arrive at Alençon before Monday. The time passes slowly, for I long to be with you. I need not say I was very pleased to receive your letter, except that I see by it that you are overtiring yourself. So I recommend calm and moderation, above all in your lace work...Once more, do not worry so much. With God's help, we shall manage to keep up a nice little home...I kiss you all lovingly, whilst awaiting the pleasure of being with you again. I hope Marie and Pauline are being very good! Your husband and true friend who loves you forever.*[10]

---

[8] *Thérèse of Lisieux, The Story of a Mission, Op. Cit.,* p. 72.

[9] *The Story of a Family, Op. Cit.,* pp. 176-177.   [10] *Ibid.,* pp. 176-177.

The first ten months of their marriage, the couple lived as brother and sister until a confessor intervened. In the next fifteen years nine children were born, seven girls and two boys of which only five daughters survived, Marie, Pauline, Léonie, Celine, and Thérèse. Four of the five were called to be Carmelites. Léonie was called to follow her aunt as a Visitation nun. Louis was actually 50-years-old when Thérèse was born while Zélie was 41. Of their marriage the Abbe Dumaine insisted that: *The union in that family was remarkable—between the husband and wife, and between the parents and their children.*[11] As to the goodness of marriage, Thérèse later wrote: *The good God had made all things good and noble. Marriage is good for those who are called to that state; only sin disfigures and sullies it.*[12]

Pope Pius XI, at Thérèse's beatification, said of her parents: *...she was born...of religious parents who were remarkable for their outstanding and constant piety.*[13] Besides their practice of daily Mass, prayers, rosary, and visits to the Blessed Sacrament, Zélie and Louis consecrated their lives to God by becoming members of the Third Order of St. Francis.

Hans Urs von Balthasar remarks that *it is to Louis and Zélie Martin that we owe the doctrine of the "Little Way" and of "spiritual childhood," for they allowed...God...to find a dwelling in the heart of Thérèse...As a result of so Christian an upbringing her whole relationship to God was always personal and never merely formal. Thus even when she is obeying she is obeying out of love for a person, never out of compulsion or a bare concern for some "law." To be good, in Thérèse's mind, means only one thing: to do the will of the father, to give joy to her mother. Guilt means only one thing: having hurt her parents. Repentance and pardon blot out misbehavior entirely, and without question...[O]ne wonders whether Thérèse really was an exception, or whether similar effects would not be produced in most children (who love God in a personal way and without fear) if only parents showed children deeper Christian love and humility.*[14] The Little Flower

---

[11] *The Search for St. Therese, Op. Cit.*, p. 47.

[12] *Ibid.*, p. 174.   [13] *Ibid.*, p. 54.   [14] *The Story of a Mission, Op.Cit.*, pp. 76-77.

herself writes, *Since I have never had any but good examples before my eyes, it was only natural that I should imitate them.*

The Martins valued children. Mme. Martin, a prolific letter writer, wrote: *...[A]s for me, my children were my great compensation, so that I wished to have many in order to bring them up for Heaven.* When Marie, their first child was christened, Louis told the priest, *It is the first time that you have seen me here for a Baptism but it will not be the last time!* Following the deaths of several of their children and stricken with breast cancer, Zélie was counseled not to have more children: *Whatever you say, we shall have another child. That is certain, unless some misfortune happens to me beforehand. But if God wills once more to take this one from me, I pray that it may not die unbaptized, so that at least I may have the comfort of three little angels in Heaven.*[15]

Just before the birth of St. Thérèse, Zélie wrote: *I love children even to the point of folly and was born to have some of my own. But soon the time for this will be ended since I will be 41 this month, and this is the time when one is a grandmother!*

Dealing With Sufferings And Crosses

The Martin family had many sufferings and crosses to deal with but these sorrows only served to deepen the parents' faith. Abandonment to the will of God became the cornerstone of their lives. Announcing the death of her son Marie-Joseph, she wrote: *My dear little Joseph died in my arms at 7 o'clock this morning. I was alone with him. He had a night of cruel suffering, and I begged for his deliverance with tears.* Upon his death she cried out, *Oh, God, must I put that in the ground! But, since You will it, may Your will be done.* When she became pregnant with her next child she wrote to her sister-in-law: *You could not imagine how I fear for the future as regards the little one I am expecting. I feel as though the fate of the last two will be its fate also. I think the dread is worse than the misfortune. It is a continual nightmare for me. When the sorrows come, I resign myself fairly well, but*

---

[15] Mme. Martin to her brother, Nov. 1, 1868.

fear is a torture to me. During Mass this morning my thoughts were so gloomy that I was thoroughly upset. The best course is to leave everything in God's hands, and await events in calm and abandonment to His will. That is what I am going to make myself do.

Their daughter, Léonie, was a worry with her difficult personality and stubborn, rebellious ways. She caused the family many humiliations. Madam Martin writes: *[I]t saddens me deeply to see Léonie as she is. Sometimes I have hope for her, but often I become discouraged. But my sister says that she is sure Léonie will become a saint.*[16] Later she again writes, *If I could make her become a saint by sacrificing my life, I would do it gladly.*[17] In a letter to Pauline she confides, *Léonie is still a heavy cross to bear.*[18]

Suffering was not any easier for Zélie than it is for us: *Oh dear! How tired I am of suffering! I have not a grain of courage left. I am impatient with everybody...I often say during the day: "My God, how I long to be a saint!" and then I do not labor to become one!* Yet in the midst of sorrow she could still see the hand of God. Writing to her brother, Isidore, Zélie confides: *When I think of what this good God, in whom I have put all my trust, and into whose hands I have resigned the care of my affairs, has done for me and for my husband, I cannot doubt that His divine providence watches over His children with especial care.*

Besides dealing with the death of four of their nine children, their surviving children were also afflicted with health problems. Léonie was afflicted with various illnesses from the time she was a toddler. When Thérèse was born, her life depended on finding a wet nurse since Zélie was unable to nurse due to breast cancer. Rose Taille, a countrywoman, agreed to nurse the baby but only if Thérèse lived with her in the country. So the Martins reluctantly gave up their baby for the first fifteen months of her life to insure her survival. They only saw her on weekends or when Rose came to town to sell her farm products.

---

[16] Marie Vaudouin-Croix, *Léonie Martin, A Difficult Life* (Dublin: Veritas Publications, 1993) p. 21.

[17] *Ibid.*, p. 25.   [18] *Ibid.*, p. 26.

Just when they began to feel easy about their new baby, their eldest, Marie, who was then 13-years-old, was brought home from school with what is believed to be typhoid. For five weeks Marie drifted between life and death. Desperate, although terminally ill herself, Zélie made a 15-mile pilgrimage on foot to a Marian shrine to beg Our Lady to spare Marie's life. Marie was cured.

As a child, Zélie had painfully injured her chest when she fell against a table. It's believed that this incident may have triggered her breast cancer later in life. For twelve years she suffered with the disease. When it first was detected, Zélie wrote to her brother, who was studying in Paris, for advice since she had little faith in the local doctors. For some reason, the matter was dropped. The disease spread to a tumor in her neck, then another tumor developed in her back. By this time it was too late for surgery. When medication and other treatments failed to arrest the cancer, she and her three eldest daughters traveled to Lourdes to beg Our Lady for a cure. The jolting carriage ride caused Madam Martin constant pain while it made her daughters nauseated. Fellow passengers making coffee over a lamp spilt it over the Martin women's clothing and belongings. Once in Lourdes, they found their hotel accommodations unavailable. Weary and sick, they had to search for another hotel. The food was wretched. To complicate matters, Mrs. Martin fell, tearing her dress and wrenching her neck. Despite taking the baths four times, her prayers for a cure were not answered in the manner the family had hoped. She wrote of her experience: *What do you want? If the Holy Virgin does not cure me, it is because my time is done and the good Lord wants me to rest someplace other than the earth.* But before her pilgrimage she confided to her brother, Isidore: *If the Blessed Virgin doesn't cure me, I shall implore her to cure my child [Léonie], to develop her mind and to make her a saint.*[19]

Adding to her suffering, at this time, was the death of her beloved sister, Sister Marie Dosithee from tuberculosis. The two sisters died within seven months of each other.

---

[19] *Ibid.,* p. 30.

The Family Life Of The Martins

Despite their great sorrows, the Martin marriage and family were happy. Louis gave Zélie the freedom to manage all the domestic and housekeeping affairs. She in turn called Louis a *saintly man* who made her *always very happy.* She told her sister that Louis *made [her] life very sweet.*

The Martins hired maids to help with the work and chaperon their daughters. Unbeknown to the family, it was one of these maids that was responsible for many of Léonie's problems.

The Martin girls were taught music, painting, and fine needlework. As a family they visited their relatives in Lisieux, took trips to the beach or country. After Mass on Sundays the family would picnic in the country then return to church later in the day for Vespers. They observed the feast days and fast days strictly, took part in retreats and pilgrimages.

In the evenings, the Martins would spend time talking and laughing together. Mr. Martin would play checkers with his daughters and teach them folk songs. The older daughters would read from **L'Annee Liturgique** *(Liturgical Year)* by Dom Gueranger. There were also readings of general interest or some carefully screened novel along with poems. Sometimes Zélie would play cards with her daughters and then have to stay up late to finish her sewing. Each daughter had her own copy of **The Imitation of Christ**. As young children the Martin girls could quote passages verbatim. Thérèse knew the book by heart before the age of fourteen.

Louis also gave daily spiritual talks to his daughters. Thérèse writes, *I always sat on Papa's knee...Papa would rock me gently, my head pillowed on his breast...and he would sing in his beautiful low voice some soothing melody as if to lull his "little queen" to sleep.*

When her daughters attended social activities, Mrs. Martin enjoyed having her daughters attractively dressed. When her sister, Sister Marie-Dosithee, protested fearing that this would teach the girls vanity, Zélie replied, *Must they shut themselves up in a cloister? In the world we cannot live in seclusion!*

Their home was comfortable, nicely decorated but had few conveniences. Oil lamps lit the home. Cooking was done over a fire and there was no running water.

The girls were not pampered nor spoiled. Treats were reserved for feast days. The younger girls were permitted hot chocolate in the morning but as they grew older it was replaced with onion soup. Coffee was reserved for feast days. Fires were not allowed in the bedrooms. When the girls had minor physical ailments or complaints, they were not allowed to complain. Luxury and luxurious items were scorned as softening one's character. Celine recalls purchasing a bracelet while on a visit to her aunt and uncle's chateau. Looking at it on the ride back to the villa from town she realized her folly. Tearing it off and tossing it away, she thought, *I will not be a slave to this.* The Martin girls, not raised to seek ease, easily adapted to the austere life of Carmel.

Besides their family, both Louis and Zélie had their businesses to run. Madame Martin writes: *It is so sweet to attend to little children. If I had only that to do, I think I should be the happiest of women. But their father and I must work to earn enough for their dowries, otherwise when they are grown up they will not be pleased.* This was a cottage industry that Zélie ran from her home.

When her lace-making business grew too successful for her to handle alone, Louis sold his own business to his nephew. He then took over the management and sales for Zélie since she preferred the creative end of the business. This continued for seven years, until Zélie died.

Marie-Pauline, their second daughter, describes their piety: *Our parents were looked upon as religious, even very devout people. In spite of her hardworking life, mother attended half-past five Mass every morning with father, and they both went to Holy Communion four or five times a week. Towards the end of his life father became a daily communicant.* [At that time it was not common to receive Holy Communion daily except with the permission of one's confessor.]

Prayer was also part of the daily routine in the Martin home. Thérèse related later that as a little girl, *I loved God very much and I offered my heart to Him very often, making use of the little formula that mother had taught me.* When the family learned of an obstinate sinner who was dying without wishing to receive the sacraments, they would pray together a novena to St. Joseph asking for the sinner's conversion. This example led Thérèse to pray for the unrepentant murderer, Prazini, who was going to the gallows. Concerned that he would go to hell, she not only prayed and made sacrifices for his conversion but she enlisted her sister, Celine, to help. Right before Prazini was executed, he asked for a crucifix and kissed it three times. Their prayers had been answered!

Fasting was also part of the piety taught in the family, particularly the Lenten fast that Mrs. Martin found so difficult.

In addition to the influence of her parents, her sisters, Pauline and Marie, also had a profound influence in the spiritual formation of Thérèse. The saint explains that Marie sat Thérèse in her lap and *[s]he explained to me that I could become a saint by being faithful over the smallest things.* This was the beginning of Thérèse's "little way." [20]   As for Pauline, Thérèse wrote: *I cannot express how grateful I am. I have to cry when I think of all you have done for me since I was a small child. Oh! How much I owe to you! But when I'm in heaven I shall reveal the truth. I shall say to the saints: "It is my little mother who is responsible for all that you find pleasing in me."* [21] Pauline taught her little sisters the different levels of happiness in heaven by filling three differing size glasses with water. Each was filled to capacity but all three had a different volume. Such are the degrees of glory in heaven. Writing to Léonie, Pauline encouraged her: *But you know, my dear, while we live on this earth we must expect to stumble, to fall on our faces. If everything*

---

[20]John Beevers, *Saint Therese, The Little Flower (The Making of a Saint)* (Garden City: Imagine Books, 1955) p. 73.

[21] *Ibid.*, p. 132.

went well-if we could tell ourselves..."I have acquired such-and-such a virtue!"- then we would become proud. Léonie, seek only one virtue: humility, which will mean that we will never be surprised by our own weaknesses.[22] Under the tutelage of Marie, Léonie, the problem sister, grew to be considerate, happy, and poised.

Concern for souls was uppermost in the minds of this family. While Isidore was living in Paris, Zélie, beseeched her brother to avoid temptations: *I beg of you, dear Isidore, to...pray, and you will not let yourself be carried along with the stream. If once you give in, you will be lost. It is only the first step that costs, on the way of evil as on that of good. After that you will be borne along by the current...You live close to Our Lady of Victories...Go in, just once a day, to say an Ave Maria to her. You will see that she will protect you in a quite particular way...*

To her sister-in-law, Celine Guérin, she writes: *Under what illusions do the majority of men live! Do they possess money? Forthwith, they want honors. And when they obtain these, they are still discontented, for the heart that seeks anything but God is never satisfied.* To her brother, during a time of financial trouble, she reassures him: *I often notice that those who have made their fortune are, for the most part, intolerably self-sufficient...Then it is certain that unvarying prosperity draws men away from God. Never does He lead His chosen by that road; they must first pass through the crucible of suffering in order to be purified. You will say that I am preaching, but such is not my intention. I often ponder over these things and I am telling them to you..."*[23]

Through the daily events in her family life, Thérèse was taught that the mystical Body of Christ was made up of the saints in heaven (the Church triumphant), the souls in purgatory and the Church militant on earth. She prayed to her four deceased siblings: *I talked to them with childish simplicity, reminding them that as I was the youngest in the family I had always been the most petted and loved by my parents and my sisters, and that they also, if they had remained on earth, would*

---

[22] *Léonie Martin, A Difficult Life, Op. Cit.,* p. 77.
[23] Mm. Martin to her brother, July 1872.

doubtless have shown me the same love. Their going to Heaven seemed to me no good reason for forgetting me; on the contrary, since they were in a position to delve into the treasures of Heaven, they must...show me that they know how to love up above.

Their Spiritual Struggles

Examining the Martin family, their life of piety and prayer seems almost effortless. This was not so. Mrs. Martin found the Church fasts and boring sermons trying. Pauline, later Mother Agnes, never was comfortable with Matens at 2:00AM. She found rising in the middle of night irksome and her prayer at that time of morning dry and distracted. Thérèse frequently fell asleep during her mental prayer and thanksgiving after Holy Mass. She found meditating on the rosary almost impossible. *The Lord has a father's pity: does He not know the stuff of which we are made; can He forget that we are only dust?*[24] Marie had no desire to become a religious. It was her confessor, Fr. Pichon, who told her after a vocation discussion, *I strongly hope that I can give you to Jesus.*[25] She entered Carmel with no enthusiasm, simply to do the will of God. *The courtyard struck her as an exceedingly bare and austere place and the garden a mean, tiny affair compared to the great enclosure of the Visitation convent where she was educated. Everything seemed poverty-stricken...Yet it came as an unpleasant shock to Marie...she did not even feel any pleasure at being reunited with Pauline. The only thing in her mind was a nagging question: how on earth could she possibly spend the rest of her life within the Carmel walls? Yet, when she was an elderly woman, she could say: "I found Our Lord within these four walls and in finding Him, I found Heaven. It is here that I have spent the happiest years of my life."*[26]

Her sister, Celine, disliked the habit. She found the veil constricting and uncomfortable. She found walking the measured pace of the nuns irksome. Thérèse herself writes about the difficulties and crosses of community life in her

---

[24] St. Therese, *The Little Flower (The Making of A Saint), Op. Cit.,* p. 138.
[25] *Ibid.,* p. 76.   [26] *Ibid.,* pp. 76-77.

autobiography, **Story Of A Soul.** The superior did not think it fair to accept such a young novice. Despite this she plunged Thérèse immediately into the rigors of Lenten penances. Thérèse developed stomachaches. Reading the details of the many misunderstandings she encountered, the irksome women she had to deal with, the lack of affection that surrounded her, the never-ending little mortifications that made her a saint, could not the tension between the body and the will of the soul be the cause of her stomach problems?

The self-willed Léonie, who found herself in and out of convents, wrote to Celine in the third person about her own lack of perseverance: *But her poor Visitandine cowardice, her reluctance to yield herself completely to love, make her unworthy. I hope that, in the end, I will surrender [to God].*[27] Later she wrote to her uncle about her vocational crisis of thirteen years: *dear God, how I have suffered!*[28] In another letter she discloses: *The fervor which I felt during the retreat has died to ashes...I eat fire every morning in Holy Communion; but my icicle of a heart is still an icicle.*[29] In another letter she admits, *It is hard for my unmortified nature to sacrifice itself constantly.*[30] But she struggled on heroically even though she stated: *I want to please God, that is all—without racking my brains over it!*[31]

Thérèse experienced aridity in prayer rather than an emotional union of hearts. She struggled to pray despite the fact she was experiencing the "dark night of the soul." Even her retreat brought only weariness. Vocal prayers were painful for her. She was troubled by temptations against faith.

While dying, Thérèse disclosed her future mission to bring souls to God via her "Little Way:" *In my mission, as in Joan of Arc's, the will of God will triumph, despite the envy of men.*[32] And there was opposition. Her family was slandered, her forbearers accused, her actions misunderstood, and her sisters accused of plotting to make her a saint.

---

[27] *Léonie Martin, A Difficult Life, Op. Cit.,* p. 60.

[28] *Ibid.,* p. 82.   [29] *Ibid.,* p. 87.   [30] *Ibid.,* p. 91.

[31] *Ibid.,* p. 59.

[32] *Therese of Lisieux, The Story of a Mission, Op. Cit.* pp. xx.

The Martin Sisters

When Zélie died, Marie, 17, and Pauline, 16, well trained by their parents, took over the spiritual and natural formation of their younger sisters. Marie, although merely a teen, was practical and competent therefore perfectly capable of running the household. Later, as a Carmelite she was responsible for the finances and purchasing for her convent. Marie died a month short of 80-years-old.

Pauline was known as firm, kind and prudent. The Holy Father, Pius XI, eventually appointed her superior of Carmel for life. Thérèse chose her as her "little mother" upon the death of Zélie and served under her when Pauline was superior. Pauline died at the age of 89.

Léonie was 9 1/2-years-old at the time of her mother's death. She was troubled with moods and impulsive behavior, besides being backward, and plain in appearance. It was difficult for her to obey. In addition she suffered from a learning disability. While her older sisters attended the Visitation school at Le Mans, where Madam Martin's sister was, Léonie was sent home twice because of poor academic work and even worse, behavior. Eventually she was kept at home. She tried several orders before finally finding her vocation. On a visit to Alençon, without telling her father or sisters, she left them and joined the Poor Clares. She stayed only a couple of weeks. When she was older, she made two attempts to join the Visitation sisters but left each time. It was only after Thérèse's death she rejoined the Visitation sisters and remained. Thérèse, in her last letter to Léonie writes: *In heaven you want me to pray to the Sacred Heart for you; rest assured that I shall not forget to give Him your messages or ask Him for all that is necessary for you to become a great saint. Goodbye, dearest sister, I want the thought of my entry into heaven to fill you with joy, for there I can love you still better.*[33]   In later years Léonie wrote to her sister Pauline: *My childhood was dreadful, disfiguring our beautiful and holy family.*[34]   She died at the age of 78.

---

[33] *The Search for St. Therese, Op. Cit.,* p. 64.

[34] *Léonie Martin, A Difficult Life, Op.Cit.,* p. 91.

Celine was eight-years-old, and four years older than Thérèse at the time of Madam Martin's death. The two youngest daughters, Celine and Thérèse were of similar temperament. They were inseparable friends sharing spiritual secrets and harboring longings to both join the Carmel. Celine was lively and spoke her mind. She loved to tinker and repair items, a talent she probably inherited from her father. Her hobby was photography. It is to her that we owe many of the photos of St. Thérèse. Celine was also an accomplished painter. She painted the world famous picture of the Holy Face, of which millions of copies exist. This painting won the Grand Prix of religious art in 1909. Strangely, Thérèse joined Carmel before her older sister. When Celine did join, Thérèse was her novice mistress. Prior to her admittance to Carmel, Celine made a solemn vow of perpetual virginity. Yet, she still went to a dance despite the entreaties of Thérèse that she not attend. Thérèse, fearing Celine was endangering her vow, tried to reason, then argued, and finally wept...to no avail. At the dance, Celine and her partner were *unable to coordinate their movements and finally retired from the floor in acute embarrassment.*[35] Thérèse's prayers won out in the long run. Celine was almost 89-years-old when she died. Growing impatient at the slowness of her approaching death she said one morning: *Well, as they don't seem ready for me in Heaven, I am going to eat.* When offered an injection to alleviate her pain she responded: *Oh, why not let the lamp slowly burn itself out, as I am not in pain and feel so peaceful.* Her spiritual director declared: *She has enough life in her for four young women.*[36]

Thérèse, the youngest of the Martin girls, was four when her mother died. The death of her mother was a turning point for her. Celine writes: *Before the death of my mother, Thérèse was a child full of warmth, alive, expansive, naturally high-spirited, but stubborn when it came to the question of displeasing the Infant Jesus.*[37] Afterwards she became quiet and withdrawn, prone to touchiness.

---

[35] *The Search for St. Therese, Op. Cit.,* p. 174.
[36] *St. Therese, The Little Flower (The Making of A Saint), Op. Cit.,* p. 82.
[37] *The Search for St. Therese, Op. Cit.,* p. 61.

While most children attain the use of reason between the ages of five to seven-years-old, Pope Pius XI, in his decree for beatification said: *She obtained the use of reason when she was barely two years old.*[38]

In *A Story of a Soul,* Therese very openly admits her faults: *her childhood stubbornness when she refused to kiss the ground for the penny; her vanity with the sleeveless dress; her "self-love"; her sensitivity; her shyness; her tears; her scruples; her strange illness; her difficulties in the convent; her reprimands from Mother Gonzague when she did her work inadequately; her temptations against faith...*[39] St. Thérèse died a painful death from tuberculosis at the age of twenty-four.

Shortly after Thérèse entered Carmel, Louis Martin experienced a series of strokes that are believed to have been cerebral arterio-sclerosis. His symptoms included paralysis, loss of memory, delirium, obsession, and finally a complete loss of his mental faculties. When he was admitted to an asylum, Mr. Martin told the sister admitting him, *[I]t is the will of God. I think it is done to break my pride.*[40]

Will your children say of you as the Little Flower said of her parents, *[O]ur Lord...allowed me to grow up in holy soil enriched with the odor of purity, and preceded by eight lilies of shining whiteness"?* Fr. Stéphane-Joseph Piat, O.F. M. writes in *The Story of a Family: Normally, the saint receives his early fashioning in the home circle.* We have seen how this was accomplished in the life of the Little Flower. The question to consider is how are you forming your own children in the light of eternity? As St. Thérèse reminds us, *Let us grasp the sword of the spirit...let us never simply allow matters to take their course for the sake of our own peace; let us fight without ceasing, even without hope of winning the battle. What does success matter! Let us keep going, however exhausting the struggle may be...One must do one's duty to the end.*

---

[38]*Ibid.,* p. 56.

[39] *Ibid.,* p. 212.

[40] John Beevers, *Storm of Glory* (Garden City: Image Books, 1955) p. 77.

HOW THE FORGIONES RAISED A SAINT [41]

"[C]hoose this day...whom you would rather serve...; but as for me and my house we will serve the Lord."

The above quote from the **Book of Josua** (24:15) describes the lives of Grazio Maria Forgione and Maria Giuseppa De Nunzio, the parents of St. Padre Pio. Before work, leisure, or personal desires they served God. Neighbors called them the *God-Is-Everything Family*. This is the simple formula of how to raise saints and foster vocations.

His Father

St. Padre Pio's father, Grazio Maria Forgione, was born October 22, 1860, to Michele and Felicita D'Andrea Forgione. When Grazio was but seven-years-old, his father died suddenly. His mother remarried and a kind stepfather, Celestino Orlando, raised Grazio and his brother, Orsola. The family, while happy, lived in poverty.

As he matured, Grazio was known not only for his piety but also for his leadership as well as his strong sense of justice. While still in his teens, he was honored by being named a "Master of the Feast"—a committee member who planned the annual festivities for his town of Pietrelcina. "Gra," as he was affectionately called, had fair skin, dark eyes and chestnut hair. Of medium height, he was strong, supple, and wiry with handsome features and a strong voice, which he used to serenade the young ladies of the village.

Gra was a man of action. He faced his problems, resolved them the best way he could and then moved on. Rather than worrying, he trusted that God would give him the wisdom to do the right thing. He instilled in his children his attitude of personal responsibility and trust in God. Six adjectives aptly

---

[41] Mary Ann Budnik, "How The Forgiones Raised A Saint," *Padre Pio The Wonder Worker* (New Bedford: Franciscans of the Immaculate, 1999) pp. 123-133.

describe him: he was simple, enthusiastic, intelligent, full of life, holy and hardworking.

Gra's conduct was virtuous and his speech free from oaths or foul words. His struggle to live the different virtues (good habits) was the root of his joyful personality, which expressed itself in singing and storytelling. It is said that he radiated *a contagious joy about him which communicated itself to others.* He instinctively knew that personal happiness consists of developing and living the virtues while at the same time learning to deal with suffering in a positive manner.

June 8th, 1881, at the age of twenty, Grazio Forgione married Maria Giuseppa De Nunzio. As was the custom, the couple was first married in a civil ceremony at the town hall and then in church. Although Maria's relatives initially disapproved of her marriage to the "humble" Grazio, it was a love match that endured for forty-eight years.

His Mother

Padre Pio's mother was, likewise, a virtuous woman. Born March 28, 1859, Maria Giuseppa De Nunzio was the only child of Fortunato De Nunzio and Maria Giovanna Gagliardi. A year and a half older than her husband, she was as tall as her husband but had light blue eyes. Maria Giuseppa was called "The Little Princess" because of her grace, elegance, and sharp intelligence. She was as slim and dainty on the day that she died as she was on her wedding day.

Maria Giuseppa matched her devout husband in putting God first. Even as a young woman she always prefaced her plans by saying, *if God is willing.* When Francesco (the future Padre Pio) was born the midwife told her,...*your son has been born wrapped in a white veil. This is a good sign because he will be either great or fortunate.* Maria simply replied, *Let the will of God be done.*

Despite her workload at home and in the farm fields, after morning prayers with the family, Maria always attended daily Mass. Known in town as Zia Beppa, she refused to criticize or gossip. Even when her beloved son, Padre Pio, was under attack she would cut short any criticism of his attackers by saying: *Who are we to permit criticism of the ministers of God? The Lord said that we ought not judge if we do not wish to be judged ourselves, and this means that we should judge neither the good nor the evil, because we can see only what people are doing, while God alone can see into men's hearts the reason why they do such things.*

She mortified herself by abstaining from meat not only on Fridays but also on Wednesdays and Saturdays in honor of Our Lady of Mount Carmel, but this did not stop her from exercising the virtue of hospitality. It is said that she *was happier when she could give than when she could receive.* Later in life St. Padre Pio referred to Maria Giuseppa as *my holy mother,* quite a complement coming from a saint!

Family Life

St. Augustine advises: *As regards the offspring it is provided that they should be begotten lovingly and educated religiously.* This was the case in the home of Padre Pio. Maria Giuseppa bore eight children, five of which survived. Of the five there were two religious vocations, one of which is a saint. Michele, the eldest was born on June 25, 1882. He married and eventually took over the family farm. Two years later another son, Francesco, was born but lived only twenty days. Next a daughter was born, Amalia, who also died in infancy. On May 25, 1887, a third son was born and given the name of his short-lived brother, Francesco. This son would be known to the world as Padre Pio. September 15, 1889, his sister Felicita was born. She married the town clerk and had three children. March 15, 1892, Pellegrina was born. When her husband left her, she became the sorrow of the Forgione family. She left the Catholic faith and lived a scandalous life. Despite her devout upbringing, she gave birth to an illegitimate son, Alfredo, who was rumored to have been fathered by her sister Felicita's husband Vincenzo Masone. Felicita forgave her and on her deathbed urged her husband to marry Pellegrina. This was impossible since no one knew whether Pellegrina's absconded husband was dead or alive. Through the fervent prayers of her family, she was reconciled to God before her death. Grazia (or Graziella) was born on December 26, 1894, and became Sister Pia of the order of St. Bridget in Rome. Maria's last child, Mario was believed to have been born March 24, 1899, but died in infancy.

The Forgiones not only taught the Catholic faith to their children but more importantly they **lived** their faith. The family attended Sunday Mass together at a time when many men stayed outside chatting or smoking while their wives and children prayed. Each day, after walking a half hour home from their farm fields, the family would stop into church to thank God for His blessings and present their needs to Him. Grazio was never without a rosary in his hands which he prayed continuously. From his example his children also developed devotion to the rosary.

The Forgione children were strongly influenced by their parents' mortified example in regard to food and drink. Imitating their example, young Francesco secretly deprived himself of food and drink for the love of God. This custom he continued throughout his life.

The Forgiones lived simply. Originally their home seems to have been two small houses since one has to go out the door of Number 27 to get into Number 28. Number 27 consists of a single room with a single window. This was the parents' bedroom. Number 28 was the kitchen and a smaller room that served as the girls' bedroom. A few doors down, the family owned a single room called "the Tower." This served as the boys' bedroom. As Padre Pio would reminisce: *We had little. But thank God, we never lacked anything.* The only decorations in the home were a crucifix and lithographs of Our Lady and the saints. These lithographs were more than decorations. The Mother of God and the various saints were considered important members of their family. It was in this atmosphere that St. Pio developed his fervent love of the Madonna.

The parents felt their main duty in raising their children was to instill the love of God and the Catholic faith into their hearts and souls. The children were disciplined by persuasion and scoldings, never by spankings. They were taught to avoid blasphemy and crude language. Working on Sunday was forbidden.

The day began for the Forgiones at daybreak with morning prayers. Then the family would set off for a half hour walk to their five acres in Piana Romana where they tended their sheep, goats, hens, ducks, rabbits, some hogs, and occasionally a milk cow. On the land itself they raised grapes, wheat, Indian corn, olives, figs, and plums. There was a cottage with a dirt floor where they kept their animals, stored their equipment, and ate and slept in the summer. The crops were picked or reaped by hand. Animals, dragging a stone behind them on the threshing floor, did the threshing. Once a crop was harvested, another was planted. Later in the season the grapes and olives were gathered. The workday would end for Gra at sundown. Maria Giuseppa, on the other hand, would rise in the middle of the night to begin baking bread. Three times a day Maria would have to climb up and down twenty steps to carry home water for the family's needs. While an exhausting life, she and her husband were content.

On winter evenings, the children would listen to stories told by their father or maternal grandmother, Giovanna Gagliardi, who lived close by. Most of the stories came from Scripture which Grazio had memorized since he was unable to read. The day would always end with the family saying the rosary on their knees. Graziella, later Sister Pia, related that prayer was given first priority in their family.

Although poor themselves, Maria Giuseppa, frugal and industrious, always donated a portion of their farm products as alms for the Poor Souls in Purgatory. She also gave the first fruits of the family harvest to the poor. It was after his mother donated an abundant amount of wheat to a friar that Francesco told his father, *"I want to be a religious."* Immediately his father gave his consent. Pio's vocation necessitated heroic sacrifices from his mother and father. They would lack his help on the farm when he went to school. Grazio would have to procure a job in the United States to earn money for his son's education. Mamma Giuseppa was left to care for five children and the farm while her husband was thousands of miles away. Their only means of communicating was by letters written by Francesco to his father. Until an American taught his father to read and write, Grazio had to rely on strangers to read his son's letters to him and to write letters for him to his family. St. Pio relates: *My father crossed the ocean twice in order to give me the chance to become a friar.*

In addition to schooling their children in virtue and prayer, the Forgiones were diligent in seeing that their children learned the teachings of Catholicism. Each Sunday evening the children attended catechism classes where they learned the Catholic faith, hymns, and pious devotions. Each made his/her First Holy Communion at the age of ten and was confirmed at the age of twelve. The sons were taught not only how to serve Mass at an early age, but also that it was an honor to serve at the altar of God.

Grazio and Maria also taught their children the importance of making pilgrimages to the various shrines. It was on one such pilgrimage with his father that the future Padre Pio witnessed a miracle at the Shrine of St. Pellegrino. The miracle taught him the power of prayer along with the power of the intercession of the Saints.

Heroic sacrifice was part of this family's everyday life. It broke the hearts of the parents to part with their son and daughter when they left home to begin their religious vocations. Grazio was unable to even attend his son's ordination on August 10,1910 since he had to return to the states to earn money. He had to rely on details in a letter written by Don Salvatore, the parish priest, to describe his son's great day for which he had labored so diligently for years.

In 1928, when she was nearly seventy-years-old, Maria Giuseppa came to spend Christmas near her son. In a short meeting with her son, Giuseppa fell to her knees and asked: *Padre Pio, how can we know if before God we are not great sinners? We confess everything that we can remember or know, but perhaps God sees other things that we cannot recall.*

Her son replied: *If we put into [our confession] all our good will and we have the intention to confess everything—all that we can know or remember—the mercy of God is so great that He will include and erase even what we cannot remember or know.*

Going out in the cold to attend Midnight Mass offered by her son, she caught a cold that turned into double pneumonia. She died on January 3, 1929. Francesco Morcaldi, a witness, relates that *her death was truly beautiful. She breathed her last serenely while they were praying. Unaided, she raised the crucifix, pressed it to her lips, [and died].*

Upon her death Padre Pio collapsed. For hours he sobbed, *Mammella! Mammella! My beautiful Mammella! My sweet, darling Mammella!* He was unable to return to the friary or even attend her funeral. For days he wept as did his younger sister, Sister Pia in her cell in Rome.

In 1938 Grazio moved to San Giovanni to be near his son. When people complimented Grazio on his son, he would humbly say, *I didn't make him. Jesus Christ did.* October 7, 1946, Gra died at the age of eighty-six. Upon the death of his father, Padre Pio again collapsed in sorrow.

Grazio and Maria Giuseppa knew the formula for raising a happy, holy family...putting the will of God first. By serving God they became Christ-like. Their son, Padre Pio, even bore the wounds of Christ. Daily they struggled to grow in the various virtues. They suffered with acceptance. They sacrificed themselves for family members and strangers alike. By living this simple formula they gave the world one of the greatest saints of the twentieth century. Can we not imitate their simple example? John Paul II reminded us in New Orleans: *Holiness is not the privilege of a few; it is a gift offered to all.*

A Profile Of The Escrivá Family

From France and Italy let us move on to Barbastro, Spain to study the family of St. Josemaría Escrivá de Balaguer, the founder of the Prelature of Opus Dei, and my spiritual father. His father, Don José Escrivá y Corzan was born October 15, 1867 in Fonz, a village a short distance away from Barbastro in the Catalonian region of Spain. He had a sister, Josefa, and a brother, a priest who was known as Don Teodoro. His grandfather worked in local government while his great-grandfather was a doctor.

His mother, María de los Dolores Albas y Blanc was born in Barbastro in 1877. She was doubly related to her cousins since her mother and aunt not only had a double wedding but they married two brothers. The two families lived in adjoining apartments. Because of their large families, the home was called by the townspeople *"the house full of children."* Dolores, a twin, already had twelve siblings at birth. Tragically, her twin sister survived only a few days. Stressing the importance of early Baptism St. Escrivá would cite the fact that both of his parents *were baptized on the very day they were born, even though they were born healthy.*[42]

Religious vocations were plentiful in María's family. Two of her sisters, Cruz and Pascuala, became nuns (Cruz joined the Carmelite order) while two brothers became priests, Don Carlos and Don Vicente. One uncle was Bishop Barón, of Avila. Two other uncles were priests as well as her cousin Mariano, who was Josemaría's godfather. Mariano was a late vocation. Ordained following his wife's death, he died a martyr during the Spanish Civil War. Another relative, Bishop Laguna, likewise was martyred during the same period.

Don José and Doña Dolores were married on September 19, 1898, in Barbastro where they took up their residence. Don José was thirty and Dolores was twenty-one.

His Father

Don José, always punctual, carried himself as a gentleman. His hat was a derby and he carried a walking stick. More important than the fact that he was always well groomed and well dressed,

[42] Andre Vázquez de Prada, *The Founder of Opus Dei, The Life of Josemaría Escrivá*, Vol. 1. (NJ: Scepter, 2001) p. 11.

he had a reputation for kindness, generosity and courtesy. Although agreeable by nature, he was not outgoing but rather reserved in his speech. Not much of a talker, he *was noted for his serene and affectionate smile.*[43] *He always showed fairness toward his subordinates, generosity toward the needy, and piety toward God. His time was basically divided between business and home.*[44]

His profession was that of a textile merchant as was the profession of the father of St. Francis of Assisi. As a merchant, he was considered part of the town's aristocracy. Financially the family was well off. Among the populace they were considered *highly esteemed.*

St. Escrivá recalls: *Thinking now particularly of my father, I recall things which make me feel proud and which have not been erased from my memory...anecdotes of a generous and hidden charity, a strong, unostentatious faith, an abounding fortitude in the hour of trial, closely united to my mother and their children. Thus it was that our Lord prepared my soul, through those examples that were full of Christian dignity and of hidden and ever-smiling heroism...*[45]

Despite the demands of his profession, José found time for God. A methodical and punctual man, he frequently attended morning Mass while still getting to work on time. He was always present for the evening family rosary. His faith influenced his business practices beginning with the welfare of his employees. *He was a great almsgiver,* recalls St. Escrivá. When hit with personal financial loss, from which he never recovered, he maintained his cheerfulness without holding any grudge against his dishonest business partner. In the growing anticlerical atmosphere of Spain he readily admitted the importance of his faith in his life.

José was also known for his kindness, spirit of service, and optimistic spirit. He was not a complainer. The grandson of a

---

[43] *Ibid.,* p. 494.

[44] Salvador Bernal, *A Profile of Msgr. Escrivá, Founder of Opus Dei* (NY: Scepter, 1977), p. 15.

[45] *Ibid.,* p. 27.

fellow employee notes: *If the son's sanctity is like that of his father's, I am sure he will be raised to the altars.*[46]

Josemaría was close to his parents; his father was his "best friend." They allowed him considerable freedom from an early age, while discreetly keeping a close watch on him and leaving his pockets relatively empty. *"I can never recall having seen [my father] look severe...I remember him always calm, with a smiling face. And he died worn out...but he was always smiling. I owe my vocation to him."*[47]

José took the role of fatherhood very seriously. He carefully watched over the development of his children. When one of the children came to him with a question or a concern, he gave them his time and attention taking their questions or concerns seriously.

The Mother

Doña Dolores is described as beautiful with elegance, a woman of great refinement, dignity, *and yet at the same time calm, simple and kind, with a very good sense of humor.* Although strong-minded, Dolores was patient, easygoing and sincere. Escrivá recalls, *Every morning and night I recited the prayers my mother taught me...She was always busy with something: knitting or sewing or mending clothes or reading...[S]he was normal, kind...a good mother who cared for her family, a Christian family, and she knew how to make good use of her time.*[48]

Dolores was prudent and frugal with the family's resources. Purchases were thoughtfully made rather than impulsively bought. In purchasing a needed item she bought the best she could afford, then made it last. When teaching her daughter, Carmen, to sew Dolores explained, *"with the threads one throws away, the devil makes a rope."*

Dolores put herself into running her home. When the family fell on hard times she saw that the family still lived with dignity

[46] *Ibid.*, p. 28.

[47] Dennis M. Helming, *Footprints In The Snow* (NY: Scepter Publishers, 1985) p. 15.

[48] *Ibid.*, p. 15.

and in good taste by especially paying attention to the little details. She used her imagination to make up for what she could no longer afford. On her feast day, the Feast of Our Lady of Sorrows, she made crespillos, which are coated spinach leaves fried in olive oil and sprinkled with sugar, as a treat for her family. Dolores would fill a huge china bowl with the crespillos then cover them with a linen napkin. The children thought they were served an expensive treat.

Their Marriage

Escrivá explains the depth of his parents' marriage: *They loved each other very much, and life brought them many sufferings, because our Lord had to prepare me...I always saw them smiling. They didn't caress in our presence, but it was obvious that they had great affection for each other...*

I cannot but bless that human love which Our Lord has asked me to renounce. But I love it in others, in my parents' love, in yours, in that between spouses. So, love each other, really! And my advice is always: husband and wife, have few quarrels. It is better not to play about with happiness. If you, wives, give in a little, he will give in as well.

*Certainly, never quarrel in front of the children: they notice everything and soon make their own judgments...*He adds, *but they quarreled when we children were not around. Nor did they behave foolishly: a kiss now and then. Be modest in front of your children.*[49]

Example makes such an impression, not only on your children but on the people you deal with on a daily basis. While we busily carry on the tasks of each day, people are watching and noting how we do things. A friend of the Escrivás observed: *They were a marvelous family, and I can honestly say that, if I have ever in my life seen a united couple, it was Josemaría's parents. Josemaría's father was a real saint. He was very much in love with his wife. He was very patient and accepted everything: he always looked cheerful. The mother was also a great lady. I remember perfectly—even though the detail may seem trivial—*

---

[49] *A Profile of Msgr. Escrivá, Founder of Opus Dei, Op. Cit.,* pp. 33-34.

the teas she prepared for us. She knew how to do it very well and prepared everything with great care.[50]

Their Children

The Escrivás had six children of which all were named María, in honor of Our Lady. On the feast of Our Lady of Mount Carmel, July 16, 1899 their first daughter María del Carmen was born. January 9, 1902 Josemaría was born. Christened José for his father and María for Our Lady, later in life St. Escrivá joined his baptismal names believing that Joseph and Mary should never be separated. María Asuncion was born in 1905; María de los Dolores in 1907; María del Rosario in 1909, and Santiage in 1919. Each child was baptized within days of his birth. Following a Spanish custom practiced since the Middle Ages, the newly installed bishop confirmed all the children of the city at the same time. Carmen was not quite three at the time and Josemaría was but three-months-old.

At the age of two, Josemaría was stricken with a severe infection. Two doctors told his parents that he would not survive the night. Characteristically his parents resorted to prayer. They prayed together for his life, and then Dolores began a novena to Our Lady of the Sacred Heart. *...[T]he couple promised our Lady that if their child recovered, they would take him on a pilgrimage to her shrine of Torreciudad.*[51] The following day the doctor stopped by to find out what time their son died. Imagine his surprise when he found a completely healthy little toddler bouncing around!

On horseback, along winding mountain trails, they traveled the fourteen long miles. [His mother] riding sidesaddle and carrying the boy in her arms was frightened by all the jolting they experienced between the crags and deep gorges which plunge to the Cinca River. Perched on a steep hilltop is the shrine of Torreciudad. There, at the feet of our Lady, they offered the child in thanksgiving. Later Dolores would tell Josemaría, *My son, it must be for something great that our Lady left you in this world,*

---

[50] *Ibid*, p. 29.
[51] *The Founder of Opus Dei, Op. Cit.*, p. 16.

because you were more dead than alive. [52]

St. Josemaría

As a child, Josemaría was shy and thoughtful but with a strong will. It was sometimes expressed with his temper. His forceful character was one of his struggles. *Throughout his life Josemaría had to struggle against the natural impetuosity of his temperament.*[53] *"Our Lord, with His grace, wanted to make use also of that defect, to teach me not to give in when the defense of God's rights demanded not giving in."*[54] The vice of stubbornness turned into the virtue of fortitude through grace, struggle, and the formation talks his father gave him on how to control his impulsive outbursts while sacrificing his wishes and wants for the good of others.

A child with a vivid imagination, he enjoyed telling stories to his friends, especially scary tales. His sister, Carmen, observed, *he was very careful not to violate the rights of others; he preferred to lose rather than have a classmate treated unfairly.* A classmate commented that he *"was not quarrelsome; he readily gave in rather than quarrel." That is not to say he was timid. That he wasn't can be deduced from a fight he had with a classmate nicknamed "Pig Foot."...[T]he two of them fought it out until both were entirely satisfied.*[55] Yet he learned from this experience that *violence never changes the mind of one's opponent, so from then on he refused to have recourse to it.*[56]

He was well liked and had many friends. *[H]e was a good companion to everyone and played all the games that kids usually played in those days, such as top spinning, marbles, handball, basketball, and pretend bullfighting.* His cousin, Pascual Albás, notes, *He got terrific grades; he was very intelligent. At home they were always setting before us as an example the good grades he got. But he was also very good-natured. He was very cheerful, faithful to his obligations, devout. His great personality was already in evidence.*[57] But his parents were very careful to avoid the problem of rivalry or jealousy among family relations. When it came time to choose a

---

[52] *Ibid.,* p. 17. [53] *Ibid,* p. 65. [54] *Ibid,* p. 512. [55] *Ibid.,* pp. 30-31. [56] *Ibid.* [57] *Ibid.,* p. 501.

secondary school, they sent Josemaría to a different school than his cousin attended to avoid intellectual competition between the two boys. Many parents unknowingly cause life-long jealousy or animosity between siblings or relatives by bragging about the intelligence, beauty, talents or sporting skills of one of their children. It's important to remember that these are simply gifts from God.

As a teen he became more outgoing. He was *extremely orderly and punctual, and he could not tolerate disorder. It made him nervous, and he was not tactful about it.*[58] During the teens his "romantic idealism" became evident which he expressed in poetry and political idealism. El Cid, the hero of Spain, captivated his imagination and inspired him. It is the story of a man who sacrificed all for the good of his Church and country. Despite El Cid's failures, the obstacles and contradictions he faced, through his death he triumphed, saving Spain from a Moslem takeover. Later in life St. Escrivá used this story to encourage people to grow in holiness. *"Having prayed, he [El Cid] then rode off." First you pray, then you ride. Riding means working, fighting, getting ready to fight. And working and fighting, for a Christian, are praying.*[59]

A Family Life Of Piety

Doña Dolores taught her children their morning and night prayers, the rosary, the angel prayer and this simple morning offering: *"O my Lady, O my Mother, I offer myself entirely to you..."* Other aspirations Escrivá learned as a child that he repeated throughout his life were: *"Sacred Heart of Jesus, I trust in you"* and *"Sweet Heart of Mary, be my salvation."* Later his mother taught him a prayer for purity and an act of self-offering to the Mother of God. His grandmothers also taught him little aspirations such as *"Yours am I, I was born for Thee,"* and *"What is it, O Jesus, you want of me?"* Escrivá returned to these childhood prayers in moments of spiritual dryness as an adult.

It was his mother who taught each of her children the

[58] *Ibid.*   [59] *Ibid.*, p. 64.

catechism even though Josemaría was already attending a school run by the Piarist priests. As one acquaintance remarked, *You could see that his parents had brought him up carefully.* In the evening José joined his children for their night prayers which included the family rosary.

On Saturdays the Escrivás used to go down to St. Bartholomew's...with other families...to say the Rosary and the Hail Holy Queen.[60]

At Christmas, the family would put up a Nativity set and sing Christmas carols together. One carol in particular, *Mother, there's a little boy at the door*, moved him because of the verse, "I have come down to earth to suffer."

St. Escrivá tenderly describes his upbringing: *Our Lord prepared things so that my life would be normal, ordinary, without anything exceptional. He brought me to life in a Christian household...I had exemplary parents who practiced and lived their faith. They allowed me a lot of freedom from an early age, yet kept a close watch on me at the same time. They endeavored to give me a Christian upbringing, and I owe more of it to them than to my schooling, though I was sent to a convent school when I was three and to one run by religious fathers when I was seven...*

The spiritual and corporal works of mercy were not only taught to the children but they were shown how to apply these works so as not to insult or offend the dignity of the poor. They were also taught how to make sacrifices of a favorite treat or their time without letting the beneficiary know of their sacrifice. As was the custom at that time in Spain, the poor would beg at the homes of the wealthy. Long lines of beggars were seen each Saturday at the Escrivá home. None left empty handed. Before the family began their walk to Mass on Sundays and Holy Days, Don José would give the children money to give as alms to the beggars at the Cathedral. Josemaría watched as a Gypsy woman came periodically to the house to speak privately with his mother. Although nothing was said, instinctively he knew Doña Dolores was helping this woman in some manner. The practice of helping the poor and the giving

[60]*A Profile of Msgr. Escrivá, Founder of Opus Dei, Op. Cit.,* p. 19.

of alms continued even after their personal financial ruin. The family still gave from their meager finances to help others..like the widow's mite we read about in the Gospel.

The founder of Opus Dei recalled: *My mother, my father, my sisters, and I always went together to Mass. My father gave us the alms that we happily brought to the disabled man who leaned against the wall of the bishop's house. After that, I went on ahead to get holy water to give to my family. Then, Holy Mass. Afterward, every Sunday, in the chapel of the Christ of the Miracles, we prayed the Creed.*[61]

Family Life

The Escrivás, like the Martin family, were financially well-off. Life was normal and uneventful. The couple were early risers but went to bed late. Doña Dolores, looked after the house with the help of a cook, María, a maid and, when circumstances required it, a nanny. There was also a manservant to take care of the heavy work. At times Josemaría would walk to his father's store to escort him home. While he waited for his father to close up, he would play with the coins in the cash register. His father took these opportunities to teach him about money, how to add and subtract. In the winter, as they walked home together his father would purchase hot chestnuts for him, giving his hand squeezes to show his affection.

Although St. Escrivá reminisced about the affection his father showed toward him, he did give his son a whack when little Josemaría refused to sit in his high chair: *It gives me great joy to be able to say that I do not remember my father hitting me except on one occasion. I was very, very small. It was on one of those few occasions when I sat at table with the grown-ups...It must have been something to do with my stubbornness. I was very stubborn: ...If this is taken to the supernatural plane, it is of no consequence; on the contrary, it can be good, because in the interior life one has to keep on insisting, isn't that so? Anyway, he gave me a ...(and he imitated a slap).*

---

[61] *The Founder of Opus Dei Op. Cit.*, p. 23.

Never again in all his life did he lay a hand on me; never.   He was always gentle with me, and it did me a world of good.   I have the most wonderful memories of my father, who was my friend.   And that is why I recommend what I have experienced: you must become your children's friends.[62]

But this does not mean that his parents were lenient with their children.   When a child was stubborn and refused to eat something, his mother would ask, *You don't want to eat this? All right, don't eat it,* but no other food was substituted.   The child went hungry.   She did not allow her children to be picky eaters, nor would she permit them to eat between meals.   *One day they set before [Josemaría] a dish he did not like.   Realizing he would then have to go hungry, he threw it against the wall, which was papered.   They did not change the paper.   For several months the splotch remained there, so that the memory of his tantrum would be impressed on the child.*[63]

Like Louis Martin, Doña Dolores taught her children the natural virtues and faith by using examples from daily living. Escrivá recalls how he hated to wear new clothes: *I hid under the bed and stubbornly refused to go out into the street when I was dressed in a new suit...until my mother gave a few light taps on the floor with one of my father's walking sticks.   I came out then because of the walking stick, and for no other reason. She then affectionately told me: "Josemaría, the only thing to be ashamed of is sin."   Many years later I realized what a depth of meaning these words contained.*[64]

When a child left his clothes on the floor or left a mess, Dolores would scold, *It's not somebody else's job to put back in order what we mess up.*   Although the family had domestic help she taught her children to pitch in and help saying, *My rings won't fall off!*   Should a child begin judging another she rebuked the child by saying, *We can easily misunderstand what other people say.*

<u>Punctuality</u> was expected from the children. When they broke

[62] *A Profile of Msgr. Escrivá, Founder of Opus Dei Op. Cit.,* p. 34.

[63] *The Founder of Opus Dei, Op. Cit.,* p. 19.

[64]*A Profile of Msgr. Escrivá, Founder of Opus Dei, Op. Cit.,* p. 16.

something, rather than throwing it out and replacing it with a new item, it was repaired or sent out to be repaired. This taught the children to live the virtue of poverty.

The Escrivás taught responsibility and self-control by giving their children very little spending money but trusting their children to act in an upright manner. They did not open their letters or eavesdrop on conversations.

In *Raise Happy Children Through A Happier Marriage* we discussed the role of the father in introducing the outside world to his children. Don José did just that. In conversation, over dinner, on outings his father discussed the issues of social justice such as unions, a just wage, and relations between management and labor. José did not just discuss the issues but he became actively involved in them. Working with other concerned Catholics, José founded a newspaper in 1903. Four years later Good Publications Reading Room was initiated. Then in 1909 the Barbastro Catholic Center was formed.

Don José...was a good employer, not only paying his workers a just wage but also tending to their spiritual needs. Every year he arranged for them a series of Lenten conferences, paid for out of his own pocket, and adjusted the work schedule so that everyone who wanted to attend these conferences could, although, out of consideration, he himself did not, lest they feel pressured to do so.[65]

World events were also discussed within the home, particularly the subjection of Ireland by the British since this involved a religious issue. *I was then about fifteen and I eagerly read in the newspapers everything about the events of the First War. Most of all, though, I prayed a lot for Ireland. I wasn't against England; I was for religious freedom.*[66]

The Crucible Of Suffering

Sorrow was no stranger to the family. Within a period of less than four years the Escrivás lost three daughters. María Rosario died before she was a year old in 1910. María Dolores

---

[65] *The Founder of Opus Dei, Op. Cit.*, p. 33.   [66] *Ibid.*, p. 66.

was five when she died in 1912. María Asuncion, nicknamed Chon, died before her eighth birthday in 1913. The surviving children, Carmen fourteen, and Josemaría, eleven years old *were deeply affected by these tragic events....Josemaría started saying that it was his turn next, since his sisters had died in ascending order from the youngest upwards. He stopped when he realized that he was hurting his mother. She assured him: "Don't worry, you have been offered to Our Lady of Torrecuidad...*[67]

Before the death of Chon, she and Carmen *liked to build castles with playing cards. One afternoon (Rosario and Dolores had both died by then) they were gathered round the table and holding their breath as the last card was being placed on one of those castles, when Josemaría, uncharacteristically, toppled them all with his hand. They were on the brink of tears, and Josemaría said to them very seriously: "That is exactly what God does with people: you build a castle, and when it is nearly finished, God pulls it down."*[68]

Financial hardship hit the family next. *José Escrivá...had worked hard and suffered much...In 1915 he uprooted the family from their hometown of Barbastro and moved to Logrono. Behind lay the graves of three daughters...also behind lay the debris of his ruined textile business, a victim of his partner's apparent chicanery. He had to let go the family servants and sell their comfortable home. Logrono represented a new start for José and Dolores, his wife of 17 years, but with greatly reduced means. The best he could offer her and their two remaining children was a cramped apartment, short on conveniences, hot in summer, chilly in winter. Try as he might at the same line of business in Logrono, José Escrivá barely improved the finances of his family. But the example of his cheerful sacrifice was not lost on the other Escrivás.*[69]

Don José, although financially ruined by his business partner, felt an obligation in justice to personally pay off all the business

---

[67] *A Profile of Msgr. Escrivá, Founder of Opus Dei Op. Cit.* , p. 23.

[68] *Ibid.*, p. 24.

[69] *Footprints In The Snow, Op. Cit.*, p.15.

debts. This brought scorn and rebukes from family members, even priests who told him he had no obligation *to compensate creditors from his personal funds.*[70] Financially the family was so poor that a friend relates how her grandmother bought them a home to live in until they could relocate to Logrono and begin their lives again. Despite the ridicule from family and friends, his parents cheerfully and with humor accepted their reduced circumstances. It was that example that triggered a point St. Escrivá wrote in his book, ***The Way:*** *Cross, toil, tribulation: such will be your lot as long as you live. That was the way Christ followed, and the disciple is not above his Master.*

But from this experience other lessons were likewise learned: *For my father, nothing ever went right when it came to business. And I thank God for this, because as a result I know what poverty is; had it been otherwise, I would not. You see how good this is? Now I love my father all the more. He was so marvelous that he knew how to have a magnificent serenity and endure adversity with the peace of a Christian and a gentleman.*[71]

Suffering is a key ingredient in the formation of all saints. St. Josemaría, as a priest, developed an understanding for its importance in shaping souls into the image of Christ crucified: *I have always made those around me suffer very much. I have not provoked any catastrophes, but the Lord, to shape me who am the nail—forgive me, Lord—gave one blow on the nail and a hundred on the horseshoe. And I came to see my father as Job personified. I saw him suffer cheerfully, without showing it. And I saw his courage. It was a constant lesson to me, because afterwards I have felt so often the ground giving way beneath me and the heavens falling on top of me, as if I were about to be crushed between two steel plates.*[72]

Suffering became such a constant reality in his life that he noted the day of his silver jubilee as a priest: *Today has been a totally happy day—something I hardly ever get for the big dates in my life. On such days our Lord has almost always chosen to*

---

[70] *The Founder of Opus Dei, Op. Cit.*, p. 505.

[71] *Ibid.*, pp. 510-511.

[72] *A Profile of Msgr. Escrivá, Founder of Opus Dei, Op. Cit.*, p. 35.

send me some kind of mishap. Even on the day of my First Communion, when they were getting me ready, fixing my hair, trying to make it curly, they burned me with the curling iron. It wasn't anything serious, but for a child of that age it was something.[73]

A Switch In Vocations

Never dreaming that their son would become a priest, Doña Dolores quoted to her son the Spanish proverb, *if you're going to marry, find you a woman neither so beautiful that she bewitches, nor so ugly that she causes twitches.* As Josemaría entered the teens a strain developed between him and his father. They shared confidences less and there was a disagreement over his future vocation. The son wanted to be an architect while his father wanted him to become a lawyer. José told his son that an architect was nothing but a *glorified bricklayer.* His professional decision was an additional financial hardship for his family which was already finding it difficult to make ends meet. *So that I could have a university-level career, my parents continued my education in spite of the family's financial ruin, when they would have had every right to make me get a job—just any kind of job—right away.*[74]

Along with his physical growth, he was also spiritually maturing. The winter of 1918, which was particularly severe, changed his life. The first week or so in January stores selling fish and meat closed because the items had frozen. Wine in casks froze, pipes burst and people died from the cold. Then a snowstorm hit that added to the misery. Josemaría, almost sixteen at the time, awoke to a frigid, snowy day. Walking down the street in the brutal cold, he was stunned to see the bare footprints of an unshod Carmelite in the glistening snow. The sight of such sacrifice, such love of God shook his very soul. Staring at the footprints, he thought, *What am I doing for the Lord?* He was already going to daily Mass and communion, frequent confession, saying the family rosary, and making sacrifices, but God seemed to be asking more of him. It seemed

[73] *The Founder of Opus Dei, Op. Cit.,* p. 503.

[74] *Ibid.,* p. 66.

an invitation to follow Christ more closely.

Looking back on this turning point in his life he commented: *I would have laughed at anyone who said I would one day be wearing a cassock. It happened all of a sudden, when I saw that some Carmelite friar had walked barefoot in the snow.*[75] Later he related, *Jesus Christ did not ask me for permission to enter my life. If anybody had told me, years ago, that I was going to be a priest...And yet, here I am!* Immediately he began praying the aspiration from Scripture, *"Lord, that I may see."* He explains: *I loved priests very much, because my upbringing at home was deeply religious; I had been taught to respect and venerate the priesthood. But it was not for me; it was for others. One fine day I told my father that I wanted to be a priest: it was the only time I saw him cry. He had other plans in mind, but he did not object. He told me, "My son, think it over carefully. A priest has to be a saint...It is very hard to have no house, no home, to have no love on earth. Think about it a bit more, but I will not oppose your decision." And he took me to speak to a friend of his who was a priest...*[76]

Initially deciding to become a Carmelite, he sensed in the coming months that God had a specific plan for his life but not as a religious priest but rather as a secular priest. Besides, as a secular priest he had more freedom. He could *take care of the needs of his family* which he felt obliged as a filial responsibility *through a secular career* such as teaching at a university.[77]

Knowing the great loss of an only son to his parents, he prayed that God would send his parents another son to replace him. His prayer was answered. *Santiago was born because of a prayer that I made to our Lord. This is obvious because he was born ten months later [on February 28, 1919]. My mother had not had any children for ten years. My parents were physically worn out by their many hardships and were also well on in years.*[78] Santiago's godparents were his older brother and sister.

---

[75] *Ibid.*, p. 516.
[76] *A Profile of Msgr. Escrivá, Founder of Opus Dei, Op. Cit.*, pp. 67-68.
[77] *The Founder of Opus Dei, Op. Cit.*, p. 516.
[78] *Ibid.*, p. 520.

In addition to his priestly studies, his father advised him to study for a law degree, which would be compatible with his ecclesiastical studies. Sadly his father, like the father of St. Padre Pio, did not see his son ordained. November 27, 1924, began for José like any other day. He had breakfast with his family, prayed his morning prayers before a statue of Our Lady, then, as he was about to leave their apartment, his heart gave out causing him to collapsed onto the floor. He passed away two hours later without regaining consciousness. José was only 57-years-old at the time of his death. His son, St. Josemaría, died in a similar manner shortly after glancing at a picture of Our Lady of Guadelupe on June 26, 1975.

In regard to his father's death, the founder of Opus Dei relates: *I love my father with all my heart, and I am sure he is enjoying a very high place in heaven because he learned how to bear the humiliation of being left in the street. It hurt deeply, but he bore it in such a dignified, marvelous and Christian way.*[79]

The Work of God...Opus Dei

On the Feast of the Guardian Angels, October 2, 1928, Fr. Escrivá finally "saw" God's plan for his life. He was 26-years-old at the time. *[W]hen our Lord wished me to begin work as Opus Dei, I had not a single resource, nor a penny to my name. I only had the grace of God and a good sense of humor. Can't you see how good this was?* God had selected him to *be instrumental in calling the laity to give themselves to God by following a clearly defined path to holiness and apostolate that wove its way through their secular occupations and preoccupations.*[80]

A friend of St. Josemaría christened this path to sanctity for lay people within the world as Opus Dei, which is Latin for the Work of God. In a ***New York Times*** interview in 1966 the founder explained: *Our Lord gave rise to Opus Dei in 1928 to remind Christians that, as we read in the book of **Genesis**, God*

---

[79]*A Profile of Msgr. Escrivá, Founder of Opus Dei Op. Cit.*, pp. 35-36.
[80] *Footprints In The Snow, Op. Cit.*, pp. 18-19.

created man to work. We have come to call attention once again to the example of Jesus, who spent 30 years in Nazareth, working as a carpenter. In his hands, a professional occupation, similar to that carried out by millions in the world, was turned into a divine task. It became a part of our redemption, a way to salvation.

The spirit of Opus Dei reflects the marvelous reality (forgotten for centuries by many Christians) that any honest and worthwhile work can be converted into a divine occupation. In God's service there are no second-class jobs; all of them are important.

*To love and serve God, there is no need to do anything strange or extraordinary. Christ bids all without exception to be perfect as his heavenly Father is perfect (**Matt**. 5:48). Sanctity, for the vast majority of people, implies sanctifying their work, sanctifying themselves in it, and sanctifying others through it. Thus they can encounter God in the course of their daily lives. The conditions of contemporary society, which places an even higher value on work, evidently make it easier for the people of our times to understand this aspect of the Christian message, which the spirit of the Work has recalled.*[81]

The Work, as its members affectionately call it, is a spiritual family. It was Josemaría's mother, Dolores, and his sister, Carmen, who taught the first members of Opus Dei how to create a family atmosphere in its various centers. Josemaría often remarked, *Without their help it would have been difficult for the Work to develop. I see it as God's Providence that my mother and my sister Carmen should have helped us so much to have a family atmosphere in the Work. Our Lord wanted it that way.*[82]

Their detachment and apostolic spirit moved them to donate their personal furniture to furnish the first centers of Opus Dei. Inherited lands were sold to raise money to build or purchase homes that could be turned into centers. Carmen took over the domestic task of administering the centers.

---

[81] *Ibid.*, p. 19.

[82] *A Profile of Msgr. Escrivá, Founder of Opus Dei, Op. Cit.*, p. 41.

Dolores died April 22, 1941, while St. Escrivá was giving a retreat to diocesan priests. Her last glance was at an Italian painting of Our Lady with the toddler Jesus offering his mother a rose. The rose is a symbol of Opus Dei. Her son recalled, *I did not know how serious the illness was, because the doctors did not think that my mother's death was imminent, or that she could not be cured. "Offer your discomfort for the work I am going to do," I asked my mother as I said good-bye. She agreed, even though she could not help saying in a low voice: "This son of mine!..."*

I went to the Tabernacle when I arrived at the seminary of Lerida where the retreat for priests was being held and said: "Lord, take care of my mother, for I am looking after your priests." The retreat was half-way through. It was midday and I had just given them a talk commenting on the unique supernatural task a mother has at the side of her priest son. When I finished I decided to remain recollected for a moment in the chapel. Almost immediately, the bishop apostolic administrator, who was also doing the retreat, approached me, his face drawn and pale, and said: "Don Alvaro is on the phone for you." I heard Alvaro say: "Father, Grandmother has died."

I returned to the chapel without a tear. I understood immediately that the Lord my God had done what was best; and then I cried, as a child cries,....Since then, I have always thought that Our Lord wanted that sacrifice of me, as an external proof of my love for diocesan priests, and that my mother especially continues to intercede for that work.[83]

Due to the spiritual faithfulness of the Escrivás, the universal call to holiness is not only understood but also promoted throughout the whole world. You and your family not only should become saints, you can become saints!

The Making Of A Martyr: The Kolbes[83A]

Our next stop is Poland to consider the family of St. Maximilian

---

[83] *Ibid.*, pp. 42-43.
[83A] Material for this section was taken from *To Weave A Garment* by Mary Felicita Zdrojewski, CSSF (Enfield, CT: Felician Sisters of St. Francis, CT., Inc.) 1989.

Kolbe. The maternal grandparents of St. Maximilian Kolbe, Anna and Francis Dabrowski were not only cottage weavers but also the parents of five children. Marianna, the mother of St. Maximilian, was their second youngest daughter. The other children included Rosalie, Casmir and Francis, close in age, who preceded Marianna while Anna was the youngest in the family.

From little on the Dabrowski's children were taught the necessity of fulfilling their religious obligations with love. Within the family circle, the truths of the faith were taught clearly, not only by word but also by the example of the parents. That included Marian devotions and the Sunday evening vesper service.

Marianna's mother, unable to afford schooling for her five children, home schooled her children in reading and writing, at the same time that she taught them how to weave. Once her older siblings became weavers and were able to contribute to the family income, Marianna and her sister, Anna, were sent to the local elementary school. In time Marianna became a skilled weaver also able to help her family financially.

Marianna Kolbe, like Zélie Martin, the mother of St. Thérèse, aspired to become a religious. Born February 25, 1870 into a Poland partitioned by Russia, Austria and Prussia, she and her family were under the anti-Catholic authority of the Czar of Russia. With convents suppressed there was no opportunity for her to join a religious order so marriage became her only option. With a burning desire to strive for holiness, Marianna prayed for a husband with similar aspirations. Her prayers were answered when she met the charming, handsome Julius Kolbe at church. He was by profession a weaver like herself.

St. Maximilian's Father

A year younger than Marianna, Julius Kolbe was born May 29, 1871 to Helen and John Kolbe, also weavers. He came from a fervent German Catholic family who lived the Christian virtues and prized their Catholic faith. The oldest of four children, he had two sisters, Theresa and Anna and a brother, Adolf. Julius' deep love of God, keen mind, and witty comments easily won Marianna's heart. *He possessed a special gift of winning the human heart and quickly made friends with everyone,* noted Francis Langer, a relative and close friend.

Wife And Mother

Marianna, a perfectionist in her role as homemaker, wife and mother, never felt that she did enough. She was obsessive about order, being on time, things out of place, cleanliness, and Christian living. She was vigilant and possessive of her children.

In addition to her busy schedule of work and family, she used her nursing skills to help the indigent. She was called upon many times to act as mid-wife. On one occasion when a new mother was dying, Mrs. Kolbe knelt at the side of the woman's bed for ten hours begging Our Lady to save the mother's life. Her prayers were answered.

Marianna was an upright, sincere person. People found her courteous, charming, yet demanding. Influential in her circle of friends, people sought her advice.

Family Life In The Kolbe Home

Julius and Marianna were marred October 5, 1891 in the Church of Our Lady of Assumption in Zduñska Wola. Marianna was twenty-one years old and Julius was twenty.

Like their parents, they made their living as skilled weavers in their cottage industry. Hardworking and frugal, they soon hired Marianna's sister, Anna, as an employee. Known for their skill, other apprentices in the town also vied to work for them.

The couple labored with their apprentices from six in the morning until eight at night in their home, taking breaks only for lunch. At noon on Saturdays all worked stopped to be resumed on Mondays. Julius wanted his workers to spend time with their families and attend church services.

While Marianna ran the home and appears to be the dominant person in the marriage, Julius ran the family business. Their marriage was happy, free from arguments and harsh words.

A Family Of Faith

Setting the tone for their family life, Marianna and Julius set up a prayer corner in their one-room rented home where they knelt to pray morning and evenings prayers. Despite their growing business, the faith still came first in their lives. It was shortly after their marriage that the Kolbes joined the Third Order of St. Francis. They strove to live his precepts as their way to sanctification. In the imitation of St. Francis' spirit of poverty, Julius went so far as to renounce his family inheritance. As a family they avoided amassing wealth or spending money foolishly. Actively involved in the activities of their parish, when their pastor initiated Sunday adoration, Julius organized the hourly adorers.

In each town the family moved to they became immersed in the activity of their parish. Julius organized holy hours, processions, and the Living Rosary. He serenaded Our Lady with his violin. The boys become members of the choir and altar boys. When a new church was planned, Julius took on the tough task of fund-raising by going door-to-door to solicit even though fellow Catholics mocked his efforts.

Marianna was conscious of the importance of small details. A neighbor related how the Kolbes went to church: *Julius and his wife made a handsome couple. Their sons' clothes were neat and spotless. With prayer books in hand, the family always walked in formation, at least to the extent the lively youths could contain themselves.*

Marianna, overly conscientious in everything, took teaching the faith to her sons seriously. She writes, *I felt my inadequacy and begged the Mother of God to substitute for me.*

The Family Expands And Moves On

Francis, their first child, was born July 25, 1892. He was named for their patron. While Julius hoped his son would follow his trade, Marianna secretly prayed that he would be a priest. Eighteen months later on January 8, 1894, Raymond was born, the future St. Maximilian. Showing gratitude to God, upon the birth of each child Julius would thank his wife by saying, *My Dearest, May God richly reward you.* Each child was baptized the day of birth.

With the growth of the industrial movement their cottage industry of weaving grew unprofitable necessitating a moved to £odz where Julius found employment in a "workhouse." It was there that their third son, Joseph, was born on January 29, 1896. Finding the conditions in the city wretched, the Kolbes soon moved again. *We left £odz so that the boys would have a decent environment to grow up in,* Julius explained to his sister Anna. He also found the greed of the factory owners distasteful. Relocating to Justrzkowa, they set up a grocery and hardware store. Until the store became established, the hardworking Kolbes not only resumed their cottage industry of weaving but they also leased land near their home for a vegetable garden. It was Marianna and their little sons who worked in the store. In 1897 Valentine was born and in 1900 Anthony, their fifth son was born.

When a financial depression hit the area the Kolbes extended credit to their customers in a spirit of charity. Many unjustly took advantage of their generosity pushing the Kolbes into bankruptcy. Undaunted by this setback, Julius and Marianna secured factory jobs. There Julius began organizing workers. He wrote articles on social justice that were printed in the local newspaper. His son, Raymond, inherited his journalist ability to write passionately. Julius also set up a lending library in his home, held secret meetings and distributed a forbidden newspaper to organize Poles as well as to educate the workers. Despite being arrested and imprisoned a short time for his convictions, Julius never wavered in his love for Poland. His sons likewise acquired his patriotism. Raymond imprudently drew Polish eagles on a public wall. Their staunch patriotism to God and country eventually claimed both their lives.

The Kolbe Boys & Their Education

The Kolbes home schooled their children in reading, writing and math, as well as the Polish language, culture and history. In the evenings, Mr. Kolbe would entertain his sons by reading stories about Polish heroes and saints. Through daily living and these stories, the Kolbe boys were taught the importance of Christian self-sacrifice. Besides school assignments and extra daily readings, the boys were assigned chores. Only when the house was in order were they allowed to play. Julius also allowed his sons to be independent thinkers along with the freedom to learn from their mistakes.

The boys inherited their father's charming, friendly personality and their mother's strong character. They were well mannered but lively and, like most boys, at times mischievous. Spankings were common in the Kolbe household. The boys were trained to bring the strap and bend over a board when punishment was needed. It was one such a time that Marianna Kolbe, upset with something Raymond did, asked in an exasperated manner that now famous question, *What will become of you!* It was when Raymond repeated his mother's question in prayer that Our Lady appeared and offered him the choice of two crowns, the white crown of purity and the red crown of martyrdom. He chose both then promptly forgot about his mystical experience. It was at this time that Marianna noticed that Raymond's personality became more subdued.

How The Kolbes Handled Suffering

Mrs. Kolbe would tell her friends, *All life is beautiful, and to live well is so important, for life is of God.* Marianna knew well the value of life. In 1898 the Kolbes lost Valentine, their fourth son when he was not quite a year old. In 1904, their fifth son, Anthony, died at the age of four. Their deaths caused Marianna to suffer not only from grief, but also gossip, and self-inflicted guilt. When no other children were conceived the couple took a private vow of chastity.

Suffering served to only intensify Mrs. Kolbe's faith. A close personal friend, Mrs. Zaleksa, explained how one day the two were praying in church when *I noticed how completely enraptured Marianna was when she prayed. I was struck with a fit of laughter. Mrs. Kolbe turned to me and said emphatically,* "Woman, do not sin!"

Vocational Choices

Upon the completion of his elementary studies, Francis, the oldest son, was sent to a business school. This was in preparation for his entrance to the seminary. In addition, a priest tutored both Francis and Raymond in Latin. When Raymond ordered a medication in Latin from the pharmacy, his knowledge of Latin so impressed the druggist, Mr. Kotowski, that he volunteered to tutor Raymond for high school in the hopes of fostering a priestly vocation. He recalled thinking, *for who knows, perhaps this youngster may enter the seminary someday.* His tutoring enabled Raymond to graduate with Francis from the business school.

When a Franciscan junior seminary opened, both Francis and Raymond applied and were accepted. While Marianna was thrilled with Francis' vocation, it took more time for her to accept Raymond's. She had hoped he would be their support in old age.

As their sons left for the seminary she hugged and kissed them, then exhorted the boys to remain faithful to Our Lady. *And your rosary, do you have it with you,* she asked? The separation broke her heart. Despite her strong faith she questioned God's will...but not for long. Julius, on the other hand, embraced them and told them, *I am honored, I am proud of you. I love you.* He insisted on being kept informed of his sons' studies and progress. Coming from a disciplined home, the Kolbe boys easily fit into the disciplined atmosphere of the seminary.

When it came time for Raymond and Francis to make their profession, Raymond was unsure of his vocation. He considered leaving the seminary and encouraged Francis to reconsider his choice also. At the hour appointed to discuss their future with the superior, their appointment was canceled because of the unexpected arrival of their mother. She brought them the glad tidings that their younger brother, Joseph, was entering the minor seminary. Raymond reevaluated his future. He remained in the monastery.

Through letters the family kept in touch. Julius wrote to his younger son: *The family that is united in love will avoid life's dangers.* From Rome, Raymond, now Brother Maximilian, wrote to tell his mother that she helped him to strive for personal holiness. At Christmastime, Julius circulated the traditional communion-like wafer to each member of his family through the mail if unable to personally visit them.

With the beginning of World War I, life dramatically changed again for the Kolbes. Julius joined the army to fight for Poland. Then Francis, a professed brother, left the monastery to fight for the independence of Poland while Joseph's vows were postponed. Marianna became distraught over Francis. She wrote to Joey, ... *Pray that he will not lose his innocence, and that by some miracle he would gain what was lost. With God, nothing is impossible...I send you...a mother's blessing and I join it with the blessing of the Virgin Mother, so she may substitute for my inadequacy. So that she who is full of grace, may unceasingly prepare you in the best way in all your works, spiritual and material. May she be your counselor and guide...*

From a distance Marianna continued to nurture the souls of her family. Fr. Maximilian credited Lourdes water and his mother's prayers for saving his finger from amputation. Joey, now Brother Alphonse writes: *I see in you Mama, and I say this with much love, the guardian angel who leads me by the hand across the steep precipice onto the eternal goal. Truly one who guides. If today, I am where I am and not blown against the walls by the winds, it is because of you, Mama. Every one of your letters has been for me new support and gives me new zeal, new strength, new hope. I feel a sense of gratitude that cannot be spoken...I must repay with sincere prayer.*

On the heels of the loss of Francis' vocation came the worry over the whereabouts of Julius. Months passed without a word from him. Later the family learned that when the Russians captured his Polish company, Julius, an officer, was hanged sometime between the end of September and the beginning of October in 1914. Marianna continually reminded her sons to pray and offer Masses for the repose of the soul of their father. On his name day, she remembered him with prayers and candles.

Marianna's son, Maximilian, helped her to enter as a domestic the Felician Convent in Krakow. While unable to become a professed sister as she had hoped, she lived as a tertiary serving in whatever capacity the sisters need. She attended the Third Order meetings in town and participated in its activities. Content with her new home, she wrote to Joseph, *I know that God will give me crosses, even here. Beginnings are sweet.*

Her day began by singing the Little Hours to praise Our Lady. She was considerate in this pious practice by not singing until the convent was officially awakened. She did not want her prayer to disturb any of the sleeping sisters. She rose early each day to give glory to God. *I never miss the six o'clock Mass, this is the time the Lord ascends His throne in our church.* (The Blessed Sacrament was exposed for all day adoration after the first Mass.)

At the convent she attended up to five Masses a day and made frequent adorations before the exposition of the Blessed Sacrament. During her prayer she remembered all the people she met and all the people she would come into contact with. Charged with running errands for the sisters, she stopped at every church she passed to make a visit. As she entered each church, she told the postulant assigned to help, *Give adoration to the Lord.* An object of jealousy to some of the sisters, she silently accepted this cross over time conquering her anger over this injustice by praying for the offending sisters.

Marianna encouraged homesick postulants to persist by promoting the beauty of religious life, prayer and perseverance. She cared for the candidates until they were admitted. Her friends said that *she was always in motion; Maria Kolbe walked with energy and spirit.* Unlike the women of her time, she rarely stopped to chat on the street. She was busy with God's work.

When her convent duties were completed, Mrs. Kolbe wrote letters encouraging each family member to support the others in prayer. To Joseph she wrote: *I assure you, My Dear Son, that I will never forget you before the Lord, for this is a mother's holiest of duties. I know that you remember us, but especially at that happy moment when you make of yourself a total sacrifice at the foot of the altar, do not forget your parents and your brothers. When we mutually support one another in prayer, then for sure we will attain our appointed goals, even if they may be most difficult, for nothing is impossible with God.*

Her son, Francis continued to worry her. His military career was cut short when he developed inflammation of the leg bone. Considered incurable and no longer fit for religious life, Francis married Irene Triebling. It was years before Mrs. Kolbe could reconcile herself to her son's marriage, wife and their daughter. Mrs. Kolbe blamed herself for his lack of faithfulness. Was it because she had not prayed nor sacrificed enough for him? Pouring out her heart to Joey, she wrote: *Oh! How difficult it is for the person who pulls himself from the hand of God and desires to fly on his own wings. Oh! That all who wish to serve God faithfully would understand this, so they would not allow themselves to believe deceptive temptations...In spite of what has happened, I deeply believe our future is in the hand of Him who rectifies everything. In spite of our unfaithfulness, and imprudence, at least we sincerely desire to serve.* Francis' life was filled with marital and employment problems.

Despite her grief over Julius and Francis, when Brother Maximilian founded the Confraternity of Mary Immaculate, known as "the Militia" or Knights of the Immaculata while in Rome, Mrs. Kolbe threw her efforts behind his Marian movement. She worked hard promoting his apostolate. Ordained April 28, 1918 in Rome, his mother did not find out until five months later that her son was now a priest.

Sorrows only increased for Marianna. Upon his return to Poland, Fr. Maximilian threw himself into his work. His run-down condition led to a serious illness. She feared for his life.

Just when he began to recover, Brother Alphonse contracted tuberculosis before his ordination. Again her prayers were answered. Her youngest son was ordained June 29, 1921. Although a priest, Marianna reminded him of his responsibility to grow holy: *May you receive more and more graces from God, so that you may attain great sanctity only in the eyes of God. Also, may you receive from the blessed Mother a holy wisdom in saving souls. May you snatch them from the power of Satan...and again, may you gain that hidden holiness, unknown to others, unknown to yourself. Only in God will it be valued and loved...*

In this same letter she also gives Fr. Alphonse pointers on the virtue of gratitude: *When you receive the package with the jacket, write and enclose in my letter a few words of gratitude to the Reverend Mother. It is very important to show appreciation. Do it discreetly, because the Reverend Mother does not want everyone in the house to know of her gift...*

Her advice to her grown sons extended also to family matters. Francis, separated from his wife, had difficulty holding jobs. In financial straights he turned to his brothers for "loans." Marianna, knowing the concern of her sons for their brother warned them not to give Francis money. She explained in letters that if they give him money their brother would never develop responsibility. Fr. Maximilian wrote to Francis telling him of his grave duty to care for his wife and daughter, citing the harm of his neglect. Francis returned to his wife but the marital relationship grew worse rather than better. Next the family worked on getting Francis to return to the sacraments.

When Fr. Maximilian with the help of his brother, Fr. Alphonse, built the City of the Immaculate, Niepokalanów, a huge complex that housed 700 religious, Marianna wrote to ask if they had a statue of St. Francis. *Indifference among the sons and daughters of Saint Francis must not exist.*

Despite St. Maximilian's spiritual accomplishments his mother continued to reiterate in letters on baptismal and name day feasts that he and his brother were to strive for great holiness, a secret holiness known only to God. At Christmas she wrote to Fr. Alphonse, *May Christ teach you the way to holiness, and when He does, write and tell me.*

When Fr. Maximilian went to Japan to found the Garden of the Immaculate in Nagasaki, Fr. Alphonse was appointed superior of the City of the Immaculate. Imitating his older brother he worked tirelessly promoting the cause of Our Lady. At the age of thirty-four he died of appendicitis only hours before he was scheduled for surgery. Marianna, devastated by this newest family tragedy, quickly regained her composure. Accompanied only by friends she attended the funeral of her baby. Fr. Maximilian was in Japan and no one knew the whereabouts of Francis. At the wake, she kissed his stole, adjusted his hood, and then traced the sign of the cross on his forehead. His funeral was on the Feast of the Immaculate Conception. Fr. Maximilian wrote her: *He lived, suffered and sacrificed himself for the Immaculata.* Her sister Anna wrote: *I share your sorrow, for I have not yet forgotten my own. It is difficult to forget. Do not take it so hard, Dear Sister, for no one can go against the will of God. We cannot see as God does; neither are we able to understand...[L]et us offer our suffering and our crosses for the persecutors of our holy faith. And your son, if the Blessed Virgin has received him, he is more fortunate than we are in the valley of weeping and tears.*

When asked to write about Fr. Alphonse, she exhibited a keen understanding of his character and spiritual struggle: *We of the kingdom...who were raised under the heel of the Russians are not docile by nature. We must gain this through grace and struggle, and at times with great difficulty. Material for struggle and conflict was not lacking in the monastery. Alphonse disregarded the opinion of others; he courageously battled against self-love and this took a personal toll on him. At times he revolted vehemently. There were occasions when he was subject to ridicule. One side of his nature was sensitive, the other side, with grace, strong and resolute. He was not known to allow for personal resentments. He complained to Our Lady and to Our Lord about his weakness...* (Fr. Alphonse suffered from a partially deformed leg due to arthritis along with a nervous disorder that triggered a spasm with his speech and facial muscles. These physical handicaps made him an object of ridicule by others.)

After six years in Japan, Fr. Maximilian, for reasons of health, was reappointed superior of Niepokalanów in Poland. When Germany invaded Poland Sept. 1, 1939 life changed again for the Kolbes. For the safety of the friars, the majority were told to leave Niepokalanów. Fr. Maximilian stayed on with a small crew to help the homeless who flocked to his city for help. On the 12th of September the Gestapo arrived to partially destroy the City of the Immaculate. Seven days later, Fr. Kolbe, considered a threat to Nazism, was arrested with all but two friars. Miraculously, on the Feast of the Immaculate Conception they were released after being detained in prison camps for three months. Throughout Poland the Nazi persecution of the Church, priests and religious grew more violent. Masses had to be celebrated in secret.

Fourteen months later, on Feburary 17, 1941, Fr. Kolbe was again arrested with four priests. Although twenty brothers drew up a petition to exchange their lives for his, the Gestapo refused their offer. This imprisonment was to lead to his martyrdom. In a letter to a priest in Niepokalanów, Mrs. Kolbe projected her humanness along with her supernatural outlook: *There seems little hope of Father Maximilian's return, and an exhausting battle erupts inside me. I want to accept the will of God, yet I am violently assaulted with temptations. How is it that others are answered and fulfilled in their prayers, while I experience the opposite? The more I pray, the more bitter are the results.*

I was tempted to forsake my trust in the protection of the Immaculate Mother. I am tormented; my son was faithful to her and she does not help him...she does not save him. I am overcome with remorse. I sense the Virgin Mary's displeasure over my infidelity in bearing crosses. I hear her speak to my heart, the greater grace is to know how to suffer, rather than passively accept suffering. I grieve because of my attitude towards the fairest of Mothers.

Physical and spiritual agony engulfs me. If my son were to die in Niepokalanów, I would at least know where he is buried.

Although with joy I would give my life for his ransom, I fear to pray impetuously for his release. I am inspired to pray for what is most important—his sanctification and the glory of God.

Vehemently and with conviction I begged, as a mother who really loves her children, for Maximilian the strong love of martyrs. A love stronger than death—love that allows one to face death with joy. I listen with a torn heart to an inner voice that whispers, "above natural love, one must place the love of God, and the desire for eternal happiness for those we love."

When Fr. Kolbe offered his life in exchange for the life of a married man, he answered his mother's prayer of a *love stronger than death.*

Coping with the sorrow of having Fr. Maximilian imprisoned, Marianna next discovered that her son Francis was forced to flee his home at the insistence of his wife and daughter because men in the Russian sector of Poland were either being kidnapped or killed. Francis, ever the Polish patriot, decided to joined the underground.

Surprisingly, the spiritual formation that she instilled in Francis was deeply rooted within his soul despite his dysfunctional life. This wayward son, once again reunited with his family, gave her spiritual counsel. He admonished his mother, Should *having a holy martyr in heaven make us sorrowful or happy? Mama, rise higher than weak self-pity. I know it hurts, but he is the happiest of our whole family...*

At the beginning of 1943 Francis was arrested by the Germans and sent to several concentration camps, among them Auschwitz where his brother was martyred. He perished in Sachsenhausen Camp on January 23, 1945.

World War I claimed Marianna Kolbe's husband. World War II claimed two of her sons. Compounding these sorrows was the fact that these three family members did not have a Christian burial.

Despite her personal grief, Mrs. Kolbe did not wallow in self-pity. She was a woman of prayer and action. She immersed herself in good works calmly hiding priests, helping the homeless, and working in the soup kitchen despite the bombs exploding around her.   <u>When the war ended the Nazis had murdered over a third of the Polish priests as well as a third of its population.</u>

Sunday, March 17, 1946, as she left the convent to attend her Third Order meeting and Vesper Service she told Sister Mary Erica Pat, *One day, I will leave and not return.* Only a few blocks away from the convent, she collapsed. Two women seeing her collapse ran to her aid.   One stayed with her while the other ran for a priest.   The priest arrived just in time to anoint her as she uttered her last words *My son! My son!* Did she see the smiling face of St. Maximilian coming to lead her into paradise?   It was only after her death that it was discovered that she slept on rough boards. Sister Mary Praxeda Mika wrote, *She was a saint in little things and small ways...*

Fr. Anzelm Kubit, a classmate of St. Maximilian, likened her to St. Teresa of Avila: *She was a strong woman who lived by her convictions and in like manner suffered for them.* Marianna Kolbe's goal in life was to achieve personal sanctity for her husband, sons, and self.   She sacrificed her desire for the religious life to become a wife and mother giving the world holy, priestly sons. From all indications, Marianna Kolbe achieved her heavenly goal for her family.

There *Is* A Formula For Raising Saints

You have studied four families that raised saints.   Each was from a different culture and nationality but each used a common formula for raising saints. Have you been able to pick up on it?   Before we consider the formula, let's briefly consider several more families beginning with Alice of Montbar, the mother of St. Bernard. Alice has an enviable track record in raising saints. All seven of her children are either beatified or canonized.

Alice was the well-educated daughter of a wealthy family. Although the lady of the manor at the youthful age of fifteen years, she quickly took charge of her new home, estate, and each child as they were born.

Alice raised her children with a specific plan in mind...they were to become saints. Each of her children was educated in the virtues, especially the virtues of humility, charity, simplicity, modesty, moderation, temperance, and generosity.

In her free time she visited the homes of the poor to leave alms. When a villager was sick, she not only visited them, but also physically cared for them. She would bathe the sick person then clean his cottage.

Back at her own estate, she taught her children to live the virtue of poverty by eating simply.   She refused to imitate the sumptuous feasts of other nobles. *She did not want her children to be spoiled or to become delicate eaters...She thought most fashions were too affected and ornate, so she went her own way in the matter of dress for herself and her children as well. Alice avoided both extremes. She was not terribly unfashionable, or did she wear the latest in styles...[Her husband's] position as the king's advisor and his...[skill] as a knight opened up every social door to the couple, but they chose to live a rather quiet life...Showing off or acting extravagantly was one thing the children knew would draw their mother's wrath. Moderation and self-restraint, even though they were rich, was more Christ-like, and therefore more to be desired.*[84]

Baroness de Chantal, known to the world as St. Jeanne-Francoise de Chantal, was widowed while still young. All alone she cared for her children, her irritable father-in-law, his estate, as well as her own estate forty miles away. Despite the demands on her, Jeanne always made time to make daily visits to the poor and sick. *She used...[these visits] to teach her children to be charitable and compassionate and brought them with her even to deathbeds. This was, as her children saw it, a reward for obedience and industriousness...She tried to teach her children that love of labor was second only to the love of prayer. This is especially noteworthy since they were independently wealthy and did not have to work for a living...Luxury and too much leisure, Jeanne well knew, led to dissipation, selfishness, and vanity. Self-denial, sacrifice,*

---

[84] Wendy Leifeld, *Mothers of the Saints* (Ann Arbor: Servant Publications, 1991) p. 94.

charity, and an ardent love of God are nearly impossible under those conditions. To counteract the prevailing cultural climate they lived in, Madame de Chantal raised her children to keep themselves occupied and busy.[85]

When her daughters were old enough to learn to sew, Jeanne put them to work hemming altar linens for churches and making clothes for the poor. Jeanne worked hard to get to know the strengths and flaws of her children so that she could encourage their strengths and help them to overcome their character flaws and vices.

The custom of taking several hours to get dressed was simply not permitted. She dressed her children simply. *She taught them to be earnest, to esteem others for their qualities, not for their dress, and to laugh at those absurd and constantly changing fashions that entail such expense and cause so much sin.*[86]

St. Thomas More[87] is another great, "down-to-earth saint." He was a great English statesman, lawyer, and scholar, but he was equally skilled as a husband and father. During his life he strove to perfect each role. His first wife, *an ideal life companion,* died within their sixth year of marriage, leaving him with four little children to raise. When he remarried, it was to an older widow. Erasmus said of their relationship: *You will scarcely find a husband who, by authority or severity, has gained such a ready compliance [from his wife] as More [has] by playful flattery.*

More was known for his great sense of humor but even more so for his ability to combine learning and Christian virtue. Although involved with the great affairs of state for King Henry VIII, More was just as involved with the education of his children. We will study his concerns in this area in a later chapter.

Erasmus writes that More was careful *to have all his children, from their earliest years, thoroughly imbued with chaste and holy morals.* In the evening the household gathered for nightly

---

[85] *Ibid,* p. 144.   [86] *Ibid,* p. 145.
[87] The following is based on Thomas J. McGovern, *Sir Thomas More: The Making of a Saint* (New Rochelle: Scepter, 1986).

prayers. Feast days and Sundays were celebrated with increased piety.

More was generous with the poor, aged and infirm to the point that he founded a home in Chelsea to care for these people. When his son-in-law acquired the ideas of Luther, More tried to reason with him without success. Finally he wrote to his daughter, Meg, *I will no longer dispute with him but will clean give him over and get me to God to pray for him.* His prayers were answered and Roper returned to the faith at considerable personal cost.

Sir Thomas More moved in the highest and most prestigious circles in Europe. He counted as friends most of the great people of his age. He was not influenced by human respect. He spoke the truth and expected the same from others. It is this characteristic for which most people remember him. At a time when most of the English hierarchy, along with *all the best learned men of the realm,* compromised their consciences, More stood firm and almost alone in his allegiance to the papacy. His example of dying for the faith kept his family Catholic.

The Formula For Happy & Holy Children

In the Introduction to **Raise Happy Children Through A Happier Marriage** I talked about "sullen childhood." The families of saints that we just studied did not suffer from this disorder. **Why?** Paul Claudel believes that *Man is only happy when he lives according to his nature and when he strives to accomplish his end.*[88]

People who are happy laugh a lot, have a sense of humor, and seem to be able to cheerfully accept the most tragic or chaotic situations in life. There is a magnetic attraction about their personality. These people seem to glow. Throughout history artists depicted this glow as halos going around the heads of the people we call saints. The secret of their happiness is their growing relationship with God. Pope John Paul II in his social writings explains that our humanism depends on our

---

[88] Henri Morice, *The Apostolate of Moral Beauty* (St. Louis, Herder, 1961) p. 88.

relationship with Christ. The more united we are with God, the more human, the more loveable, the happier we become. The reverse is also true. The more we separate ourselves from Christ, the less human we become, the less happy. Can't you see this in society today? Turn on MTV for a second. Eavesdrop in a public high school. Glance at a magazine rack or video rental shelf. Look at the teen who waits on you at the store. Need I say more?

Shakespeare, who scholars think may have been Catholic, in his play, **As you Like It**, writes, *O, how bitter a thing it is to look into happiness through another man's eyes!* How can we avoid such a fate? How can we be happy and in turn, raise a happy family? The formula is simple but precise. I call it the four S's. Families that possess happiness base their family life on these four points:

1. Striving to deepen one's prayer life as an individual and as a family;
2. Struggling to grow in virtue which involves the cultivation of good habits;
3. Suffering with acceptance; and,
4. Sacrificing oneself for family members and strangers.

Living these four points **is** necessary to achieve holiness and happiness. These four points **must** also be lived with constancy, perseverance and patience **daily.** This is how the parents of saints and married saints structured their families. As St. Augustine exhorts us: *Cannot I do what these men and women did?* Let's consider what happens if one or more of these key points are missing in family life.

THE VISIONARIES OF LA SALETTE[89]

Jesus points out in Scripture, *It is not the healthy who need a physician, but they who are sick. For I have come not to call the just, but sinners (Mark 2:17).* His statement was not just for His immediate listeners but for us as well. God uses a

[89] Mary Ann Budnik, "The La Salette Seers—Faithful to Their Mission," *"You Will Make This Known To All My People,"* (New Bedford: Franciscans of the Immaculate, 1998) pp. 71-75.

variety of means to touch souls. In La Salette, France, He sent His Mother to call people to convert. There Our Lady's chosen messengers were two French children, Maximin Giraud and Melanie Mathieu, who were representative of the religious indifference prevalent in France in the mid 1800's.

Neither of these children has been canonized although they did fulfill the mission given to them by Our Lady to make her message ... *known to all my people.*   Despite their obedience to the request of Our Lady, their lack of spiritual formation as children prevented them from achieving the sanctity we associate with saints. Granted, they were not given the message because they were holy, but rather, they were given the divine assignment to call **us** to holiness. As the parish priest of Corps, Father Melin, explained: *Many people would like to see the children more mystical, at least more perfect. But the Blessed Virgin has left them their own natures and there is nothing we can do about it. What has been confided to them, it seems to me, can be compared to an orange in a jar. The orange does not change the jar, will not make it crystal.*

The children warned the French people and Church officials that the French people would be severely punished if they continued to work on Sunday and to take the name of God (Jesus) in vain. Their crops would be destroyed. They would endure a famine. A strange illness would kill young children. But, *If they convert, the stones and rocks will change into wheat, and potatoes will be found sown in the earth.*

Who were these children? Françoise Melanie Mathiew and Peter Maximin Giraud were both born in Corps, a small town of not more than 1,000 inhabitants in the southern French Alps. Surprisingly, they never met until the day before the apparition. Melanie, the eldest of the two, was born November 7, 1831. Maximin, four years younger, was born August 27, 1835. Both children were born into poverty. Neither of their families was considered devout. As a young child, Melanie contributed to the support of her family by grazing cattle and shepherding for farmers in the area. This left little opportunity for her to even attend Mass on Sunday or holydays. Her contact with the

Catholic Church was the sound of the church bells tolling in the valley while she labored as a shepherdess watching her sheep or cows on the mountains. When Our Lady asked, *Do you say your prayers well, my children?* Melanie truthfully replied, *No, Madame, hardly at all.* Later in life she would muse, *Isn't justice served that I, the least of all creatures, who did not begin to pray until the age of 15, suffer more and am more humiliated than others?*

It was a lonely, spiritually deficient life for such a young child. This possibly accounts for her timid, moody, sulky and introverted personality. There was no time for schooling for the little girl who spent her days out in the scorching summer heat and the frigid mountain winds of autumn.

Her employer at the time of the apparition, Baptiste Pra, reported that she was *excessively timid, and so careless of herself, that on returning from the mountain, drenched with rain, she never thought of changing her clothes. Sometimes, and it was a part of her character, she would sleep in the cattle-sheds; and at others, if not observed, she would have passed the night under the stars.* Pra also described Melanie as idle, disobedient, inclined to pout, and moody. He also noted that following the apparition, Melanie changed. She became more active and obedient. She began to pray. The young visionary struggled to control her moodiness. (See the power of grace in a life?)

Maximin's father was a cartwright, who by reputation was known to be undependable. In Corps, he was viewed as a spendthrift and drifter. Maximin's mother had died when he was small. His stepmother disliked the high-spirited little boy so she beat him frequently yet her abuse did not apparently affect his cheerful disposition.

Maximin preferred activity to study, which possibly explains why he could neither read nor write at the time of the apparition. In fact, his father claimed that it had taken the young boy three to four years to memorize the *Our Father* and *The Hail Mary*, prayers that toddlers today easily learn. Was it Maximin's short attention span or the fact that his father was teaching his son the prayers in the local cabaret? Like

Melanie, Maximin received no direction, no spiritual formation, had no positive role model, and worst of all, had no training in the natural or supernatural virtues. He was known to lie and swear previous to the apparitions.

At the time of the apparition, Melanie, fifteen, was hired out to Baptiste Pra of Les Ablandins, to watch his cows. Maximin, eleven, was similarly hired by Peter Selme to temporarily replace a little boy who had fallen ill.

The day before the apparition the children met for the first time on the mountain in the area of La Salette. While Melanie, shy and accustomed to the solitude, would have preferred to spend the day alone, Maximin craved companionship. Seeing her on the mountain, he hailed her, then spent the day chattering away. As they parted that day, they agreed to meet the next day on the mountain.

Saturday, September 19, 1846, began as any other day until the two children beheld the apparition of Our Lady sitting in the little hillock crying. That vision was to change their lives. As Maximin would later say to pilgrims questioning him about the apparition: *From there, she [Our Lady] rose into the air, disappeared, and left me with all my faults.* At another time he emphasized: *The apparition and I are two different things. I was only an instrument...We have been only conduits, only parrots who have repeated what we have heard. We were stupid before the apparition, we were stupid after, and we will be stupid all of our lives.*

When news of the apparition spread, the two children were placed for four years in Providence, a convent school in Corps, to be protected, educated, and prepared to make their First Communions. Melanie's family was given a small pension by Church officials so that Melanie would no longer have to work nor her sister beg for food on the street. She was allowed to make her First Communion only after her parents made their Easter duty.

Unlike other visionaries who entered the religious life, Maximin and Melanie never seemed to find their niche. Maximin wanted to become a priest but his years at the different seminaries proved that he was not interested in studying. The Superior of Providence explained that *Maximin has but ordinary abilities; he is sufficiently obedient, but light, fond of play, and always in motion.* His attention span was limited. He tried his hand as an apprentice mechanic. He unsuccessfully tried to obtain an arts degree, to become a doctor, or a pharmacist. Nothing worked out for him. There were months that he was so poor in Paris that he went hungry. Like his father, he was unable to handle money. At the age of thirty he became a Papal Zouave, a volunteer soldier of the Holy Father, then a French soldier. Imprudently he lent his name to a liquor venture headed by a swindler. March 1, 1875, at the age of forty, Maximin died from tuberculosis. Though of an unstable nature, he retained his innocent, childlike faith to the end of his life. When asked before his death, *Hasn't the apparition produced something special within you? I mean, hasn't it brought you a particular grace to improve you, to inspire you to live in a saintly way?* Maximin responded: *I can't say that. I never felt anything special. But the Blessed Virgin did grant me the grace of a very Christian education with the good Sisters of Corps. She surrounded me with very edifying priests. My childhood and youth were spent in a milieu that encouraged me to do good and to avoid evil. Without the apparition I could have strayed far from God and become really bad. I might even have become a member of the Internationale, or the Commune. By keeping me in this milieu and giving me the religious convictions I still have, she bestowed a wonderful gift on me.*

Melanie likewise led a wandering existence. She was in and out of various convents, beginning with the Sisters of Providence in Corps. At this convent her experience brought not only acclaim but adulation, both of which are deadly to spiritual growth. Comfortable with being the center of attention, Melanie began telling the sisters about her other "mystical experiences." Despite the fact that the stories were spectacular and grandiose, her mistress novice, Sister Therese de Jesus, encouraged Melanie's tales. Without a wise spiritual director or confessor working with the young woman, Bishop Ginoulhiac was unable to curb this spiritually dangerous development. When it was time for Melanie to take her vows, the bishop refused permission. Upset over his decision, she left that convent and was taken to England by Fr. Newsham where she joined the Carmelites only to leave to return again to France. In France, she stayed at the Marseille convent of Our Lady of Compassion. It was here that she became a teacher. After a year, the order sent her to work at their orphanage on the Greek isle of Cephalonia. After two years, Melanie returned to Marseille hoping to have her "secret" published. She was unsuccessful. When it was finally published it caused intense controversy. To silence the ever-growing controversy, the Holy See placed the "secret" on the Index of Forbidden Books and ruled that the "secret" was not connected to the authenticated apparition of Our Lady of La Salette.

During this controversy, disappointment and growing ill health plagued Melanie as she trekked back and forth between Italy and France. She spent the last months of her life in Altamura, Italy where she died December 14, 1904 at the age of seventy-three.

While Melanie and Maximin became faithful Catholics after the apparition, they were never canonized because of their lack of heroic virtues. These children, never educated in the 4 S's, led unhappy lives.

The Importance of Your Domestic Church

What lessons can you draw from these examples of family life? In studying the lives of saints, you can see that their formation, for the most part, began within the home, within the "domestic church" as the Holy Father refers to the family. The parents of saints and saintly parents not only taught their children how to pray, but they prayed with their children, took them to the sacraments frequently, pointed out the practical aspects of living the faith, taught them catechism, discussed the faith and how it impacted the issues of the day, kept Sunday holy, lived and encouraged their children to live the spiritual and corporal works of mercy. In addition, they trained them in the various natural virtues such as work, order, perseverance, charity, etc. They disciplined their children and taught their children the spirit of service, self-sacrifice, mortification and the purpose of suffering.

When parents do not educate their children in the faith and virtues at an early age, the children will have less chance to respond to God's calling. We see this so clearly in the case of the visionaries of La Salette. Their spiritually and emotionally dysfunctional families produced children who grew up to be dysfunctional adults. It was not until after Our Lady's appearance that they were instructed in the Catholic faith, and outside their homes at that. If Melanie and Maximin had been taught the Catholic faith and Christian virtues from their parents when they were little children, what a different ending their story would have had. Possibly we would call them saints today. As the convert G. K. Chesterton observed, *The Christian idea has not been tried and found wanting. It has been found difficult and left untried.* Don't you think it's time to peel off the bumper stick that reads: *My child is an honor student at_____* and replace it with one that reads: *My child is striving to be a saint and so am I!?*

Additional Helps

✓ Use the lives of the parents of saints and saintly parents as case studies. Discuss with your spouse and/or other married couples the parenting techniques of each saintly family. Begin by listing on a sheet of paper the similar methods they used to raise their children. What contributed to the growth and development of their children that led their children to become saints? Questions to consider:

❑ How did they live the 4 S's?

❑ What was their common goal for their children?

❑ How did these parents fight the vice of human respect?

❑ How did these parents live the 3rd commandment: *Thou shall keep holy the Sabboth?*

❑ What pious practices were practiced in the home and taught to the children?

❑ How can you teach your children similar practices?

❑ How did these parents instill love for prayer and the sacraments in their children?

❑ Specifically how can you imitate their example?

❑ How did these parents discipline and correct their children? What did you learn from their example?

❑ Consider the spiritual life of each father and each mother. How did they live their faith? How can you imitate their spirituality in your own life?

❑ How did these families specifically live the spiritual and corporal works of mercy? See Chapter 5 for a listing of the works of mercy.

❑ How did these parents live and teach the virtues of charity, work, sincerity, simplicity, order, industriousness, audacity, flexibility, fortitude, friendship, generosity, humility, justice, loyalty, modesty, moderation, obedience, optimism, patience, patriotism, perseverance, prudence, respect for others, responsibility, sociability, and understanding. Consult Dr. David Isaac's book, *Character Building* for help in understanding these virtues.

❑ Specifically, how can you begin to imitate their example in each of the above areas?

❏   How did these parents handle suffering? How did they teach their children to accept suffering and contradictions?

❏   How can you utilize suffering to grow spiritually and help your children to accept their daily crosses?

❏   How did these parents teach their children mortifcations, the spirit of self-sacrifice, and spirit of service?

❏   Explain in what areas the parents of the La Salette seers neglected to spiritually form their children. How can you avoid similar pitfalls?

✓   Introduce your children to the angels, saints and heroes/heroines of the Old Testament. Catholic Resource Center (800-874-8453) or www.Catholicresource@aol.com carries a wealth of books for children, particularly the St. Joseph series whose themes deal with 1. The teaching of the Church; 2. The Christian way of life; and 3. Catholic worship. Call for a catalog. Most books come in English, Spanish and French. These books I highly recommend. The artwork is excellent.

✓   View the video *El Cid* with your children if you have not already done so.

✓   Read **Don Quixote** with your teens and discuss it with them.

CHAPTER 2

THE STORY OF TWO LIVES: THE ROLE OF FAITH IN CHARACTER

"Sow a thought and you reap a desire; sow a desire and you reap a deed; sow a deed and you reap a habit; sow a habit and you reap a character; sow a character and it grows into your destiny."　　　**Anonymous**

For the last several years there has been a national discussion on the importance of "character." First of all what is *character?* Character is defined in the dictionary as *moral excellence and firmness.*[1] In other words, character means a person of integrity, one who holds firmly to set moral values, a person who is incorruptible. Author James Stenson, who writes extensively on the topic of character, further defines it as *strengths of intellect and will whereby people direct their lives. These include faith, hope, charity, prudence (sound judgment), justice (fairness), fortitude (capacity to withstand discomfort), and temperance (self-control).*[2] Note that all these characteristics are virtues (good habits). Stenson adds that character is developed in three ways:

---

[1] *Webster's New Collegiate Dictionary*, 1980, p.185.

[2] James Stenson, "Fatherhood: The Dynamics of Character Formation" Lecture.

✓ By **example**: by what the children **witness** in the lives of their parents and other adults whom they admire—for children (like the rest of us) unconsciously imitate people they admire.
✓ By **directed practice**: by what the children are repeatedly **led to do**, or **made to do**, by parents and other respected adults.
✓ By **word**: **by verbal explanation** of what they witness and are led or made to do.[3]

I would add a fourth point:

✓ By enduring **hardship and suffering**.

Unless a child learns how to suffer, the firmness needed to sustain integrity of character will be lacking. Let me give you a scientific example from Biosphere Two. This was an experiment to see if man could live in a man-made environment. Biosphere was completely self-contained. What was discovered is that as the trees in this artificial environment grew to a certain height, they toppled over because of a lack of root structure. Scientists further discovered that the lack of a root system was caused by the absence of wind in this man-made environment. Trees need the friction of wind to stimulate their rooting capacity just as we need trials and sufferings to stimulate the virtue of fortitude within ourselves. By protecting your children from the sorrows and disappointments in life, you are destroying opportunities for them to develop courage and fortitude.

The character of a child is pretty well formed by the age of reason. Motivational writer Zig Ziglar maintains that by the age of five character is 80% developed. These early years are critical in forming your child spiritually and morally.

Is character important? Think about it. If you owned a business could you trust an employee who lacks moral integrity? Would you hire a babysitter who lacks moral integrity? Would you want a repairman in your home, alone with your wife, who lacks moral integrity? Would you buy a pre-owned car from

------

[3] James Stenson, *Lifeline* (NY: Scepter, 1996) p. 27.

someone who lacks moral integrity? Of course not. Character *matters*. ***A good name is better than great riches: and good favor is above silver and gold*** according to the book of ***Proverbs*** (22:1). The truly great men and women of history **had** character rather than **being** characters. Abigail Adams, the wife of the second President of the United States, used Shakespeare's quote, *Take his character all together, and we shall not look upon his like again*, to describe George Washington.

What about character in government? Is it necessary? According to the Thomas Jefferson Research Center located in California, *Some things are common in all great civilizations and religions—wisdom, integrity, love, freedom, justice, courage, humility, patience, industriousness, thriftiness, generosity, objectivity, cooperation, moderation and optimism.* Many people, out of a mistaken loyalty to a political party insist that the personal conduct of a government leader does not influence the direction of government. This is naïveté. The character or lack of character of political leaders impacts government either for good or for evil. One of our founding fathers, John Adams also authored the *Constitution for the State of Massachusetts.* In this document he pointed out: *Wisdom and knowledge, as well as virtue, diffused generally among the body of the people [are]...necessary for the preservation of their rights and liberties...[I]t is the duty of legislators and magistrates...to countenance and inculcate the principles of humanity and general benevolence, public and private charity, industry and frugality, honesty and punctuality in their dealings, sincerity, good humor, and all social affections and generous sentiments among the people.*[4] This was a consistent theme in Adam's writings and speeches. When the seat of the U.S. government was permanently moved to Washington, D.C., President John Adams gave the first invocation in the Capitol praying, *May this territory be the residence of virtue and happiness! In this city may that piety and virtue, that wisdom and magnanimity, that constancy and self-government, which adorned the great character [Washington] whose name it bears, be forever held in*

---

[4] David McCullough, *John Adams* (NY: Simon & Schuster, 2001) p. 223.

veneration! Here, and throughout our country, may simple manners, pure morals, and true religion flourish forever![5]

Character is based on how one lives personal morality. Morality is conforming to a standard of right and wrong behavior based on the natural law of God, which is written within the soul of each person and promulgated in the Ten Commandments. How can we expect children, teens, and adults to be morally excellent if they are ignorant as to what moral excellence, character, entails? In addition to teaching your children the Ten Commandments and moral standards at home, your efforts likewise must be supported by the educational systems you entrust your children to because their free will must be carefully nutured so that they choose good over evil. Since the Supreme Court ruled that the display of the commandments is unconstitutional, we have been plagued with school shootings. In addition to the wrongful exercise of free will in these situations is there a cause and effect relationship at work here?

Morality is living a virtuous life; having the habit of performing good actions rather than evil actions. It is based on living a life of virtue. One must live these virtues consistently no matter what situation one finds himself in. One must live a virtuous life when one is healthy as well as when one is sick. But virtues can only be lived consistently when they are united to a living, ever deepening faith. When it is not, a person's morality tends to become subjective rather than objective. Situation ethics, "feelings" or emotions triumph rather than principle. Right and wrong becomes arbitrary rather than a universal standard. This is the situation with abortion, contraception, pornography and the "gay rights" controversy. What you consider morally acceptable may be objectionable to me. A Gallup Poll taken in 1998 showed that 37% of employees approve of minor "employee theft." In 1969 a Gallup Poll showed that 68% of Americans found premarital sex morally wrong. By 1999 70% of these same Americans gave President Clinton a high approval rating despite his blatant immorality

---

[5] *Ibid.,* p. 554.

in public office. In May 2001 a Barna survey found that 58% of Americans *say cohabiting, watching a sexually explicit movie, and having sexual fantasies are morally acceptable behaviors.*[6] This same poll found that 37% of Americans feel that profanity is morally permissible while 70% of mainline Protestants believe that divorce is not a sin. *Researchers found that almost three-quarters of American adults are concerned about the moral condition of the nation. About one-quarter said their moral decisions are primarily based on religious principles and biblical teaching, while 44 percent said their moral choices were based on a desire to do what brings them the most satisfying or pleasing results.*[7] Pretty scary, isn't it?

While the natural law of God is written in the heart of every person, the effects of original sin intrude so that we use our free will many times for evil rather than for the good. We can curve our tendency to sin through a living faith added by the exercise of natural virtues (good habits). St. Paul told the Romans, *...[T]he Law is spiritual but I am carnal, sold unto the power of sin. For I do not understand what I do, for it is not what I wish that I do, but what I hate, that I do...Therefore, when I wish to do good I discover this law, namely, that evil is at hand for me* (7:14-18). This makes it difficult for us to live morally upright lives so as to be people of character. It makes consensus in society impossible. That is why our Pledge of Allegiance very specifically maintains the importance of *one nation under God indivisible with liberty and justice for all.* If not under God, the nation is divided by self-interests. The Founding Fathers of the United States understood this principle well. At a critical point during the War of Independence, notwithstanding the lack of financial resources, the Continental Congress passed a bill allocating $300,000 to purchase Bibles to be distributed to the Colonists living in the thirteen colonies. Note well the date this bill was passed...September 11, 1777.

Totalitarian governments also understand this principle.

---

[6] *The Atlanta Journal-Constitution*, Sept. 15, 2001. p. B2.
[7] *Ibid.*

During the height of Nazism, SS officials felt threatened by Blessed Titus Brandsma, a Carmelite. The SS thought Brandsma *genuinely a man of character and firm convictions,*[8] so acting from an evil premise within themselves they used their free will to exterminated him in Dachau. His good character was perceived as a threat to them.

Self- Esteem & Character

In the Gospel of *St. Luke* (14:1, 7-14) Jesus is invited to a dinner. While there, He observed two character flaws: the host only invited **the** best people while the dinner guests selected **the** best seats for themselves. Father Edward J. Thein, the pastor of Holy Family Parish in Marietta, Georgia used this gospel to give a deeper insight into the related topics of self-esteem and character. The following are the notes from his homily.[9]

The host and the guests portrayed in this Gospel were simply seeking self-esteem. It is part of human nature. When defined, self-esteem is based on the drive to exist and to be significant. *Look at me...I count! I'm somebody. I am.* These are basic human drives and needs.

Jesus does not tell us to ignore our self-esteem, He asks us to consider what criteria we use to make ourselves feel important, significant. The criteria of both the host and the guests were all wrong—competition and external status. Genuine self-esteem is based within us.

There are five major categories that we use to measure our self-esteem:

- ✓ Significance to others.
- ✓ Competence in my job performance.
- ✓ Power to influence people.
- ✓ Body image.
- ✓ Possessions.

---

[8] Matthew, Margaret, Stephen Bunson, *John Paul II's Book Of Saints* (Huntington: Our Sunday Visitor, 1999) p. 353.

[9] September 2, 2001.

Let's consider each of these categories.

Significance to others: We really do not have "self"-esteem as much as "other"-esteem; that is, what others think about us ultimately leads us to think the same thing about ourselves. We call this peer pressure. This raises the question, to whom have I given control over my sense of self-esteem? PROBLEM: If my self-esteem is based on what someone else thinks about me, what happens if that person is no longer in my life? This "other"-esteem creates an ongoing co-dependency preventing my true self from emerging, that is, who I am and what I stand for. I can never learn to be my own person.

Competency: If my self-esteem is based on what I do—and do well—this is equally fragile. Sooner or later work and ability falter, destroying my self-esteem since our culture values people for what they can do, not for who they are. PROBLEM 1: The unborn are not valued because they cannot "do anything." We devalue the handicapped, the retired and the elderly likewise. We are often praised for our competency, but never praised simply for who we are.

PROBLEM 2: Being praised for competency is just not enough. Suspicions arise that when I lose my competency, I will lose respect, I will lose value, and I will lose the esteem of other people. I will even lose my identity.

Power over other people: This works for a while as a source of self-esteem for parents, employers, politicians, stars, and even leaders of youth gangs. PROBLEM: When people begin to grow they need to get out from under that control. If one's self-esteem is based on this category, who are you then when you no longer have the power to influence others?

Body image: In this category inner virtue and character are considered negligible and external image is everything. A whole body related industry creates this illusion. Body image becomes crucial for a sense of self-esteem. Obsessions with weight, skin, hair, and clothes are a national pastime and have spawned a multi-billion-dollar market. We look for products that will "cure" whatever is wrong with our appearance. Bulimia and anorexia thrive as the dark side of this culture of body image. PROBLEM: To be "in," people will suppress what is nobler in the human spirit. God forbid you have the wrong "look" on the first day of school! You'll be dubbed a nerd forever.

Possessions: The more possessions we have, the louder the applause or greater the envy, the bigger the boost to self-esteem. The rule seems to be that the less sense of inner worth one has, the more one must display lavish outer worth. It's not a strong, loving and supportive family that is important. Look at the late model cars and designer clothes our children must have. PROBLEM: Let the market crash, and people who identified themselves with their possessions can also crash. Some commit suicide, several have gone on homicidal rages. Who remembers the last funeral procession followed by a U-Haul full of the deceased's possessions?

In the end, all these criteria betray us; that is the point behind the gospel story. Self-esteem, self-worth, is centered elsewhere. It is centered in being a child of God, being beloved by God, in doing the Godlike things of our nature such as telling the truth, keeping your word, giving to those who cannot repay, and taking the lowest seat. **Self-esteem is what we used to call having "character," an inner anchoring in truth, a sense of the "deep within," an awareness of our core identity as being made in the image and likeness of God.**

Fr. Thein concluded his homily by stressing that there is a reward for those who strive for an inner character that reflects God's image; there are words for those who learn that using external criteria as a basis for self-esteem will ultimately betray them: *My friend, come up higher.*

Faith & Character

In the first chapter we examined the character and faith of saints and the parents of saints. In the beginning of this chapter we discussed the importance of character and government. Let's now consider the faith and character of five famous men from the last century: Thomas Edison, Henry Ford, Harvey

Firestone, Alexis Carrel and Charles Lindbergh.* All were men of integrity, outstanding character and men of strong faith, although only Alexis Carrel was a Catholic. They were all close friends of James Newton, one of the founders of the Moral Re-Armament Movement whose goal was to infuse the importance of character back into our culture. The following information is based on his book, ***Uncommon Friends.***

It has been said of Thomas Alva Edison that he "invented the twentieth century." He owned *1,093 patents for his inventions— that is, a patent for every ten to twelve days of his adult life.*[10] Among his thousand of inventions, Edison found a substitute for rubber in his Edison Botanic Research Corporation, the electric light bulb (and everything related to it), the phonograph, the motion-picture camera, talking movies, a forerunner of the television tube, tin foil, wax paper, and the carbon transmitter to make telephones possible for general use. He never took personal credit for his genius. Instead he said, *When you see everything that happens in the world of science and in the working of the universe, you cannot deny that there is a "Captain on the bridge."*[11]

When Henry Ford, Harvey Firestone, and he got together the three discussed science, philosophy, government, and religion. All three felt that religion was at the core of character and progress. Right before he died, he awoke from his coma and told his wife, *It's very beautiful over there.* He must have had a glimpse of heaven.

It was Thomas Edison who gave Henry Ford his start. Introduced at a dinner in New York, Ford explained to Edison that he had designed a gas car. Edison was intrigued with him since he himself was doing work to improve the electric car. During their discussion Ford drew sketches of his design that impressed Edison, *he then banged a fist on the table and said,*

---

*Lindbergh was falsely accused of endorsing the Nazis when he was forced into accepting an aviation award from them while in Germany gathering intelligence information for the U.S. government.

[10] James Newton, *Uncommon Friends* (San Diego: Harcourt, 1987) p.19.

[11] *Ibid.*, p. 30.

"Young man, that's the thing. Your car is self-contained, no boiler, no heavy battery, no smoke or steam. Keep at it!"

"You can imagine how excited I was, the man who knew most about electricity in the world—my boyhood idol—telling me my car was better than an electric car! He was the first to give me real encouragement that my dream would work! Well, that boyhood idol became my manhood friend." [12]

Not only did Ford design the automobile as we know it today, but he made it financially within reach for the common man through his assembly line, another first in industry. A quiet man of faith, Ford insisted that *When fear seizes us, it's a sign that the body has taken over the soul.* He also maintained that *there's enough goodwill in people to stop fighting, class war, and economic slump. Governments lack that kind of power. We have to find ways to turn our private moral convictions into public policies.* [13] To James Newton, Ford sent a bible with a line from **Hebrews** 11:1 underline: ***Now faith is the substance of things hoped for, the evidence of things not seen.***

During World War II, Charles Lindbergh worked with Ford Motor Company on developing fighter planes. In a letter of congratulations to Ford, Charles wrote:...*You combine the characteristics that I admire most in men—success with humility, firmness with tolerance, science with religion—I shall not attempt to make a longer list. Possibly the thing I admire most about you is that you have built one of the world's greatest industries without letting it change your own outlook and character.* [14]

Harvey Firestone was the giant of the tire industry. His business relationship with the Ford Company grew into a personal friendship with Ford. Harvey felt that *fundamental honesty is the keystone of business.* He applied his faith in God to his personal and business transactions. On more than one occasion Firestone observed, *Elections don't make much difference any more. We've gotten away from things that matter in this country. We need a much deeper moral and spiritual*

---

[12] *Ibid.*, p. 10. [13] *Ibid.*, p.30. [14] *Ibid.*, p. 267.

change than politics can give us.[15] This conviction grew even
stronger when his son Bud, an alcoholic, finally turned his life
over to God and become sober. This spiritual conversion led
Bud Firestone to work with others to found Alcoholics
Anonymous. Faith also rebuilds character.

The French surgeon, Alexis Carrel, a Catholic, won the Nobel
Prize in 1912 for the transplantation of organs and the suturing
of blood vessels. He is also known for developing tissue and
cell culture. Carrel worked with another genius but from the
world of aviation, Charles Lindbergh, on the perfusion pump
that kept organs free from infection and alive outside of the
body, as well as an artificial heart. Although a scientist of great
repute, he was not afraid to tell his associates that God
permeated everything in the world. *You understand that man
does not live by bread alone. Nor does society. It needs
equilibrium between material and spiritual nourishment,* he
insisted.[16] *[T]he point is to <u>concentrate your attention on
something beyond the self—then comes inner peace.</u> Man
integrates himself by meditation and by action. <u>And most of all
by bending all his energies in a moral and a spiritual quest.</u>*[17]
While Carrel felt that character was key, he also felt that man
*must also seek ways to know the will of God...Today, anything
in the way of spiritual endeavor is regarded with great suspicion
by most scientists and intellectuals. <u>But the real obstacle to
following that path is the strict discipline it requires. Just as an
athlete has to go into physical training, someone who follows the
road to the mystical and spiritual must accept a discipline of
the physical appetites.</u>*[18]

In another conversation, Dr. Carrel, pointed out: *We have
put too much emphasis on intellect and so little on moral
sense....Moral sense is so much more important than intellect.
When that disappears from a nation, everything else begins to
crumble. You see it every day when you read the newspaper—in
your country and mine...[C]hange in society has to begin in the
motives of men. But how is it to be done on a great enough scale
to reverse the flow of materialism in our civilization?* His listener,

[15] *Ibid.*, p. 57.   [16] *Ibid.*, p. 123.   [17] *Ibid.*, p. 131.   [18] *Ibid.*, p. 127.

James Newton, responded, *Well, the only way I know is for people to start with themselves...*Carrel agreed and called for a *renaissance of values in the life of modern man.*[19]

When World War II erupted, Dr. Carrel became involved in medical preparations for the wounded. He again wrote to Mr. Newton from France: *There would be an immense material progress in this country if there was a spiritual change. It is quite surprising to witness the effect of antagonism, fear, jealousy, selfishness on the results of the work of those entrusted with the defense of the nation.*[20] At another time this great man, now involved with chemotherapy, blood transfusions and other innovative aspects of medicine wrote to his friend, *I want to be like smoke in the wind at God's disposal...God's love is the great reality. It is the mortar that holds the bricks of civilization together.*[21]

Charles A. Lindbergh, the aviation hero who put transcontinental air travel within the reach of every person was also a test pilot, a designer, an inventor, a consultant to the Air Force, a member of the committee to develop ballistic missiles, a member of the Strategic Air Command, a diplomat, as well as part of the commission to select the site for the Air Force Academy. Following World War II he observed, *We will always be on the defensive unless we commit ourselves to vigorous and positive moral policies. We need to reach beyond materialism to a philosophy springing from the character of man and the truths of God.*[22] Later he added, *a solution to instability in the world has to come at a deeper level. The quality of a civilization depends on a balance of body, mind, and spirit in its people, measured on a scale less human than divine.* This balance can be imposed by government or by individual self-control. Self-control comes from *the acceptance of certain human values— you would call them Christian values—love, honesty, purity of motive, regard for others.*[23]

Anne Morrow Lindbergh, the daughter of an ambassador and a noted author, joined the discussion by observing that

[19] *Ibid.,* pp. 142-143. [20] *Ibid.,* p. 187. [21] *Ibid.,* p. 194. [22] *Ibid.,* p. 292. [23] *Ibid.,* p. 294.

St. Francis of Assisi was not only important because of the foundation of the Franciscan order or because of his powerful preaching of the virtues but rather because *he had taken Christianity out of the church and into the streets and the marketplace and the kitchen. Ordinary people by the thousands responded to his call—they had been ready. That joyous flowering of the human spirit had led to the Renaissance...It had all come from within.*[24] Charles Lindbergh believed *the solution [to change our culture] lay in each individual, through the standards he held, not in political parties, movements, or laws, but in human values. In other words, the solution lays within ourselves. It was not an intellectual question but one of will and desire.*[25]

When Lindbergh was awarded the Guggenheim medal he told the audience: *We have measured success by our products rather than by ourselves. A materialism that overemphasizes short-term survival detracts from the humanism essential to long-term survival. We must remember that it was not the outer grandeur of the Roman, but the inner simplicity of the Christian that lived on through the ages.*[26]

Author James Newton sums up his observation of his five friends: *[T]heir greatest legacy to us would still be their faith, expressed by each in his own way, that we place our body, mind, and spirit at the disposal of our Creator, who will use them to fashion mankind in ways beyond our wisdom or imagination.*[27]

Character Is Perfected By Grace

St. Paul explained to the Romans, *For I am delighted with the law of God according to the inner man, but I see another law in my members, warring against the law of my mind and making me prisoner to the law of sin that is in my members...Who will deliver me from the body of this death? The grace of God through Jesus Christ our Lord...*(**Romans** 7:21-25).

The graces that St. Paul writes about are actual graces, sacramental graces and sanctifying graces. Fr. John Hardon,SJ,

---

[24] *Ibid.,* p. 294.   [25] *Ibid.,* p. 297.   [26] *Ibid.,* p. 304.   [27] *Ibid.,* p. 357.

explains:...*The supernatural life is capable of increase and depth, depending on the frequency and fervor with which the sacraments are received, on devotion to prayer and, in fact, on the whole gamut of good works performed, which merit growth in sanctifying grace and advancement in the soul's nearness to God.*

*It is not a passing remark when the Council of Trent described justification as a "renovation of the interior man through the **voluntary** reception of grace," since <u>our free wills have much to do with setting limits to divine generosity</u>. St. Francis de Sales observed that in the measure to which we divest ourselves of self-love, so that our heart does not refuse consent to the divine mercy, God "ever pours forth and ceaselessly spreads His sacred inspirations, which ever increase and make us increase more and more in heavenly love." He then <u>asks how it happens that we are not so advanced in the love of God as some of the saints: "It is because God has not given us the grace. But why has He not given us the grace? Because we did not correspond with His inspirations as we should have. And why did we not correspond? Because being free we have herein abused our liberty."</u>*

Living in grace, therefore, is a vital process from the divine side and from ours: God is free to confer this life and in the degree that pleases His unfathomable will, and <u>we are free to receive what He offers and as much as we choose according to our generosity.</u>[28]

The development of character in a child/person has spiritual and temporal benefits. Lutz Gabriel, M.D., a Catholic psychiatrist, writes *I will always marvel at the amazing effects on how a deepening faith and love of God in patients have strengthened their character and re-integrated their personalities.*[29]

Thomas Monaghan, who you will meet later in this chapter,

---

[28] John A. Hardon, S.J., *The Catholic Catechism* (NY: Doubleday & Company, Inc., 1975) pp. 182-183.

[29] Lutz Gabriel , M.D., "The Roman Catholic Psychiatrist," *The Catholic Faith,* March/April 1996, p. 17.

found that a *disproportionate number of CEO's in the U.S. are Catholic numbering at least 100,000.* Motivational writer, Zig Ziglar, describes an interesting study made by **Who's Who In America**. What type of people make this prestigious list? *Researchers discovered that it took 25,000 laboring families to produce 1 child who would be listed in **Who's Who**. It required 10,00 families in which that father was a skilled craftsman, 6,000 Baptist preachers, 5,000 lawyers, 5,000 Presbyterian preachers, 2,500 dentists, and 1,200 Episcopalian priests to produce someone listed...However, every seventh Christian missionary family produced a member...*[30]

Ziglar surmises that these children became successes because of the sacrifices lived to promote their faith, the lack of material luxuries, the close family unity, the dedication and example of their parents, and the scarcity of negative outside influences such as TV and newspapers. He then ends by saying, *we teach what we know, but <u>we reproduce what we are</u>.*[31]

The Holy Father reiterates that the Christian family is called to evangelization, to bring about the reign of Christ in the world now. You and your children are called to be the missionaries to the world, to change it in the manner desired by Edison, Ford, Firestone, Carrel and Lindbergh but unless you and they have character all efforts will prove fruitless.

Let's put flesh on Dr. Gabriel's observation by studying the lives of two internationally known billionaires, Thomas (Tom) S. Monaghan and Robert Edward (Ted) Turner III. This is a fascinating but difficult comparison to write. The intimate working of God's grace in souls is mysterious, and God never gives up; so it would be unjust for us to classify any human being still on this earth—or even after death—as either lost or saved. This applies both to Ted Turner and Tom Monaghan. Both men must ultimately face their Maker, and it is **He** who will judge who is truly worthy, based on the graces and

---

[30] Zig Ziglar, Staying *Up,Up, Up In A Down, Down, World* (Nashville: Thomas Nelson Publishers, 2000) p. 3.
[31] *Ibid.,* p. 4.

opportunities that He gave to both men during their lives—along with the sorrows and pains that He sent them.

Nevertheless it is legitimate to look at the world and people's lives candidly, in order to learn something important for ourselves and for our families, and to appreciate more the transforming nature of faith in human actions...or what can happen when it is apparently lacking. And so, without the desire either to "demonize" or "canonize" I begin this section with an earnest prayer for the good of both of these men, Ted and Tom, and for their families.

Close in age, wealth, and prominence, the lives of Ted and Tom have incredibly striking parallels despite the divergent paths their lives have taken. Both owned/own major league baseball teams, raise bison, have been invited to the White House by a president and were named by **Forbes** as part of the *"400 Richest People In America."* While both Ted and Tom should have been raised Catholics, only Tom was raised in the faith. Let's begin with Ted Turner.

The Impact Of Faith On Character

"My departure from Christianity was slow, meticulous, and without crisis or fury or anguish. Progressively I ceased being Christian, because when still very young I took religion very seriously. Otherwise I would have remained a Catholic."
Belgian playwright, professor and politician Francois Perin[32]

Ted Turner, the founder of CNN, is a mixture of English, Scottish and French on his father's side while on his mother's side he claims Dutch, Irish and German ancestry.[33] His mother, Florence Rooney Turner Carter, was from a prominent Catholic,

---

[32] Perin's explanation on his apostasy from Christianity and his belief in older, pagan gods in an interview in *Hindus Today Magazine*, Feb. 1999. From the wire services.

[33] Porter Bibb, *It Ain't As Easy As It Looks* (New York: Crown Press, 1993). All information on Mr. Turner is taken from this biography.

Cincinnati family. It was her grandfather, Henry Sicking, who founded the first chain of grocery stores in the Midwest. Raised as a Roman Catholic, Florence attended exclusive convent schools. Her storybook life ended when her parents divorced in 1915, a rare occurrence in those days.

Engaged at the age of twenty, Florence's fiancé suffered an acute appendicitis attack the night before their wedding. He died two days later. When she was almost thirty, her brother introduced her to a southerner, Robert Edward (Ed) Turner, Jr., a car salesman from Mississippi. Ed Turner, although raised a strict Methodist, did not practice his faith. Their eight-month whirlwind courtship culminated with their marriage at St. Francis de Sales Cathedral in Cincinnati. Little did Florence realize that her elegant, society marriage would cost her the loss of her Catholic faith. As the two rode away from the Cathedral following their wedding, Ed told Florence that she was never to step into a Catholic church again. So Florence joined a high Episcopal church.

Without a vibrant living faith, their marriage was a difficult one. November 19, 1938, their son, Robert Edward (Ted) Turner III was born. Mary Jane, their second child was born three years later.

Then began a list of moves around the country for the family, first when Ed joined the Navy, then later for business reasons. While the Turners took Mary Jane with them, Ted was left behind at the age of three to live with his maternal grandmother until he was sent to a boarding school at the age of six. During the next fifteen years he spent all but one year away from his family. His only year spent with his family was when his father relocated to Savannah, Georgia. Ted was in sixth grade at the time.

A discipline problem at the boarding schools, Ted's father sent him Georgia Military Academy, a school with the reputation of straightening out troublesome well-to-do young men. His summers were rotated between his two sets of grandparents rather than with his parents and sister.

Turner, not interested in studying, was next sent to board at McCallie, an exclusive school in Chattanooga, Tennessee, where he was the only seventh-grade boarder. Students his age were day students. He was a discipline problem there as well.

On returning home after his first year at McCallie, Turner learned that his sister, Mary Jane, was stricken with a rare form of lupus that not only affected her body but also her mind. This began a heart breaking five-year ordeal for the Turner family. His mother, consumed with the burden of caring for Mary Jane, was unavailable for Ted, leaving him to feel completely rejected by his parents.

Influenced by McCallie's strong Presbyterianism, Ted spent one summer reading the Bible through...twice. Moved by the scriptures, when he was a sophomore he announced his intention to become a missionary. His faith was shattered when Mary Jane died of systemic brain damage in his junior year. She was just fifteen. Unschooled in the acceptance of suffering and the cross, Ted rejected God, imitating the example of his father.

While his father expected Ted to attend Harvard, his C-average earned him only entrance to Brown University in Rhode Island. There he majored in classics until he was expelled. He never completed college.

At twenty-one he married Judy Nye, of Chicago, but by the time he was twenty-three, Ted was the divorced father of two children. This began a string of broken marriages. While he had the Midas touch for business, as a spouse his efforts were sadly lacking. He was simply imitating the example of his parents who had divorced in 1959. In 1960 his father remarried but, fearing he would lose his substantial fortune, he committed suicide. He was fifty-three years old at the time.

Ted, taking control of his father's business, set to work to build an empire. From billboards, Ted turned to acquiring radio stations and then TV stations. In reflecting over his life, Turner muses: *When I was a young man I was a good man. I worked hard. I was always honest and a good patriotic citizen, paid my taxes, had never been indicted for anything. But I was more interested in my own pleasure, in making money. I was interested in winning sailboat races, primarily. Gradually, over a period of time, I would see what was happening.*[34]

Originally a political conservative, Turner, influenced by Castro, as well as girlfriends who were Marxist, New Agers or Radical Leftists, became a radical liberal. His views toward Christianity grew verbally more antagonist. He attacked the Ten Commandments as outdated. Then he publicly stated that *Christianity is for losers.*[35] Ash Wednesday of 2001 he harassed employees wearing ashes by demanding, *What are you, a bunch of Jesus freaks?* This comment moved Stuart Varney, co-anchor of CNN's "Moneyline News Hour," to quit. While Turner later apologized for his comment, for Varney it was the last straw.[36]

Ted believes that the government should limit families to two children. To meet his goal, he pledged $1 billion to the UN, which among other things will be used to fund population control, i.e., abortion, forced sterilization. In addition, in 1999 the Turner Foundation gave $3.3 million to the National Abortion and Reproductive Rights Action League (NARAL). As the founder of the Better World Society (BWS) in 1985, whose slogan is *Harnessing the Power of Television To Make A Better World,* his networks are used to change the belief systems of its viewers. In 1985 and 1989 over forty documentaries were funded by BWS. These were then broadcast on CNN, Ted's Superstation, TBS, or other cable networks. BWS's programming is distributed free to the Soviet Union and China. Through documentaries for TBS, made-for-TV-movies and specials, he pushes his radical environmental themes, the myth of overpopulation, and "the new world order."

On a mission to save the world from itself, Turner boasts, *I intend to conquer the world but instead of conquering with bombs,*

---

[34] Ted Turner, "Talking with David Frost," Television interview aired on PBS, Jan. 2, 1991.

[35] Zenit, Aug. 29, 2000.   [36] Zenit, March 18, 2001.

I intend to conquer with good ideas."[37] Unfortunately, one cannot make a silk purse out of a sow's ear.

Idealism is only sound when based on the natural law of God. The Turner family biography seems a perfect case study depicting the tragic results of abandoning the faith and the laws of God for personal convenience. A person's actions affect one's spouse, one's family, along with all the people one influences in the course of a lifetime. God is the source of interior happiness, *not* great wealth. Pope Pius IX told U.S. Cardinal James Gibbons, *The American people are much engrossed in worldly things and in the pursuit of wealth, and these things are not favorable to religion; it is not I who say it but Our Lord in the Gospel.*[38]

Considering Ted Turner's, immense influence and wealth, what good he could have done in the world if he had been raised as a solid, practicing Catholic! But even more important, how much happier and fulfilled his life would have been along with the lives of his first wife and children. If Florence had been taught by her parents the importance of living the Catholic faith, she would have persisted in the practice of her faith rather than capitulating to the unreasonable demands of her husband. In doing so she would have imitated St. Monica possibly winning her husband's conversion and saving his life. *If...if...if...*

Yes, it's heroic to practice the faith in the face of disapproval from someone we love but *that's* the stuff of saints. In the eyes of God it is not permissible to deny our faith for a bowl of porridge as Esau did. Despite Ted's desire *to conquer the world...with good ideas,* only people with character can change the world for the *better.*

But let's not give up on Ted. Only God can judge the human heart based on the graces, opportunities, and sorrows that He sends us. Prayer is all-powerful, and our Catholic faith teaches us to continue praying for everyone, especially for those who

[37] *Atlanta Constitution,* Sept. 1, 1982, p. D-5.

[38] Arline Boucher and John Tehan, *Prince of Democracy: James Cardinal Gibbons* (NY: Hanover House, 1962) p. 16.

seem the farthest away from God. With the mercy of God and prayer there is still time for Ted to "turn around."

The Power Of A Faith-Filled Life...

"There is an impression prevalent that worldly success and Roman Catholicism are not compatible... That is only an extra reason why Catholics should make themselves more proficient in their respective trades and professions...And if he shines in his Catholicity as he does in his profession, then the cause of Catholicity will benefit in proportion." Rev. Thomas J. Gerrard[39]

Thomas S. Monaghan, founder of Domino's Pizza and chairman of the Ave Maria Foundation begins his autobiography, *Pizza Tiger*,[40] with a dedication to his life-long sweetheart, his wife, Margie:

> *To Margie,*
> *whose help and support sustained*
> *me in the struggle to build Domino's*
> *Pizza and whose love makes it all*
> *worthwhile.*

He only then begins: *My most visible accomplishment in life has been the building of Domino's Pizza from a single store into the world's largest pizza-delivery company.*

I'm an entrepreneur, but I'm also an idealist. So while I thoroughly enjoy the things money can buy, such as private jets, a helicopter, a yacht, a big-league baseball team, an Indy race car, some of the world's finest classic cars, and a northwoods resort, they are all just frosting. To me, the real substance of life and work is the constant battle to excel. I am determined to win...and beat the competition. But to my mind, winning in business is nothing unless you do it strictly according to the rules... [41]

---

[39] Thomas J. Gerrard, *Marriage and Parenthood, The Catholic Ideal* (NY: Joseph F. Wagner, 1911) p. 177.

[40] Tom Monaghan with Robert Anderson, *Pizza Tiger* (New York: Random House, 1986) [41] *Ibid.*, p. 4 .

...I bought the Tigers, the realization of one of my long-standing dreams, in 1983...In team play, the 1984 Tigers outdid those storied Yankees, and they capped their fabulous summer by winning the World Series.

To commemorate that championship season, I was awarded a World Series ring. It's big and a bit gaudy, but for a long time I wouldn't leave home without it. I wore it on the same finger as my wedding band, and I enjoyed the contrast. The plain wedding ring cost me $12, and I guess you could say the World Series ring cost me $53 million, which is what I paid for the Tigers.

In many ways, the contrast is symbolic of me and my life. The wedding band reflects the simple and enduring values that are my greatest strength. The World Series ring represents my flamboyant side...My flamboyance isn't an ego trip, it's showmanship. It gives me the kind of public relations benefit Bill Veeck used to get from his stunts.[42]

Mr. Monaghan's comments to a meeting of franchisees are equally telling: Because *you're successful, people come to you with all kinds of deals...But for gosh sake, you're working your tail off in Domino's, and if you have any spare time you ought to get away from the pizza business and take care of your health and your family.* **There's more to life than making money.**[43] [Editorial emphasis]

Monaghan ends his book by saying, *...I feel a strong sense of wanting to be a good Christian and wanting to help convert the whole world...I always try to stress the importance of spirituality when I give a talk or am interviewed by the press. I keep it low key; I don't want to turn people off; I just want to plant a seed.*

I also try to spread the good word by example. I don't hide the fact that I go to Mass every day—maybe that fact alone will get someone else thinking that it's not a bad idea. I know I was inspired when I read that a guy I admired a lot, Miami Dolphins' coach Don Shula, went to Mass every day. I was even inspired by Mayor Daley of Chicago...when I read that he went to Mass

---

[42] *Ibid.*, pp. 3, 6-7.   [43] *Ibid.*, p. 275.

every day...I told myself, "That guy can't be that bad."

*...I believe there's something in life that's a lot bigger and more important than Domino's. I have faith that God will help me find it, and that he'll show me the way to **my ultimate goal, which is to go to heaven and take as many people as possible with me.***[44] [Editorial emphasis]

Let's take a closer look at this dynamic gentleman. Tom's mother, Anna Geddes, was a Lutheran of German and Scotch ancestry. She lived in Chelsea, Michigan a small town not far from Ann Arbor. Her father, Warren Geddes, was in the movie business. He traveled by train around southeastern Michigan lugging two-reel movies from theatre to theatre. Eventually his professional efforts paid off and he was able to purchase two of his own theaters, the Princess Theater in Chelsea and the Electric Theater in Almont.

On his father's side Tom is Irish. His paternal grandparents, Stephen and Mary Monaghan were both Catholic. The Monaghans, for unknown reasons, separated leaving Stephen with the care of the seven children. When Stephen died at the age of thirty-nine, Tom's father, Francis, being the eldest, quit school in 8th grade to help support his family by running the farm. He also became the surrogate father for his brothers and sisters. *Besides being a hard worker, Dad was a great athlete. In fact, he pitched for a professional baseball team. One day a big guy came into my store to order a pizza. When he heard my name was Monaghan, he asked my father's name then told me "Your dad pitched on my team. He had a heart of gold."*[45]

Francis Monaghan worked on a dairy farm, worked for a time at a Ford Motor Company generator plant and baled hay for farmers. In 1932 when he was eighteen years old, he met Anna at a Christmas party. Anna was sixteen and a junior in high school. His quiet manner, sense of humor and curly hair won her heart. She converted to Catholicism from the Lutheran faith

---

[44] *Ibid.,* pp. 345-346.

[45] Personal interview Feb. 21-22,2000. All quotes not footnoted come from this interview.

at the time of her wedding. The couple married in Ann Arbor April 14, 1936 while she was still in nurse's training. Tom relates:

I was born on March 25, 1937. My mother likes to tell about how my father came to see her in the hospital, and held me for the first time. She says he stood there by her bed looking down at me and said, "he's worth a million dollars."

By this time, Dad had found a fairly steady job driving a tractor-trailer rig for the Interstate Company, and he and my mother had moved into the tiny three-room house he'd built on land purchased from Grandmother Monaghan. Dad never did finish that house, though he kept working on it whenever he could...But even though the house must have been drafty and uncomfortable and its little rooms must have been crowded after my brother, Jim, was born in August 1939, it remains in my memory as warm and as spacious as a mansion.

Dad was a gentle man. He was very patient with me, though my mother says I was a "holy terror" who needed watching every minute...But Dad only punished me once that I can recall, and that was when I was about four-years-old. He intended to drive down to some neighbors' house with a block of ice for their icebox. My mother said I couldn't go, but I believed Dad would want me with him and made up my mind to go anyhow. When Dad pulled out of our yard in our '37 Pontiac, I jumped onto the rear bumper beside the block of ice and clung there as we lurched along the deeply rutted gravel road. It never occurred to me that I might fall off and be injured or killed. After Dad parked in the neighbor's yard, I went running around the car to surprise him, shouting "Here I am!" I'll never forget the stricken look on his face. And I'll never forget the spanking he gave me, either.[46]

In the Monaghan home Tom remembers *a lamp with the picture of the Little Flower painted on the base. I also remember kneeling in church next to my Dad but being disappointed in my father. He wasn't kneeling up straight. Instead he was half kneeling and half sitting.*

---

[46] *Pizza Tiger*, Op. Cit., pp. 24-25.

The saddest day of my life was when my father died on Christmas Eve in 1941, the year I was four-years-old. He was only twenty-nine. He died from peritonitis caused by bleeding ulcers. I still get misty-eyed when I think of his loss.

My mother was very fragile and overwhelmed by her responsibilities of being both mother and father to Jim and me. To support us, she realized that she would have to go back to school to become a registered nurse. It was impossible for Mom to go to school and take care of two pre-schoolers so we were placed in foster homes. She promised that once she got a good job she would take us back to live with her again. I was twelve and a half years old when I finally got to go home, and then it was just for one year.

While Ted Turner made the rounds of boarding schools, Tom and his brother, Jim, made the rounds of foster homes. While in foster care, the Monaghan boys had no contact with the Catholic faith. Concerned that her sons were not being raised Catholics, Mrs. Monaghan, decided to place the boys in St. Joseph's Home for Boys, an orphanage run by the Felician nuns. *Though I hated the institution,* Tom reminisces, *I loved its architecture.* St. Joseph's was housed in a huge Victorian mansion complete with ornate cupolas. His new home away from home triggered Tom's life-long interest in architecture.

At the orphanage, Tom was introduced to a rigid schedule. In addition to going to school, each boy was expected to do chores. The assigned chores not only kept the home humming, but the nuns used the chores to develop various virtues in the boys. Tom learned to cut the grass, scrub and polish floors, clean the carved banisters of the main staircase, and iron shirts and trousers. *I prided myself on being the best and fastest ironer in the orphanage. That dexterity stayed in my fingers and came out in my ability to make pizzas fast.*[47]

I had the most prestigious job in the orphanage...cleaning the chapel. I would scrub the floors and do anything else that needed to be done.

---

[47] *Ibid.*, p. 298.

Sister Berarda was Tom's surrogate mother until he was eight years old and in third grade. Along with being his teacher, she was also his housemother who lovingly disciplined him. It was Sister Berarda who taught Tom his prayers, the Catholic faith, instilled the virtues, and made sure he attended Mass each day. *I took to Sister Berarda's religious training. It made sense to me. Every morning we said long prayers and attended Mass. Every evening we had benediction. The sisters talked about God all the time. I was really taught the faith in the orphanage. It made me think about being a priest when I grew-up. It was at St. Joseph's that I learned that the bottom line is to get to heaven. If you die with a mortal sin on your soul, you go to hell. It's a selfish reason that I practice the faith. I don't want to go to hell.*[48]

I remember telling the class that when I grew up I wanted to be a priest, an architect, and shortstop for the Detroit Tigers. The other kids laughed and said that was impossible...Sister Berarda quieted them down and said, "Well, I don't think it's ever been done before, Tommy, but if you want to do it, there's no reason you can't." That was inspiring.[49]

Under her warm guidance, Tom became the star of his class. He advanced so rapidly that Sister Berarda asked his mother for permission to skip him from second to fourth grade. Mrs. Monaghan refused for social reasons.

In third grade, Tom joined the older boys who walked to St. Mary's parish school.   He also was given a new housemother, a nun much stricter with little warmth. *She ruled by the strap. We were whipped for the slightest infraction; there was no leniency, never a reprieve. That housemother was as tough as the strictest drill instructor I ever had in the Marine Corps...Under her regime, I lost interest in outside activities. My school grades slid and other kids started surpassing me in sports. I went into a gradual slump. I managed to keep about a B average, as I recall, but I never regained the enthusiasm for class work that Sister Berarda had given me.*[50]

---

[48] Inteview.

[49] *Pizza Tiger, Op. Cit.*, p. 30.

[50] *Ibid.*, p. 30.

Although Mrs. Monaghan visited her sons often, the visits only made Tom more miserable. He wanted to live with his mother in a normal family environment.

I disliked the orphanage. We were so different from the other kids in school who lived a normal life although we did have a gym where we could play basketball. We also played baseball and football in season. One of my favorite activities was to play "store." In the summer we went to camps such as the Boy Scout Camp or the YMCA camp. We always had a day at the lake, an annual Christmas party with presents. There was also a Christmas play. The food wasn't very good and I was always envious of the kids who got out.

Just as Ted Turner spent his only year home in sixth grade, Tom was told he was going home after he completed sixth grade.

When I was in sixth grade my mother told me she was taking Jim and me to live with her in Traverse City. She found a job there working as nurse at Munson Hospital. She purchased a house and we moved back with her in August. From a regimented life to total freedom...it was wonderful but it only lasted a year. This time I attended Immaculate Conception school where I became friends with the pastor, Fr. Passeno, who recruited me to serve as an altar boy. He became a surrogate father, even interceding with my mother to smooth over our problems. Fr. Passeno also gave me odd jobs around the school to do. My aspirations about becoming a priest vanished though. Lois, the girl who sat in front of me, made me forget the priesthood. Although I asked her out, her mother said she was too young to go out in 7th grade.

While Ted's parents could afford to send their troublesome son to Georgia Military Academy, Mrs. Monaghan had to rely on foster homes instead. *My mother and I did not get along too well. We were always arguing so that summer I kept busy doing odd jobs such as picking cherries, selling fish I caught and selling the **Traverse City Record Eagle** on a corner. Keeping out of my mother's way did not ease the tension between us, so off I* *went to another foster home for 8th grade where I attended a little country school. Jim was closer to Mom so he stayed behind with her. At the orphanage we had been taught to roll with the punches so that's what I did.*

When I entered high school, Jim again joined me in foster care. This time we were sent to a farm family by the name of Johnson. A couple of months later I was sent to another farm owned by Mr. and Mrs. Edwin Crouch while Jim went back to live with Mom. The farm was humble. It did not even have electricity so I did my homework by kerosene lamp. I liked everything about this wonderful place. Besides, I didn't want to be with my mother.

Each day I'd walk a mile and a quarter to catch the bus to St. Francis High School. Along the way I'd dream about becoming an architect. I'd even take out library books on the subject. That's how I became a life-long student of Frank Lloyd Wright. His work intrigues me.

Around the same age that Ted decided to become a missionary, Tom decided to pursue his dream to become a priest. *At the end of my freshman year I was shoveling manure in the barn when the thought hit me "How did I get so off track?" Not only was I shoveling muck in the barn, but I was stuck in the muck of the world when I should have been concentrating on my spiritual quest. It was right then that I decided to become a priest. I contacted Fr. Passeno who arranged for me to enter St. Joseph's Seminary in Grand Rapids, Michigan. I wasn't the least bit homesick while the rest of the guys were. Unfortunately I only lasted to Easter vacation. I was devastated when Rector Monsignor Falicki told me that I "lacked the vocation."*

Both Tom and Ted had difficulty following the rules in school. Each held records for infractions at their respective schools.

Although my grades were good, except in Greek, it seems as if I was always in hot water at the seminary for pillow fights, talking during the "Grand Silence" and study hall, being late for something, climbing a fence, not writing home to my mother. In fact Monsignor Falicki chewed me out for not writing home. I preferred to write to my Aunt Peg since I had spent a week or two every summer while I was in high school with my aunt and uncle. The Rector knew I had stretched the limit of infractions, four were the usual number for dismissal and I had eleven, so he was firm in his decision. My problem was that I wasn't as uptight as the rest of the kids. Still, I was serious about becoming a priest and I wanted to be a good priest.

But it was a good experience for me. It fueled my faith because we were submerged in orthodox, disciplined religion night and day. It was like my religious experience in the orphanage.

Once again back home, I borrowed my mother's car when I was a junior in high school without telling her. That did it! She called the police. When I refused to apologize I found myself spending a night in jail. The next thing I knew I was put into a detention home for six months. My mother had signed the order to lock me up like a common thief. It was a terrible nightmare. By day I continued to go to St. Francis High School doing everything I could so my classmates would not find out, but by night I was locked up with juvenile delinquents and criminals. After six months of living like this, my Aunt Peg found out about it and won custody of me. I was so grateful to be taken into their home. It was the highlight of my life to be in a family, to finally be in a warm, family situation...to be in a normal home. My uncle and aunt were the closest things to real parents. Uncle Ed gave me a Jeep to drive while I worked in the office of his construction company. Working for him I had visions of being a big contractor.

My senior year was spent at St. Thomas High School. All I wanted to do was play sports and date girls. I rarely cracked a book. In my yearbook the caption under my picture reads, "The harder I try to be good, the worse I get; but I may do something sensational yet."

I was an optimist because of my self-confidence. I was always ambitious but wouldn't sell my soul for a dollar. I couldn't wait until I got to the point when I could control my own life. I knew that I would be successful and wealthy. After high school I got the chance to be on my own.

Tom's dream to become an architect was hindered by a lack of finances. His goal was to attend Ferris State College which had an architectural trade school. By attending Ferris, working nine years in the field and then taking a test he could eventually become a licensed architect. That was his plan. Unfortunately, this phase of his life is similar to the character, George Bailey, that Jimmy Stewart played in the movie *"It's a Wonderful Life."* No matter how hard Tom tried to earn and save money for college, insurmountable obstacles interfered with his goals. He worked hard. He carefully saved his money. Then he enrolled in the architectural trade school but was turned down because there was no room. He reapplied for college the next quarter and was surprised when he was accepted into pre-engineering. His grades were excellent but shortly into the school year serious dental problems wiped out his savings. Penniless, but determined to stay in school, he was forced to scrounge for food. One week he existed on stale popcorn and a little wine he found in the upstairs of a house he shared with some guys. *...I managed to struggle throughout the balance of the year. Luckily, the landlord allowed me to work off my share of the rent by doing yard work.* [51]

Tom's grade point average at Ferris permitted him to transfer to the School of Architecture at the University of Michigan. All he needed to attend the U of M was the tuition money. Determined to land a well paying summer job to finance his university education, he began his job search by hitchhiking first to Detroit, then on to Chicago where he landed in Harvey, Illinois, a southern suburb. By the middle of June he realized that *I didn't have time now to save the kind of money I'd need to go to school in Ann Arbor. One day I was walking past the Harvey post office and noticed what I thought was an Army recruiting desk inside. That reminded me of an advertisement I heard or saw about receiving a free college education if a person joined the Army. So I walked into the post office and talked to the man at the desk...*[52]

---

[51] *Ibid.*, p. 41.

[52] *Ibid,*, p. 42.

It was only after he filled out all the forms and was accepted that he discovered he had joined the Marines at the age of nineteen...not the army.

While in the Marines in 1957, I began to have doubts about my faith. Before that time I never missed Mass on Sunday. In fact, throughout my Catholic school training I went to Mass daily with my class. On Sundays I might be late but I always got there before the Offertory. Then I began to think more deeply about the faith. Did Jesus really arise from the dead? Questions like that bothered me. For a period of around six months I missed Mass periodically on Sunday. While I was troubled with these doubts I spent my free time reading any good book I could get my hands on. I read almost every book in the base library that could help me achieve my aims to become wealthy and successful. Rarely read a novel unless it could help me. My favorite books were biographies and inspirational books by such authors as Norman Vincent Peale and Dale Carnegie. One of the books I found in the library was **Rebuilding A Lost Faith** *by John L. Stoddard.[53] This book removed all my doubts forever. It takes every criticism of the Catholic Church and explains it. Sometime after I read that book I put my list of five priorities together on a long voyage back to Japan.[53A]*

Tom's list of five priorities included spiritual (God first), social (a good marriage), mental (a good conscience and questioning mind), physical (exercise and counting calories) and financial (business success based on the golden rule and hard work). *I want to get A's in all five areas.*

At the end of his hitch, Tom, now twenty-two, had saved enough money for the first couple of years of tuition at the University of Michigan. Hitching a ride back to his base one day, he met an individual who invited him to invest in an oil business. If the deal was as good as the fellow thought it was, Tom would be able to complete his education. Tom invested, then reinvested, draining his savings until he realized that he

[53] John l. Stoddard, "An American Agnostic," *Rebuilding A Lost Faith* (New York: P. J. Kenedy and Sons, 1922).
[53A] Interview, *Op. Cit.*

had been "taken." His oil partner just sent promises, no repayment.

Although accepted by the University of Michigan, Monaghan was again unable to pay the tuition. Determined to get his degree, Tom attempted to attend school while working full-time even though he could not afford to buy his textbooks. Just when things could not get any worse, he suffered a ruptured eardrum. Reluctantly he dropped out of school hoping to save-up for the following semester.

The next semester he again dropped out due to the lack of finances as well as his inability to study since he was working three jobs. Rather than giving up, he enrolled in night courses in refresher algebra in the evenings at the local high school. The following fall when he was in the process of enrolling in college again, his brother Jim, who worked at the post office, came up with the idea of a business partnership. He wanted to buy a pizza place in Ypsilanti from Dominick DiVarti.

The store only operated seven hours a day, from 5 PM until midnight. Jim would work three and a half hours, and I would only have to work three and a half hours thus giving me the time I needed to study. The income from our business venture would be enough to put me through college. We got a loan for the $900 we needed to buy the store from a credit union.

I thought Jim cared about the business as much as I did, so I was surprised when one day, about eight months after we'd formed our partnership, he came around and said he wanted out...

With Jim stepping out of the picture, my hope of running the pizza business part-time and going to the U of M full-time flew out the window for good. It was a setback, but I took it in stride...[54]

Fourteen months after Tom began his pizza business, Margie Zybach entered his life. Despite the objections of Margie's mother, they were married at the church of St. Thomas in Ann Arbor on August 25, 1962, just before the colleges were back in

[54] *Ibid.*, p. 61.

session and their business started picking up.

We met February 1961...I was making my first personal delivery from a new store I'd opened...The address on the order was Sweeny Hall, a dormitory at Central Michigan University, and Margie was working the switchboard at the reception desk when I walked in. She was cute, and I started a conversation with her...

I was smitten with her right off the bat. I sang and hollered as I drove back to the store...After our second date, I gave Margie a heart-shaped pizza for Valentine's Day and when I looked into those big blue eyes, I realized I was in love.[55]

I knew after our second date that she was the girl I wanted to marry. She was wholesome and decent and unpretentious, and those blue eyes of hers were absolutely electrifying. So I went to a jewelry store and bought a four-hundred-dollar engagement ring, the most expensive one I could charge with no money down. The diamond was only half a carat, but it looked bigger because it had a lot of ornamentation around it. The jeweler assured me that if my girl didn't accept it, I could bring it back.

I had the ring in my pocket when I picked Margie up for our third date...We went to a competitor's pizzeria and sampled its pizza...I told her I was going to be a millionaire by the time I was thirty...When we got back to her dorm, I didn't ask her to marry me. I didn't know how to get the words out. I just handed her the ring. "I can't take it," she said... "Please"...Well, she might wear it while she was sleeping, but she wouldn't show it to anybody. I considered that a victory. And sure enough, a week later, she said yes, she would marry me.

Since Margie was a Lutheran, she took instructions in the Catholic faith, but she did not convert.

At first we lived in house trailers. I was only taking a salary of $102 a week out of the business, and we lived very simply. After our first two daughters were born—Mary in May 1963 and Susie in May 1965—Margie helped me in the Ypsilanti store.

[55] *Ibid.*, pp. 11-12.

Our babies slept in cardboard boxes in the corner while Margie answered telephones and did the bookkeeping. She worked in Domino's accounting department, and personally handed out paychecks to every employee in our headquarters. Our four daughters have grown up with Domino's as a sort of extended family. They've done baby-sitting for franchisees, worked at various jobs in stores and around the office, and they've shared some of the heartbreaks and triumphs of people in the company.[56] [The Monaghans' other two daughters are Maggie, born in 1969 and Barbara in 1973.]

Both Tom Monaghan and Ted Turner faced business setbacks, takeover attempts, and financial crisis. While Ted turned to racing sailboats, Mr. Monaghan turned to his faith.

Throughout my professional career my prayer life was steadily increasing. It was the only thing that kept me going...particularly in 1991 when everything was in crisis. It was in 1973 that I resumed going to daily Mass. Although I had been saying the daily rosary for a while, when I bought the Detroit Tigers I increased my rosaries to three a day.

All of my apostolates are named for Our Lady because of my deep love for her. My faith has never been an obstacle to my success. It has fueled it. Around 1989-90 I read C. S. Lewis' book **Mere Christianity.** *It made me take stock of my life. There is an excellent chapter in the book on pride. After reading that book I realized that I worked harder so that I could have more. I wanted to impress people. That was pride.* **Mere Christianity** *made me realize that a lot of the things I thought were good were actually manifestations of pride. I had a lot of toys and distractions that took me away from the day-to-day operation of my business. I got rid of them along with the Detroit Tigers. I immediately took the "Millionaire's vow of poverty." I still have comforts and conveniences but I got rid of anything ostentatious. I sold the plane, helicopters, yacht, my hunting/fishing lodge, the championship golf course, and immediately stopped construction on my new home. It was way too luxurious. I built*

---

[56] *Ibid.*, pp. 11-12.

a more humble house about four years ago.

The book also taught me that I needed to work on the virtue of humility. A person who is humble is too busy battling problems to think about himself. As a matter of policy I do not put my name on any building or entity.

An article in the **New York Times** provides further insight: *He [Mr. Monaghan] also became an outspoken advocate of a traditional, politically conservative brand of Catholicism. In 1988, his faith based politics and his business collided when the National Organization for Women led a nationwide boycott of Domino's to protest Mr. Monaghan's support of anti-abortion groups. The controversy—along with boycotts by homosexuals and other groups—angered some Domino's franchisees and colored the company's image...*

Mr. Monaghan is indifferent to such talk. "The things I do always bring out praise and criticism...[I]t doesn't bother me. You have to do God's will."[57]

That boycott by NOW did not hurt us in the least, although it did make some franchisees nervous. I decided to sell Domino's Pizza for two reasons. I did not want my activism to possibly hurt the livelihood of any of my franchisees and I needed the money to fund the works of my Foundation.

The Fruits Of A Character Based On Faith

"More than ever, now there is a need for a genuine witness of faith, made visible through the life of the lay disciples of Christ, men and women, young and old. There is a need for committed witness to fidelity to the Church and responsibility towards the Church, which for twenty centuries has brought salvation to every people and nation, announcing the immutable teaching of the Gospel."

John Paul II[58]

---

[57] Alex Prudhomme, "For Domino's Founder, a New Mission" in *The New York Times* (NY), Feb. 14, 1999, p. 13.
[58] Poland, June 10, 1999.

While Ted Turner uses his money for social engineering and environmental issues, Tom Monaghan uses his financial resources for the evangelization of souls. *I want my contributions to be made in the most meaningful way possible.*[59] His foundation, originally called Mater Christi but later changed to Ave Maria, funded numerous apostolic initiatives, among them a Catholic mission in the mountains of the Central American country of Honduras. Working with Father Enrique Silvestre of Spain, Mr. Monaghan has constructed or repaired fifteen to twenty small churches which had been closed for years; brought in minimal electricity to small towns; has a model training farm; an experimental farm; medical clinic; ceramics factory; chicken hatchery; sewing factory that makes quilts; uniform company; a cooperative store; and two Spiritus Sanctus grade schools. The goal is to be able to train the workers not only to run the businesses but eventually to own them.

When an earthquake destroyed the Cathedral of San Diego (St. James) in Managua, Nicaragua, Cardinal Law of Boston asked Tom to help Miguel Cardinal Obando y Bravo build a new cathedral for that diocese. *The cathedral was an important symbol for the people, the Cardinal, Nicaragua, and in the peoples' effort to stem the tide of communism.* Tom paid 80% or $3.5 million of the $4.5 million construction cost of the new Cathedral of the Immaculate Conception. He also supervised the construction. A Mexican, Mr. Ricardo Leggeretta, was the architect for the project. For his work on the cathedral he won the American Institute of Architects (AIA) gold medal in 1999.

Over the years, Tom has likewise given of his time to be on numerous boards: Madonna College, Christendom College, NY Medical College, Catholic University of America, Franciscan University of Steubenville, The Institute for Religious Life, Catholic Campaign of America, Catholic Alliance, Culture of Life Foundation, Father Gabriel Richard High School, Fellowship of Catholic University Students, St. John Vianney Seminary in Denver, Ave Maria Catholic Values Fund and many

---

[59] *Pizza Tiger, Op. Cit.*, p.339.

others.

Late in 1998, Monaghan sold 93% of his stock in Domino's so that he could devote all of his time, effort, and financial resources toward the spreading of the Catholic faith. *...I don't want to take my money with me when I go, and I don't want to leave it for others. I want to die broke.*[60]

While he remains chairman emeritus of Domino's Pizza and continues to serve on its Board of Directors, his efforts are focused on his Foundation of which he is Chairman. In his "retirement" he is concentrating his efforts, through his foundations, in five areas: Catholic education, Catholic media, pro-life, evangelization of Ann Arbor, Michigan, and Legatus (an international organization of Catholic CEO's.) The ***Detroit News*** notes that Monaghan *is well on his way to setting up a large Catholic education system in Metro Detroit, mostly funded from a large chunk of his pizza fortune.*[61] Mr. Monaghan explained to me: *Right here in the Ann Arbor area we have the best Catholic education in the country with a network of eight Christ-centered schools to choose from. Each school is faithful to its effort to follow Christ in the fullness of the Catholic faith. The schools all feature strong family involvement, character formation, a positive peer environment, devoted staff, solid catechesis based especially on the new **Catechism of the Catholic Church**, frequent Mass and daily prayers and devotions.*

While all the schools share these basic values, each school has its own flair and flavor. The schools also have different structural models and configurations. We have two Montessori schools called Shepherd Montessori, one of which is in our headquarters. These schools have a child driven curriculum.

When Mother Assumpta, the prior superior general of the Nashville Dominicans, completed her tenure as mother superior, Cardinal O'Connor of New York asked her to help him to found a new order of sisters dedicated to pro-life. This new order is the

---

[60] "For Domino's Founder, a New Mission," *Op. Cit.*, p. 1.
[61] "Monaghan merges 2 colleges," *The Detroit News*, June 7, 2000.

Sisters of Life. Once this was accomplished, Mother Assumpta was drawn to start a new Dominican teaching order. It took her about a year to discern where to settle. I coaxed her to come to Ann Arbor. Her order, the Sisters of Mary, Mother of the Eucharist, now runs four Spiritus Sanctos grade schools [which Tom financed and built in the style of a farm]. Each of these schools has daily Mass, weekly confession, and monthly Eucharistic Adoration. These schools have small, multi-grade classes: K, 1 & 2, 3 & 4, 5 & 6, 7 & 8. The carefully structured curriculum is presented via a traditional educational approach. The two sister Spiritus Sanctus schools in Honduras host visiting students from our U.S. schools.

Agnus Dei Academy is a "one room school" concept with a strong home-schooling spirit. Students can work at different grade levels in different subjects so the students can progress at their own rate, but within a traditional Catholic curriculum. This is a "three room" school with students divided into pre-K and K, grades 1-3, and grades 4-8. In its second year of operation it had 60 students.

We also sponsor Huron Valley, a parent-run independent grade school K-8, with an 18-year tradition that has recently become Catholic yet retaining its strong ecumenical and charismatic values.

Ave Maria College is expanding each year. It has received state approval as a four-year college. Seven men are enrolled in the new Pre-Theologate Program for the formation of priests under Fr. Dave Testa. Our purpose is to foster vocations to the ministerial priesthood in the Roman Catholic Church. This goal is achieved through the full implementation of the Program of Priest Formation of the National Conference of Catholic Bishops...We believe that through this program, young men, with the help of God's grace, the dedication of their faculty and advisors, and their own good will, may discern and grow in a vocation to the ministerial priesthood. It is not to be construed as a "seminary," but as preparation for a seminary or religious community.

In memory of Fr. John Hardon, S.J., a Catholic Catechetical Institute, with diplomas in Pastoral Catechetics, has been instituted. This program is fully accredited by the United States Conference of Catholic Bishops and recognized by all the dioceses in the U.S. Distance education opportunities are also available.

*The fall of 2000 saw the beginning of the law school with Judge Robert H. Bork as one of the professors. The Dean of the Law School is Bernard Dobranski, most recently Dean of Catholic University's Law School. We are only hiring the top people in each field. Each must be in tune with our mission as well as take an oath of fidelity to Magisterium of the Catholic Church as prescribed by the 1990 apostolic constitution on Catholic higher education, **Ex Corde Ecclesiae.***

Recently we purchased St. Mary's College at Orchard Lake, Michigan. With a variety of educational choices from pre-school through college every child in this area has an opportunity for an authentically Catholic education.

In San Marcos, Nicaragua we purchased a Baptist college that we renamed Ave Maria College of the Americas. Not only is it our Central American campus but it is also the only U.S. accredited four-year college south of the border. It offers majors in aquaculture, biology, agribusiness, and business administration. With the alliance of Ave Maria College with St. Mary's College and Ave Maria College of the Americas in Honduras, Ave Maria University was created. This university is a fully accredited Catholic University.

Living the faith was an important aspect of life for the Monaghans. *Our four daughters attended Catholic schools. We went to Mass as a family every Sunday. We said evening prayers together and grace before meals.*

Trying to find a daily Mass at the same time each morning in Ann Arbor became challenging for Tom. *My time is valuable and I spent a lot of it running around trying to find a Mass.* So in 1980, Tom, with the permission of his bishop, turned a conference room into a chapel at Domino Farms with the help of Tom Gordon Smith, Dean of the Notre Dame School of

Architecture. Later the bishop granted Tom permission to reserve the Holy Eucharist in a tabernacle in the chapel. Besides morning and evening prayer, there are four daily Masses in this chapel, in addition to the daily Mass at Ave Maria University and two daily Masses at Ave Maria School of Law. Each grade school likewise has daily Mass. In all, Tom is responsible for thirteen daily Masses with an attendance of 700. At Domino Farms the sacrament of reconciliation is available twelve hours a day. Where does he find the priests?

I simply got on the phone and called some African bishops and Lebanese bishops. In return for them sending me priests, I send the priest a round trip ticket, pay for his education at Eastern Michigan University, provide him a place to live, a car to drive, and a monthly stipend for living expenses.

In the future we will have master and Ph.D. programs for clergy and laity at Ave Maria University. Then we won't have to import priests but will be able to have Masses and confessions around the clock...

Tom's Ave Maria Foundation is heavily involved in Catholic media. Ave Maria Communications, a division of Ave Maria College, includes a new publishing house for books as well as a new Catholic magazine entitled, you guessed it, *Ave Maria Magazine.*

In January 2000, a year-old venture, Catholic Singles On Line (Catholicsingles.com) was purchased by the Ave Maria Foundation. Within the first nine months of its existence a total of 25 marriages resulted from the website. In order to participate through the website, browsers answer questions that are used to screen the participants so that only authentically Catholic singles participate. It has grown from 1200 members to 3500 members throughout the U.S. and in many countries.

A weekly, award-winning, Catholic newspaper, **CREDO**, is sent free to 40,000 Catholics in the Ann Arbor area. Also housed in its offices at Domino Farms is a radio station WDEO which covers the Ann Arbor and Detroit area. Another radio station, WMAX, has been started in the Bay City/Saginaw area. The two stations broadcast to nearly 40% of Michigan's listening audience. Al Kresta, a convert to the Catholic faith manages Ave Maria Radio and **Credo**.

Mr. Monaghan personally funds various pro-life activities that include state and national PACs. Since these PACS are political, they are not part of the Ave Maria Foundation, nor are they funded by the Foundation. These are the only Roman Catholic PACS in the U.S. In the 2000 election these PACS supported 19 federal and 24 state and local campaigns. *The mission of The Ann Arbor Political Action Committee is to support, promote and elect candidates for federal, state and local office who are dedicated to promoting and defending laws and public policy which support the value of life, family and private initiative through financial support and through the mobilization of grassroots volunteers. In doing so, we will begin to turn back the culture of death and restore America's greatness, with unlimited opportunities for all.*

The Thomas More Center for Law & Justice, a law firm that defends cases brought against plaintiffs by the A.C.L.U. and others, receives grants from the Foundation. This national, non-profit, public interest law firm and educational organization is dedicated to the defense and promotion of the religious freedom of Christian family values and the sanctity of life. It takes part in some of the largest cases in the U.S. regarding religious freedom and right-to-life issues.

In 1987, Legatus, an organization of Catholic CEO's, was *an inspiration* following Tom's first meeting with the Holy Father. It was Cardinal Szoka who invited him to attend Pope John Paul II's private Mass and to meet the pontiff afterwards.

Legatus, which is Latin for ambassador, is structured along the lines of the Young Presidents' Organization (YPO). The monthly meetings for practicing Catholic executives and their spouses begin with an opportunity to go to confession before Holy Mass. Dinner and a lecture by a prominent speaker follow the Mass. *The idea is to give executives and their spouses a chance to pray and reflect, to talk about integrating faith into their secular lives and to be educated.*[62] *Our mission is to study, live and spread the Faith in our business, professional and personal lives.* As a group, Legatus is not involved in any projects. *The real project is the members themselves. We get them in, then zap them with religion. Legatus provides proven leaders for our Church. They in turn will motivate others to not only live their faith but also use their talents to evangelize. Our members are in a visible position of importance. As such they give good example as Catholic lay people.*

The mission statement explains that the goals of the organization are to encourage Catholic executives to *study, live and spread the Faith in our business, professional, and personal lives.* Ten percent of the membership fee is sent yearly to the Holy Father for his charities. The average age is 56. *We have members like Roger Staubach, former Dallas Cowboys' quarterback, John Harrington, president of the Boston Red Sox, Peter Lynch of Fidelity Investments, Ed and Virginia McCaskey, the owners of the Bears, William Bidwell, owner of the Arizona Cardinals, and Wellington Mara, owner of the New York Giants.*

Legatus continues to grow with over 1,300 CEO's in 44 chapters in the US and Canada with at-large-members in Mexico and Honduras. *A disproportionate number of CEO's in the U.S. are Catholic, and there must be at least 100,000 that would qualify for membership,*[63] according to a ***New York Times*** article. To qualify for membership, a CEO must run a business with at least $5 million in annual sales with a minimum of 30 full-time employees. A CEO of a financial service company who employs ten full-time employees can join if the company does $100 million in annual business. Chairmen, chief executives and presidents of companies who are practicing Catholics in good standing with the Church (especially in regard to the sacrament of matrimony) can join.

Ave Maria Catholic Values Fund is an investment fund for

---

[62] "For Domino's Founder, a New Mission," *Op. Cit.*, p. 13.   [63] *Ibid.*

individuals, dioceses, parishes and other institutions begun in May 2001. It seeks long-term capital appreciation by investing in companies whose products, services and activities are consistent with the core values of the Roman Catholic Church.

Ave Maria Missions is a charity that provides scholarships for poor children in Honduras. There is also Ave Maria House that provides Catholic dorm housing for coeds who attend the University of Michigan. Activities at Domino Farms includes the Ave Maria First Friday Breakfast with speakers, the Catholic Men's Tuesday Breakfast with featured speakers, Heart to Heart, a Catholic women's group, and the Ann Arbor Catholic Men's Movement. The above are just *some* of the apostolates of Mr. Monaghan. A book is needed to explain everything. There are also secular interests such as the Ann Arbor Antiques Market; the Ave Maria Fine Art Galley; Domino's Petting Farm that hosts 45,000 children and adults each year; St. Nicholas Light Display that entertains over 72,000 visitors at the indoor light display and others.

To fully understand the power of his impact one needs to travel to Ann Arbor, Michigan to experience the vibrant, dynamic Catholic faith that is expanding out from his headquarters at Domino Farms. All meetings begin and end with prayer. Most employees attend daily Mass and pray the Divine Office together. In addition, many attend the Holy Hour on Thursdays, Stations of the Cross on Friday, and the daily recitation of the rosary.

The vision of Tom Monaghan's Ave Maria Foundation is not limited to the Ann Arbor region. Rather, its goal is the evangelization of our country and the world for Christ. This is all being done in a prayerful, highly professional, and well thought-out manner. Tom insists on high internal standards. Part of the standards includes an executive dress code (suits and ties for men, modest suits, skirts and dresses for women). He feels that professional dress is an important part of doing business.

Using the same expertise, professionalism, and attention to detail that made Domino's Pizza the world's largest pizza delivery company, Tom has put together a team of immensely talented executives to head each division of his Ave Maria Foundation. These executives are not only committed to excellence and orthodoxy but they share his vision of spreading the Gospel throughout the world. Observing a meeting of Tom's Foundation Executive Team, I experienced a potent, Catholic powerhouse that is seriously committed to reaching out to convert non-Catholics and bringing home fallen away Catholics. In addition, his team is diligently working to deepen the faith of practicing Catholics besides striving to re-Christianize our culture. These are ambitious goals in the "culture of death" atmosphere in which we live. As Bernard Dobranski, formerly the Dean of Catholic U's Law School, remarked, *We all took risks to come here.*

Not only do Tom and his executive team hire the best person available in each field but Tom ensures top performance by establishing challenging goals, with monthly reviews with each of his executives. Each week the team meets to keep the goals on track besides constantly updating their strategic plan. Just as in any top business, there is a pro forma for measuring effectiveness in spreading the faith and winning souls for each division.

Can you *see* the dramatic contrast between the current lifestyle of Ted Turner and Tom Monaghan? Both men were raised in highly unusual family circumstances. Their youth is almost a mirror image. The Catholic faith is the key difference between the two men. Ted should have been raised a Catholic, but he was not. Tom's biography shows the powerful impact of faith not only on a person's life but also on everyone that person influences. Moreover, Tom's continuing struggle to deepen his own faith makes him an outstanding *Catholic* leader, a leader of character and of integrity. Could one say it's a "domino" effect?

Anyone who has noble thoughts, deep convictions and high principles, which he retains even when it cost him some sacrifice, is a man of character, writes Fr. Joseph Massmann. *It is a law of the mind that what a man thinks, he is or soon will be. The man who constantly thinks good thoughts becomes good or is so already. He who has bad thoughts and only sees the dark side, soon becomes gloomy and bad. The man whose mind constantly revolves upon worldly things becomes worldly, restless and egotistical. But he who concerns himself with God becomes saintly.*[64]

Each of us wants our children to be men and women of character, of integrity, to be leaders. Isabel O. Lopez, of Lopez Leadership Services, a Denver management-consulting firm, ties together these ideas in her article "Leadership Defined."[65] These are suggestions we should take to heart as parents while teaching them to our children as well. She writes: *Leaders I would follow have: wisdom; the ability to love and be loved; authenticity; trustworthiness; fun; and a sense of purpose. [C]an we learn integrity and ethics? How?...[T]hey are only learned through reinforcement as children and through experience as adults. However they are learned, we need to have these qualities to lead with wisdom.*

My favorite definition of integrity is trustworthiness. The person with integrity is congruent—their actions match their words. Their actions come from their ethics...Often we mistake ethics for legality and our first questions are, "Is it legal?" and "What are the rules?" Basing our ethics on these questions alone puts us on shaky ground: The outcome will not necessarily be integrity...

Wise leaders...are past the level of basing their decisions strictly on personal rewards and consequences. They are past the stage of doing what others expect them to do to fit in. They are at the level of making decisions for a higher purpose. Their decisions consider others.

...Given a choice, people choose, in my experience, to follow those with integrity, those who are authentic, those who have a sense of purpose, those who are balanced, those who have fun

---

[64] Rev. Joseph Massmann, *Nervousness, Temperament and the Soul* (Ft. Collins,CO: Roman Catholic Books, 1941) p. 141.

[65] *Colorado Business Magazine*, June 1990.

doing what they do, those who allow others to succeed, those who love. They have ethics, value individuals, and are comfortable with ambiguity and paradox. In other words, they are wise. Wise leaders: They do not use the techniques of fear, of manipulation, or of position and images. They move to leadership through trust and integrity, they move to leadership through vision and they end up being followed because of wisdom...My bias is that true leadership is wise leadership.

Let me emphasize, true leadership depends on character. And yes...character counts.

Additional Helps

- ✓ Read *Upbringing, A Discussion Handbook For Parents of Young Children* by James Stenson. It can be purchased from Scepter Publishers at (800) 322-8773.
- ✓ Read *Lifeline—The Religious Upbringing of Your Children* by James Stenson. It can be purchased from Scepter Publishers.
- ✓ Read *Uncommon Friends* by James Newton (Harcourt, Inc.).

CHAPTER 3

TEACHING THE FAITH...
TO YOUR CHILDREN

"Rejoice not in ungodly children; if they be multiplied: neither be delighted in them, if the fear of God be not with them. Trust not to their life, and respect not their labors. For better is one that fears God than a thousand ungodly children. And it is better to die without children then to leave ungodly children." **Ecclesiasticus** (*Sirach* 16: 1-4)

Is it really possible to raise **your** children to be godly...to be saints? Yes, it is. In fact the most perfect Father, God who created heaven and earth, gave you a guidebook, the Bible that is filled with instructions, and an institution, the Catholic Church, to guide you, as parents, in this serious responsibility. Within the Church there are also various organizations to help you in this task such as Opus Dei, Regnum Christi, Pro-Sanctity, Miles Jesus, the Neocatechumenal Movement, the Militia of the Immaculata, the Apostolate for Family Consecration, the Blue Army and others. Everything you need to know for the job is available. You just have to

1. Have the will and determination to raise your children saints accompanied by a lot of prayers and trust in God;
2. Learn and live the Catholic faith with intensity;
3. Make the effort to learn how to teach your Catholic faith through personal example, doctrine and conversations with

your children;
4. Instill a desire in your children to become saints;
5. Then persevere in the task of passing your living Catholic faith on to your children.

When God created us, He created us with a body **and** a soul. Our bodies, which have a limited "shelf" life, is biodegradable. But our souls live on for eternity either in perpetual happiness or perpetual agony. The Church calls attention to this fact by celebrating the feast days of the saints on the day they died which is the day they entered eternity, rather than on their birthdays. There are only three feasts that celebrate birthdays. We celebrate the births of Christ, Our Lady and St. John the Baptist.

Now back to the soul. Within the soul lies the intelligence and will. The soul, unlike the body, never ages. If fact, one of the frustrations of growing older is wanting to do things that the body is no longer capable of doing. The spirit is willing but the body aches! Since length of life is uncertain, the wise person puts his efforts into preparing for eternity, which after all, is the purpose for our existence. Fr. John Hardon, S.J., stressed that *there are only two classes of people. Those who belong to God and those who belong to Satan. When we belong to God we become channels of grace for others. The depth of the grace in our soul is the degree to which God can use us.*[1]

The next important lesson that you should teach your children is that **life is to be lived so as to gain heaven. Nothing else really matters.** Nothing else is important. Nothing else counts in life. No other pursuit will make your children happy. As Pope John Paul II reiterates over and over again: *Every Christian is called to holiness, namely to live the beatitudes. The Church points out, as an example for all, the brothers and sisters [i.e. saints] who have been outstanding in virtues and instruments of divine grace.*[1A] St. Bernadette would say, *We are going to heaven, we are working for heaven, everything else is nothing.* The great British martyr, St. John Fisher claimed

---

[1] "The Liturgy and the Sacraments" audio tape.   [1A] Zenit, Nov. 4, 2001.

that *the joys of heaven incomparably surpass all the joys that can be devised in this wretched world.* Fr. M. D. Molinié, O.P., explains: *As a matter of fact those who really love [God] have a more passionate thirst for happiness than an egoist. Egoists fatally shrink their heart's desires, gradually sacrificing the joy of living to their own comfort—growing increasingly negative and petty...A strange paradox, well confirmed by experience, has it that only those who give themselves entirely are able to enjoy and desire, simply because really being alive always involves running risks that no man could possibly face if he spent all his time protecting himself against invasion by others...*

More profoundly, much more profoundly, do the saints yearn for happiness. However, they love God more than they thirst for happiness...The intense desire for happiness is harnessed by their desire to please God...[2] In other words, to be truly happy give God your life as a blank check, and teach your children to do the same. *Even though all faith, hope, and confidence are a gift of God,* wrote St. Francis Xavier, *the Lord gives them to whom He will, but usually to those who strive to overcome themselves and take the means to do so.* St. Francis continues, *There is a great difference between one who has confidence in God when he has all that he needs and one who has confidence in Him when he has nothing.* This is another key teaching to be instilled in your children. Faith must be lived just as intensely when God "seems to abandon one" as during times of spiritual consolation. When a person "feels" that God has deserted him, God is actually closer to that person. God is simply testing one's faith. Writing in the early 1700's, Fr. Jean-Pierre De Caussade, S.J., addressed this spiritual mystery: *We must realize that it is in order to stimulate and sustain this faith that God allows the soul to be buffeted and swept away by the raging torrent of so much distress, so many troubles, so much embarrassment, and weakness, and so many setbacks. For it is essential to have faith to find God behind all this...*[This is similar to the importance of the friction of wind to the root structure of trees discussed in the last chapter.] *But God, who*

---

[2] Fr. M. D. Molinié, O.P., *The Struggle of Jacob* (Ramsey, NJ: Paulist Press, 1977).

comforts the humble, always gives us, however great our feeling of desolation, an inner assurance that we need be afraid of nothing as long as we allow Him to act and abandon ourselves to Him...[H]e walks beside you, He surrounds you and is within you. He lives with you and yet you try to find him...All you suffer, all you do, all your inclinations are mysteries under which God gives Himself to you while you are vainly straining after high-flown fancies...God disguises Himself so that we may reach that pure faith which enables us to recognize Him under any appearance.[3]

In reviewing Mother Teresa's diaries and letters for her beatification it was found that she sometimes *felt rejected by God, helpless and tempted to abandon her work caring for the poor and dying.*[4]

If your children do not aim for sanctity, besides living unhappy, miserable lives, they could end up losing their souls. One cannot treat God with indifference and then expect to get to heaven. We simply would be out of place, uncomfortable there. It would not be heaven for us but rather hell. Let me give a personal example. Last fall friends invited Bob and me to stay with them in their villa in Naples, Florida. We have stayed at beautiful hotels and luxurious condos before but those experiences did not prepare us for our friends' exquisite villa. Each room could have been featured in *Southern Living*. The couple greeted us with sincere affection, and did everything to make us feel at home yet my desire to flee the villa never left me the entire time I was there. I simply did not belong there because I'm prone to spill things, break things, and bleed at the most inappropriate times. The stress of being out of place became so unbearable that we left our friends two days earlier than planned. God used that experience to teach me how we will be the ones to determine where we will spend eternity. Rationalizing our lives or trying to bully God to get into heaven

---

[3] From *Abandonment to Divine Providence* by John Beevers (NY: Doubleday, 1975).

[4] "Mother Teresa expressed doubts," *The Atlanta-Journal-Constitution*, Sept. 15, 2001, p. C4.

simply won't work. Unless we live as true sons and daughters of God heaven will be off limits...by our own choice.

Life has its limits. How you live each day determines what happens to you at the moment of death. Your primary duties as a parent are not only to teach your children that they were created to be saints and apostles, but to **educate them in the faith so they can fulfill their vocation to become saints. Nothing takes precedence over this responsibility.** Christ insists, *Your light must shine before men so that they may see goodness in your acts and to give praise to your heavenly Father (Matt.* 5:16). Unless your children are growing more holy on a daily basis they cannot be this "light" to others.

J. R. R. Tolkien, the author of *The Hobbit* and *Lord of the Rings*, was profoundly moved by the sacrifices his mother made to convert to the Catholic Church and to raise him as a Catholic. An Anglican by birth, his mother had to suffer the scorn of her family when she converted to Catholicism. To feed her own faith and nurture the faith of her family, she chose to live close to Catholic churches so she could walk to daily Mass. The sacrifices his mother made to raise him a Catholic had an intense effect on his subsequent life and his writings.

Vatican II called attention to the fact that Christian _couples are instruments of grace and witnesses to the Faith for themselves, their children and relatives. They are their children's primary teachers and educators in the Faith, molding them in a Christian and apostolic life through their word and example. They guide them wisely in choosing their vocation,_ and they carefully stimulate the call to the religious life, if it is found in their children.[5]

Our attention is easily diverted from this urgent responsibility by living in a world blanketed with practical atheism that knows that God exits but insists that it does not need Him. Along with practical atheism, we live with the added evil of humanism. According to the late Fr. Malachi Martin, the humanist *shares the view that mankind is **not** called to be*

---

[5] Vatican Council II, *Apostolicam Actuositatem,* no. 11.

144 Raise Happy Children...Raise Them Saints!

holy; it is called to be happy, in the certainty that all the glory of life is right here, and right now. Happiness lies within the ambit of material development. Each of us is called to be a happy consumer of the world's goods, living in a bountiful world. That is our supremest right and our only common destiny.[6] But from what Fr. Molinié, O.P., told us previously, we know that this is a terribly erroneous concept that only contributes to unhappiness.

Practical atheism wedded to the pervasive spirit of humanism, seen in the consumer mentality, can cause us to lose track of the purpose of our lives and the lives of our children. For example, one couple we know would never think of missing Sunday Mass or anticipated Mass when they are home but when on vacation, they vacation from God. On vacation they want to be happy, not holy. But **to be happy, one has to be holy**. Other humanistic excuses for not attending Sunday Mass include *I'm too tired, I was too busy, I don't get anything out of it.* **We go to Mass to give glory to God, to give of ourselves...not to get.**

If you are serious about teaching your children to develop a personal relationship with God you must carefully **limit** their **outside activities to make time for God.** Many parents have the mistaken notion that when their children are not in school, they must have every free minute programmed. So children are signed up for endless activities. **Beware**...this is one of the most effective ways to separate your children from God. Another way is to allow them to spend all their free time watching TV, cruising the Internet, listening to the radio, or giving their lives to a sport or hobby.

Recently a mother told me about her five-year-old daughter's extracurricular activities. That poor child! From the moment this little one gets home from all-day kindergarten, she is carted all over town from one activity to the next, even on the weekends. She does not have a free minute to even think. This tyke is enrolled in art classes, ballet classes, Brownies, swim

---

[6] Malachi Martin, *The Keys Of This Blood* (NY: Simon and Schuster, 1990) p. 293.

team, piano lessons, soccer practice, and gymnastics. (Note there is nothing involving the Catholic faith.) As unbelievable as this sounds, this is not uncommon today. The parents, themselves good people, only want the best for their child, yet they are giving her the worst. Furthermore, the mother is in turmoil trying to plan carpools while getting dinner on the table in time for the little girl to leave promptly for her next activity which daddy chauffeurs. The parents do not have time for each other. Without realizing it, this couple is destroying family life and family unity. If the marriage remains intact, the disruption of family life can result in serious consequences down the road for the child. One consequence is a false sense of values. This little girl is learning that her interests take priority over everything else in life and in her family. That it is okay for art, dancing and gymnastics to become her gods. She is being taught to be self-centered rather then at the service of those around her. She is being taught a distorted view of life and leisure. Unknowingly, her parents are teaching her that every minute of her life has to be filled with activity. But in this rush of activity there is no time for solitude with God. There is no time for prayer or for catechism lessons. Dad is simply the chauffeur and Mom the activities director. If this continues, this little girl will grow up to be one of the adults, we all know, who runs from one activity to another as a means of escaping responsibility, and ultimately from God.

This frenzy of **programmed free time is also a serious obstacle to the parents' personal growth in holiness.** Mothers and fathers cannot get to confession, attend retreats, Days or Evenings of Recollection because of the conflict with carpools and scheduled games. Teens cannot make frequent confession, retreats or doctrinal classes because of ballet practice, chorus or football. When these parents and teens are faced with some trauma, they may not be able to turn to God because they were too busy to make His acquaintance.

Going back to the example of the little girl, psychologically the child herself may be headed for future counseling since she is being taught that her happiness lies in her interests rather than in the fact that she is a child of God put on earth to serve others. She will only know happiness when she learns the purpose of her life then strives for the ultimate goal of heaven.

Your faith, your struggle to grow in virtues and your prayer life cannot be put into neat little compartments. They must interweave the 24 hours of each day. This is called unity of life. Also, it is through the example of the interaction within the family that children are taught to sanctify their work and offer it to God. If there is no family life how can this be done?

Nancy Kennedy, wife of Martin De Porres Kennedy who is the author of **A Philadelphia Catholic In King James Court,** confides, *nothing is more important to me than raising my children saints. We don't have a TV. In the evening, when the children are ready for bed we say the family rosary. After the rosary we talk about God, the Holy Eucharist, Our Lady, read the lives of the saints, discuss the good things the children did that day and the not so good things they did. This is the most important twenty minutes of my day.*

Nancy and Marty also skillfully mold the characters of their children through home schooling. In talking with Nancy I was impressed with how serious she and her husband are about protecting the innocence of their children from outside negative influences. Her concern coincides with this insight: *Some Catholics do not pray because they have allowed their mental processes to be taken over by radio and television. Most adult Americans make their first mistake of the day right after they get out of bed. They turn on the news. This is a harsh way to start the day—with war, riots, killings, pollution, violence, hatred, crises. The list is endless.*

Bad news, commercials, beat music—these are all destructive of tranquility and prayer life. Constant emphasis on bad news can destroy our values, inhibit emotional growth, and increase depression. In Boston during a newspaper strike the suicide rate went down 22%. When Seattle had no newspaper or TV, suicides there dropped 43%. The wise person, consequently, controls the baneful influence of the media. The person who wants to pray must control the media even more carefully.[7]

The Virtue of Religion

"[W]ithout faith our children will never be rich; with faith they will never be poor."   Bl. Joseph Tovini

Teaching the faith to your children is the practice of the virtue of religion. When practicing the virtue of religion make it **attractive** to your children. Teach them to imitate the example of St. Thérèse who called our Heavenly Father, *the Good God.* Lead them to fall in love with God simply because He is God, not for what He can give them or do for them through "gimme prayers." When a child only turns to God in time of need, should God not respond in the manner or in the time frame that the child sets, the child will rebel and abandon his faith. Don't you see adult examples of this all around you?

In talking with your children, refer to God, as *the Good God.* For example, *Mary, look what a beautiful day the good God gave us today.* Or, *Michael, look at the beautiful sunset the good God created for you tonight.* By connecting "good" with God, a natural love and appreciation for God will develop within their hearts and souls.

Daily point out to your children the wonderful things that God does for you and your family. This helps the children to develop the virtues of gratitude and appreciation. John Paul II asks us *to praise God and see the imprint of His love in the beauty of creation. [The] beauty of nature impels the soul to recall God's goodness. [It is] the first book that God has entrusted to the mind and heart of man.*[8]

After pointing out all the large and small caresses the good God lavishes on you, lead your children in aspirations of praise and adoration. *Thank you, Jesus, for the place we live. Thank you, Jesus, for the food you provide for us. Thank you, Jesus, for Daddy's job. Thank you, Jesus, for our grandparents. Thank*

---

[7] *The Vatican II Weekday Missal* (Boston: Daughters of St. Paul, 1975) p. 453.
[8] Zenit, "Pope Links Beauty of Creation To God's Love," July 15, 2001.

you, Jesus for the air we breathe. Thank you, Jesus, for our Catholic faith. Thank you, Jesus, for the priests who minister to our family. Thank you, Jesus, for all of your goodness towards us, even the help we are unaware of. Even teach your children to thank the good God for the sufferings or contradictions of each day asking Him to use them to convert sinners, for peace in the world, for the return of family members who have left the Church. Find it difficult to pray prayers of adoration with your children? Teach your children the ***Canticle of the Three Children*** and ***Psalm 150***. Pray them with your children in the morning or at bedtime. Alternate saying the lines of the prayer between you and your children or take turns letting your children lead the prayer and you respond.

Canticle of the Three Children

Ant. Let us sing the hymn of the three children, which these holy ones sang of old in the fiery furnace, giving praise to the Lord. (P.T. Alleluia).

1. Bless the Lord, all you works of the Lord; praise and exalt Him above all forever.
2. Heaven, bless the Lord; angels of the Lord, bless the Lord.
3. All you waters that are above the heavens, bless the Lord, let all the powers bless the Lord.
4. Sun and moon bless the Lord; stars of heaven bless the Lord.
5. Every shower and dew, bless the Lord; all you winds, bless the Lord.
6. Fire and heat, bless the Lord; cold and heat, bless the Lord.
7. Dews and hoar frosts, bless the Lord; frost and cold, bless the Lord.
8. Ice and snow, bless the Lord; nights and days, bless the Lord.
9. Light and darkness, bless the Lord; lightnings and clouds, bless the Lord.
10. Let the earth bless the Lord; let it praise and exalt Him above all forever.
11. Mountains and hills bless the Lord; everything growing from the earth, bless the Lord.
12. Seas and rivers, bless the Lord; fountains, bless the Lord.
13. Whales and all that move in the waters, bless the Lord; all you

fowls of the air, bless the Lord.

14. All you beasts and cattle bless the Lord; sons of men bless the Lord.
15. Israel bless the Lord; praise and exalt Him above all forever.
16. Priests of the Lord, bless the Lord; servants of the Lord, bless the Lord.
17. Spirits and souls of the just, bless the Lord; holy men of humble heart, bless the Lord.
18. Ananias, Azarias and Misael, bless the Lord; praise and exalt Him above all forever.
19. Let us bless the Father and the Son, with the Holy Spirit; let us praise and exalt Him above all forever.
20. Blessed are you, Lord, in the firmament of heaven; and worthy of praise, and glorious above all forever.

Psalm 150

1. Praise the Lord in His holy place, praise Him in His mighty heavens.
2. Praise Him for His powerful deeds, praise His surpassing greatness.
3. O praise Him with sound of trumpet, praise Him with lute and harp.
4. Praise Him with timbrel and dance, praise Him with strings and pipes.
5. O praise Him with resounding cymbals, praise Him with clashing of cymbals. Let everything that lives and that breathes give praise to the Lord.

Glory be to the Father...
Ant. Let us sing the hymn of the three children, which these holy ones sang of old in the fiery furnace, giving praise to the Lord. (P.T. Alleluia).

Lord have mercy. Christ, have mercy. Lord, have mercy. Our Father who art in heaven...

V. And lead us not into temptation.
R. But deliver us from evil.
V. Let all your works praise you, Lord.
R. And let your Saints bless you.
V. Your saints shall rejoice in glory.

R. They shall rejoice in their resting place.

V. Not unto us, Lord, not unto us.

R. But unto Your name give glory.

V. O Lord, hear my prayer.

R. And let my cry come unto you.

Let us pray: God, who did allay the flames of fire for three children, grant in your mercy that the flame of vice may not consume us your servants.

Direct, we beseech you, Lord, our actions by your inspirations, and further them by your assistance: that every word and work of ours may begin always from you and by you be likewise ended.

Quench in us, we beseech you, Lord, the flame of vice even as you did enable blessed Lawrence to overcome his fire of sufferings. Through Christ our Lord. Amen.

If the concept of a **good God** is planted in your children's mind at a young age and cultivated through their youth, they will remain firmly attached to Him throughout their lives. If they also develop gratitude and appreciation toward Him as young children, these virtues will likewise grow as they mature. One Protestant friend of mine grieves that her two adult children do not possess the love of God that she has. Now a new grandmother, she is making sure that her grandson will love God. Although he is only one-year-old, she told me that by the age of two he <u>will</u> know the *Our Father*. She sings him lively hymns teaching him how to raise his arms in praise when she sings "alleluia to God." It's precious to see this little one praising God in this manner.

Just as we teach our children to say "please" and "thank you" to those around them, we have to also teach to them say "please" and "thank you" to God for all of His goodness to them. One father in New York taught his toddler son to greet each day with, *Jesus, thank you for a nice day.* The father explains to his son that even though it may be raining, it's a nice day because God sends the rain to help the farmers grow our food. Teaching appreciation of the goodness of God is a key foundation stone in your children's spiritual formation. Unless they learn to appreciate the goodness of the *good God* your children cannot love Him. Let's take this to a personal level. Recall the times you have heroically spent yourself to help another yet no true appreciation was expressed by the person or group. Weren't you hurt by the indifference? Recently I found myself in such a situation. Crushed by the person's indifference, I found myself also attacked by the person for my efforts. Turning to God in tears I asked *why*? Immediately came the response, *You were treated badly but look how people treat Me. I give them air to breathe, food to eat, graces to enhance their lives, jobs to provide their means of support. Everything good that they possess comes from Me but consider how they treat Me...so little appreciation, so little gratitude. If they treat Me, their Creator so poorly, why are you surprised that they treat you, a creature, with contempt?*

After instilling the concept of appreciation for the goodness of God, love and trust of God should follow next. Explain to your children that God's love is truly beyond their comprehension. Fr. Hardon, S.J., reminds us that God created us...but He did not have to. He simply created us out of love. God came down to earth to redeem us...but He did not have to. He sacrificed Himself for us out of love. Explain in detail this aspect of God's love. *Christ **willfully** died for our salvation*, Fr. John Hardon, S.J., explains, *to show us how to use our wills.* Contrast the life of Christ on earth as similar to one of your children becoming an ant to save an ant colony or use some other comparison so that your child can understand the enormity of His sacrifice. Jesus' incredible self-sacrificing love should move your children to love Him intensely. Keep reiterating this theme in various ways throughout their lives.

Teach your children that God is actively involved in every aspect of their lives. Quoting the works of the Prophet Isaiah (45:15) John Paul II during a weekly audience told us *"Truly with you God is hidden..." With these words, the prophet invites us to realize that God intervenes in history, even if it is not immediately apparent. It might be said that He is "behind the scenes." He is the mysterious and invisible director who respects the liberty of His creatures, but at the same time holds the thread of the world's events. The certainty of the providential action of*

God is a source of hope for the believer, who knows he can count on the constant presence of Him, "maker of the earth..."

Read books on the history of the Church and Bible history yourself then pass on the fascinating information to your children. It will inflame their faith. Your research will make scripture and the story of redemption come alive for both you and for them. For instance, at the time of the Annunciation historians believe there were probably about 150 people who inhabited Nazareth...about 20 families more or less. People basically lived in caves building a front on to them with wood and roofing them with palms. Families lived in the front part of the caves and slept on carpets. The middle part of the cave was used for cooking and the back part of the cave was used for housing livestock. Recall the parable of the neighbor who came to borrow some bread and the man told him he could not give him any bread because his children were sleeping. In order for the man to get to the bread, he would have to climb over his sleeping children to reach the kitchen and then climb back over them to reach the door to give the bread to his neighbor. In this process he might awaken his children. Anyone who finally gets a toddler or baby to bed doesn't want to do anything to wake that child! That is why the man first refused but due to the neighbor's persistence he probably felt that if he did not chance giving the man the bread the man's loud arguing would awaken the children anyway.

It was in such a cave that the Incarnation took place over 2,000 years ago. Nazareth was such a humble little town that it was not even listed on ancient maps. Following the Incarnation, Our Lady went to visit her cousin Elizabeth in Ein Karem, who at the age of 60 or 61, was expecting St. John the Baptist. Elizabeth, being married to a high priest, Zachary, was of the wealthy class so the couple owned a home in the mountains and another in the city. Historians believe that during her confinement, Elizabeth lived in her mountain home (again a cave) that is reached by climbing 320 exhausting steps. It was there that the Visitation took place. How did Mary, pregnant at the time, climb that mountain! In the cave of the Visitation there is a large boulder which pius legend says hid St. Elizabeth and St. John from Herod's soldiers as they swept through Israel slaughtering the Holy Innocents. It is believed that Herod wiped out a whole generation of males in his attempt to kill Jesus since the killing was not limited to the region of Bethlehem but encompassed the whole country.

Christ, Himself, was born in a cave, not a barn as we think of barns. The mountains are riddled with caves, large and small. The "inn" that *had no room* was actually a series of caves. All of the front caves were occupied in Bethlehem so Mary and Joseph had to go back into a back cave reserved for the livestock. It was in that windowless, smelly place that Jesus was born. There are two places to venerate in this cave: the location of the birth of Christ, inlaid with a star located under a small altar, and the nearby location of the manager.

In Shepherds' field, where the angels appeared to the shepherds to announce the birth of Jesus, the caves are so large that they could contain 100 sheep. Shepherds were considered the lowest of the low but God the Father determined that it should be they who learned of the birth of Jesus first. God isn't status conscious.

These are just a sampling of some of the interesting facts about our faith. See how interesting your faith can be when you make the effort to learn the details surrounding scripture and the life of Christ?

Explain The Rules Of Life

"God forbid that we should forsake the law and the commandments."   (*1 Maccabees* 2:22)

Explain to your children that everything that is created, either by God or by man has a set purpose and comes with a set of instructions to explain how best to use creation. Your personal "how-to" instructions explain that your purpose is to do the will of God and only then will you function happily and efficiently. God's will for you is not something arbitrary or ruthless. As your Creator and Father, only He knows what will make you truly happy and joyful on earth and in eternity. His will guides you through the pitfalls of life, keeps you on the path to holiness and then rewards you with eternal bliss. Venerable Cardinal John Henry Newman pointed out that *Christ bids us do nothing that we cannot do.* Unfortunately, the pride that caused the fall of Adam and Eve, then mankind in general, is evident in our personal actions. We want to do what we want, not what God wants although in the long run we cause ourselves terrible misery. St. Paul, in his letter to the Philippians, laments that **they all seek their own interests, not those of Jesus Christ (Phil.** 2:21).

Teach your children that God is not obligated to do their bidding nor be manipulated by their wishes. Because of God's intense love for them, He knows best what is for their good and likewise what can harm them. Because of His love, many times, like any good parent, He has to say "no" to their pleas. Remind them that their happiness depends on doing His bidding. Christ tells them in the Gospel, **Your business is to follow Me (John** 21:23), not vice versa. Just as children are to honor their parents (the fourth commandment) we are called to honor God and accept His decisions.

Before Pope John Paul I became pope, he wrote a book in the style of letters to various famous people, entitled **Illustrissimi.** In one of those letters he relates: *The great Tolstoy wrote of a horse which, halfway down a slope, rebelled and reared up, saying: "I'm tired of pulling the carriage and of obeying the driver. I'm stopping!" He was quite free to do so, but it was to cost him dearly. From that moment on, in fact, all turned against him: the driver whipped him, the coach slammed into his legs, the passengers in the coach yelled and cursed.*

So it goes. When we take the wrong road and rebel against God, we overturn order; we break the pact of alliance with the Lord: we renounce His love; we become irritated with ourselves, discontent with what we have done, gnawed by remorse.

Yes, sin becomes, willy-nilly, the master of the sinner. Perhaps at first it pays him compliments and caresses him, but the sinner remains its slave and sooner or later will get a taste of the whip.

Let me give you another example of how doing "my will" can destroy personal peace and joy and that of those who deal with us. "Ginny" was trying to work with her family on how best to celebrate Christmas. One part of the family thought the holiday should be celebrated at the family cabin in the Upper Peninsula. From past experiences Ginny knew the cabin was not equipped for entertaining. It would be hard to setup, everything would have to be transported, and if something was forgotten for the meal they were out of luck. Clean-up likewise was a problem so she was relieved when another family member offered to host the holiday. Then, without consulting Ginny, the family decided to change the location to the country cabin despite her prior objections. Hurt that her family would exclude her from the planning, she was even more upset because she knew it was a holiday disaster in the making. On Christmas morning one daughter called to say her children had chickenpox so they would not be going up. Ginny's husband was running a fever. Should they go or stay home? If they stayed home, family members might not believe Gary was sick and think the couple was bowing out because they were upset over the location change. They decided they better go to keep family peace. They drove six hours up in a snowstorm with Gary getting progressively sicker. From the moment they walked into the cabin, Ginny was attacked because there was "no TV", someone had forgotten to bring sugar, etc. etc. Everything she feared and tried to warn about was realized. Not only were most of the family members unhappy, it actually caused a rupture in the family with some members stomping out early in anger. Ginny cried all the way home while Gary ended up with walking pneumonia for his heroic efforts. Ginny knew what was best for her family but they resisted her efforts and the result was a holiday disaster. God knows what is best for us, what will make us happy and give us joy, but we likewise go behind His back to rearrange our lives to suit ourselves and then wonder why we are so miserable. Then like Ginny's family, who blamed her for the disaster, we turn on God and blame Him when our lives fall to pieces. Use the events in your daily lives to point out to your children how their will caused problems and how if they had followed God's will or your advice as God's stand-in they would have been happier.

Fr. John Hardon, S.J., raises an important point: *We only have the right to ask God two questions: What do You want me to do? How do You want me to do it?* This can actually be used as an aspiration to pray during the day. Why not teach your children to pray from little on: *Good God, what do you want me to do now? How do You want me to do it?* When they are fighting or in a cantankerous mood, ask them, *Is this how the good God wants you to act?* Teach your children that unhappiness results from putting their will before God's will. St. Paul adds, ***Do all things without murmuring and without questioning, so as to be blameless and guileless, children of God without blemish in the midst of a depraved and perverse generation. For among these you shine like stars in the world...(Phil.*** 2:14-16). Blessed Edward Poppe (1890-1924) was declared blessed because of his *exact fulfillment of the will of God.* Sanctity is that simple.

Explain The Symbolism Of Catholic Art...

Explain the symbolism in holy pictures to your children. This symbolism teaches lessons. For example, the picture of Christ dressed as a shepherd, with a staff in his hand, carrying a lamb around His neck is a powerful picture story. First of all, why do shepherds carry a staff with a hook on the top? The reason they do not use merely walking sticks is because the hook is used to pull straying lambs back into the fold. It is customary for shepherds to use the hook up to five times to pull the same straying lamb back. If the lamb persists in defying the shepherd, the shepherd is forced to take more drastic measures to save the lamb from wandering away or being eaten by wolves. The shepherd uses a rock to break the feet of the lamb. He wraps the lamb's feet in an old rag then carries the lamb around his shoulders. Likewise, God keeps pulling us back to Him when we stray but when it becomes habitual, for our own good He permits some great sorrow or tragedy to break our self-will.

But God never abandons us. Rather, He binds us up lovingly then carries us on His shoulders. Likewise, a bishop uses the symbol of the shepherd's staff with a hook to remind Catholics that part of his vocation is to pull in straying members of the Church.

Explain relics to your children. One important relic is the Shroud of Turin. During Lent, as a family, study or view a video on the Shroud of Turin. Viewing the Shroud, believed through intensive research to be the burial cloth of Jesus, one can see that His body, front and back is covered with bloody wounds. He was scourged from the base of His neck to His ankles. The crown of thorns was a cap that enclosed His forehead to the nap of His neck. There are bruises visible on His shoulders from carrying the cross. Tests on the Shroud indicate that His blood type is AB. His height about 5 ft. 10 inches and His weight is about 175 pounds. Viewing the Shroud leaves a personally moving realization of God's passionate love for us.

What Is A Priestly Soul?

"What are we in this world for, if not to love God and help to save souls?" Bl. Mary of St. Euphrasia Pelletier

One of the graces every baptized person receives is that of a priestly soul. While only an ordained priest can offer the sacrifice of the Holy Mass, as possessors of priestly souls we are called to generously sacrifice ourselves. In fact, the depth of our love for God is measured by the depth of our self-giving, our self-sacrifice. How? By sacrificing our free wills to God. As Fr. John Hardon, S.J., reiterated repeatedly, to truly live a Christian life *is to be a living martyr.* He always added, *the Catholic Church today needs Catholics who are living martyrs. Paganism is Christianity without the cross.* To do God's will rather than one's personal will is to be a martyr. To suffer ridicule for obeying the will of God is to be a martyr. To live the commandments and the moral teachings of the Church in today's culture is to be a martyr. To defy peer pressure is to be a martyr. If you teach this fact to your children from little on, the junior high years through college will not be so difficult for them to endure as Catholic Christians. The words of Bl. Julia Louisa, a Carmelite martyred during the French Revolution are just as apropos today as they were in 1794: *We are the victims of the age, and we ought to sacrifice ourselves to obtain its return to God.*

Teach your children that living heroic love of God did not begin with Christianity but has precedent in the Old Testament. Read the second book of **Maccabees** to them. This book has two powerful examples of heroic love of God to the point of martyrdom. The first is the story of Eleazar (6:18-31), an elderly scribe, who chose death rather than violate God's law prohibiting the eating of pork. His friends, trying to save his life, suggested that he pretend to eat the sacrificed meat but instead eat meat of his own choosing. Eleazar pointed out to his friends that this not only would give scandal and bad example, but also would be a betrayal of his God. He corrects them saying, ***At our age it would be unbecoming to make such a pretense; many young men would think the ninety-year-old Eleazar had gone over to an alien religion. Should I thus dissimulate for the sake of a brief moment of life, they would be led astray by me, while I would bring shame and dishonor on my old age. Even if, for the time being, I avoided the punishment of men, I shall never, whether alive or dead, escape the hands of the Almighty. Therefore...giving up my life now, I will prove myself worthy of my old age, and I will leave to the young a noble example of how to die willingly and generously for the revered and holy laws.*** For his faithfulness he was tortured to death but before he died he witnessed to his persecutors: ***"The Lord in His holy knowledge knows full well that, although I could have escaped death, I am not only enduring terrible pain in my body from this scourging, but also suffering it with joy in my soul because of my devotion to Him." This is how he died, leaving in his death a model of courage and an unforgettable example of virtue not only for the young but for the whole nation.***

In the same book but in the next chapter of *2 Maccabees* (7:1, 20-42) we read of the brutal martyrdom of a mother and her seven sons when they refused offers of wealth and position if they would forsake the law of God. It was the mother who urged her sons to be faithful to God even to the point of death telling them: *I do not know how you came into existence in my womb; it was not I who gave you the breath of life, nor was it I who set in order the elements of which each of you is composed. Therefore, since it is the Creator of the universe who shapes each man's beginning, as He brings about the origin of everything, He, in his mercy, will give you back both breath and life, because you now disregard yourselves for the sake of His law.* After all but the youngest had been savagely killed before her eyes, she told her youngest son, *I beg you, child...Do not be afraid of this executioner, but be worthy of your brothers and accept death, so that in the time of mercy I may receive you again with them.* He likewise went to his death saying, *What are you waiting for? I will not obey the king's command. I obey the command of the law given to our forefathers through Moses...I too, like my brothers, surrender my body and life for the laws of my ancestors...calling on God to show His kindness to our nation and that soon, and by trials and afflictions to bring you to confess that He alone is God...*With that the young man was brutally killed followed by the martyrdom of his mother.

The above family prefigured the martyrdom of St. Felicity and her seven sons who lived in the second century. Felicity, known for her life of charity and intense prayer life was arrested <u>because</u> of her goodness. When urged to sacrifice to the Roman gods to save the lives of her sons, Felicity replied, *My children will live eternally if they are faithful, but must expect eternal death if they sacrifice to idols.* She then encouraged her sons to be faithful by saying, *My sons, look up to heaven where Jesus Christ with His saints expects you. Be faithful in His love, and fight courageously for your souls.* Shortly thereafter, Felicity and her sons Felix, Philip, Silvanus, Alexander, Vitalis and Martial entered heaven as martyrs. This is the type of courageous, unyielding faith God expects you to instill in your children. Fr. John Hardon, S. J., adds, *teach your children to die to self for the love of those God put into their life. This is the essence of love. God who died for us provides the grace for every person to live according to His laws. Grace is the power we receive to do the humanly impossible. Christians are the soul of the world. This is our responsibility. What the soul is to the body, giving it life and direction, the Christian is to the world. We are to be the light of the world, the leaven in society, and the salt that gives it flavor. We have a grave responsibility to teach this to our world. Selfless charity isn't possible without the cross. Love without pain is a lie. Inspire your children with the ideal of true love, which is self-sacrifice.*[9]

Also, instill in your children the desire to be apostles, to bring their friends to the Catholic faith or back into the Church if they have left. Encourage them to invite their friends to come along when you take your children to confession or Holy Mass. Teach them how to offer their work and sufferings for the conversion of their friends or fallen away family members. Give example to their friends by saying grace before and after meals. For birthday party gifts why not give a video or book of a saint, a statue, rosary, medal or other sacramental? When our youngest daughter was in third grade she was a Blue Army Cadet. At one meeting she was given a handful of scapulars and encouraged to give them to her friends to wear. She did not understand that one has to be enrolled in the scapular to receive the benefits. Mary Terese simply explained to her friends that it was like having the arms of the Mother of God around them for protection. Attending a public school, she had even her Protestant and Jewish friends wearing one for a while!

Four examples come to mind of how parents who taught their children the Catholic faith led their children to become apostles to others. The first concerns a little girl. There was a diocesan curia Christmas party and one of the women brought along her five-year-old granddaughter. After the party, a tour was given

---

[9] John Hardon, SJ, audiotape #12, "How to Preserve the Catholic Family" from *The Sacraments and The Marian Catechist* (Bardstown, KY: Eternal Life) 1998.

of the newly renovated rectory. To get to the rectory the group had to walk through the church. When the little girl reached the altar, she knelt down in front of the tabernacle and folded her hands in prayer. The people behind her continued talking as they walked by. The little girl, turning to the adults, put her finger to her lips saying, *Shhh.* Immediately the adults became quiet. My friend, who related the experience, told me, *I was so moved by her example. That little girl had more sense than the adults there.*

A Springfield, Illinois, woman enjoyed taking in exchange students. One of the students was a seventeen-year-old boy from Spain. Although she was a Protestant, each Sunday she not only drove the teen to Holy Mass but stayed with him through Mass. Then one evening he was out late. When he came home she felt sorry for him having to get up for Sunday Mass the next day. She told him, *Your mother isn't here and she won't know if you sleep in tomorrow and skip Mass.* Her words shocked the Spanish teenager. *I don't go to Mass to please my mother. I go for myself,* he replied. The next day she drove him to Mass but this time she followed along with the prayers. She was intrigued by what the teen found so important in the Mass. Over the coming weeks she found herself falling in love with the Mass. Through his example she converted to the Catholic Church. Now she attends daily Mass.

The third anecdote relates to a young business professional in Milwaukee who began dating a young Catholic woman. As their relationship progressed he asked to take her to church on Sunday. Wisely she replied, *Since you are Protestant it doesn't matter which Church you go to on Sunday but it only counts for me if we attend a Catholic Church.* He agreed to take the young woman to Sunday Mass. While he did not fall in love with the Catholic woman, he did fall in love with the Catholic faith. He has since converted to Catholicism and attends daily Mass.

My final example concerns a college coed from Florida, Lisa Demidovich, who attends Notre Dame University. Lisa, raised in a devout Catholic family, told a visiting college friend her yearning to learn more about her faith. In answer to her request for help, her friend sent her books to help in her spiritual quest, one of which was my book, *You Can Become A Saint!* Another college coed, familiar with the book, worked with Lisa helping her to deepen her interior life. Lisa began going to daily Mass, retreats, the Sacrament of Penance, saying the rosary, and going to adoration and spiritual direction but she was looking to deepen her faith even more. When Lisa left to spend a semester in Russia, she took along the book. While in Russia she began initiating conversations about the faith with her host family who are nominally Russian Orthodox. The twenty-year-old daughter of the family, Natasha, a senior at Moscow Linguistics University and fluent in English, noticed the book and asked to read it. Lisa writes, *She spent the last two months I was there reading it. She really dove into each chapter and would ask me five to seven questions from each one.* By the time Lisa left Russia, Natasha asked to keep the book. Besides this, Natasha's mother began living a mini plan of life daily in addition to accompanying Lisa to Sunday Mass at the Catholic Church. Natasha, unbaptized, considered baptism in the Orthodox Church but is holding off. While visiting in the U.S. she attends Sunday Mass at Catholic churches.

But the story gets even more interesting. Lisa next wrote asking for permission for Natasha to translate *You Can Become A Saint!* into Russian: *I remember my wanting to share the book with my host mom and other friends, but their English just wasn't good enough...There are not many religious books in Russia. I have met so many Russians who want something more and are searching for that "Good" in New Age cult, because they don't know any better. The churches are very poor and have nothing to distribute, although there is a constant flow of people wanting to know more. Because of the exchange rate and poverty in Russia, I know this project could never make money or even come out even but personally I know there are ways when there are so many souls starving over there. I know we can help!!*

Within five months Natasha had the book translated, six months ahead of her projected deadline. Lisa writes, *She recognizes her work progressed so swiftly because of the many prayers and graces she has received.* These two college coeds are now researching Russian publishers and working out a distribution plan through Catholic churches in Russia. Truly these two young women are apostles to Russia. But it was also two other young college women, spiritually well-formed by their parents, that enkindled the apostolic zeal of Lisa and Natasha. I can't wait to read the next chapter of this story! Each of Lisa's letters is more apostolically exciting than the previous ones. These young women understand what St. Francis of Assisi meant when he said, *Nothing is more important than saving souls!*

Discuss pertinent topics with your children and their friends so as to give them a Christian perspective. For instance, discuss the importance of modesty and chastity with your children and their friends in a natural way in regard to swimsuits, prom dresses, short skirts, shorts, and tight pants. Our home had a large in ground swimming pool that we thought would be fun for the girls to use with their friends. It was a very natural way to teach modesty by stating our policy of one-piece swimsuits only. If a friend did not have one, she had two options. She could borrow a suit from us or wear a long shirt that covered her two-piece suit. When a friend protested that only girls were present and that our yard was enclosed, I would point out that our neighbors' two-story home overlooked the pool and their teenage son should not see them dressed immodestly because it could be an occasion of sin for him.

Rather than having your children join a scouting troop why not start a club for girls and a club for boys that appeal to their interests. In addition to a specific activity, give a short, practical talk on a specific virtue. Before I moved to Springfield, I worked with some moms on a cheerleading club for girls' kindergarten through fourth grade. The high school cheerleaders taught the little ones once a week, a mom gave a virtue talk and the high school allowed the little girls to perform at their games. There was also a ballet club with a similar format. In St. Louis there is a club that teaches boys how to build rockets. Here in

Springfield we had a "Pot Rattlers" Club that taught the young girls cooking and baking skills. In the Milwaukee area an artist is teaching painting to a group of girls.

The importance of being apostles is pointed out by Christ very graphically in the *Gospel of St. Matthew* (3:10-11): *Every tree therefore that is not bringing forth good fruit is to be cut down and thrown into the fire.*

Catholicism Develops A Moral Sense...

"I will always marvel at how a deepening faith and love of God in patients have strengthened their character and re-integrated their personalities."

Dr. Luz G. Gabriel, M.D.

The Roman Catholic Church is the largest religious denomination in the world. The next largest group of Christians is fallen away Catholics. Isn't this chilling information? Fr. John Hardon, S.J., insisted that *it's the infidelity of Catholics in every vocation that has caused the destruction of our culture and family.* One recent example of this is the case of John Walker, a Californian and member of the Taliban, who fought against his country and celebrated the destruction of innocent life in the September 11, 2001 terror attacks. The *Wall Street Journal* notes that he was *Named for John Lennon; the son of a Catholic father and a mother who embraced Buddhism; a graduate of an alternative high school who converted to Islam after reading The Autobiography of Malcom X.*[10] If Walker's father had practiced his faith and brought his son up to love God would he had used his free will for evil? Would Walker had fallen into the 20% that would do evil despite the best Catholic formation or the 80% that are influenced for the good by such formation?

I believe that millions of Catholics left the Church because they were never actually taught the Catholic faith. We are told that most Catholics leave the Church over moral issues such as abortion, contraception, homosexuality, fornication,

---

[10] "Sons of Liberty," *The Wall Street Journal*, Dec. 7, 2001, p. w21.

divorce and remarriage. I disagree. If these Catholics had been diligently taught a deep faith and how to live the faith daily as children and young adults, the great majority of them would not have fallen away.

Professor Gerardo Castillo of the University of Navarre explains that we should help our children *develop a moral sense. Early on they are incapable of understanding morality, although they do have an innate ability to distinguish good from evil. Children easily accept moral norms, but only as rules and because of the authority of those who enforce them. Initially they are not capable of discerning the reason behind a particular norm.*[11] I believe that most Catholics were never educated beyond this point. They were neither taught the principals nor the reasons behind the various moral laws. If they were it is more likely that they would use their free will to obey and defend the laws rather than dispute them.

On the other hand, what if a parent does everything right and the child still leaves the faith? Remember God's gift of free will. Consider the family of St. Roderick who lived in Spain during the 9th century. Roderick had two brothers, one of whom left the faith to become Muslim while the other left the faith out of indifference. When Roderick tried to stop his brothers from fighting, they turned on him beating him senseless. While he was still unconscious, his Muslim brother handed him over to the Muslim authorities to be killed. What a family! Closer to our era is the family of St. Maximilian Kolbe. Their three sons entered the Franciscan seminary. Two became priests, while the eldest, Francis, left the seminary to fight in World War I. Recall how rather than returning to the monastery after the war, he married but his life was dysfunctional.

Funeral eulogies lead us to believe that every person goes immediately to heaven, even fallen away Catholics. Ah, if it were only so! Eternal bliss takes heroic virtue and diligent daily effort. If we are baptized into the Catholic faith or convert

---

[11] Professor Gerardo Castillo, "Educating In the Faith," Instituto de Ciencias de la Educación, University of Navarre, 1987.

to the Catholic faith we have to also die in the faith. Without the sacraments how can one grow in sanctifying grace? Without frequent confession how can one grow in virtue? Without confession, how can one be cleansed of his mortal sins? Confessing our sins to God in the great outdoors may be your will, but it is not God's will. Without prayer how can you have interior peace and joy?

The book of **Joshua** warns *if you leave the Lord, and serve strange gods, He will turn, and will afflict you, and will destroy you after all the good He has done you* (24:20). Strange gods can include one's will, materialism, the occult, the New Age, obsession about work, sports, success, sex or anything else that is not of God.

While the thought of having one of our children leave the faith causes us to shudder, we also have a personal interest in keeping our children Catholic. When we die, it will be our children who decide our funeral arrangements. If our children do not practice the faith there is little chance we will have a Funeral Mass or be buried in consecrated ground. Sound absurd? In the last month three different fallen away Catholic families we know dispensed with the Funeral Mass, cremated the bodies and left the ashes *blowin' in the wind.* It saved the kids' money. On a purely natural level, why pay for something one does not believe in?

Up until now we have discussed the importance of faith on a spiritual level, but it is also important to teach your children the importance of faith on a natural level. ***Reader's Digest*** ran an interesting article maintaining that man's *brain [has] been wired to experience the reality of God.*[12] (Are you really surprise by this?) The author, a fallen away Catholic has been working with Andrew Newberg, a professor at the University of Pennsylvania. *Newberg...[is] a leading figure in the emerging science of neurotheology, which explores the links between spirituality and the brain.*[13] By using a SPECT scanner, Newberg was actually able to map the brains of people in prayer.

---

[12] Vince Rause, "Searching for the Divine," ***Reader's Digest,*** December 2001, p.143.
[13] *Ibid.*, p. 142.

Scientists are actually able to see the effect prayer has on the human brain. In addition to this, there have been frequent articles in 2001 about the importance of faith in regard to one's health. *Harvard Women's Health Watch* in November 2001 found that those who have resilience in the midst of traumas or setbacks hold a belief in God. They urged readers to *Make decisions that affirm your values and standards...Practice your beliefs...[s]pend more time in prayer or meditation...[while] helping others may be the best way of healing ourselves.*[14] In an article written by Tara Parker-Pope for the *The Wall Street Journal,* the author points out that there are *more than 600 papers dealing with the issues of spirituality and health* [in the] *Medline database of medical articles.*[15] She adds that *Increasingly, the medical profession is promoting the notion that a person's spiritual well-being may be as important a factor in long-term health as are diet and exercise.* As for relieving stress, *The body also can evoke a relaxation response that triggers a variety of chemical and body changes, including decreased brain activity and lower blood pressure and heart rate. The response can be evoked by repetitive thoughts during meditation....or repetitive prayer, such as saying the rosary.*[16] The author then notes that Associate Professor Herbert Benson of the Harvard Medical School is currently doing a study on *the effects of daily prayer on physical health.* *Reader's Digest*[17] also ran a fascinating article entitled "Faith Heals" by Lydia Strohl. She found that those who practice a life of piety and attend at least weekly church services benefit in the following ways:

- ✓ Live longer life spans by seven years;
- ✓ Hospitalized for shorter periods of time;
- ✓ Experience fewer health problems;
- ✓ Recover faster after surgery, particularly open-heart surgery;

---

[14] "At the Heart of Recovery, Personal Resilience," *Harvard Women's Healthy Watch,* Nov. 2001, Volume IX, #4.

[15] "More Physicians Make Spiritual Well-Being Part of Health Profiles," Tara Parker-Pope, Fall, 2001 (no date).

[16] *Ibid.*

[17] May, 2001, p. 108.

✓ Have 70% less likelihood of having coronary heart disease;
✓ Have lower blood pressure;
✓ Experience less depression and anxiety thereby better mental health in general;
✓ Are less susceptible to illnesses in general because they experience less stress overall.
✓ Faced with terminal illness/death there is peaceful acceptance rather than fear.

For your children to benefit from all the above, teach them:

❑ To call God *the good God;*
❑ To show appreciation and gratitude to God daily;
❑ To love God for Himself, not for what He can do for them;
❑ To study the biblical and historical context of the Catholic faith.
❑ To get up in the morning with the determination to live God's will each day;
❑ To be an apostle by bringing their friends closer to God;
❑ To live love of God and love of neighbor through self-sacrifice and self-giving.
❑ To accept the fact that God knows best in every situation;
❑ To adore God daily.

"Holy Parents Produce Holy Children."
Fr. John Hardon, S.J.

Fr. Stéphane-Joseph Piat, OFM, the biographer of St. Thérèse's family, believed that nature rarely takes sudden leaps. *In order to cause appeal of sanctity to emerge, God works at and raises up a whole series of generations. Giants of holiness who rise up in isolation and detached...from the family territory are rare...Normally, the saint receives his early fashioning in the home circle.*[18]

Researching various saints, his theory bears out. If the saints did not come from a family of saints, most of the saints came from "pious parents" or "holy parents." Consider the family

[18]*The Story Of A Family, Op. Cit.,* p. x.

and extended family of Jesus. His Old Testament lineage is rich with holy men and women. His grandparents, Ann and Joachim are saints. His parents, Mary and Joseph, are saints. His cousins, uncles and aunts are saints. To begin with there was the family of St. Zachary, St. Elizabeth, and St. John the Baptist. St. Mary of Cleophas is thought to be the sister of Our Lady. Her children included St. Salome (mother of the apostles St. John and St. James the Great), St. Joseph (Barsabbas, called Matthias who was chosen to replace Judas as an apostle), St. Simeon (second Bishop of Jerusalem), St. Jude and St. James the Less (first bishop of Jerusalem). The last two sons were apostles. Her husband, St. Cleophas, is thought to be the brother of St. Joseph. It was St. Cleophas and his son St. Simeon who were believed to be the disciples that met Our Lord on the road to Emmaus after His resurrection.

Among the apostles there are three sets of saintly brothers, St. Jude and St. James the Less (the cousins of Jesus), St. James the Greater and St. John mentioned above, along with St. Peter and St. Andrew. Another apostle, St. Philip, was the father of several daughters, three of which are considered saints. Rather than stopping here, let's go through the centuries to see the wealth of saints whose faith was nurtured and brought to fruition in holy families. St. Paul writes to St. Timothy: *I find myself thinking of your sincere faith--faith which first belonged to your grandmother Lois and to your mother Eunice, and which (I am confident) you also have* (2 *Tim.* 1:5). In this same century we have the example of the Roman martyr St. Felicula and her foster sister, St. Petronilla

In the **2ⁿᵈ century**, St. Cecilia converted her husband, Valerian, who in turn converted his brother Tiburtius. All three became saints by winning the crown of martyrdom sometime between the years 161 and 192. St. Getulius was married to St. Symphorosa. He was martyred along with his brother St. Amantis. Later his wife Symphorosa and their seven sons were also martyred. St. Philemon to whom St. Paul writes is married to St. Apphia. Sanctity also ran in the family of St. Eustathius, a martyr. His wife, St. Theopiste, and their sons Sts. Theopistus and Agapius are also counted among the saints.

St. Felicity, a widow, and her seven sons (who we discussed earlier) are all canonized for their faithfulness to God. St. Vitalis and his wife, St. Valeria, are the parents of twin saints, Gervasius and Protasius. The martyr St. Plutarch, a student of Origen, was the brother of St. Heraclas, the bishop of Alexandria. St. Potamiaena and her mother St. Marcella were martyred with St. Plutarch.

During the persecution of the Emperor Maximian in the **3rd century**, St. Donatian converted to Christianity. His example so edified his brother, St. Rogatian, that he also wanted to be baptized. Rogation was martyred before he could be baptized so his baptism was that of blood. Sts. Felix and Fortunatus of Vicenza,Italy were brothers who also were killed during this same persecution. Sts. Timothy and Maura, a young couple married only twenty days were likewise martyred for the faith. Two brothers became saints in Ethiopia; St. Frumentius and St. Aedesius. In Spain two brothers became saints by proclaiming the faith in an anti-Catholic environment. First they were scourged to scare them into repudiating the faith. When they refused to renounce the faith, Sts. Justus and Pastor, the patrons of Madrid and Alcalá, were beheaded. <u>What is so unique about these two brothers and their courageous stand is that they were only thirteen and nine-years-old.</u> Would your children give their lives for Jesus? St. Tranquillinus, a Roman, was converted when he witnessed St. Sebastian miraculously healing St. Zoe, a mute woman. Troubled with gout, he was miraculously cured from his infirmity upon his baptism. He is the father of another set of the twin saints, Sts. Marcus and Marcellianus.

In the **4th century** St. Saturninus and four of his children were martyred for the faith. They are all saints. All six members of this next family are saints. St. Basil the Elder and St. Emmelia are the parents of St. Basil the Great. His sister, St. Macrina helped to educate her three saintly brothers: St. Basil, St. Peter of Sebaste, and St. Gregory of Nyssa. In Turkey, St. Carina, her husband, St. Antonius, and her teenage son, St. Melasippus, became saints by being martyred for the faith. Talk about a perfect family! In this same century we have the famous mother-son saints, St. Monica and St. Augustine. St. Monica refused to permit the soul of her son Augustine to be lost. She followed him from Africa to Italy imploring the great St. Ambrose *to do something!* What is little known is that St. Monica had three children. The two lesser-known ones are beatified. Talking about St. Ambrose, his sister St. Marcellina is also canonized. The strong faith of St. Nonna converted her pagan husband who is now known as St. Gregory Nazianzen the Elder. He eventually became a bishop. All three of their children were canonized: St. Gregory Nazianzen, St. Caesarius of Nazianzen and St. Gorgonia. St. Gorgonia married and her son is St. Caesareus. St. Paula's daughter, Blessilla, and her son-in-law, a Roman senator, Pammachius, are both canonized. They were close friends and helpers of St. Jerome. St. Chrysanthus, an Egyptian, married St. Daria, a Greek maiden. When they moved to Rome their dedication to God attracted the attention of the pagans who martyred them.

In the **5ᵗʰ century** we have the example of St. Romanus and St. Lupicinus, two brothers who founded monasteries in Gaul. In France the family of St. Celine, the mother of St. Remigius. includes three other saints

Famous brother and sister saints include St. Scholastica and St. Benedict who lived in the **6ᵗʰ century** in Italy. Also in Italy we find the saintly parents of St. Gregory the Great, St. Sylvia and St. Gordian. St. Gregory's two aunts are also canonized, St. Tarsilla and St. Emiliana. In France we find St. Desideratus, Bishop of Bourges, and his two brothers, St. Desiderius and St. Deodatus. Their parents, Auginus and Agia gave all their possessions and time to caring for the poor. It was their example that moved their three sons to strive for holiness. South Wales also had family saints. St. David, the patron of Wales was the son of St. Non, the Queen of South Wales. St. Keyne, also of Wales, was the aunt of St. Cadoc. There is also the husband and wife team of Sts. Gundleus and Gwladys and their son St. Cadoc. Scotland boasts of St. Blane, the nephew of St. Cathan.

Multiple family saints seem to be theme in the **7ᵗʰ century**. In Spain, St. Isidore, his brothers, St. Leander and

St. Fulgentius and their sister St. Florentina are numbered among the saints. The King of East Anglia (England) matches St. Isidor and his family in sanctity. While history writes about the sanctity of the king, it is his daughters Sts. Sexburga, Ethelreda, Ethelborga, and Withburga who are canonized saints along with a half sister, St. Sethrida. This saintly family line continued for three generations. Queen St. Sexburga's daughter, Queen St. Ermengild, also had a child who is canonized, St. Werburga. Another niece is St. Ebbe, the daughter of King Ethelfrith of Northumbria. Also in England, St. Ermenburga, a princess from Kent married King Merewald. Their daughter is St. Mildred. In the same century is the family of St. Walburga. Her two brothers, Willibald and Winebald are canonized saints. Bl. Itta and Bl. Pepin are the parents of St. Gertrude of Nivelles and St. Begga. St. Begga married the son of St. Arnulf of Metz. St. Guthlac, a priest and monk was the brother of St. Pega, a nun. St. Ethelburga of the English town of Stalington was the sister of St. Erconwald who was the bishop of London. France has three notable families. St. Rictrudis and St. Adalbald are the parents of St. Eusebia. Her great-grandmother is one of the St. Gertrudes. St. Angadrisma is the cousin of St. Lambert. She was bethrothed to St. Ansbert of Chaussy. The daughter of St. Salaberga and St. Blandinus is St. Anstrudis. St. Anstrudis refused an offer of marriage at the age of twelve to enter her mother's convent in Laon, France. Her grandmother is St. Salisverga. Ansturdis' suitor, so impressed by her resolve, imitated her example by becoming a cleric and renouncing his wealth. Belgium boasts a generation of saintly relatives. St. Waldetrudis and St. Aldegondis were the daughters of Sts. Walbert and Bertilia. Their daughter, St. Waldetrudis married St. Madelgar. This couple had four children, all of whom are saints: Sts. Landericus, Dentelinus, Aldetrudis, and Madelberta. St. Amalburga of Brabant is the mother of three saintly children: St. Gudula, St. Reineldis,and St. Emerbert of Cambrai. In Austrasia we have St. Faro who is the brother of Sts. Chainoaldus and Burgundofara. Ireland has its share of saints: St. Foillan and his two brothers, Sts. Fursey and Ultan. In Wales St. Winifred was the niece of St. Beuno.

In the 8th **century** we have St. Richard, prince of West Saxons who had three children, all of whom are saints. His two sons, Sts. Willibald and Winebald worked with their famous uncle St. Boniface to evangelize the Franks. His daughter St. Walburga was an abbess who ran a school. During this same century in Spain, Sts. Nathalia and Aurelius, a Moslem couple, converted to the Catholic faith. Their example inspired Aurelius' relatives, Sts. Liliosa and Felix to practice their faith openly, which lead to the martyrdom of the four. Also in Spain two sisters, Sts. Nuilo and Alodia died for the faith. In Rome two saintly brothers became popes. St. Paul I succeeded his brother Pope Stephen III. In Flanders St. Alberic was named Bishop of Utrecht upon the death of his uncle, St. Gregory of Utrecht who previously held the post.

Sts. Cyril and Methodius were brothers who lived during the 9th **century.** Not only were they missionaries to the Slavic countries, but St. Methodius is credited with the Slav alphabet into which he translated Scripture. Her grandmother, Maud, a widow and Abbess of a monastery, raised St. Mathilda, the future queen of Germany. Of her three sons, one became St. Bruno, the Archbishop of Cologne.

In Russia, at the beginning of the 10th **century,** we have a dynasty of saints. St. Olga, the ruler and queen of Kiev, Russia, is the grandmother of St. Vladimir. Two of St. Vladimir's sons, Boris and Gleb are also saints. They were killed by their older brother and stepbrother. St. Boris is the patron of Moscow. Toward the end of the 10th century St. Ludmilla, the grandmother of St. Wenceslaus, king of Bohemia, was in charge of his education. Unfortunately his mother, Drahomira, a pagan, hated Christianity and initiated a persecution. When Wenceslaus was old enough to take over reins of government, the country was divided between Wenceslaus and his pagan brother Boleslaus. While Wenceslaus was praying in church his brother slaughtered him. We sing about him at Christmas.

The 11th **century** is likewise filled with saintly families. St. Henry and his wife St. Cunegundes became the Emperor and Empress of the Holy Roman Empire. They did not have any children since Cunegundes made a vow of perpetual virginity before her marriage. Blessed Gisele, another queen, was married to St. Stephen, the king of Hungary in 1008. Their only son was St. Emeric. St. Stephen's granddaughter or grandniece (history is a little murky here) is St. Margaret of Scotland. Sandwiched in the middle of this century is Alice of Montbar, the mother of large family of saints that spanned the 11th and 12th centuries. She raised St. Bernard of Claivaux, Bl. Guy, Bl. Gerard, Bl. Andrew, Bl. Humbeline, Bl. Batholomew, and Bl. Nivard. Don't you wish she had written a how-to book on raising saints! Her son St. Bernard led all of his brothers and thirty of his relatives into the monastic life. He is also a doctor of the Church. St. Jeanne-Francoise de Chantal is related to this family. Blessed Charles the Good is the son of St. Canute, the Danish king who was martyred in 1086. Upon the murder of his father, his mother spirited him out of Denmark to Flanders, her home. Upon his cousin's death, he assumed the throne and ruled with compassion, justice, and wisdom. He enforced truces and fought against black marketers who were extorting high food prices from the people. In revenge the black marketers murdered him while he was praying in church. As an ailing child, St. Hildegard of Bingen, Germany was placed in the care of Bl. Jutta, her aunt. She corresponded with famous clergymen, King Henry II of England, several emperors, and four Popes. Because of all her accomplishments, she is considered one of the greatest figures of this century. Her abilities spanned medicine to mysticism. Then there is St. Agnes of Assisi who is the sister of St. Clare.

In the **12th century** we have the example of St. Hildegund who was married to a count. They had three children, one of whom died young. The other two are Bls. Hedwig and Herman. St. Vitale's sister is Blessed Adeline. They lived in Savigny.

The **13th century** canonized family members were more extended. St. Sanchia was the king of Portgual. His three daughters are all saints: Mafalda, Sanchia and Teresa. His eldest daughter St. Teresa married the king of Leon,Spain. St. Elizabeth of Portugal, queen of Portugal and St. Kinga, queen of Poland, were both nieces of St. Elizabeth of Hungry, who was also a queen. St. Agnes of Bohemia was also related to St. Elizabeth of Hungry. St. Elzear, the Count of Ariano in Naples, married Bl. Delphina when both were sixteen. Their marriage was blissfully happy. King Bela IV of Hungary is the father of four daughers who are declared blessed. Among them is Blessed Yolande, who married a Polish duke. In France Blessed Blanche of Castile was the mother of King St. Louis IX who founded the University of Sorbourne besides leading the last crusade. Although the crusades have fallen into disfavor because of Protestant revisionists, the purpose of the crusades was to win back the Holy Land from the Moslems who had taken over the country by force, defiled our sacred shrines and were slaughtering the Catholics inhabitants. It is important to keep this historical epoch in perspective.

In the 14th century we have the great Scandinavian saints, St. Bridget and her daughter St. Catherine of Sweden. Catherine was the youngest of Bridget's eight children.

The 15th century saw family martyrs such as we saw in the first three centuries. Bl. Margaret Pole was imprisoned when her son, Reginald Cardinal Pole, protested the Act of Supremacy. King Henry VIII executed the Cardinal's mother, Bl. Margaret Pole, and two of her sons. In Portugal St. Beatrice Da Silva Meneses and her sister St. Amedeus were daughters of the Count of Viana.

Bl. Joseph de Anchieta was a cousin of St. Ignatius of Loyola. They both lived in the 16th century.

In 18th century France we have the family of Rev. M. Charles Balley, who prepared St. John Vianney for the priesthood. Fr. Balley was the youngest of sixteen children. While none of the family is formally canonized yet, they lived very holy lives. His brother, Dom Etianne, a Carthusian was martyred for the faith during the Reign of Terror. His sister, Sister Marie Joseph Dorothée, was forced to leave the convent when the government closed it. She spent the rest of her life caring for her brother Fr. Charles. Another brother, Fr. Jean-Alexandre Balley, apostatized by signing an agreement with the government. He later repented of his actions. Claudine Thévent, known as St. Mary of St. Ignatius saw her two brothers martyred for the faith by the French Revolutionaries. Two other brothers, John and René Lego were guillotined in 1794. Also in France, Bl. Josephine Leroux, a poor Clare, was martyr along with her sister, Mary Scholastica who was an Ursuline nun during the French Revolution. When Josephine was being lead to her death she remarked, *Could anyone fear to leave this place of exile when he reflects on the beauty of paradise?*

In the late **19ᵗʰ century** we have the Martin family whom we discussed earlier. Both Louis and Zelié Martin are Venerable, while their daughter, St. Thérèse of the Child Jesus, is a Doctor of the Church. Her four sisters also lived lives of heroic virtue. In Korea we have the married couple, Damien Nam Myong-hyok and his wife Mary Yi Yon-hui, who were martyred for the faith. St. Michael My Huy Nguyen was the father-in-law of St. Anthony Dich. They were martyred in 1838 for hiding St. James Nam, a priest.

October 21, 2001 John Paul II beatified the first married couple from the **20ᵗʰ century**, Luigi (1880-1951) and Maria (1884-1965) Beltrame Quattrocchi. What was unique about this beautification is that the spouses were beautified together rather than separately, as has been the custom in the past. The miracle needed for their joint beautification came through their joint intercession. The postulator for their cause, Fr. Paolino Rossi noted that *there was nothing apparently extraordinary about Luigi and Maria. What singled them out was the extraordinary way in which they lived. The two spouses were Christians of conviction, consistent and faithful to their own baptism. They knew how to accept God's plan for them and respected its priority; they were very loving people, with one another, with their children, and with their neighbor, promoting goodness and justice. They were people of hope, who knew how to give the right meaning to earthly realities, while always contemplating eternity...In recognizing their "joint intercession," we can say that the theologians underscored that the spouses* *are not only united in a human but also in a spiritual dimension.*[19] John Paul II selected their anniversary, November 25th, as their feast day.

The Quattrocchis, married fifty years, were the parents of four children, three of whom lived to see their parents beatified. Their two sons, Filippo (95) and Cesare (92), both priests, concelebrated the Mass of Beatification with John Paul II. Of their two daughters, Stefania and Enrichetta, only Enrichetta (87) remains. During Maria's pregnancy with Enrichetta a famous gynecologist urged her to abort the baby to save her life. Although Maria had only a 5% chance of surviving the pregnancy, she refused. After Enrichetta was born, Maria lived for forty-one more years! Stefania (Sister Maria Cecilia) who died in 1993 was only five years old at the time. She recalls her father taking her, along with her two brothers, to church where they remained outside the confessional as he talked to the priest. *He stayed and spoke with the priest a long time. Perhaps he told him about our mother's condition. At one point, he raised his hand to his forehead...weeping. We were quiet, sad, scared. We prayed as children...*

Her brother Filippo, now known as Fr. Tarcisio recalls *the aspect that characterized our family life was the atmosphere of normality that our parents created in the constant seeking of transcendental values.* Enrichetta muses that *It is obvious to think that at times they had differences of opinion, but we, their children, were never exposed to these. They solved their problems between themselves, through conversation, so that once they came to an agreement, the atmosphere continued to be serene.* [20]

Cesare, now Fr. Paolino, noted, *Although I never imagined that one day they would be proclaimed saints by the Church, I can sincerely say that I always perceived my parents' extraordinary spirituality. There was always a supernatural, serene and happy atmosphere in our home, but not excessively pious. No matter what the issue facing us, they always resolved it by saying that it had to be appealed "to the heavens."*

[19] Zenit, Oct. 22, 2001.
[20] Zenit, July 30, 2001.

There was kind of a race between father and mother to grow in spirituality. She began in the "pole position," as she already lived an intense faith experience, while he was certainly a good man, just and honest, but not very practicing. Through their marital life, with the decisive help of his spiritual director, he also began to run, and they both attained high levels of spirituality. To give an example: Mother would recount how, when they began to go to daily morning Mass, father would say "good morning" to her as they came out of the church, as if the day only began then. The intensity of their love emerges in the many letters they wrote one another, which we have been able to find....For example, when my father would go on a trip to Sicily, no sooner he arrived in Naples he would send a message, in which he told his wife how much he missed her. This love was transmitted as much within—during their first years of marriage the parents of both of them lived in our apartment, as did her grandparents—as it was without, by welcoming friends with all kinds of ideas, and helping anyone in need.

*Education, which led to the consecration of three of us, was our daily bread. I still have an **Imitation of Christ** that my mother gave me when I was 10-years-old. The dedication still stuns me: "Remember that Christ must be followed, if necessary, unto death."[21]*

Who were the Quattrocchis? Luigi Beltrame, a middle class lawyer known for his brilliance, was appointed assistant attorney general of Italy. During World War II he and his wife took refugees into their home. Following the war, he worked hard for the rebirth of Italy. His wife, Maria Corsini, not only was a professor but was the author of articles and books on educational topics. A lover of music, she was also involved in Scouting and Catholic Action. In explaining the example of the newly blessed, Pope John Paul II stressed that the couple *lived an ordinary life in an extraordinary way. Among the joys and concerns of a normal family, they had an extraordinarily rich spiritual life. Daily Communion was at the center, to which was added filial devotion to the Virgin Mary, invoked by praying the rosary every night, and reference to wise spiritual counsel.*

---

[21] Zenit, Oct. 21, 2001.

These spouses lived conjugal love and the service to life in the light of the Gospel and with great human intensity. They assumed with full responsibility the task of collaborating with God in procreation, dedicating themselves generously to the education, guidance and direction of their children in discovering His plan of life.[22] This couple is only the beginning. In November, 2001, the process of beatification of Marcello and Anna Maria Inguscio opened in Sicily. Anna was a convert to the faith. To read their story see www.Zenit.org (11/16/2001).

John Paul II calls the 20th century the century of martyrs. Edith and Rosa Stein are two Jewish sisters who converted to Catholicism. While Edith is canonized, Rosa, a third order Carmelite, was also martyred for her faith along with her sister, in Auschwitz, the Nazi prison camp.[23] This is the same concentration camp that gave us St. Maximilian Kolbe. Most of his family members died in the odor of sanctity themselves. The beatification process has begun for two brothers who died in the Flosenburg, another Nazi Concentration Camp. Flavio and Gedeone Corra were members of Catholic Action. When a cellmate asked if Gedeone was frightened of the future, he responded, *What does it matter? I have done my duty completely; I am in the Lord's hands. Even if death came, it would be the means to arrive sooner in paradise.*[24]

Bl. Joseph Allamano, a priest, followed his uncle St. Joseph Cafasso as the head of Consolata, an ecclesial order in Turin, Italy. Bl. Jacinta and her brother Bl. Francisco Marto were children who lived heroic virtue after the appearance of Our Lady of Fatima. Their cousin, Sister Lucia, will mostly likely be declared blessed after her death. Blessed Fr. Miguel Pro was martyred for the faith along with his brother, Humberto Pro. His seventy-five-year-old father, Miguel Pro not only led the funeral procession of his sons followed by thousands of Mexicans shouting *Long Live the Catholic Church! Viva Cristo*

---

[22] *Ibid.*

[23] Information on the saints is taken from *Lives of the Saints Vol. I and Vol. II* by Rev. Hugo Hoever, SO, Cist., Ph.D. Catholic Book Publishing Company, NY:1999.

[24] Zenit, Sept.14, 2000.

Rey! Long Live The Pope! But at the gravesites of his sons he lead the massive crowds in singing the *Te Deum*, a hymn of joy and praise. Mary Theresa Ledochowski and her sister Ursula are both blessed. Mary Theresa founded the Missionary Sisters of St. Peter Claver while her sister founded the Ursuline Sisters of the Sacred Heart. St. Katharine Drexel, foundress of the Sisters of the Blessed Sacrament that ministers to the Indians and Afro-Americans, was supported in her work by her three married sisters Elizabeth, Louise and Katharine. Louise established an industrial school for black males while Katharine founded a school for black girls. Elizabeth established an industrial school for orphans. All the schools were Catholic.

In researching the lives of the above saints what was notable was the fact that almost all of the saints came from fervent Catholic parents. While some of the family members were canonized, with few exceptions the rest of the family members were holy lay people, priests, religious, and bishops. Each of the saints was joyfully happy. Isn't this what we want for our families? St. Augustine asks *why cannot we do what these people have done?* If you do, you can be listed in the roll call of family saints for the **21st century!**

How Generations Pass On The Faith...

"You're best buddies with God, aren't you, Dad?"
Four-year-old son to his father, Tom Gustafson

Generations of pious, holy people do generate saints. Let's go a bit deeper to see how this works. For our example, let us use the Martin family. Their sanctity is not a bolt out of the blue. Ancestors on the Martin and the Guérin side of the family laid their spiritual foundation. On the Martin side, St. Thérèse's grandfather, Pierre Martin, married the second daughter, Marie-Anne-Fanie, of the staunch Catholic family of Monsieur Boureau. The priest of the area wrote that *M. Nicholas-Jean Boureau...with his wife and two daughters, had led a life grounded upon principles of honor, right conduct and religion, and that on account of its virtues this honorable family is worthy of the esteem and admiration of the citizens of this town.*[25]

Pierre himself had a deep love for the Eucharist. When the chaplain of his military unit asked Captain Martin why he remained kneeling so long after the Consecration, he responded, *Tell them that is because I believe!*[26] It was also noted that he prayed the *Our Father* with intensity. When a young man asked Pierre's permission to marry his niece (possibly he was her godfather), Pierre wrote the young man a letter. Note his spiritual tone: *...I desire, with all my heart, that our divine Master may deign to bless your union with my beloved niece...and that when you draw your last breath God may receive you into His mercy and place you among the number of the blessed, there to live forever...*[27] Is this how you write to your godchildren?

In addition to an active prayer life, Pierre and his wife, Marie-Anne, spent their days doing works of charity. There is a wealth of wonderful letters that capture the spirit of the family. When Louis Martin, their son, was in Brittany learning the craft of a watchmaker, his mother wrote: *Dear Son...How often I think of you when my soul, upraised to God, follows my heart's longing, and soars to the foot of His throne! Therein I pray with all the fervor of my love that God may pour out upon all my children the happiness and peace which we need in this stormy world...Be ever humble, my dear son.*[28]

St. Thérèse's mother, Zélie Guérin, also came from a long line of fervent Catholics. Her father, Isidore, raised during the French Revolution, reminisced about secret Masses and hiding clergy such as his priest-uncle, Abbé Guillaume-Marin Guérin. When Revolutionaries raided Isidore's home, Abbé Guérin hid inside the kneading trough. Acting quickly, little Isidore jumped on top of the lid spreading out his toys next to him. His actions saved his uncle's life. He also guided his uncle to the places where Catholics waited to be baptized and married, or to where they waited to go to confession and attend Holy

[25] *The Story Of A Family, Op. Cit.,* p. 7.   [26] *Ibid.,* p. 10.
[27] *Ibid.*   [28] *Ibid.,* p. 12.

Mass. Once when the Abbé was taking the Holy Eucharist to parishioners, ruffians accosted him in the woods. Putting Our Lord down carefully, he told Him, *My God, take care of yourself alone, whilst I settle these fellows.* He knocked the three fellows down, and then dumped them into a pond. He then picked up the Holy Eucharist and continued on his way. Eventually he was captured and tortured but was saved from martyrdom by political changes.

While in the military, Isidore married Louise-Jeanne Macé. They had three children, Marie-Louise, Zélie, and Isidore. Louise-Jeanne had a fervent faith but was given to sermonizing. Despite this draw back, she and her husband instilled in their daughters the desire to seek sanctity.

The grandparents of St. Maximilian Kolbe instilled in their children the importance of fulfilling their religious obligations regularly with love. The truths of the faith were taught clearly. Devotion to Our Lady was infused through the example of the parents. Everyone in the family was enrolled in the scapular of the Immaculate Conception and wore it daily. As is the custom in Poland, there was a family altar in a corner of the house with a picture of Our Lady of Czestochowa enshrined. It was here that the family said their daily prayers as well as the fifteen decades of the rosary. On feasts of Our Lady and certain days of the week oil lamps burned before her picture.

As a little girl, Marianna Kolbe, Maximilian's mother, attended various Marian devotions. She and her sister spent time praying before the family shrine along with their friends.

The father of St. Maximilian, Julius Kolbe, was also a fervent Catholic. Annually he made the eleven-mile walk to the Shrine of Our Lady of Czestochowa. Once married, Maria and Julius set up a prayer corner in their home where they knelt to pray during the day. Shortly after their marriage the Kolbes joined the Third Order of St. Francis, striving to live his precepts as their way to sanctification. *Years later, Maria Kolbe wrote to Fr. Cezar Baran, that they were especially careful not to amass money or to spend it foolishly.*[29]

St. Josemaría Escrivá was a descendant of St. Joseph Calasanz and Michael Servetus *who was burned by the Protestant inquisition of Calvin.*[30] Escrivá enjoyed quoting St. Calasanz who said, *If you want to be holy, be humble; if you want to be holier, be more humble; if you want to be very holy, be very humble.*[31]

Josemaría came from a family filled with religious and priestly vocations. There were even several bishops in his family, one of which was martyred during the civil war as well as a priest-uncle who was martyred. He wrote in his diary following the death of his father: *As of yesterday I have a small crucifix, with the image very worn down, which my father (may he rest in peace) always carried with him, and which was given him on the death of his mother, who used it all the time. Since it is very poor and worn out, I don't dare give it to anyone, and so the holy memory of my grandmother (a great devotee of the Most Blessed Virgin) and that of my father will increase my love for the cross."*[32]

His grandmother, as mentioned in an earlier chapter, taught him many of the aspirations that he not only prayed himself throughout his life but likewise taught others around the world to pray also.

"I want to be a saint, cost what it may."
Bl. Tommaso Reggio

The background of these saints demonstrates again that the holiness of our children depends on our own ongoing personal struggle to grow holy. If we are lukewarm Catholics of little piety, we will raise children without **any** faith. Remember, the second largest group of Christians after Roman Catholics is fallen away Roman Catholics. According to St. John Vianney, *If a child goes to hell because of the neglect of his parents to teach him his faith, you can be sure the parents will follow.* A terrifying thought, isn't it?

---

[29] *To Weave A Garment, Op. Cit.,* p. 11.

[30] *The Founder Of Opus Dei, Op. Cit.,* p. 491.   [31] *Ibid.*   [32] *Ibid.,* p. 542.

As the Holy Father makes so plain, ordinary Catholics will not even survive, not to say thrive, in our day. Only heroic Catholics will preserve the Catholic Church. Only holy Catholics will be the seedbed of vocations to the priesthood. Hear it, and I am quoting our Holy Father verbally, this is the age of martyrs. We have confidence that God is providing and will provide such graces as the world has never before received, but we must cooperate with these graces. You mothers and fathers, you are the ones from whom vocations to the priesthood must come, reiterates Fr. John Hardon, S.J.

He adds, *God's grace is assured, but we are Catholics; we believe God's grace must be cooperated with. We must recognize the grace with our minds, and correspond with the grace with our wills. We shall have only as holy priests as we Catholics ourselves live holy lives.*[33]

Teaching The Faith...
"Christians aren't born, they are made."
St. Jerome

The purpose for teaching our children Catholic doctrine is to help them develop a deep, personal relationship with God. Doctrine and pious practices are the kindling that ignites the graces they received in baptism, as well as in the other sacraments, into a love of God so intense that the child could actually die a martyr for the love of God. The role call of the saints is filled with child martyrs and teen saints. St. Justus of Beauvais was only nine years old when he died for the faith while both St. Grimonia and St. Reparaya were but twelve. Chrisopher, Anthony, and John, the first martyrs of the New World likewise were children. St. Tarcisius, just thirteen, was taking the Blessed Sacrament to condemned Christians when he was killed by a mob. He refused to allow the Holy Eucharist he was carrying to be desecrated. Upon his death the Blessed Sacrament disappeared. In 1940 Bl. Bibiana Khamphai, fifteen, and Bl. Maria Phon, fourteen, were martyred for the faith in

---

[33] Fr. John A. Hardon, S.J., 50th Anniversary Homily.

Thailand. St. Dominic Savio was but fifteen when he died a natural death. This is just a small sampling of children who loved God "unto death."

While our children may never be called to give their lives for the faith, they **are** called to be contemplatives, to be able to raise their minds and hearts to God throughout the day. Bl. Nazaría Ignacia, of Mexico, was only nine when she told Jesus, *I will follow you, Lord, as closely as a human creature can.*[34] If we start to train our children to fervently live the faith when they are young, it is not likely that they will rebel against the faith during their teens, nor leave the faith when they enter college.

Fr. Robert Smith, in one of his columns, wrote about the scene in the Gospel where Jesus calls a little child over to him (*Matt.* 18:2-4, 10). He points out that it was not just any child that Christ called but the child of His followers, His believers. *We tend today to think that a child cannot be a real believer until he reaches what we call the age of reason, seven years old or so. But it happens much earlier with children in a devout family.*

In a sense, the faith puts its mark on them. A little child with faith believes in angels, in praying for the dead, praying to God, praying to the saints, has total acceptance of God's law without quibble of any kind, and has total humility in the right sense. He has vitality and a sense of wonder about him, as if he is about to meet an angel just around the next corner.

...The children with [faith] are a miracle, magic; the children without it are a sad and forlorn lot...[T]his shows the tremendous special care that God gives to those who commit themselves to the pursuit of holiness, a special protection which does not exist to that extent toward those committed to disregarding the path toward holiness.[35]

If we lay the groundwork of the faith in our children, the

[34] Margaret Matthew and Stephen Bunson, *John Paul II's Book Of Saints* (Huntington: Our Sunday Visitor, 1999) p. 316.

[35] Fr. Robert D. Smith, "The Mark of Faith," *The Wanderer*, no date.

Holy Spirit and Our Lady will make up for any deficiencies on our part. Marianna Kolbe takes no credit for teaching the faith to her sons: *I felt my inadequacy and begged the Mother of God to substitute for me.*[36] She and her husband, Julius, taught their sons that the faith required self-sacrifice and personal discipline. This spirit of self-sacrifice moved St. Maximilian to give his life in ransom for the life of a husband and father.

Molding your children into saints begins with your prayer, self-surrender and sacrifice. Your children cannot become the mirror image of God if they do not learn what the image should look like from you.

Your children's minds are recording your actions like a video camera. What you do or don't do, what you say or don't say, and how you do it is all being imprinted on their minds. If a husband and a wife yell at each other, the children will become yellers also. Children observe, then imitate how you handle problems, sufferings, work, and leisure. They note your piety as you dress for church, genuflect before the Blessed Sacrament and receive Holy Communion. It is those impressions that will motivate their actions in the future either for the good or for the bad. To educate your children to be saints you need to:

- ✓ know your faith doctrinally,
- ✓ live your faith,
- ✓ give good example,
- ✓ be people of upright character and moral integrity
- ✓ desire to be saints and raise your children to be saints.

Women of the past were more in tune to the spiritual significance of pregnancy. The soul, created by God, is present at the time of conception. So just as a mother cares for herself and avoids anything that could harm her growing baby, she should equally care for her soul. Over fifty years ago Msgr. Gray advised ...*[D]uring the months immediately preceding the birth of her child, the mother should keep close to God, of whom the infant she bears within her is the image, the handiwork, the gift and the child. She should be for her offspring, as it were, a temple, a sanctuary, an altar, a tabernacle. In short, her life*

[36] *To Weave A Garment, Op. Cit.*, p. 148.

should be...the life of a living sacrament, a sacrament in act, burying herself in the bosom of that God who has so truly instituted it and hallowed it, so that she may draw that energy, that enlightening, that natural and supernatural beauty which He wills, and wills precisely by her means, to impart to the child she bears, and to be born of her.[37]

In the past many parents consecrated their children to Our Lady before their birth. Such was the custom in the family of St. John Vianney. Having lost all of her previous children at birth, the mother of Barbe Acarie (Bl. Marie de l'Incarnation) dedicated her daughter to Our Lady before her birth. She hoped that this would insure a safe delivery. It did.

When you learn you are pregnant, why not make a visit to the Blessed Sacrament or to a shrine of Our Lady to consecrate your child? After your first child, make it a family tradition to make a pilgrimage to consecrate your unborn child. What an impression it will make on your older children! There is also a special Church blessing for expectant mothers. Ask your pastor when it would be convenient for him to bestow this blessing on you.

Pray to the various saints during your pregnancy for a healthy baby. One prayer that I tack on to my Morning Offering is *Keep my daughters healthy in mind, body and soul.* As our family grows my prayer also includes our sons-in-law, grandchildren and parents. Pray to St. Gerard or to St. Robert Nonnatus for a safe and easy delivery. Get into the habit of using the spiritual helps available in every aspect of your life. Your children will then imitate you.

When St. Maximilian Kolbe's older brother was born, his father, Julius, planned that the little one would follow his trade of weaving while his mother, Marianna prayed that he would be a priest. Sometimes when parents daydream about the future of their unborn baby the mind goes wild.*He will do this, she will be that.* Rather than thinking of the secular, think in terms of the spiritual. *I want my child to be a saint! Wouldn't it be wonderful if our son became a priest! What a joy to have a*

[37] *The Story Of A Family, Op. Cit.,* p. 49.

daughter who gives her life totally to God!   Then plan how to accomplish this. This is more important than getting the right border for the nursery or the perfect crib set. The spiritual has to infuse every area of your life. Before Zélie Martin was even married she prayed: *I beg of You to give me many children and to let them all be consecrated to You.* The Martins longed for sons who would become priests and daughters who would become religious.

As The Due Date Approaches...

Along with packing your suitcase for your hospital stay, prepare spiritually by asking family, friends, priests and religious to pray for your safe delivery and a healthy baby. If you are scheduled for a C-section ask a priest to say a Mass for you that day.   If you aren't sure what day you are going, have a Mass said close to your due date. The usual stipend is $10.00. When a relative or friend is due, give the gift of a Mass prior to the delivery. When our daughter, Mary Kate, recently had her fifth baby we got the early morning call to start praying. When the labor dragged on, I ran over to the priests' retirement home to ask one of priests if he could offer his Mass that day for her. He postponed his original intention to pray for Katie and asked the congregation to likewise pray for her. One of the families attending Mass that day was the Popovich family, who you will meet in a later chapter as well as on the cover of the next book in this series. Ange and her five children prayed and fasted the rest of the day for Katie and her baby. The birth was difficult because Kathryn was born face up with the cord wrapped around her neck twice. Yet with the prayers, Mass, and sacrifices of everyone, Katie and her baby came through it all safely. Oh, the power of prayer and fasting!

Organize a prayer chain among family and friends for those in labor. Then after the baby is born, organize meals for the new mother. Besides being a wonderful act of charity it's also one of the corporal works of mercy (to feed the hungry).

I find that the *Agnus Dei* is a powerful sacramental to use for childbirth. Pin it to your hospital gown but don't lose it because they are difficult to obtain. The custom of this sacramental dates from the 8th century. The *Agnus Dei* is a waxen disc imprinted with the figure of the lamb and blessed by the Holy Father in a specific liturgical ceremony. It is then encased in a petite leather pouch or on the back of a medal. Pope Pius XII was the last pope to distribute the *Agnus Dei* so their availability is limited. There are six promises attached to the Agnus Dei. It can:

1. Banish languor of soul by fostering piety.
2. Through Divine aid strengthen us to bear good and evil fortune; that, through the mysteries of the Life and Passion of Jesus Christ, we should be delivered from human or diabolical deceits; from a sudden and unprovided death; and, finally, from whatsoever evils threaten mankind.
3. Wards off the menaces of lightning, thunder, floods, and hailstorms. Raging storms shall cease; whirlwinds, lightning and hurricanes should be dispelled.
4. Help one overcome adversity; and be immune from plague or pestilence, poisons and from contagious disease; injury at sea, from fire, from floods, and from the malice of men.
5. Protect the mother in bringing forth her offspring and shields the newborn child.
6. Repel by Divine intervention the snares, wiles, and frauds of Satan.

There is a final note that warns, *if however, the desired result is not always obtained, this should not be attributed to want of efficacy on the part of the Sacramental; but rather to the lukewarmness of suppliants; or to some hidden cause in accordance with the counsels of the Most High.* Besides this sacramental there are many other sacramentals and devotions that are helpful in our growth in holiness.

Once The Baby Is Born...

At the birth of each of Marianna Kolbe's sons, her husband

would thank his wife by saying, *My Dearest, May God richly reward you.*[39]　How is God present when you give birth?　In the excitement of seeing your new infant, do you remember to thank Him for this cherished new life?　Alice of Montbar, upon the birth of each child, held the baby up in her arms and consecrated the infant to God.

Zélie Martin consecrated each of her daughters to God saying: *Lord, grant me the grace that she may be consecrated to You, and that nothing may ever come to tarnish the purity of her soul. If ever she is to lose it, I prefer that You take her at once.*

It's All In The Name...

Naming your child is an important consideration.　While fad names are cute, choose the name of a saint so your child will have a holy patron to help guide him or her along the path of sanctity.　This has been the custom in the Church since the fourth century. Then teach your child about his patron saint and how to pray to him.　Carol Kelly of Illinois adds a litany of saints to the family's *Morning Offering.*　She uses the family baptismal names, confirmation names and any saints she feels the family needs for specific helps at that time.

Why not celebrate your children's saints' feast days with a special dinner, dessert, or party?　Each saint, while living all the virtues, usually has one that stands out.　Help your child to learn what that virtue is and how he can live it.　Call on the saints to protect, guide, and inspire your children along the path of holiness.　In today's world, we need all the spiritual help we can get, and the aid of a namesake saint is essential.

The Martins had a deep devotion to the Blessed Virgin.　Each of their children was given the name of Marie regardless of sex, as had been the custom in Zélie's family.　They chose Joseph as the secondary name for their first son.　To avoid confusion, the children were called by their secondary patrons except for the eldest daughter who was called Marie.　No secular names for the Martin family!　They wanted patron saints for their

---

[39]*To Weave A Garment, Op. Cit.,* p. 13.

children for protection as well as an example for their daughters to emulate.

The Kolbe's named their first son after St. Francis since they were Third Order Franciscans. The second son, as is a European custom, was named for the saint of his birthday. So St. Maximilian was named Raymond. St. Josemaría Escrivá was named for St. Joseph and Our Lady. His three youngest sisters were named after various titles of the Mother of God.

From the 1880s through 1950 Mary ranked first as the name most given to girls. In fact, in 1905 *one out of every 20 girls born in the U.S. was being named Mary.* Now Mary has fallen from favor and ranks as 47th with one in 330 girls being named after the Blessed Mother. Jennifer, a derivative of Guenevere from Camelot, now ranks #1. In the top 10 baby names in Illinois in 2001 there were only three female saints' names. Boys fared better with 8 out of ten names being male saints. *The Catholic practice of giving children religious names had declined substantially over the past two generations...*[40] Don't you think it's time to reverse this trend?

In our country we have the freedom to give our children Christian names. Not so in other parts of the world. Shockingly, in the Holy Land, the birthplace of Christianity, Christians are quietly persecuted. To name a child after a saint is to limit his opportunity to get into a good school or even to get a job.

Next, Baptize The Baby...

Once the baby is born, parents switch into high gear to care for the child. Not to be forgotten is the care of the infant's soul. Within a week or two the baby should be baptized. Why? The infant needs to become a child of God as soon as possible. To deny or put off the graces of baptism for months or years is to deny the child God's presence within him. Just as we would never think of starving a baby, by delaying baptism a parent

---

[40] "In naming kids, Catholic parents pick Jennifer over Mary," *Catholic Times*, Oct. 28, 2001, p. 2. "Jacob, Emily most popular names," Tony Cappasso, *State-Journal Register,* Jan. 18, 2001.

spiritually starves his child.   We'll discuss this sacrament and its purpose in depth in the next chapter.

St. Edith Stein makes clear how the sacrament of baptism is just the beginning: *Grace in the child is like a hidden little flame, which must be painstakingly tended and nursed.*[41] Parents, begin fanning that little flame immediately.   Imitate the example of the parents of saints we have discussed earlier. Recall how Marianna Kolbe gave her life to sanctify her husband, her sons and herself. Her three surviving sons would never have entered the seminary if Marianna did not cultivate their vocations from little on by instilling the faith.[42]   Before he was ordained, Fr. Alphonse wrote to his mother: *I will tell the Christ Child, that if up until this moment, I have been able to serve Him, it has not been my merit but my mother's. So there should be no reward for me, but for my mother...So we continually support one another, and somehow we will safely spend the days of our earthly pilgrimage and joyously greet each other in the Kingdom.*[43]

Right from infancy familiarize your children with images of the supernatural.   Let the first images your infant sees be pictures of Our Lady, angels, saints and a crucifix. How cold is a home with no statues or pictures to remind the inhabitants to lift their minds and hearts to God! As you teach your toddlers to talk, point out pictures and statues of Jesus, Mary, St. Joseph, angels, and saints.   Help them to pronounce the name of each object.   Teach them to make the Sign of the Cross. Marie Vianney began the spiritual training of her children when they were little more than infants. *So soon as... [St. John] began to notice things, his mother took pleasure in pointing out to him the crucifix and the pious pictures that adorned the rooms of the farmhouse. When the little arms became strong enough to move with some ease, she guided the tiny hand from the forehead to the breast and from the breast to the shoulders. The child soon grew into the habit of doing this, so that one day—he was then*

---

[41] Freda Mary Oben, Ph.D., *Edith Stein, Scholar, Feminist, Saint* (NY: Alba House, 1988) p. 52.

[42] *To Weave A Garment, Op. Cit.*, p. 103.   [43] *Ibid.*

about fifteen months old—his mother having forgotten to help him make the sign of the cross before giving him his food, the little one refused to open his mouth, at the same time vigorously shaking his head. Marie Vianney guessed what he meant, and as soon as she had helped the tiny hand the pursed-up lips opened spontaneously.[44]

As the child grows teach him to lift his little mind and heart to God when he sees these reminders such as *Good Jesus, I love you. Good Jesus, help me to be a good little boy/girl. Mother Mary, I love you. Good Jesus, I offer you my day.* St. Charles Borromeo prayed the simple aspiration, *O my God, I give myself entirely to you.*

From early on take the children to Sunday Mass since Jesus insists, **Let the little children be, and do not hinder them from coming to me, for of such is the kingdom of heaven** (**Matt.** 19:14.). While you may feel that you don't get much out of the Mass feeding a hungry infant or wrestling with toddlers to keep them quiet, both you and your children obtain spiritual benefits. Explain to the toddler that *we are going to visit the good Jesus who made you and loves you so much.* Explain how Jesus eagerly waits for him to come to church *because He has presents of graces to give you. You can't see them with your eyes but your angel can!* Show toddlers how to bless themselves with Holy Water. Bless your infants too. It may prevent Satan from agitating the little ones.

Don't limit Mass attendance to Sunday. You and your children need a continuous influx of graces. Try to get to daily Mass. If morning Mass is difficult, look for a noon Mass (many hospitals have them) or an early evening Mass. Sometimes a Catholic nursing home will have a 10 AM Mass. Check around for a convenient time for you. While it takes an effort to get organized and out to Mass daily, God will heap blessings on you and your family for doing so. One such mother who makes a daily effort is Jan Thomas, who is the mother of seven children. Her children range in age from sixteen to 18 months. When her baby is three days old, she and the baby along with her other

[44] *The Curé D'Ars, Op. Cit.,* pp. 5-6.

little ones are back at Mass. It's very edifying to see her example.

A neighbor relates how the Kolbe's went to Mass: *Julius and his wife [Mrs. Kolbe] made a handsome couple. Their sons' clothes were neat and spotless. With prayer books in hand, the family always walked in formation, at least to the extent the lively youths could contain themselves.* [45]

Daily Mass was likewise important for the Martins. As the children grew up, they accompanied their parents. After their thanksgiving after Holy Mass, the Martins returned home to breakfast and morning prayers with their daughters. On the way home from Mass, Mr. Martin would not join his daughters' conversation. Instead he told them, *You will excuse me, children, for I am continuing my conversation with the Lord.* Even when Zélie was near death from cancer, she would struggle to get to daily Mass, almost passing out before reaching the church doors. Likewise, Louis one day suffered a small stroke before Sunday Mass. He still went to Mass with the help of his daughters, Thérèse and Celine, by dragging his leg. What a powerful example this was for the Martin girls and for us. On the way home he told his daughters, *We are as frail as the blossom on the trees. Like them, we look splendid one evening, but in the morning, after a frost, we lie withered on the ground.* It was a good lesson about one's mortality.

St. Vincent Pallotti was taken to daily Mass, along with his nine brothers and sisters from an early age. St. Paula Frassinetti who lived between 1809-1882 became the mother of her four younger brothers at the age of twelve when her mother died suddenly. Although burdened with the responsibilities of her family at such a young age, she still found time to attend daily Mass and do mental prayer. In time, all four of her brothers became priests. Paula eventually founded a religious congregation.

How valuable is a Mass? Decades ago, in a small town in Luxembourg, a starving woman went to the butcher shop to

---

[45] *To Weave A Garment, Op. Cit.,* p. 13.

beg for a piece of meat. *I am sorry I have no money but I'll hear Mass for you.* The butcher and his friend, the Captain of the Forest Guards laughed at the woman. To get rid of her the butcher told her, *All right then. You go and hear Mass for me and when you come back I'll give you as much as the Mass is worth.* The woman left then later returned. The butcher to amuse himself and his friend, the Captain, wrote on a small piece of paper *I heard a Mass for you.* He placed the piece of paper on one side of the scale and a tiny bone on the other. Nothing happened. Next he put a piece of meat on the scale. Still the paper was heavier. Each time he added to the scale the paper was heavier than the meat. *What do you want my good woman? Must I give you a whole leg of mutton?* Still the paper outweighed the mutton. That was the moment of the butcher's conversion. From that day on he vowed to give the woman her daily meat. Likewise, the Captain left the butcher shop a changed man. He became a daily communicant. Two of his sons became priests, one a Jesuit and the other is the late Fr. Stanislaus SS.CC who told this story. The captain counseled his priest-sons to always say a daily Mass *and* say it well.[46] Because as St. Bernadette Soubirous of Lourdes explained, *Know that a priest at the altar is always Jesus Christ on the cross.*

Celebrating his 50th anniversary in the priesthood, Fr. John A. Hardson, S.J., gave us a glimpse of the faith of his mother and how it impacted his life: *I never once remember my mother, never, missing Mass or Holy Communion, every day of her life. Holy people are not only an example of sanctity to others; oh no, holy people are channels of grace to others. I am speaking to all of you, and through you to the tens of thousands of professed Roman Catholics. In the name of Jesus Christ, live lives of close union with God.*

Remember, Wheaties may be the breakfast of champions, but the Holy Eucharist is the breakfast of the saints.

---

[46] Sr. M. Veronica Murphy, *Catholic Society of Evangelists Newsletter,* August, 1999.

Church Manners...

Dress your children up for church. Jeans, shorts, cutoffs and other beach and picnic attire are not appropriate for the House of God. Dress like you truly believe you are going to honor a King. Also, before leaving for church make sure everyone has gone to the bathroom. It's a distraction for the priest and the congregation to watch a parade of people going back and forth to the rest room. Granted, at times it cannot be helped but a little preplanning can cut out needless trips. Be on time for Holy Mass and stay until the priest leaves the church. Then try to develop the habit of staying for a ten minute thanksgiving after Mass. Our Lord is physically present within one for about fifteen minutes. Use this time to praise, adore, thank and petition your God rather than hurrying out the door to your next activity. Your example in this regard is necessary for your children to see.

Upon entering the church turn off your cell phone. Teach your children to carefully make the sign of the cross on their foreheads with holy water as they enter church. Show the little ones how to genuflect reverently (all the way down to the ground rather than a little half-hearted knee bend) in the direction of the tabernacle as a sign of their love for the good Jesus. Why do we genuflect? St. Paul responds, ***At the name of Jesus every knee must bend, in heaven, on earth, and under the earth; every tongue should proclaim to the glory of God the Father: Jesus Christ is Lord*** (**Phil**. 2:10-11).

If you teach your children church manners when they are little and eager to learn, you will avoid the problem of unruly older children disrupting Mass. Explain that they are only talk to Jesus in Church. *You don't want to insult Jesus by ignoring Him and talking to others. Wait until you are in the vestibule or outside to talk to anyone else.* Rather than amusing children with secular books during the priest's homily, bring little picture books of saints, the Mass, etc. Purchase a book on the Mass for your child that explains the Mass. Go over it with him before Mass. Then, during Mass point out pictures of what is happening as the Mass progresses in the toddler's Mass book. Check Appendix A for suggestions on various books. Instead of noisy toys bring a rosary, a handkerchief doll, or a stuffed toy such as Noah's Ark or the Nativity. Rather than letting the children play with these toys during the week, put them away to be used only on Sunday at Mass. This keeps them "special." Avoid giving children candy to keep them quiet. It causes a sugar high that triggers tantrums, irritability and crying.

Teach them how to whisper *I love you, Jesus! I love you, Mary* when they go into church, pass a church or see statues of Jesus and Our Lady. Why not show them how to blow a kiss to Jesus in the tabernacle? When passing a Catholic church explain how one bows one's head to show reverence to Jesus in the Blessed Sacrament.

Before or after Holy Mass take them to see the Stations of the Cross and the statues of the saints. Explain the story behind the statue or picture. In time they will understand. When our oldest daughter was three we attended a Chicago parish where St. Francis Cabrini attended Mass. The church has a life-size statue of the saint in her black habit. Never having seen a nun in habit before, when our daughter saw the statue she yelled out in shock, *there's a witch over there!* I had not prepared her to see a nun in habit.

Children love the statues and stained glass windows of the saints. Just as they were used in the early centuries to teach the unlettered, they can now teach your children the faith. If your parish church is devoid of the sacred, take your children to visit parishes that do have stained glass windows and spiritually uplifting artwork.

Explain to your children in simple terms why you go to Mass. Holy Mass is the unbloody re-enactment of Jesus' sacrifice on Calvary. It's like being in a time machine. We are truly present, kneeling, along with Our Lady, St. John and the holy women, at the foot of the Cross as Jesus dies to save us from our sins.

Don't be shocked or disappointed if your child resists going to Mass, misbehaves despite being disciplined or keeps asking,

Can we go home now? Or, *We go to too many holy things!* This is normal, but in time, and with patience, the child will learn to behave and participate. Help your child to appreciate the gestures and prayers of the Mass by explaining in words they can understand. Teach your teens that the church is not a place to chat with friends, put his arm around or steal kisses from his girlfriend.

When children are a little older take them to holy hours. My youngest daughter hated going to the monthly holy hour but was always happy afterwards that she went. Tangible graces are given when we pray before the Blessed Sacrament.

While back pews are great for crying babies, when the children are a little older, sit in the front pew so that they can see what is going on. Out running errands? Make a visit with your children to Jesus in the Blessed Sacrament. Your parish church will then become just an extension of your home. Mr. Martin's devotion to the Blessed Sacrament was evident to his daughters by his frequent holy hours and Nocturnal Adoration. Daily St. Thérèse and her father would take a walk that would lead them to a different church for a visit to the Blessed Sacrament. This laid the foundation for her devotion to the Holy Eucharist. Julius Kolbe was also devoted to the Blessed Sacrament. Each week he arranged adorers for Sunday adoration.

Teach Your Children The Power Of Prayer

"God will not fail to bless the family that prays united in the name of His Son, our Lord Jesus Christ."
                                                                John Paul II

From little on, include all the children in morning and evening prayers. St. John Bosco insisted that *It was by prayer that the saints reached heaven; and by prayer we too shall reach it.* Try to have a set time for prayers and say the prayers with your children. This serves the dual purpose to insure that prayers are not skipped as well as teaching through your example how important praying is. *From the age of eighteen months, when the family met for night prayers, [St. John Vianney] would, of his own accord, kneel down with them...[H]e knew quite well how to join his little hands in prayer.*

Prayers ended, his pious mother put him to bed, and, before a final embrace, she bent over him, talking to him of Jesus, of Mary, of his Guardian Angel. In this way did the fond mother lull the child to sleep. [47]

It was the custom of the Martin family to say morning prayers before a statue of Our Lady. This custom was ingrained in the lives of the Martin girls. When Zélie was dying Thérèse and Celine spent the day at a friend's home. Thérèse, only four at the time, later wrote ... *Celine whispered to me on the way home: "Ought we tell her we haven't said our prayers?" I said yes, and she explained...to Madame Leriche, who replied: "Never mind, you'll say them now," and went off, leaving us together in one of the big rooms. Celine looked at me and we both agreed: "Mamma would never have done that. She always made sure we got our prayers said."* In the evening, Thérèse knelt next to her father: *...I had but to look at Papa to learn how the saints prayed.* Hopefully your children have a similar experience.

Marie Vianney taught her little ones their prayers by rote as she worked around the house. As your children begin to talk, teach them the *Hail Mary*, the *Our Father*, the *Prayer to the Guardian Angel*, and *grace* before meals. These are all easily learned through repetition. When you pile the kids in the van turn off the radio and teach them prayers. You have a captive audience! Carefully teach the meaning of the words for each prayer otherwise the child may not understand. Our daughter Marianne surprised us one day when she led the Angelus. At the second part she prayed *Behold the Handmaid of the floor* instead of *the Lord*. We also should explain the words of Christmas carols. After singing *Silent Night* one Christmas, one of our daughters asked what *round yon Virgin* was. What we take for granted is new for our children.

When children are three to four-years-old use your driving time to teach them the *Angelus, the Memorare,* The *Act of*

---
[47] *The Curé D'Ars, Op. Cit.,* p. 6.

Contrition, The Acts of Faith, Hope and Charity, The Creed, the Ten Commandments, The Laws of the Church, The Spiritual and Corporal Works of Mercy.

A simple Morning Offering taught to a toddler will stay with the child forever. It is actually the first step in teaching your child to become a contemplative. Explain in simple words how the child can offer everything he does to the good Jesus such as his playtime, sports, chores, naps, and schoolwork as a prayer. This makes a prayer out of all of his actions. It helps him to become a contemplative in the midst of the world. From little on, this gives meaning to his day and ours too. St. Thérèse writes that as a little girl, *I loved God very much and I offered my heart to Him very often, making use of the little formula that mother had taught me.*

In addition to offering one's work and saying vocal prayer, teach your children how to do mental prayer. This is a necessary aspect to developing a personal relationship with God. Mental prayer is simply talking to God with one's thoughts via the heart. My two-year-old niece, Bridget, was in a restaurant having breakfast with her parents and grandparents one Sunday. Everyone was talking when suddenly the little one piped up and demanded, *Be quiet! I'm thinking.* When asked what she was thinking about, she replied, *Jesus.* She was doing mental prayer.

Fr. John Hardon, S.J., had the custom of saying a *Hail Mary* as he buckled his seat belt. Then he said an aspiration to Our Lady related to the trip. We can imitate his example. As you drive the kids to school, *Our Lady, Seat of Wisdom, pray for us.* Going to the doctor, *Our Lady, comforter of the afflicted, pray for us.* For other reasons use, *Our Lady help of Christians, pray for us.* Going to a family outing or party, *Cause of our joy, pray for us.* Select aspirations from the *Litany of Loreto.*

When the children are young, vocal prayers should be short. As the children grow older, begin adding a decade of the rosary in the evening until you can say a complete family rosary together. When children develop the habit of praying the rosary when they are young, they do not rebel. It becomes a family custom. If they become silly or obnoxious during it, gently correct them and continue. Our Lady is not offended. The day I took the cover photograph for this book our three-year-old grandson, Michael, who was staying with us was so homesick that he had to go home. His father offered to meet us halfway since we live two hundred miles apart and it was already late in the evening. As we started to drive the children to meet their father, Bob remembered that we hadn't said our rosary. When my husband began to lead the rosary, I noticed this little voice responding with me. Michael was praying **from his heart** to Our Lady to **get him home!** He said every prayer but the Creed and the Hail Holy Queen. It was amazing. Too many times we underestimate the abilities of children.

Why say the family rosary? Our Lady asks us to say it to protect our families and bring about the conversion of the world. Since the early 1200s Our Lady has been requesting the daily family rosary. Our pastor wrote in the church bulletin: *It is our custom to put the Holy Rosary into the hands of our deceased relatives and friends when we lay them to rest. God forbid that we should wake up in eternity and wonder what it is that we have in our hands!* If we teach our children when they are young to say this powerful prayer, they will say it as adults. Juan and Josefa Claret, the parents of St. Anthony Mary Claret were Spanish weavers. They worked from early in the morning until 9:00 PM yet three times a day they stopped their work to say five decades of the rosary. By the end of the day the family had prayed all fifteen decades. They also stopped three times to say the Angelus on their knees.

Is it easy to get the family rosary started if your children are older and you are not doing it already? No. But anything worthwhile is a struggle. It only takes 12-15 minutes out of your day. Say the rosary before a beautiful picture or statue of Our Lady. You are not praying to the statue but to the person it represents. In our family we had the custom of saying the rosary individually. We only said it together when we traveled. So it was not easy getting the family rosary going. One night our daughters wanted to watch a TV show first and say the rosary afterwards. But after the show they were tired and wanted to go to bed. In the midst of an argument about saying it, I got a phone call. This delayed the rosary even more. The girls went wild. Complaining loudly, they were tossing their rosaries in their hands as they waited for me. Suddenly, the links of their rosaries turned gold. Shocked, they all settled down and willingly said the rosary everyday after that experience.

One October our pastor spoke at an all-school Mass about the importance of the rosary. He told the children that he would give a quarter to every child who had his rosary with them. They just had to hold it up and show him. There were about 500 children at that Mass but only one child had a rosary. It was a sad commentary on the lack of devotion to the rosary and to Our Lady's wishes.

Give each of your children a blessed rosary. Large rosaries are even sold for babies to suck on. Tell them to carry it with them always. Once your children make their First Communion they should be enrolled in the brown scapular of Our Lady of Mt. Carmel. Teach them to wear the scapular always. When they wear it, it is like having Our Lady's arms around them. She protects them from physical and spiritual harm. If the cloth is too difficult to wear, give your child a medal on a chain to wear. Help them to overcome negative peer pressure by explaining the importance of the Scapular. It is the badge of Our Lady. Just as a knight of old wore the badge of the lady he loved, we wear the badge of our heavenly Mother. When my brother, Tom, was in high school, the guys would tease him about his scapular. They called it his "tea bag." Such ridicule only strengthened his devotion to Our Lady.

Have your children wear the Miraculous Medal. It is actually called the medal of the Immaculate Conception but because of the countless miracles attached to it people call it the Miraclous Medal. Don't leave home without it!

Need help in teaching your children prayers? There are

beautiful children's prayer books listed in the Appendix to help you to teach your children to pray.

Little ones are so open and interested in the majesty of God, His mother, Mary, and the guardian angels. As mentioned earlier in this chapter, point out the beautiful sunsets, rainbows, the juicy oranges and the chocolate for candy that God makes for them because He loves them so much.

Make prayer and the supernatural world come alive for your children through the normal events of each day. Years ago many people in Central Illinois were worried about a predicted earthquake. When it did not occur, some people blamed the scare on the faulty reasoning of a scientist. We, on the other hand, felt strongly that prayer spared us. Was it preparation and *prayer* that prevented the Y2K disaster?

Explain to your children how they can pray to help other people or for special intentions. Teach them to pray for their grandparents, aunts and uncles, brothers and sisters and friends in need. Remember, God hears the prayers of children and the sick first. Your children can become spiritual powerhouses. One of my close friends is suffering from Lou Gehrig's disease. The disease has progressed so far that my friend is no longer able to speak. She communicates through a machine. At Christmas time each of my daughters went to visit her with their children. Mary Kate's three-year-old, Elizabeth, has prayed every night since then that *Mrs. Mack can talk again.*

Point out to your children answered prayers. When a prayer is not answered, explain that prayers are not magic. Emphasize that God will work things out in a better manner for the spiritual good of the soul. At other times, prayers may take many years to be answered. Sts. Ann and Joachim, the parents of Our Lady waited many years for a child. Then look who God sent them! Explain the story of St. Elizabeth who prayed for a child for decades. God finally answered her prayer when she was past childbearing age. When St. Gabriel told her husband, Zachary, he was to be the father of St. John the Baptist, Zachary's disbelief caused the angel to strike him dumb until after the birth of the baby. In the Old Testament there is the similar story of Abraham and Sarah. She was also childless and past the age of childbearing. When visiting angels told Abraham she would have a child within a year, Sarah, overhearing the conversation, laughed because it seemed so ridiculous to her (**Genesis** 18:15).

When sorrows or disappointments hit, help your children to discern the lesson that God is teaching. Contradictions are usually spiritual lessons in acquiring a virtue we lack. The sooner one learns the lesson or virtue, the sooner the suffering ends. It may not be the way we want things to work out but God knows best. He sees the big picture. When a family prays together for a special intention, it firms up the faith of everyone. When we relocated to Springfield, we found selling our home in the Chicago suburbs difficult. Our whole family was earnestly praying for ten months for this intention, still nothing happened. Mary Terese, age seven at the time, was especially discouraged that her prayers went unanswered. Along with finding a buyer for our house, she added to her prayer list that she wanted to fit into a pair of her favorite jeans that had become too snug. One day she tried on the jeans and found they fit. Joyfully she ran to me exclaiming, *I think my prayers are starting to get warm!* Teach your children never to give up praying because their prayers are always *warm.*

Shortly after the birth of Mary Terese we were told she had leukemia. We asked our extended family and friends to join us in saying a novena to St. Padre Pio that she would not have leukemia. At the end of the nine days her blood work came back normal. Just as we were breathing a sigh of relief, her pediatrician told us that she would never walk. Mary Terese had been born with a hip deformity. We marshaled family and friends to join us in saying another novena to St. Pio. After a round of specialists and extensive x-rays we were told that yes, she does have a deformed hip but somehow (!) there is movement and she would walk. She not only walked, she played tennis, volleyball and basketball in grade and high school. When she began to talk we noticed another problem. Her sounds were all confused. Since no one could understand her, she acted out what she wanted. After two years of speech therapy, Mary

Terese was not improving. Her therapist informed me that because of her speech problems she was not ready for kindergarten. During the three summer months before school began I said a continuous novena to St. Dymphna, the patron of brain dysfunction. When we met with her speech therapist the first day of school she was incredulous at Teresie's fluency. She kept asking me what I had done. She could not believe that *all I did was pray.* Before becoming the mother of three little girls (three and under) Mary Terese was a mechanical engineer.

When our oldest daughter, Mary Kate, was in fourth grade she developed a chronic kidney disorder that would necessitate surgery if she did not outgrow it. After two years of daily medication and biannual nuclear tests, her specialist decided that she needed immediate major surgery. Again we marshaled our family and friends to join us in saying a nine-day novena to St. Pio. The ninth day of the novena she was cured.

Our second daughter, Marianne, was stricken with Bell's Palsy when she was a junior in high school. At the time the paralysis hit she was running for a student council office. Her paralysis was so severe that a classmate had to give her campaign speech because Marianne could not talk. Her beautiful face was terribly distorted. She was lent a first class relic of St. Escrivá. Family, friends and classmates prayed his prayer card for her recovery even though seventy percent of her facial nerve had been destroyed. Ninety-eight percent eventually regenerated due to the intercession of St. Escrivá.

Several years ago my husband, Bob, became so ill that family members thought he was dying. The doctors in our medical community felt that his only option was to take a dangerous drug that could cause cancer or heart disease. Prayer found us a doctor several hundred miles away who restored him to health. His spiritual director, a dentist who had consulted with medical experts in St. Louis about Bob's case, claims his restoration to health *was a miracle.*

These family sorrows taught our children to pray for each

other and for others from a very young age. They *know* the power of prayer. For every situation in our lives and the lives of our children, God has help available to us. We only have to ask. A year before our daughters were eligible to attend a wonderful private Catholic girls' school, my husband was promoted and transferred up to Alberta, Canada to run a huge manufacturing complex. After discussing the ramifications the promotion would have on the Catholic education of our children, my husband refused the promotion and took a job as the chief operating officer for a smaller company. His first day on the job he realized that the company was bankrupt. The company did go under leaving Bob to find another job. Each evening over dinner we discussed the worrisome situation and prayed for help. As the weeks dragged by with no job in sight, our third grade daughter, Marianne, suddenly asked if she could go up to the attic to pray. When we asked why, she responded, *the closer I get to God, the more He will hear my prayer for a job for Dad. I want to go up to the attic and pray on my tippee toes.* Needless to say, God answered her prayer.

We also have to teach our children to understand the reason behind seemingly unanswered prayers. As I mentioned earlier, when we moved to Springfield it took us thirteen months to sell our home. I used no fail novenas. We buried St. Joseph in every conceivable position. Every known saint's medal was planted. In centuries to come archeologists will think the ruins of our former home was a church! Nothing worked until I personally learned the virtue of detachment. Only then did St. Escrivá sell our home. He prefers to teach lessons along with his miracles.

Sometimes prayer is not answered in the manner that we hoped because God needs our suffering for the conversion of sinners. My husband suddenly developed rheumatoid arthritis when he was thirty. The disease progressed so rapidly that doctors told us that he would be bedridden within a matter of months. We again gathered our prayer weary family and friends. This time, while there was no permanent cure there was help. The crippling disease left his lower extremities allowing him mobility. It relocated though to his right hand and wrist making them unusable. When his pain became extreme we went to Lourdes in search of help. After bathing in the miraculous waters, the disease left him for a year, only to return on Ash Wednesday. The date that it resurfaced confirmed Bob's original belief that his suffering is meant to be permanent but redemptive.

Prayers may not be answered because one lacks faith. I have a speech impediment. I stutter. I have tried gadgets, the newest techniques, and speech therapy all to no avail. After the birth of my second child it became so severe that talking on the phone was impossible. When I needed a babysitter, our eldest daughter, four-year-old Mary Kate, would call the sitter for me and make the arrangements. She took all my phone calls and returned phone calls for me. In desperation I turned to the intercession of St. Pio for a cure. He *did* obtain the cure for me. I became fluent. Terribly excited I was also terribly frightened. *What if it came back? What would I do?* I simply did not trust that God could be so generous towards me. As the months went by my fears grew until I knew that since I could not develop trust, it was senseless for me to have the gift of fluency. The gift was withdrawn. It was a painful lesson to learn but God is good. He compromised. I can at least function. Besides, the impediment keeps me humble and quiet in groups. To teach me trust in God, God puts me on the dreaded lecture circuit, on radio and TV. The most terrifying experience for a stutterer is to speak before a group. *Will I be able to say the things I want to say? Will I be fluent or stutter through the whole lecture?* As long as I agree to do His will in this regard, He *always* gives me the miracle of fluency during lectures or interviews so that I can talk about Him. Before or after the lecture or media interview...I'm on my own!

The mothers of saints *relied* on prayers. St. Bonaventure was deathly ill as a child. His mother, frantic with concern, ran to St. Francis of Assisi to beg prayers for her son's recovery. As St. Francis prayed he was given a premonition of the spiritual greatness of the sick little boy. He prayed *O buona venture* which means "good fortune" thereby giving the child his new name. Bonaventure became a Franciscan, a Cardinal and a doctor of the Church. He counted among his friends King St. Louis of France and St. Thomas Aquinas.

In the last chapter we learned how, at the age of two, St. Josemaría Escrivá became gravely ill and was not expected to survive the night. It was the prayers of his parents to Our Lady of Torreciudad that saved the toddler's life. Today, the restored shrine entrusted to the Prelature of Opus Dei welcomes millions of pilgrims each year.

As our children grow older, we need to continually reinforce the idea of a loving God who **is** actively involved in all aspects of our lives. One little boy was well tuned in to the power of God. Desperately wanting a bike, he decided to write a letter to Jesus requesting one. He started his letter several times. *I'll promise to clean my room for a month. No, that's too much. I'll promise not to fight with my brother. No, that's too hard. I'll promise to obey my mother. That's too impossible.* He got up from his desk, took his mother's statue of Our Lady and wrapped it in a towel. Going over to his toy chest, he hid the statue at the bottom under all his toys. He again sat down at his desk and began to write, *Dear Jesus, if you ever want to see your mother again, please bring me a bike.*

When students are studying for exams, remind them to pray to the Holy Spirit to enlighten their minds, to their guardian angel and to St. Thomas Aquinas for help. For young adults looking for the perfect mate recommend St. Raphael and St. Nicholas. If something is lost, pray to St. Anthony. Need a prom date? Try St. Thérèse. She sends a rose when a novena petition is going to be granted.

Point out to your children articles in the newspaper or news stories in the media that refer to answered prayer. During the aftermath of 9-11 there were many stories of prayers being answered, angels protecting people, etc. Dayna Curry and Heather Mercer, two young Christian women who were captured by the Taliban, explained upon their release how prayer protected their lives and their virginity during their three months of terrifying imprisonment. In 2001 a severe drought in Western Texas threatened not only the water supply of 22 communities but also the crops in that vast area. Bishop Michael D. Pfeifer of San Angelo asked the mayors of the communities to declare Sunday, Aug. 26th as a day of prayer for rain. Parishes were asked to offer prayers for this intention that day. All denominations joined in the effort and it rained almost an inch. This was not the first time Bishop Pfeifer requested a day of prayer for rain and got it. In January 2000 the Bishop asked for a day for prayer while Catholics prayed a nine-day novena. It rained. Bishop Pfeifer maintains that *praying brings no magic guarantees but we've done this several times, and we have received rain.*[48]

How To Teach The Faith In The Home

St. Edith Stein felt strongly that *[t]he mother has to lay a secure foundation for religious education or else the school has a hard time. It is because the woman has a special affinity for moral values that this responsibility is hers* writes Dr. Freda Mary Oben.[49]

Put together a library of Catholic resource books. Get a Catholic Bible such as the **Douay-Rheims** Version[50] or the **New Jerusalem Bible**. For the New Testament purchase the **Navarre Bible** along with the **Pentateuch**[51], which has a rich commentary on each verse of Scripture. Also include the **Catechism of the Catholic Church, The Catholic Catechism** by John A. Hardon, SJ,[52] **The Faith, A Popular Guide Based On The Catechism of the Catholic Church** by John A. Hardon, SJ,[53] **The Question And Answer Catholic Catechism** by John A. Hardon, SJ,[54] and **The Faith Explained** by Leo Trese.[55] All these books can also be used to teach your

---

[48] "Downpour greets day of prayer for rain in parched West Texas," *Catholic Times*, Sept. 9, 2001.

[49] *Edith Stein, Scholar, Feminist, Saint, Op. Cit.,* pp. 52-53.

[50] Tan Books & Publishers.   [51] Scepter Publishers (800) 322-8773.

[52] Doubleday & Company.   [53] Servant Publications.   [54] Image Books.

[55] Scepter Publishers.

children the faith. In fact, by the time your children reach junior high these books can be used as their textbooks. Fr. Hardon's books are very clear, concise, and enjoyable to read. It's like having an understandable theologian-in-residence. Another good book to add to your library is *Father McBride's Family Catechism*[56] by Alfred McBride, O.Praem. This is a non-threatening introduction to the *Catechism of the Catholic Church.* Each four-page chapter contains a story, a reflection section, some questions and answers taken from the *Catechism,* questions for personal reflection, prayer and a glossary of terms. Fr. McBride also has written *Father McBride's Teen Catechism* and *Fr. McBride's College Catechism* all by Our Sunday Visitor. Teens and adults can also use my book and workbook, *You Can Become A Saint!* and *You Can Become A Saint! Workbook* to go deeper into the faith. Call Eternal Life (800-842-2871) for their catalog of audiotapes by Fr. Hardon, S.J.

Begin to teach your little ones a more structured faith starting at the age of three-years-old. Children this age are hungry to learn about God, Our Lady and the Saints. They absorb everything like an ink blotter. Don't wait until they start school. Begin now. Tell them about the miracles of Jesus. Read them Bible stories. Purchase toys and games with a spiritual flavor. Infuse their world with the faith. My daughter, Mary Kate, related how her son, Michael, at three suddenly became aware of death. One night, as she was tucking him and his two-year-old-brother, Matt, into bed, Michael kept asking her questions such as *are you going to die? If you die, who will take care of me?* Rather upset, he continued on in this vein for a while. Katie, trying to be honest and yet not scare him, explained that she did not know who physically would take care of him if she died, but she did know that Jesus would take care of him from Heaven. At that point two-year-old, Matt, waving his little finger at his brother piped in and said, *and remember your Mother Mary. She loves you too.* Katie was dumbfounded by his remark. She did not realize her younger son was listening in on her talks about God and Our Lady. Recently her four-year-old daughter,

---

[56] Our Sunday Visitor.

Margaret Mary (the baby on the cover of this book) told her paternal grandmother, *When you are home by yourself, Grandma, you aren't alone because God is always with you.* As you teach the older children, your younger children will learn also, although they may not understand everything. As I ran errands I would quiz the girls on doctrine. One day when I asked the older girls to name the three persons of the Blessed Trinity, my youngest, who was three, insisted on answering, *God the Father, God the Son, and God the bird.* She still needed a little work on that one.

Please refer to Appendix A for additional teaching aids for this age group.

Since parents are the **primary educators** of their children by the time your children go to school, they should know their prayers and the basic truths of the Catholic faith. If your child attends a Catholic school or the CCD program its function is to *supplement* what you have already taught your children.

By kindergarten begin a formal program of catechism at home. Get a good catechism series and work with your children at home. Work as a team with your husband if possible. Personally I am partial to the ***Baltimore Catechism*** with the question/answer format. If an answer is memorized, it is retained for life. When a person is asked a question about the faith, the memorized answer pops into mind. From there one has a foundation from which to elaborate. But without a definitely worded answer, most Catholics fumble around in confusion. They know the answer but can't quite express it. A priest, St. Jerome Emiliano, first devised the question/answer catechism format in 1532. He found this to be a most effective way to teach children the faith.[57] This methodology was used successfully for 400 years. Here is an approach you might consider: with our daughters, we used the ***Baltimore Catechism*** for the foundation and then supplemented with other texts such as the ***Faith And Life Series*** for grade school. Dr. Scott Hahn uses this series for his children. These texts

---

[57] Rev. Hugo Hoever, SO Cist., Ph.D., *Lives of the Saints Illustrated Part I* (NJ: Catholic Book Publishing Co., 1999) p. 65.

will help your children be able to explain their faith in class, to friends who are confused, or to people who are non-Catholics.

Dad, it is **so** important for you to be involved in the Catholic education of your children. Read bible stories or the lives of the saints to your children for bedtime stories. Teach them the catechism. Children need to see that faith is not something just for women. Besides seeing their father pray, children need to be taught the faith by their father as well. What is important to you becomes important to them. If Dad's not involved, the children may rebel against the faith. One friend explained that her husband converted to the Catholic faith simply because their daughter refused to go to church *because Dad doesn't go.* Once Dad converted, the daughter willingly went to Sunday Mass. Dion, the Italian heartthrob of teenage girls in '60s writes that his parents weren't *too interested in religion and found the Church unnecessary...Catholicism seemed suited for old women and sissies. Real men don't need it.*[58] Without any faith foundation he wandered through life and various Protestant denominations. In 1997 he just "happened" to turn on EWTN. He became engrossed in *The Journey Home* with John Haas, a former Protestant clergyman, who was Marcus Grodi's guest. It encouraged him to come home to the Catholic Church. You certainly do not want your children to be wanderers, do you Dad?

Fun Ways To Teach The Faith

Make the faith attractive to your children. At Christmas time use a religious Advent calendar to count the days to Christmas. Emphasize St. Nicholas rather than Santa Claus. Have the children put their shoes outside their room the evening of December 5th. Surprise them with shoes filled with candy or treats when they awaken on December 6th, his feast day.

Pull names from a hat for Christmas angels. The Christmas angel does secret works of service for the person he selected. On Christmas the angel is unmasked.

---

[58] Dion DiMucci, "The Wanderer Comes Home," *Envoy*, May-June 1999, p. 34.

Begin to collect a beautiful nativity scene with many pieces. Let it be the focal point for your holiday decorations. How about rewarding each good deed with a piece of straw for the Baby Jesus' manager?

Put together a food basket for the poor, have each child give one of his nice toys to Toys For Tots; or adopt a child, a nursing home resident or a poor family for Christmas.

The Christmas season begins on Christmas Eve and ends with the Baptism of Jesus. Keep your decorations and tree up during that period of time. If possible, plan your holiday parties **after** Christmas so as to keep the penitential spirit of Advent. Celebrate the twelve days of Christmas and the Feast of Epiphany. Epiphany should be an important feast for us for Christ was shown to the Gentiles (our ancestors) on that day. Maryann Schicker of Maryville, Illinois relates how as a child, on the eve of the feast, it was the custom in her home to place a round cake pan under her bed. In the morning she eagerly awoke to see what the Three Kings left in the pan. It could be unshelled nuts and coins, a small gift or other trinkets. She suggests reading to your children the O. Henry story, "The Gift of the Magi," and the poem, "Journey of the Magi," by T. S. Eliot. She also suggests viewing the opera *Amal and the Night Visitors* and the movie *The Fourth Wiseman.* She notes that *in the Church's calendar, the Feast of the Epiphany is equal in importance with Christmas, the Ascension and Pentecost— ranking only after the Easter Triduum in order of precedence.*[59] By the way, Maryann adds that the Cathedral in Cologne German holds the relics of the Three Kings in a large silver casket. If you are ever in Cologne, stop to view their relics.

So many of our holidays owe their origins to the Catholic Church. These include St. Valentine's Day, St. Patrick's Day, All Saints Day, St. Nicholas Day as well as Christmas and Easter. Teach your children the origin of these feast days and how to celebrate them as Catholics. At St. Francis by the Sea Parish in Hilton Head, South Carolina, on the Sunday nearest

[59] Maryann Schicker, "Epiphany is feast rich in church, family traditions," *Catholic Times*, Jan. 6, 2002, p. 4.

to all Saints Day the second graders come to Mass dressed as saints. They process in with the main celebrant. Before Mass begins many of the children introduce their saint by giving a concise biography that explains which virtues their saints excelled in. The homily centers on the universal call to holiness. During the petitions other children give a short bio of their saints and petition God that we imitate the main virtues of that saint. The saints include Mary, Joseph, bishops, priests, religious, and lay people. The purpose of this custom is not only to teach the children about the saints, but it was a clever way to educate all the parishioners. Maybe you could introduce this custom to your parish. Halloween on the other hand is of pagan Celtic origin that centered on the return of the spirits of the dead and witches. The French bishops, on the advice of Bishop Hippolyte Simon of Clermont, hope to change the focus of Halloween by asking parents to use the night of trick-or-treating to explain to their children *how the Church has freed us from these fears and ghosts. One should explain to children the passage from the gloomy, hopeless night of spirits, to the brilliance transmitted by the saints who enjoy the infinite happiness of heaven.*[60]

Make family pilgrimages to Marian shrines or churches in May and October. Have a May crowning in your backyard and invite your friends and their families to participate.

For Lent, encourage the children to do something extra for Jesus and to give up something they like for Him. Our youngest daughter, who aspired to the stage, gave up putting on nightly shows for her father one Lent. Collect money for the poor by cutting back on carryouts and by abstaining from movies or videos for Lent. Make it a game to see just how much you can save for the poor. Remember the "Jesse Tree" for Christmas? Leaflet Missal sells "The Jesus Tree" for Lent.[60A]

A word of caution, if your child is overindulged with secular toys, watches hours of TV or secular videos, religious themes

---

[60] Zenit, Oct. 30, 2001.

[60A] or contact Scripture Trees at P.O. Box 715, Willernie, MN 55090-0715. E-mail scripturetrees@usfamily.net will not be attractive. As Fr. John Corapi, multimillionaire-drug addict turned priest warns *Don't let MTV raise your children. You raise your children. Don't let the spirit of the world raise your children.*[61]

The Bible...

Did you know that the Catholic Church compiled the Bible, which is the inspired word of God? God inspired the books of the Bible, the Church canonized it. Since the Catholic faith is based on Scripture and Tradition, our children need to have an understanding of both the Old and New Testament. St. Augustine explains the unity of the two: *the New Testament is hidden in the Old, and the Old becomes visible in the New.* The sacraments and the moral law are rooted in the Bible. St. Paul tells Timothy: **All Scripture is inspired by God and is useful for teaching, for refutation, for correction, and for training in righteousness, so that one who belongs to God may be competent, equipped for every good work** (2 **Timothy** 3:16-17). Furthermore St. Jerome tells us that *to be ignorant of the Scripture is not to know Christ.*

When we say that the books of the Bible are inspired, the Church means that God chose certain people to write whatever He wanted written but no more. The writers *made full use of their own faculties and powers so that, though He acted in them and by them,* the human instruments are the actual authors of their writings.[62]

Rabbis between the second or third century AD definitively determined the books of the Old Testament, composed over a period of 1,000 years. Even then there was a difference of opinion between the Hebrew Jews and the Jews in Egypt who used the Greek Old Testament as to the number of books to be included in the Old Testament. The Greek Old Testament contains the books of Tobit, Judith, Wisdom of Solomon, Sirach or Ecclesiasticus, Baruch, 1 and 2 Maccabees, and parts of Esther and Daniel. Christians selected the Greek Old

---

[61] "Thousands Attend Fatima Family Congress," *The Wanderer,* June 25, 1998.
[62] *Catechism of the Catholic Church*, no. 106, quoting *Dei Verbum,* no. 11.

Testament that has forty-six books. During the Protestant Revolt, the Protestants reverted back to the Palestinian Old Testament that only has thirty-nine books. The New Testament is composed of twenty-seven books that most Protestants accept.

The New Testament was written between 51-100 AD yet it was three to four centuries before Christians actually had an approved list of books considered to be inspired. The solemn declaration giving the definitive list of Sacred books was not made until the Council of Trent in 1546. It was St. Jerome, along with his team of helpers some of whom are canonized saints, such as St. Paula and her daughter, St. Blessilla, who translated the books of the Bible into the Latin Vulgate. Reading Scripture strengthens our faith and nourishes our souls...It has also made many saints.

The Bible contains the whole truth and can only be read and understood within the Tradition of the Church. And where do we find the teachings of Sacred Tradition? Mainly in the teachings of the universal Magisterium of the Church, in the writings of the Holy Fathers, and in the words and customs of the Sacred Liturgy. The life of the Church itself shows us that the heretics of every age—acting just as the devil did when he tempted Christ in the wilderness—have had recourse to Sacred Scripture to support their beliefs. And the experience of centuries shows that when one dispenses with Tradition it is very difficult to maintain the integrity of the message of revelation. Thanks to Tradition, for example, the Church knows the canon, or list of sacred books, and understands them with increasingly greater depth...

The main reason for an incorrect understanding of Sacred Scripture is usually ignorance rather than malice. To avoid this, the Magisterium of the Church makes three recommendations. First, we should meditate, study, and contemplate the Scriptures, going over them in our heart, and scholars especially should strive for a deeper knowledge of revealed truth. Second, we should listen to the pope and to the bishops in communion with him, because they are the successors of the apostles in the charisma of truth. Finally, we should try to interiorly understand the mysteries that we are living.[63]

Introduce the Bible to your children when they are young by not only reading Bible stories but also explaining them. Read three minutes of the **New Testament** to children five and older and explain what is happening in the scene and what God is teaching us. Older children can be taught a more disciplined approach by encouraging them to read three minutes from the New Testament then discuss with them how they can apply what was read. Point out how they can live what they read at school, at work, at play. Or, consider reading Scripture as a family for ten minutes each day. Eventually you and your children will be able to quote Scripture as well as any Protestant! Be sure your children comprehend what you are teaching. I overheard a little boy asking his mother what type of car God drove. The mother replied that God was a spirit so He did not have any car. But the little boy kept insisting that God has a car: *The Bible says God drove Adam and Eve out of Paradise!*

Scripture can have a profound effect on the fabric of our lives. When we moved to Springfield my fourth grader came home crying from school everyday. She had been such a happy child from birth until our move. Since the move, no matter what I tried, nothing worked. Finally I decided that we would read five minutes of scripture each day. That even made her more miserable, yet I insisted. Then one day it dawned on me that she was no longer crying after school. When I asked why she shyly said, *"You know why." "No I don't,* I replied. *Why aren't you crying anymore?"* She hemmed and hawed then said, *"It's reading the New Testament. I'm not sad anymore."*

Scripture helps us to relate to everything that happens in our lives. In our family we jokingly refer to a bad day as having a "Mary Ann Day." When Mary Terese was seven we read the story of Job together. When we finished, I asked her what she thought about the story. Solemnly she replied, *He had a Mary Ann day.*

---

[63] Josemaria Monforte, *Getting To Know The Bible* (New Jersey: Scepter, 1998) pp. 14-15.

Don't let your teens leave for college until you go through the books of **Proverbs, Ecclesiastes, Wisdom** and **Ecclesiasticus** (or called **Sirach**) with them.

Guardian Angels...

Through your natural interaction with your children you can point out God's help in all their needs. For example, once a child learns about his guardian angel, you can point out occasions to your child when his guardian angel helped him. For instance, we can say, *see how your guardian angel saved you from getting badly hurt when you fell,* or *look how my angel found us a parking place at the grocery store.* Impress on your children how the spiritual is intimately intertwined with the natural. Fr. John Hardon, S.J., in his fascinating 12 tape series on *Angels & Demons* explains that the holier a person is, the more power his angel has to intercede for him.[64]

Children are so open to the mystery of the angels. Observing the moon as we drove home one evening, Mary Terese who was five at the time commented, the *moon is following me home. Guess my angel is pushing it.*

When our eldest daughter was in kindergarten, she had to cross a four-way stop street to get home. One day, while walking home a car ran the stopped sign just as she was crossing the street. The car braked at her knees. It was a miracle that she was not hit. When she burst into the house to tell me what happened, she told me that her angel saved her life. Another time we had joined my parents for Sunday brunch. On the way home, we were following my parents' car until another car cut in between us. All three cars were stopped at a light by an exit ramp of a Chicago expressway. A car coming off the ramp, lost control and ran into the car between my parent's car and our car smashing in the side where our children would have been sitting. Instantly we all thanked God and our angels for protecting us. Then the girls asked why we had been protected and not the people in the car in front of us. All we could answer was *maybe they didn't ask for protection.* This thought impressed

---

[64] Angels & Demons can be purchased from Eternal Life (800) 842-2871.

them as to the importance of praying to their angels for protection. On the other hand, God may have allowed the accident and injuries as part of His larger plan, a plan that we may never know in this life. Make prayer and the supernatural world come alive for your children through the normal events of each day.

While a grandmother was watching her grandchild the child darted out the door, into the street into the path of an oncoming car. The grandmother frantically called to the child but the child kept running. When the woman could not reach the child she prayed, *Guardian Angel of that child save him!* When she looked again, the car was gone and the child was safely walking back to her.

Another woman was alone at her summer cottage. Her front door was open and through it she saw a car pull up. An evil looking man jumped out of the car. He rushed up to the cottage and started to open the door. Paralyzed with fear, all the woman could do was pray for help. Suddenly, the man stopped, looked up, turned pale, ran back to his car and left. This woman believes her angel became visible to the would-be intruder.

Teach your children to pray daily to their angels, not only for protection but also for guidance in everything that they do. Suggest they name their angels to make their relationship more personal. Did you know that angels have the ability to work on a person's personality? Having a difficult time with a child? Pray to the child's guardian angel to resolve the problem. Teach your child to greet the angels of his friends; to ask his angel's help with problems or in difficult situations. When a person develops a sensitivity to angelic inspirations it can save one from problems and even death. Haven't you had the experience of planning on doing something, being warned interiorly not to do, then have done it anyway and have lived to regret it? That warning came from your guardian angel.

Besides teaching your children how to utilize the help of his guardian angel, warn your child about the fallen angels. Angels are powerful beings. While the good angels influence us for the good, the fallen angels tempt us to do evil. They can trigger upsetting or impure thoughts. They can tempt us to be moody or to despair. They can incite us to anger, to judge others, to fall into all types of vices. They can cause mischief by misplacing our things, causing items to break down or malfunction or turn people against us. Read the ***Book of Job*** in the Old Testament. God allowed Satan to test His servant Job. Likewise, He allows Satan to test our faithfulness. In fact, the more a person strives for holiness the more Satan will attack him. St. Padre Pio was physically beaten by the devil as was St. John Vianney. Sr. Lucia of Fatima writes: *This is how it is: where God is, the devil appears stirring up conflicts, battles and contradictions. All these things are a sign of the presence of God. If they did not come from God, the devil would have nothing to fear as he would not be in danger of losing his domain.*

Satan has no need to make the life of his friends difficult. He already controls their lives. Instead he attacks the friends of God hoping they will sin, lose heart, turn from God and finally despair. Fr. John Hardon, S.J., notes that there is only one hint of demonic possession in the ***Old Testament*** but with the birth of Christ demonic possession becomes a reality. The battle for souls began in earnest with the ***New Testament.*** To safeguard your children and family, say the *Prayer to St. Michael the Archangel* daily. St. Michael vanquished Satan from heaven. Likewise he will protect your family if only you ask.

Lives Of The Saints...

When I was a little girl my father nightly read me fairy tales so of course I wanted to be a princess. Mom brought me down to reality by explaining that my chance of becoming a princess was zip *but* I could become a saint, which was *so* much more exciting than being a princess. Haven't we seen this dramatically portrayed by the media when Mother Teresa and Princess Di died the same week? The funeral of each was a media event. While Mother Teresa continues to grow in stature, less and less is heard about the princess.

It is through the lives of the saints that we can give our children true heroes and heroines to imitate. Reading the lives of the saints motivates young people to emulate their lives of prayer, mortification, and struggle to grow in virtue. Example, as mentioned before, is one of the most powerful ways to influence others. If all our children see are action figures, or rap stars on TV, that is what they will aspire to be. Introduce your children at least weekly to the daring exploits of the saints, the courage of the martyrs, the self-sacrifice of young men and women for a greater goal than a touchdown. It will change their lives. My oldest daughter fell in love with the saints at a young age. She decided that she wanted to be a saint...but not a martyr. Yet her young sons and their friends love to watch the videos of martyrs and listen to their stories...the gorier the martyrdom the better.

Are you aware that some saints were motivated to become saints by reading about the saints? St. Ignatius of Loyola was a nobleman of Spain. He was raised at the Court of Ferdinand of Aragon, the husband of the Servant of God, Queen Isabella. Wounded at the battle of Pamplona, he was forced out of sheer boredom to read *The Lives of Saints* for want of anything else to read. It changed his life. This book led him to dedicate his life and efforts to the King of Kings rather than an earthly king. He gave up his worldly interests to become a saint by founding a spiritual army known as the Jesuits.

Reading the biography of St. Ignatius of Loyola brought about the conversion to the Catholic Church of the great philosopher, Dr. Dietrich Von Hildebrand.

St. Edith Stein, a great Jewish intellectual, had decided to become a Christian but was undecided as to which denomination to join. Staying with friends, one night her friends went out leaving her home alone to amuse herself. Perusing their library, *she picked up a German translation of St. Teresa of Avila's autobiography and did not close the book until dawn. She tells us herself that she said then, "This is the truth."* [65] When the stores opened the next morning she purchased a missal and a catechism. In less than six months she was baptized.

---

[65] *Edith Stein, Op. Cit.,* p. 17.

222 Raise Happy Children...Raise Them Saints!

Servant of God, Fr. Walter J. Ciszek, S.J., who spent twenty-three years as a priest in Soviet prisons and labor camps in Siberia, confides that it was reading the life of St. Stanislaus Kostka that changed his life: *I wanted to smash most of the plaster statues that showed him with sickly sweet look and eyes turned up to heaven; I could see plainly that Kostka was a tough, young Pole who could—and did—walk from Warsaw to Rome through all sorts of weather and show no ill effects whatsoever. He was also a stubborn young Pole who stuck to his guns despite the arguments of his family and the persecution of his brother when he wanted to join the Society of Jesus. I liked that. I thought perhaps I ought to be a Jesuit.*[66]

The saints also teach us about Church history. For instance, some identify St. Veronica, the woman who wiped the face of Jesus on His way to Calvary, as the woman in Scripture with the *issue of blood*. French legend reports that she married Zacheus, also a New Testament character.[67]

Read the lives of the saints as bedtime stories or on Sunday afternoons. When the children can read by themselves, give them books on the saints to devour. It's such fun to spend an afternoon or evening with a saint! They uplift one's spirit. Why not put together a summer reading program of the saints for your children? In researching this series of books I have spent several years with the saints as companions. What fun it will be to meet them in person!

Peter Kreeft insists that *Saints "sell" to teenagers better than abstract principles. Morality is taught best by concrete examples and stories. It's not so much taught as caught—like a good infection. Saints "sell" to teenagers because saints are great lovers, and teenagers are beginning to explore love. Saints show that love is more than sex, better than sex, happier than sex.*[68]

St. Philip Neri insisted that the best preparation for prayer

[66] Walter J. Ciszek, S.J., *With God In Russia* (NY: Image Book, 1966) p. 2.

[67] *Lives of the Saints Illustrated Part I*, *Op. Cit.*, p. 61.

[68] Peter Kreeft, "Being Catholic," *Talking To Your Children About Being Catholic* (IN: Our Sunday Visitor, 1995) p. 6.

is to read the lives of the saints. Start your preteens reading *The Story Of A Family...The Home of St. Therese of Lisieux* by Fr. Stephane-Joseph Piat, O.F. M. Then move them on to the autobiography of St. Thérèse (*Story of A Soul*). Next have them read *Illustrissimi* by John Paul I, *Journal Of A Soul* by Blessed Pope John XXIII, *With God In Russia* and *He Leadeth Me* by Walter J. Ciszek, S.J. Another fascinating book is *The Founder Of Opus Dei, The Life of Josemaría Escrivá* by Andrés Vázquez de Prada. Spiritually well-formed teens should be able to read *The Collected Works of St. Teresa Of Avila Vol. 1,* and *The Curé D'Ars* by Abbé Francis Trochu.

Stimulated by scripture and the lives of the saints, developing a relationship with God will be natural for your children.

Spiritual Reading...

From the first three chapters of this book did you notice the spiritual reading book that was mentioned by almost all the saints we have studied so far? It is *The Imitation of Christ*. If you recall most of them were reading this book by the age of ten and many even memorized complete passages from the book by that age. Why not start your children with this book around that age, possibly reading it with them at first until they are comfortable with the style. Then move on to *The Devout Life* by St. Francis de Sales. Give your children a copy of *The Way* by St. Escrivá then follow it up with some of his other books such as *The Forge* and *Furrow*. Young people will also be attracted to *He and I* by Gabrielle Bossi. As your children grow spiritually, share spiritual reading books with them that you found valuable. But don't wait until a set age for specific books because the maturity of children differs. What we think may be above their comprehension may not be at all. Lucia of Fatima recalls having the three volume series, *Practice of Perfection and Christian Virtues*, by Alphonsus Rodriquez, S.J., read to her as a child. While there was much she admits she did not undersand, the examples did stick with her. My grandson, Michael, who is seven, just made his first confession. As a memento of the occasion I sent him a book on

St. Tarcisius,the first martyr of the Holy Eucharist and my book for adults, ***Looking For Peace? Try Confession!*** thinking he could read it when he was older. He immediately read the saint book. That night when his mother went to tuck him into bed, she found him reading the confession book! He keeps the book under his bed and reads bits from it at night before he goes to sleep.

Examples From Life...

Incorporating the spiritual and corporal works of mercy into your children's daily lives is crucial for their spiritual formation. Our faith is not just warm feelings or spiritual highs. Love is action. Remember, *actions speak louder than words.*

Teach your children that charity is more than writing an occasional check. It's getting involved, getting one's hands dirty, giving of one's time. St. James is pretty forthright in this regard: ***What will it profit, my brethren, if a man says he has faith, but does not have works? Can the faith save him? And if a brother or a sister be naked and in want of daily food, and one of you say to them, "Go in peace, be warmed and filled," yet you do not give them what is necessary for the body, what does it profit? So faith too, unless it has works, is dead in itself*** (*James* 2:14-18).

Take your children to visit nursing homes, campaign for pro-life politicians, work at soup kitchens, volunteer at the pro-life office, help out a new mother, donate money to the poor and to the Church. Imitate the example of the saints and parents of saints.

Each day, Mr. Martin gave St. Thérèse money to disperse to the needy she and her father met during their walks. On Monday evenings beggars would gather at the gate of the Martin home. It was Thérèse who was given the task of dispersing alms to them. Her mother, despite long days spent with her business and family would spend hours at night nursing sick neighbors, or helping poor families with money, food, and clothing. Orphans and widows also received help as well as businessmen in financial straits.

The Escrivás and the Vianneys were likewise generous in the giving of alms even when they had to do without themselves to help others with food or clothing.

Marianna Kolbe, like Zélie Martin, donated her time and expertise to helping the less fortunate through her skill of nursing. She even acted as mid-wife. When the doctor gave up on one mother, Marianna knelt at her bed for hours begging the Mother of God to preserve the woman's life. Her prayers were answered.

Use the events of everyday to teach spiritual lessons. Louis Martin once made a toy for St. Thérèse that was a set of weighted cones that she could knock down but would spring back up. He pointed out to her *in the trials and shocks of life, you must...rise up again after every fall and keep looking up!* On one of their walks, Thérèse's puppy jumped into a pond then rolled in the dirt getting his white and brown fur filthy. Louis used this illustration to teach his daughter about sin: *See, that reminds us of a spotless, white soul which becomes soiled by sin.* These lessons made such an impact on Thérèse that she wrote about them in her autobiography. Mr. Martin daily gave his daughters a talk on some aspect of the faith. You can do the same by using the problems and joys of life to teach some spiritual truth to your children.

When my daughter Marianne was nine, I took her shopping with me to the Loop in Chicago where we got stuck in an elevator. We were both scared to death. After the experience was over I thought I'd teach her a supernatural lesson. I asked, *"What did you think of doing first when the elevator stopped?"* *"Grab your hand, mom."* *"Then what did you think of?"* *"Leaning back against the wall for support."* *"And what next?"* She looked at me puzzled. *"Didn't you think to pray?"* I asked exasperated. *"No, I didn't think of it. But I did see my guardian angel in the corner of my mind and he was just as scared as me!"* We spent the rest of the afternoon discussing the strength and the courage of angels.

Prudent parents instill in their children that the measure of all things is what God thinks. Motivate your children to do good because this is pleasing to God. For example you can encourage your son or daughter by saying, *Give a gift to God by cleaning up your room* or *doing your homework.* At first they will look at you strangely but as you reiterate this same theme over and over they will begin to think, *I'll do this to please God.*

It is so important to teach children, when they are young, to please and not to offend the good, loving God. I have a three-year-old niece who is going through a difficult stage. She was especially naughty one day so she was punished. Later that night her parents heard her crying up in her room, *I'm so sorry, Jesus, I'm so sorry!* If a child is taught in this manner from little on, as the child grows he will be guided by a well-formed conscience that will be activated whether you are around or not.

To raise your children saints today requires diligence and dedication on your part. Drugs, sex, drinking and Satanism are rampant even in grade schools. Children are easily swept up into these deadly activities if parents are not vigilant. Witchcraft is permeating our schools. Anything dealing with the demonic is dangerous. My six-year-old grandson was invited to a birthday party of a fifth grade neighbor. One of the "toys" the little girl requested was a Ouije Board. Not only should we be concerned about our children, but also the children of our friends, relatives, neighbors, etc. We are our brothers' keepers.

TEACH YOUR CHILDREN SELF-SACRIFICE

The Martin girls were taught to make little sacrifices (mortifications) to the Child Jesus so that they could add "pearls" to their crowns in heaven. Marie recalls her first mortification at the age of four or five years old. She had asked her father to make her a saucer out of her orange peel. When she showed it to Pauline ...*it made you envious and, to have a pearl in my crown (that was the way mother used to make us do things) I gave it to you. It seemed to me that I was accomplishing a heroic act, because that famous orange skin seemed all the more precious to me because you wanted it. Then, running quickly towards mother, I said: "Mama, if I gave my orange skin to Pauline. Will I go to heaven?" Mother smiled and answered: "Yes, my little daughter, you will go to Heaven." That hope alone was able to console me for the loss of my fortune.*

When Grandfather Guerin died, nine-year-old Marie faced the dentist bravely hoping to get her grandfather out of Purgatory.

St. John Vianney, when four years old, had a favorite rosary that his younger sister, Marguerite wanted. There was a screaming, pulling session over the beads but John won. Running to his mother, he was dumbfounded when she told him to give the beads to his sister: *Yes, my darling, give them to her for love of the good God.* Obediently but sadly he gave his rosary to Marguerite. As a reward for his sacrifice his mother gave him a small statue of Our Lady. *Oh! How I loved that statue...the Blessed Virgin was the object of my earliest affections; I loved her even before I knew her.*[69]

Teach your children that sacrifices are gifts they can present to Jesus. Each sacrifice done for the love of God strengthens the will besides developing the virtue of fortitude. Children as young as three can offer things up. If your children are not accustomed to doing little mortifications now, ask them individually to do or give up something on Saturdays for Our Lady's intention. Another day they could do a sacrifice for the Holy Father or to end abortion. Up until age fifteen train your children to do short term sacrifices such as drinking water rather than soda; selecting the smaller pieces of food they enjoy; delaying a drink of water; cleaning the table off; doing the dishes; watching the baby; anything at all.

After the age of fifteen, teens can make and keep long term resolutions such as *couldn't you keep your bedroom clean this week for the love of God?* Or, *could you be cheerful this evening for the love of God?* If the teen agrees but forgets, gently remind

[69] *The Curé D'Ars, Op. Cit.,* p. 8.

your son or daughter by asking how the resolution is going or by encouraging your teen "to begin again." Teach your children to use reminders to help them to live their resolutions daily. My niece, Elizabeth who is in high school, paints only her thumb with nail polish to reminder her *to be nice to my family.* Also use the penitential seasons of Lent and Advent to help your children grow in the spirit of sacrifice.

Fr. Hardon, S.J., maintained: *Barring an extraordinary grace from God, He generally calls those persons to follow Him as priests or religious, who have been taught the value of sacrifice from childhood. The experience of self-denial in the use and enjoyment of material things is the normal predisposition for a lifetime practice of evangelical poverty. Training in self-control of the senses, especially in the use of the media, is the ordinary preparation for a lifelong dedication to consecrated chastity. Careful and loving nurture in self-denial, almost from infancy, is God's usual way of conditioning the human will for commitment to the counsel of obedience.*

Every vocation is born of sacrifice, is maintained by sacrifice and is measured in the apostolate by the sacrifice of those whom God calls...In fact, the more intimate is one's vocation to the service of Christ, the more demanding will be the sacrifices required.

Sacrifice is finally the condition and norm of apostolic work...Who have been the great achievers in the vineyard of the Lord over the centuries? Have they not been the men and women who never said, "Enough" in their zeal for souls; who labored, like St. Paul, in season and out of season, selflessly and exhaustingly; who never counted the cost in time or effort or personal preference; in a word, who lived lives of heroic sacrifice?[70] Although Fr. Hardon's words were addressed to priests and religious, they apply as well to us since we are all called to live lives of heroic sanctity.

---

[70] John Hardon, S.J. "Sacrifice and Vocations", *Call to Holiness News,* Vol. 5, No.1, Winter 2001.

The Faith Of Your Child Will Impact Countless Lives

In forming your children to be saints you have the help of your parish along with wonderful orthodox Catholic organizations that sponsor activities for children and teens to reinforce the Catholic faith. I mentioned these organizations at the beginning of this chapter but I will name them again. They include Opus Dei, Militia of the Immaculate, the Legionaries of Christ, Regnum Christi, Schoenstatt, Miles Jesu, Pro-Sanctity, the Neocatechumenal Movement, the Blue Army and the Apostolate for Family Consecration. These organizations put forth tremendous resources and effort, not to mention expense, to help *you* raise your children to be saints. They are not doing this because they have nothing better to do. They are doing this to serve God by serving you. Take advantage of these golden opportunities for your children. Don't just check them out but make the sacrifice to utilize them. Check out the websites of each.

The faith you teach your children will not only have a lasting impact on their lives but also on the lives of all those they touch. Sir Alec Guinness, the recently deceased actor, owed his conversion to the faith to a little child. Playing the part of a priest in France, he decided to walk back in costume to his hotel after the day's shooting. As he walked along a quiet country lane, a little boy ran up to him. The child grabbed his hand, kissed it and began chatting happily to a man he thought was a priest. Guinness, not able to speak French, simply smiled at the happy child. When the child ended his conversation, he again kissed the actor's hand and ran off. Alec Guinness was so touched by the reverence the little boy had toward the "priest" that it moved him to convert to the Catholic faith.

The Parents of Lucia of Fatima

Let's conclude this chapter by showing how the parents of Lucia of Fatima lived their family life. Sr. Maria Lucia agreed to write an account of her family *because I remember my parents as admirable examples of a Christian family, united in faith, hope and love...And may God assist me, and may my father, who sees me from Heaven, take my hand again, as he did when I was a child, guiding it and teaching me to trace on my forehead the sign of the Redeeming Cross of Christ Our Saviour.*[71]

Lucia's Father, António dos Santos

Although Fatima is a poor village, the Santos family, to which Lucia's father belonged, were landowners. As such they were considered wealthy. Her father not only farmed his own property but also his Aunt Teresa's property that adjoined his. This aunt married a friend of Lucia's father, Anastácio Vieira. *They had no children. When I was born, my father invited Anastacio to be my godfather at Baptism, something he and my Aunt Teresa accepted with great pleasure. They asked my parents to give me to them, so they could bring me up as their own child and adopt me, but this my parents did not want. However, they did allow them to take me to their home whenever they wished, which happened frequently, always with the hope of fulfilling their desire. My godmother Teresa said that it was also to relieve my mother, who, in her charity, was at this time raising a little orphan [a niece]...*[72]

Lucia's mother, Maria Rosa, described her husband as *always a good Christian, practicing Catholic and a good worker, even as a youth. Therefore, I liked him very much and we were married. He was always very faithful to his religious duties and to his state, and a very good friend to me and the children. When I told him that God was going to grant us a seventh child, he responded: "Don't be troubled! It is one more blessing from God. Therefore, there will be no lack of bread in the drawer nor oil in the pot."*[73]

Lucia recalls how her father loved children and enjoyed having

---

[71] *Fatima In Lucia's Own Words II-5ᵗʰ and 6ᵗʰ Memoirs*, Edited by Fr. Louis Kondor, SVD, (Fatima: Portugal, 1999) pp. 8-9.

[72] *Ibid.*, p. 10-11. [73] *Ibid.*, p. 21.

the village children play on their patio. He would read them stories after his work. *My father was of a calm nature, kindly and joyful; he liked music, fiestas and dances....He had no disputes with anyone...He loved to please everyone and to see everyone happy...[My father gave a] little patch of land with fig trees...to a certain family, because they lamented not having a fig tree near their home from which to gather figs to eat.*[74]

António was a devoted and loving husband. He praised and complimented his wife before his children to teach them appreciation for their mother telling them, *"God has given me the best woman in the world!" That is what made me believe that my mother was the best in the world.* Likewise, he treated her with tenderness and thoughtfulness. He never permitted her to carry heavy pitchers or carry buckets of water from the well. That was his job or the older children's. *[W]hen the new babies were born and they cried during the night, it was my father who got up to attend to them and carried them to her bed...*[75] If someone came at night for my mother to care for the sick, it was António who answered the door. As his wife dressed, he would prepare a drink of egg yolks, honey, and brandy to keep her healthy. He would then light her lantern, *wrap her cloak round her, pull her hood over her head, and opened the umbrella for her so that she would not get wet or catch cold.*[76]

Lucia's Mother, Maria Rosa

Maria Rosa Ferreira Rosa was the youngest of seven children with three brothers and three sisters preceding her. When she was baptized twelve days after her birth, her parents followed the Portuguese custom of naming Our Lady her godmother then having a family friend stand in for her. (What a beautiful custom to resurrect today!)

Lucia describes her maternal grandparents as *very cheerful and willing to be of service, good singers and guitar players, sponsoring parties and dances, so they subsequently became very popular with all the young people of the district.*

---

[74] *Ibid.*, p. 15. [75] *Ibid.*, p. 27. [76] *Ibid.*, p. 69.

Her family had the reputation of a large, practicing Catholic family. Lucia recalls, *The Ferreira Rosa family distinguished itself by the practice of charity.* The family helped to tend the fields of elderly farmers and nursed the sick. *My mother's aunt, Maria Isabel...taught children to read...* Some of the books she used to teach Lucia's mother and later Lucia herself to read were the three volume series by Alphonsus Rodriguez, S.J., entitled the **Practice of Perfection And Christian Virtues.** Aunt Maria Isabel *gathered abandoned children to care for them and afterwards placed them in the homes of good families who would love them and help them through life.*[77] Besides her goodness, Maria Isabel was known for her great beauty. When the occupying French troops were leaving Fatima her mother had to hide her in a chest covered with sacks to prevent General Junot from taking her back to France with him.

The Ferreira Rosas lived next store to the dos Santos family into which two of their children married. Maria Rosa Ferreira Rosa married António dos Santos's while her older brother, José, married Olympia dos Santos. Before his marriage, on a voyage to Brazil, José's ship sank. His prayers to Our Lady of the Rosary saved his life after he spent days clinging to debris in the sea. Married only eight years, he died from an illness leaving his wife, Olympia, with two small sons to care for. Olympia later married Manuel Pedro Marto and had seven more children. Her two youngest from this marriage are Bl. Jacinta and Bl. Francisco Marto. Grandchildren from this marriage include two priests (one a missionary to Africa) and a religious sister.

Lucia recalls that her mother fits the description of the virtuous woman in the **Book of Proverbs** (31, 10-11; 20-22; 26-27; 30-31). She was gentle, calm, cheerful, outgoing, affectionate, humorous, serene and *always punctilious and industrious in the performance of her duty towards God, the members of her household and those outside it. The Commandments of God's Law were her rule of life. She inculcated these into everyone...*[78] In the village she was called "a second mother" to all in need. *She*

---

[77] *Ibid.,* pp.12-13.   [78] *Ibid.,* p. 47.

Teaching The Faith...To Your Children 233

*generously accepted all the children that God sent her...*besides taking in orphans and children whose parents could not care for them. Likewise she took in unwed mothers and their children. One such illegitimate child, she cared for until she could reconcile the young woman with her parents, later married her daughter, Carolina. This marriage gave the Church a priest and a religious sister. When a neighbor asked Lucia's mother how she *could bear to receive into her house all the human wretchedness that came knocking at [the] door...my mother replied: "Look! What do we do when we see someone fall down? Don't we run at once to give them a hand to help them up, and then support them so that they won't fall again? Well, that's what I do. I give a helping hand so that someone who has fallen once won't fall again...*[79]

Her husband and children were her main priorities after God. When called away to care for the sick, she always let her husband know where she was going then instructed one of her daughters to take over her work and cook the meals so that António would not be inconvenienced. After work, António would seek her out to see if she could come home for dinner. If this was possible, he would wait to walk her home. *Thus, being absolutely sure of her fidelity, honor and honesty, my father allowed her to go everywhere without the least worry or suspicion, convinced that she was going to sacrifice herself, for the sake of charity, in order to help and assist whichever neighbor had turned to her for help.*[80]

Lucia explains, *She was not rich in the things of this world, nor in the human sciences that people set so much store by, but she was rich in the gifts of nature and of grace, of faith, hope and love, those gifts which most enhance our value, which do not fade, and the fruits of which abide with us in time and in eternity.*[81] One priest described Maria Rosa as *all that a woman should be: worth her weight in gold; she had tact, and intelligence.* Another priest felt that Lucia's mother *is a saint.*[82] Lucia herself describes her mother as *humble, a woman of great faith, who loved justice and truth, was full of charity, and was always*

[79] *Ibid.*, p. 125. [80] *Ibid.*, p. 69. [81] *Ibid.*, p. 89. [82] *Ibid.*, p. 49.

*ready to help people both in the household and outside it...I had
the happiness of living with her and receiving from her such
wonderful teaching, such good and affectionate example, always
inspired by a living faith, hope and love.*[83]

Family Life...

Maria Rosa and António dos Santos were the parents of seven
children, one of which was stillborn caused by a carting accident.
The five daughters and one son who survived were Maria dos
Anjos (a weaver who married and had eight children), Teresa
de Jesus (a dressmaker who married and had six children),
Manuel (a farmer who married, emigrated to Brazil and had 11
children), Gloria de Jesus (a domestic who married and had
five children), Caroline de Jesus (weaver, seamstress, and
farmer who married and had six children), and the visionary,
Lucia de Jesus (a Carmelite). Maria Rosa was the baby who
was stillborn. From this family and extended family came many
large deeply devout Catholic families as well as many priestly
and religious vocations.

   As soon as the dos Santos children were able they were taught
to cook, clean, help with farm tasks (such as feeding the
chickens, tending the sheep and milking the cows), weaving,
sewing and crocheting clothing. *My mother taught me to crochet
when I was very small, first narrow bands of lace to decorate
one's underclothes; later she taught me to work with wool.*[84] When
Lucia wanted new clothes, Maria Rosa would agree but rather
than making the garment for her taught Lucia how to make the
garment herself. On one occasion, Lucia not only received a
sewing lesson but also lessons in self-sacrifice and charity. After
she painstakingly completed her first sewing project, a dress
she wanted for herself, her mother asked her to give it to a
little girl who stopped by their home to beg. Seeing the other
child cold and dressed in tatters, Lucia reluctantly agreed. Her
mother sweetened her sacrifice by promising to teach her how
to make the next dress even prettier. As they worked in the
home and in the fields, the parents and children discussed issues

---

[83] *Ibid.*, p. 50.　　　　　　　　　　[84] *Ibid.*, p. 83.

of faith and morals in a natural manner.

Truthfulness was a virtue promoted in their family. Their mother *took advantage of every opportunity to urge us always to tell the truth. She said that she herself had always to tell the truth, even if it were against herself...It was for this reason that she was so upset at the time of the apparitions, as it seemed to her that such a thing could not be true. "Are we worthy of such a thing? Get this out of your head, child, and tell the truth!"*[85]

Although affectionate, Maria Rosa did not put up with the *whims and lack of courtesy [of her children].* When Lucia refused to eat a meal she was told, *in this house you don't eat only what you like, but what there is to eat, like everyone else; so until you eat your beans, you'll get nothing else.* When Lucia continued to refuse to eat her beans after everyone had finished their lunch, her mother put her beans in a drawer and all the other food out of her reach. At dinnertime, Lucia was again presented with her dish of uneaten beans. Only when she finally forced herself to eat half of them was she allowed to eat the dinner that was prepared for the rest of the family. Her mother explained, *You have conquered your caprice, so now eat what the others are eating...It was a lesson for a lifetime I was never again tempted to say: "I won't eat this or that because I don't like it." At the time, I did not yet know about offering sacrifices to God, but He was preparing me. Thanks to Him and to the mother He chose for me.*[86]

On Sundays and holydays the family assisted at Holy Mass together. Then friends and relatives spent the day at the Santos home. The older daughters were courted on Sundays under the watchful eyes of their parents as the women chatted together while the men played cards. Between the rounds of cards the men would drink a glass of wine. To avoid having the men drink too much, Maria, in an very unobtrusive way, would take a platter of fruit and replace the wine jug with a cool lemon drink saying, *Here's some fruit for you all to eat and a nice cold drink; the more wine you drink, the hotter you'll be.*[87] The men,

---

[85] *Ibid.*, p. 87. [86] *Ibid.*, p. 99. [87] *Ibid.*, p. 113.

none the wiser, expressed their gratitude. Sometimes she would join the men for cards suggesting they all put in a little wager which she usually won. *At sunset, when the bells of the church rang for the Angelus, my father got up and, with him, all the others. Removing his cap, my father led the three Hail Mary's to which they responded.*[88] Then everyone left for his own home.

Weekday meals included all members of the family. It was a time to exchange experiences and to discuss the events of the day. It was a time of laughter and peace. Arguments were never allowed.

The couple supported each other's decisions. When any of the children needed permission they were required to ask both parents for that permission. If one said "no" or "yes" the other spouse supported the decision. *My father was responsible for the work in the fields, while my mother looked after the house. Together they decided what was best for each one to do, and were always in agreement.* At times this meant that the older girls who helped in the home were needed in the fields leaving Maria with an abundance of work to accomplish. Rather than being perturbed or upset she would say, *It doesn't matter. The first thing is to help Father with the work in the fields, then we will all help with these things in the evening, and everything will get done with the help of God.*[89]

A Family Of Faith

Maria Rosa was 38-years-old when Lucia was born. She recalled that Lucia *was born on the 28th of March 1907. It was Holy Thursday; in the morning, I went to Holy Mass and received Holy Communion, thinking I would return in the afternoon to visit the Blessed Sacrament, but it was not to be, since on that afternoon, she was born...Her father made the arrangements for her Baptism immediately.*[90] Lucia was baptized on March 30th, Holy Saturday although it was the custom to christen children eights days after birth. Lucia's godmother, Maria Rosa Marto, was a young neighbor girl. The young woman's father would only permit his daughter to take on this spiritual

[88] *Ibid.*, p. 22.   [89] *Ibid.*, p. 116.   [90] *Ibid.*, p. 14.

responsibility if the baby was named Lucia, rather than Maria Rosa the name her parents gave her. And so it was agreed that the infant would be named Lucia.

Charity was an outstanding feature of the Santos home. *Neither my father nor my mother wished that any poor person should go away from our door without something. If my father was at home, it was he who gave; if not he it was my mother; if it was neither...it was the oldest son or daughter who would give the alms...*[91] *It seemed as if my mother could only say "yes". She never refused her services when asked, and, on many occasions, it was she herself who offered her help.*[92]

If someone needed farm produce but could not pay, it was given to them: *Don't worry about having to pay. God will pay me. Take your chicken and if you need any more, come and ask and God grant that the invalid may recover...*[93] They also extended credit or lowered prices to fit the pocketbook of the customer.

Her mother, observant as to the needs of others, would put together baskets of gifts. So as not to embarrass the recipients, she would send Lucia with the baskets of firewood, chestnuts or other necessities to the elderly and the sick. At the same time she did not believe even the elderly should be idle. She would encourage the elderly men to do small chores around her home and the elderly women she would set to work rocking babies or helping with easy tasks.

Once Lucia's father gave a beggar a black pudding after asking his wife's permission. The beggar prayed an *Our Father* and a *Hail Mary* over António and Lucia then said, *May the Lord grant good fortune to you and to your little girl.* When Lucia told this to her mother, Maria Rosa asked, *And for me nothing?* António quickly responded, *For you also, because you and I are one; everything that is mine is yours and our children's.* Her mother was pleased with his reply.

Neighbors came to borrow loaves of bread or other staples. Knowing this, her mother always baked extra bread to give to

[91] *Ibid., p. 15.*   [92] *Ibid., p. 90.*   [93] *Ibid., p. 103.*

others. In times of drought, when their neighbors' wells dried up, they would ask to draw water from the Santos' well. *God blessed it, because the water of our well never failed.* When the hogs were slaughtered, the village priest and the elderly in the village who had no family were given portions. Sick neighbors turned to Maria for help. When told by a relative she was wearing herself out, Maria Rosa replied, *Never mind, I help others and God helps me.*

Mrs. Santos, hearing a neighbor man screaming at his wife, went to investigate the cause. She found that the woman had just given birth the night before and was too weak to get out of bed. The husband, enraged that the house was in disorder, that no meals were prepared, that the children were not dressed nor the animals cared for, verbally abused his poor wife. Maria immediately took charge. She sent for her older daughters to clean his house and care for the older children. She herself washed the wife, took the baby home to care for while she prepared food for the wife. Maria then invited the husband and children to eat with her family until the poor woman was back on her feet. The Santos furthermore invited the husband to sleep the next several nights in their home while their daughter, Teresa, stayed with the wife to care for her and the children. Maria's quick thinking and generous response to the needs of that family restored peace and harmony.

When the flu epidemic of 1918 struck their village, Antonio's brother warned him not to allow his wife to nurse the sick for fear she would catch the disease and infect her family. It was this epidemic that took the lives of their niece and nephew Bls. Jacinta and Francisco. Maria Rosa, busy nursing the sick and making meals at home to bring to the sick, asked her husband to accompany her saying, *Look, you have a good point...But...how can we leave those people to die, without anyone there to give them a glass of water? It would be better if you came with me to see how these people really are, and, then, if it's alright to leave them alone.* [94] António agreed and, generous man that he was, found himself staying to care for the ailing in

---

[94] *Ibid.,* p. 19.

different homes. In families were both parents were ill, he brought the babies and toddlers back to his own home to be cared for by his older children. Lucia's parents even permitted her to care for a sick widow whose son was dying from tuberculosis. When neighbors questioned Antonio's prudence in this matter he replied, *God will not repay me with evil for the good that I do for Him!*

Lucia's parents also made it a practice to teach their children how to care for the poor and the sick so if they were not available, the children could help those in need. Their training bore fruit when their daughter Teresa de Jesus was called to assist at the birth of a child. The doctor pronounced the baby stillborn and told her to bury the infant. Instead Teresa *placed the child's mouth on her own and began to breathe into it and warm it. Little by little it began to move. She wrapped it in warm blankets and put a few drops of milk into the mouth.* The child lived. *This was the fruit of the charity taught in the school where my sister learnt it: to love our neighbor as ourselves, to respect and preserve the gift of life that God has given to us, in ourselves and in others, and that God alone has the right to take us from time to eternity.*[95]

The family also had a set prayer life. Grace was said before meals and a thanksgiving was prayed after them. Following dinner in May the family prayed the rosary together on their knees before the crucifix. Neighbors would join them, sometimes so many that all could not fit into their home so the overflow prayed outside on the patio or in the street. (This was prior to the apparitions of Our Lady of Fatima.) May devotions at this time could not take place in church because of government persecution. The Santos children participated in processions and brought gifts of food to the Infant Jesus on Christmas Eve.

António, after working in the fields, hunting, caring for the sheep or pigs would return home when the Angelus chimed to pray with the family and await dinner. As he waited, he would tell the children stories, teach them dances or sing them songs.

---

[95] *Ibid.*, p. 60.

Lucia's mother would ask, *What are you teaching this little one!*
If only you would teach her doctrine! Her father would reply
kindly, *Let's do as your mother wishes! And he took hold of my*
little hand, teaching me to trace the Sign of the Cross on my
forehead, mouth and heart. Afterwards he would teach me to
pray the Our Father, Hail Mary, the Creed, how to prepare for
Confession, the Act of Contrition, the Commandments of God,
etc. Later on, when we were all together at supper, he made me
repeat what I had just learned.[96]

Evenings were devoted to teaching the faith to the family
with António being expected to answer catechism questions
along with his children. Lucia recalls that her mother *began*
with the Ten Commandments..."First to love God above all things.
This is the one that confuses me most because I never know
whether I love God more than my husband and children, but
God is so good that He will forgive me and have mercy on me."
When she came to the sixth, which requires us to be chaste, she
would stop again and say: "We have to be very careful about
this, too, because there are many temptations and many dangers.
And you," turning to my brother and sisters, *"must be very careful*
not to let yourselves be deceived, nor have any dealings with
anyone who suggests such things to you. The grace of God first
and foremost, [then] our good name, our own personal honor and
dignity. God gave me the grace of offering Him the pure flower
of my chastity on the day I was married, when I placed it on His
altar and received, in exchange, other flowers, namely the new
lives which He wanted to give me. In this way, God has helped
me and blessed me." Then she would go on, reciting, after the
commandments...those of the Church, the theological virtues, the
works of mercy, and so on...[97] When António tried to protect
Lucia from having to answer due to her young age, Maria Rosa
would reply, *she has to have it all on the tip of her tongue.* Lucia
recalls that while she memorized everything but understood
little at the time, it was absorbed *by my spirit and stored in my*
memory. Maria also enjoyed telling stories, with a moral, to
her own children as well as to their friends.

---

[96] *Ibid.*, p. 25.   [97] *Ibid.*, p. 47.

My mother used to say that matrimony was the tree of life that God planted in the garden of the world, and that the fruit of these trees were the children, who had to be brought up with great love and educated with great care because they had come to bring on earth the new life with which God enriches us, and it is they who, in turn, will take care of their parents, in sickness and old age, until God chooses to transfer them from earth to Heaven.[98]

Days of fasts and abstinence were *scrupulously* kept. By the time each child was seven, he was required to observe the fast days during Lent on Wednesday, Fridays and Saturdays. When António protested that a child was too young and not obliged to fast, Maria would respond that it was good for the child to get use to the fast because *you can only bend a cucumber when it's young. When it's fully grown, it will split rather than bend.*

When the children were sent to the village on errands or to visit friends, they were instructed not to return home without first making a visit to the Blessed Sacrament at church.

Before bed, António would take Lucia outside to view the stars saying, *Look, up above, it's Our Lady and the Angels; the moon is the lamp of Our Lady, the stars are the lamps of the Angels, which they and Our Lady light and place in the windows of Heaven, in order to light up our way at night. The sun...is Our Lord's lamp which He lights every day to keep us warm and so that we can see in order to do our work...[W]hen there was a thunderstorm, it was Our Heavenly Father scolding men because of their sins.*[99] During one intense storm that blew up, Lucia's father grabbed her hand and ran for home. When she questioned him who had sinned to cause the storm he replied, *It was I and others also. Let's pray to St. Barbara, to deliver us from the thunder and lightening.* The family then knelt before their crucifix and prayed for protection.

One day after Lucia had been disobedient her mother told her that she was naughty. She challenged her mother by saying that her father said she had come from heaven. *So then, are*

---

[98] *Ibid.*, p. 72.   [99] *Ibid.*, p. 25-26.

there bad things in heaven also? Her mother used the opportunity to teach more doctrine: *Well, yes, the demons were angels who were in Heaven but, because they were bad, God put them out, and now they go about tempting everyone. As for you, He sent you here below to see if you'll be good, so as to be able to return there.*[100]

Spiritual reading was also important in the family. Besides the three volume series by Alphonsus Rodriguez, S.J., entitled the *Practice of Perfection And Christian Virtues* mentioned before, the family read together *Missão Abreviada.* After the apparitions ended and Lucia was sent away to school, her mother sent her a copy of the *Imitation of Christ. The Imitation of Christ I have always carried with me,* recalls Lucia.

Times of Trial

When prayers for serious intentions went unanswered rather than turning away from God, Maria would say *I still haven't managed to win this grace from God. It must be because of my sins, because we are all sinners and we have to be patient.*

The apparitions of Our Lady to Lucia caused intense suffering for her family. Lucia's mother never truly believed that her daughter was gifted to see the Mother of God. She thought it was a trick of the devil, that her daughter was lying. *This was the doubt that tortured her, perhaps to the very end of her life.*[101] Prior to the apparitions the family was happy, now there were financial worries and sorrows. Her father watched in shock as the pilgrims destroyed his crops in the field of apparitions. Their actions threatened the family's livelihood. Yet António remained calm in the face of financial ruin keeping his faith and trust in God. He consoled his wife by explaining that once the apparitions ended, the people would stop coming to their fields and they could replant. When the reverse proved true he told her, *If it was Our Lady who appeared there, she will help us get along without the Cova da Iria [property].*

---

[100] *Ibid.,* p. 27.   [101] *Ibid.,* p. 192.

With pilgrims clamoring to see Lucia and no one else available to watch the sheep, the family was forced to sell their flock, another great financial loss. It meant they no longer had wool from the flock from which to make their clothing. Then their two eldest daughters married, who through their weaving and sewing had augmented the family income. Their income was now lost to the family. The Santos became impoverished. The apparitions did not financially affect Bls. Jacinta and Francisco's family since Our Lady never appeared on their property.

Despite their difficult circumstances, the Santos continued to help the poor. Maria would say, *We ourselves have little, but this little will have to stretch to help those who have less even than we have.*[102]

People mobbed their home insisting on talking with Lucia at all hours of the day and night. The family could not carry out their daily duties. This triggered tension between the family members. When António came home in the evening for dinner and saw mobs of people at his home he escaped by going to the tavern to play cards leaving Maria to fend off the mobs. He would only return home when he was assured that everyone had gone. The strain of the situation caused Maria to break down sobbing in the evenings asking, *My God, where has all the joy of our home gone?* While his actions worried Rosa Maria because she was use to having her husband home at dinner time, Lucia defends her father by stating that *my father never went to excess, nor [failed] in the awareness of his duties as a Christian and practicing Catholic, always maintaining the dignity of his personality as head and father of the family, faithful to his matrimonial promises, friend of his wife and children, preserving peace and serenity in his home.*[103]

When a legal situation arose involving some pilgrims and his land, friends advised António to sue the individuals involved. He replied, *No, I am not going to do this. I prefer to forgive them so that God may forgive me my sins too; all I want is to live in peace and harmony with everybody.*[104]

---

[102] *Ibid.*, p. 149.   [103] *Ibid.*, p. 40.   [104] *Ibid.*, p. 144.

Pressure was exerted on Lucia to admit the apparitions were lies. *"What shall I do? If I say that I lied in order to put an end to it all, then I shall be telling a lie. If I don't, my mother will die of sorrow, and it will be impossible to live in our house! To say that I saw nothing is to tell a lie, and to tell a lie is to offend God, and I don't want to offend God. I'd rather die and He can take me to heaven."*[105] Yet, on October 13th when rumors spread that a bomb might be thrown during the upcoming apparition, both parents accompanied Lucia saying, *If she is going to die, we want to die also at her side.*

Next, illness struck the family. The stress and overwork took a toll on Maria's health. She was dying. At the urging of her sisters, Lucia went alone to the apparition site to beg for the life of her mother. Although her prayers were answered, her mother still refused to believe in the apparitions although she did believe she was cured through the intercession of Our Lady.

Pilgrims left money at the apparition site to compensate the family for the loss of the farm fields but António refused to accept the gifts saying, *God forbid that I should keep this money! It doesn't belong to me. It belongs to Our Lady! Neither do I want anyone in my family to keep as much as five pennies of that money! As for the loss of the land, it is Our Lady who will repay me and she will help us.*[106] Later he donated the land for the Chapel of Apparitions. When Maria Rosa would become discouraged by their dire circumstances, he would remind her, *As many sacrifices as we make, we will never be able to repay God for the grace of sparing us from the influenza epidemic which did not enter our home, nor did He allow any of the children who were here during those days to become ill.*[107]

When wealthy people from outside Fatima offered to take Lucia into their home to raise and educate her, Maria thought this might be the way to restore tranquility in their family. António thought otherwise causing their first disagreement: *[W]e can't hand over a child of ours who is still so young just like that without knowing what might be the outcome.*[108]

---

[105] *Ibid.*, p. 131.   [106] *Ibid.*, p. 34.   [107] *Ibid.*, p. 35.   [108] *Ibid.*, p. 165.

April 4, 1919 their nephew Bl. Francisco died. Maria was grief stricken by his death. She considered him and his sister as part of her family. Three months later on July 30, 1919 her husband developed double pneumonia. He died within twenty-four hours. Before his death, he asked for a priest to hear his confession and to administer the last sacraments. The priest delayed coming so he died in the arms of Maria Rosa and his sister, Olympia, repeating the aspirations they suggested to him, *Jesus, Mary, Joseph save my soul which belongs to you! Lord Jesus, have mercy on me, by the merits of Your life, Passion and Death on the Cross!; Father into Your hands I commend my spirit.*

Maria's response to these sorrows was, *I don't know what else God wants to ask from me, but may He give me the grace to give Him everything He asks of me.*[109]   Her troubles were not over. Following the death of her husband, her niece, Bl. Jacinta, died. She herself was diagnosed with displaced vertebra, cardiac problems and a displaced kidney. Next, at the request of the bishop, she permitted Lucia to be sent away to be educated at Porto. Maria's final cross was her inability to have any contact with Lucia before her death. Lucia, at the time a Dorothian nun, received a letter from her mother asking that she visit her as she was dying. Lucia's superiors refused Maria's request. Lucia was told *to write to my mother and urge her to offer the sacrifice [of not seeing me] to God.* Lucia appealed to the Bishop of Leiria but he reinforced her superior's decision saying that her mother was well cared for. Maria, sobbing, cried out, *So they won't let her return to Fatima even to be present at my death! If I had known that that's how it would be, I would never have let her go there! However, I'll offer this great sacrifice to God so that He will keep her in His care and help her always to be good.*[110]

Days later, Maria asked her daughter, Teresa, to call Lucia's convent so that she could at least say "good-bye" to her daughter on the phone. When this request was also refused, Maria sobbed, *This is the last drop the Lord kept for me at the bottom of the*

---

[109] *Ibid.*, p. 168.   [110] *Ibid.*, p. 194.

chalice and which I had yet to drink on earth. I'll drink it for love of Him.[111] She died in Lucia's room on July 16, 1942, the Feast of Our Lady of Mt. Carmel, whose scapular she wore. A priest from the Shrine brought her the apostolic blessing for a happy death. Only after her mother's death did Lucia learn about her mother's final phone call.

When the Bishop of Leiria told Lucia that she should *thank God for giving you such a good and holy mother,* Lucia responded: *Yes, I thank God for the good and holy mother He gave me, while at the same time I mourn bitterly over so many others who deliver their children to death even before they are born...I am the last of the seven children that God gave to my parents; if that had been their attitude, I would not be here today.*[112]

Your Vocation Is To Raise Saints...

"...Choose this day that which pleases you, whom you would rather serve...but as for me and my house we will serve the Lord."   *Joshua* 24:15

There is no greater accomplishment than to raise your children to be saints. This is the vocation God has given to you. He provides you with grace and unlimited help. It's simply up to you to utilize them. L. D. Weatherhead once wrote: *The trouble with some of us is that we have been inoculated with small doses of Christianity which keeps us from catching the real thing.* May God prevent this from happening to your children!

What To Do At Each Age...

Following is a rough breakdown by age of what to teach your child. Each child in the family will develop differently. Some learn rapidly, others more slowly. Patiently adjust what you are trying to teach your child to his ability. The object is to teach your child to love God, not to resent Him. Once a concept or pious practice is introduced, such as explaining that one's purpose in life is to become a saint, this needs to be built on in a deeper manner throughout the child's life. It cannot simply

[111] *Ibid.*, p. 194   [112] *Ibid.*, p. 195.

be introduced, checked off the list then forgotten. Note that if you start this program when your children are small the faith and striving for holiness will seem natural. If your children are older, simply play catch-up in a natural manner so as not to arouse animosity in them.

And most important: respect your child's freedom. He or she may rebel or complain at times—but patiently, in a positive manner, help them to see the goodness and beauty of these practices. Do not become angry or frustrated if they do not do all you want them to do. God's grace takes time and operates in a different manner for each child. Instead, pray and try to guide them in such a way that they **freely want** to do these practices—not only because you tell them to.

Infant to six-months-old: Consecrate your child to God. Baptize the baby within two weeks of birth. Hang a crucifix on his bedroom wall. Use holy water to bless the child daily. Pray vocal morning and night prayers over the child. Have good religious art and statues scattered throughout your home. Try to get to daily Mass and take the child along. Pray that your child will desire to become a saint.

Six-months-to-twelve months old: Point out the crucifix, statues and religious pictures in your home. Name each item. Explain them simply. Teach your child to fold hands in prayer for morning and evening prayers and for grace. Teach child to shake hands at the sign of peace at Mass. Show child how to put hand in holy water font at church. Point out the Stations of the Cross, statues, and stained glass windows at church. Let the child play with an oversize rosary. Begin telling the child he is a child of God (Divine filiation).

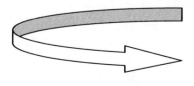

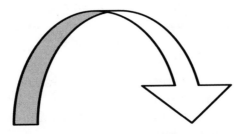

One-year-old to Two-years-old: As child begins to say words, teach him the name of the Good God, Jesus, Mother Mary, angels and saints. Work on keeping his hands folded during grace and other prayers. Teach the Sign of the Cross. When the child can put words together teach small aspirations such as "Jesus, I love You;" "Mary, help me;" "Jesus I offer my day to you;" "Angel, protect me." Have him say a little morning and night prayers as well as a simple grace before meals. Tell the child simple stories about God, Our Lady, angels and saints. Begin reading basic bible stories at night showing the child the pictures. Tell him how much God loves him. Explain how God helps him and watches over him. Point out the gifts God gives. Teach him to say "thank you, God..." Show him how to genuflect before the tabernacle. Point out where "Jesus lives." Teach him to share his toys and put things away, to help out by fetching something or setting the table. When the child can understand, suggest he put his toys away as a gift for Jesus. "Can you give a gift to Jesus? Why don't you put your toys away?" or "give a gift to Jesus and let your sister play with that toy." Explain how the child is a child of God. At Mass use a toddler's Mass book to point out the actions of the Mass.

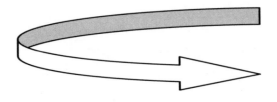

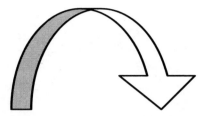

Two to Three-years-old: Teach your child to praise and thank God. Begin to teach the *Hail Mary, Our Father,* and *The Glory Be.* Explain what the words mean. By three children can say a decade of the rosary with you. Teach your child to pray for others during night prayers. Explain how "to talk to Jesus in your heart" (mental prayer). Show the child how to offer sacrifices to the Good God such as a chore done cheerfully; giving something one wants to another without crying, etc. Point out how to turn the day into prayer by saying a simple morning offering. Instruct the child in what is good and what is bad. Point out the confessional and explain how when you offend God you go to confession because doing bad things hurts Jesus who is so good. At night go through a simple examination of conscience and then have the child say he is sorry to Jesus for the things that were displeasing to God. Educate your child to ask his guardian angel for protection and help. When the child won't cooperate in something ask him what Jesus would do or say about the situation. Each morning ask the child what he can give the Good God as a gift of self-sacrifice. Inaugurate specific practices in your home for Advent and Lent. Read the lives of the saints and bible stories pointing out that *God wants you to become a saint.* Begin to teach simple doctrine such as "Why did God make you?" Point out the wonders of God's love everywhere. Make visits to the Blessed Sacrament. Talk about doing special things for people for love of God. Teach church manners.

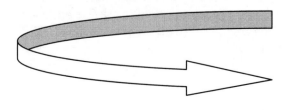

Three to Four-years-old: Teach more prayers by rote such as the *Angelus*, the *Creed*, simple *Acts of Faith, Hope, and Love, Act of Contrition* and *Morning Offering*. Explain what the words mean. Encourage child to make a daily sacrifice for the Good Jesus. Talk about offering up sacrifices to Jesus. Increase the morning and evening prayers. Pray to the patron saints of the family. Talk about how God created him to be a saint. Encourage the child to say at least one decade of the rosary with the family. Explain about the different types of prayer: praise, adoration, thanksgiving and petition. Reinforce God's love for him. Begin to teach the Ten Commandments. Introduce videos and CDs of the saints, angels, the rosary, bible stories and hymns. Give your child his own rosary. Take the child with you to have the rosary blessed. Talk about the miracles Jesus performed. Add more structure to the doctrine you teach. In addition use fun ways to teach the faith such as Catholic games, puzzles, dot-to-dot, coloring books, etc. Teach Marian devotions. Place a flower by a statue of Mary. Have a May crowning with friends in your yard. Explain the Mass in simple terms. Instruct child that everything he does should be done for the honor and glory of God (unity of life). Explain who the Holy Father is.

Four to Five-years-old: Continue teaching simple doctrine and the Ten Commandments and the laws of the Church. Explain in simple terms about sin. Encourage your child to do more sacrifices during the day to help Grandpa or someone who is ill. Include more little chores for the child to do to develop the spirit of service. Talk about virtues (good habits such as cheerfulness) and vices (bad habits such as fighting, pouting, refusing to help when asked.) Keep working on prayers. Read the lives of the saints and bible stories. Make it clear that the purpose of life is to become a saint. Teach the child to ask God each day what God wants him to do and to also ask how he should do it. Talk about modesty and truthfulness. Explain a bishop and cardinal.

Five to Six-years-old: Child should know all the basic prayers such as as the *Morning Offering, Angelus, Memorare, Apostles Creed, Acts of Faith, Hope, and Charity, Our Father, Hail Mary, Hail Holy Queen* and *Prayer to St. Michael, The Archangel.* Begin preparing your child for his first confession and First Holy Communion. Go deeper into the Ten Commandments and the laws of the Church. Teach the theological and moral virtues as well as the spiritual and corporal works of mercy. Teach doctrine in a more formal, disciplined manner by selecting a text and workbook. Work together with your child at a set time each day. Refine the evening examination of conscience. Help the child to select a particular area that he needs to work on such as helpfulness, cheerfulness, or order. Set small goals that he can achieve. Have the child check each evening how his struggle to grow in that area is going. Help him to make concrete resolutions for the next day. Show the child the inside of a confessional. Have him informally talk with a priest. Begin to talk more about the Blessed Sacrament and how to prepare to make his First Holy Communion. Explain more the concepts of divine filiation and unity of life. Teach child about sacramentals such as holy water, medals. Help child to understand the Mass and how to make a thanksgiving.

Six to Seven-years-old: Is your child ready to make his first confession? Is he prepared to make his First Holy Communion? After First Communion enroll him in the scapular. See that he wears it daily. Talk about the concept of suffering, how it helps one to grow spiritually and brings one closer to Christ. Teach child to offer sufferings and to make sacrifices for specific intentions such as for the Holy Father, for peace in the world. Teach child to use disappointments to grow holy. Purchase books on the lives of the saints that the child can read himself. Read with your child three minutes of the New Testament and ask the child how he can apply it to his day or next day. Explain how the child in his role to become a saint must also become an apostle...to bring his friends to Jesus. Ask him how he can do this and give him suggestions. Stress frequent confession. Can you take your child to daily Mass? A weekly holy hour?

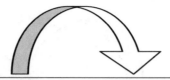

Seven to Eight-years-old: Begin to teach the concept of Divine Providence. Everything that happens is part of God's plan. Catholics do not believe in "fate." Re-emphasize Divine Filiation, the importance of being a child of God and the responsibilities that this requires. Explain the importance of the *Morning Offering* prayer and how this turns work, joys, sorrows, even breathing into prayer. But work must be done well for the love of God. One cannot give God shoddy work or half-hearted efforts. This is part of "unity of life." Teach child to pray each morning, "Lord, what do you want me to do today and how should I do it?" Teach the child to make visits to the Blessed Sacrament on his own. Take your child to at least monthly confession.

Eight to Nine-Years-Old: Concentrate on teaching your child the spiritual and corporal works of mercy in depth then work with your child to practice them. Go deeper into the meaning of each of the Ten Commandments. Use the *Catechism of the Catholic Church.* Emphasize the importance of striving to become a saint. Discuss the different types of prayers and how to pray them (praise, adoration, thanksgiving, petition). Take your child to at least monthly confession.

Nine to Ten-Years-Old: Stress the importance of being orderly and doing one's work well for the love of God (unity of life). Begin to teach the child the cardinal virtues and the capital sins. Further develop your child's spirit of mortification (little sacrifices). The saints read *The Imitation of Christ* at this age. Can your child? Train your child to do 10 minutes of spiritual reading everyday. Find spiritual reading books that will appeal to the maturity of your child. The child should be able to put together his own nightly examination of conscience geared to his struggle. Help your child to realize his strengths (virtues) and weaknesses (vices). Then assist your child in making concrete resolutions how to fight his vices. Select one vice at a time to work on. Give tips to your child as how he can fight vice.

Ten to Eleven-years-old: Teach, in detail, the seven gifts of the Holy Spirit and the Fruits of the Holy Spirit in preparation for the Sacrament of Confirmation. Make them understandable. Educate your child in the beauty of married love rather than the cold "facts of life." Teach the sacredness of marriage and how it's tied in with the virtues of chastity and modesty. How is the child living the spiritual and corporal works of mercy? Take child to at least monthly confession. Is your child striving to become a saint?

Eleven to Thirteen-years-old: Re-emphasize the capital sins and the cardinal virtues. Go deeper into the meaning of the Ten Commandments touching on the topics of abortion, drugs, contraception, fornication, homosexuality, drunkenness, suicide, and divorce. Keep the child on a specific spiritual schedule of vocal prayer, mental prayer, spiritual reading, gospel reading, frequent confession and examination of conscience. It is important to make the effort to take your child to daily Mass as well as frequent confession. View videos of the Holy Land. Emphasize the purpose of life is to grow holy...to become a saint.

High School Years: Make sure the teen makes a yearly retreat. Take the teen to World Youth Day. Get him involved in pro-life groups, Catholic youth groups, and charitable activities. Re-enforce the Ten Commandments and the Laws of the Church. Explain the purpose of dating—to find a spouse. Point out clearly what is acceptable conduct on a date and what is not. Be firm with curfews. Check out your child's friends. Emphasize that your child must be an apostle to friends. Daily Mass and at least monthly confession are critical for this age group. Reinforce your teen's prayer life and spiritual reading. Research Church history. Stress the purpose of life, divine filiation and unity of life.

John Paul II warns us: *It is easy to be consistent for a day or two. It is difficult and important to be consistent for one's whole life. It is easy to be consistent in the hour of enthusiasm; it is difficult to be so in the hour of tribulation. And only a consistency that lasts throughout the whole of life can be called faithfulness.*[113]

Does this program sound too demanding? Bishop George J. Lucas of Springfield, Illinois writes: *...I am reminded that those of us who are a little older have a serious responsibility to give sound teaching and good example to the young...There [seems] to be a reluctance at times to give the young good, solid food...When I really listen to young people, I hear them asking for solid teaching, real piety and a church community that stands for something. They have a right to know the demands of the Gospel and the traditions of the Catholic Church. My sense is that such knowledge will not scare them off. Rather, it will inspire them to want to share in the saving mission of Jesus Christ in the 21st century.*[114]

Additional Helps

✓ To learn more about the Bible purchase the book *Getting To Know The Bible* by Josemaria Monforte (Scepter 800-322-8773).
✓ Devise a weekly schedule for reading the lives of the saints and scripture to your children as well as teaching prayers and doctrine.
✓ Read the book *Talking To Your Children About Being Catholic* from Our Sunday Visitor.
✓ Most dioceses have a lending library. Check out yours for videos on the saints and bible stories.
✓ Read *Fatima In Lucia's Own Words II.*

---

[113] Address, 26 Jan. 1979.
[114] Bishop George J. Lucas, "Energy, enthusiasm of young Catholics example for all," *Catholic Times,* Dec. 16, 2001, page 2.

CHAPTER 4

THE SACRAMENTS HELP CHILDREN GROW HOLY!

"The Sacraments enable us to do deeds and attain levels of moral perfection that are unimaginable without grace. Not to frequent them often would be to deny ourselves the very gifts that He who loves us most would give us." [1]

Dr. Janet E. Smith

Our soul is the principle of life. When the soul leaves the body we die. Just as food nourishes our bodies, the sacraments nourish our souls. For example, unless the Holy Eucharist nourishes us our soul dies. Christ is very firm about this: ***[U]nless you eat the flesh of the Son of Man, and drink His blood, you shall not have life in you*** (*St. John* 6:54). A dead soul in a living body can be brought back to life through the Sacrament of Reconciliation. St. Augustine believed that it was a greater miracle to bring a dead soul back to life than restoring life to the dead Lazarus.

The seven sacraments—Baptism, Confirmation, Penance, Holy Eucharist, Matrimony, the Anointing of the Sick, and Holy Orders—are the basis of our Christian life. Three of

---

[1] Dr. Janet E. Smith, "The Sacraments and the Moral Life," *Magnificat,* Vol. 3, No. 8, Oct. 2001, p. 7.

the sacraments, Baptism, Confirmation and Holy Orders, leave a permanent seal on our soul called a character. As such, these sacraments can only be received once. Fr. John Hardon, S.J., points out that these three sacraments actually alter our spiritual personality. We become totally changed individuals through the reception of them. Baptism is the basic sacrament. It is the sacrament of spiritual regeneration. It gives one supernatural life, God's life, the indwelling of the Blessed Trinity. Supernatural means above one's human nature since natural life cannot bring one to heaven.

The Sacraments of Reconciliation and Holy Eucharist on the other hand should be received frequently. Their graces are powerful in helping us to live as followers of Christ. The Sacrament of the Anointing of the Sick can be received when we are chronically ill, seriously ill, elderly, dying or undergoing surgery. The Sacrament of Matrimony can be repeated only if our spouse dies or if our marriage is annulled. These sacraments provide the restoration of God's graces, spiritual growth, healing and endurance.

The sacraments are the means given to us by God to help us to grow holy, to become saints. Each sacrament infuses our souls with sanctifying and special sacramental graces, which are a share in God's life. These graces raise us from a merely human condition to a supernatural condition. Quite frankly, we cannot grow holy or happy without them. Dr. Janet Smith explains why: *The grace of baptism restored order to my soul and permits me to receive more graces; the grace of the Sacrament of Reconciliation frees me from slavery to my own sins; the grace of the Sacrament of Confirmation strengthened my power to endure in seeking and defending what is good; the Eucharist fills my soul with the ineffable intimate union with the divine.*[2]

During these troubling times, it is important to note that the effectiveness of the sacrament in producing graces **does not** depend on the holiness of the priest nor the bishop who administers it. St. Catherine of Siena emphasized, *It is Christ who gives and administers the sacraments to us.*

[2] *Ibid.*

Each time we receive a sacrament we receive varying amounts of sanctifying and sacramental graces. It is vital that each sacrament be received with the right attitude, intention and proper preparation so that we receive as much of God's grace as is available. Why receive a drop when we can, with preparation and proper disposition, receive a bucket of grace?

Along with the graces from the sacraments, we receive an additional infusion of the theological virtues of faith, hope and charity as well as the other infused virtues of prudence, justice, fortitude, temperance, and the gifts of the Holy Spirit (wisdom, understanding, counsel, knowledge, fortitude, piety, and fear of the Lord).[3]

Each sacrament empowers *you* to live an outstanding Christian life. People who frequent the sacraments are more sensitive to living upright lives as well as details of love toward God, Our Lady, and neighbor. They more easily avoid being drawn into the pagan culture around them. In the sacraments you meet Jesus Himself. Besides the sacraments, when you are in the state of sanctifying grace, God also infuses additional graces into your soul when you pray, when you practice acts of penance, as well as when you do good deeds. The more sanctifying grace you possess, the more Christ-like you become, the holier you grow.

The sacraments are outward signs instituted by Christ to give grace. The sacramental sign consists of two elements, the material element (water, bread, wine, oil, etc.), which is called the matter, and the formal element (the words which specify the meaning of the material element), which is called the form.

Two of the sacraments, Baptism and Penance, confer grace on persons who do not already possess sanctifying grace such as a baby in the state of original sin and a person in the state of mortal sin. For this reason they are called the sacraments of the dead (spiritually dead). (The Sacrament of Penance is also received by people in the state of grace.) The other five

---

[3] For a deeper understanding of these virtues read *YOU CAN BECOME A SAINT!* by Mary Ann Budnik.

sacraments are called the sacraments of the living since they should be received in the state of sanctifying grace. The Sacraments can also be categorized as the three sacraments of Christian initiation (Baptism, Confirmation and Holy Eucharist), the two sacraments of healing (Penance and Anointing of the Sick) and *the sacraments at the service of communion and the mission of the faithful* [Matrimony and Holy Orders].[4]

Should a person receive a sacrament of the living in the state of mortal sin, besides committing a sacrilege (a grave mortal sin), no graces or infused virtues are received. In fact, St. Paul tells the Corinthians: *Whoever eats this bread or drinks the cup of the Lord unworthily, will be guilty of the body and the blood of the Lord...For he who eats and drinks unworthily, without distinguishing the body eats and drinks judgment to himself. That is why many among you are infirm and weak, and many sleep.*[5] During the early days of the Church people who received a sacrament in the state of mortal sin were inflicted with sickness and death as a temporal punishment from God.[6] Could this be why we have so many strange illnesses and rare cancers afflicting our population today?

There are special sacramental graces attached to each sacrament to correspond to the different moments in our supernatural journey toward union with God. In Baptism we are born to the supernatural life. In the Sacrament of Confirmation we are strengthened to face temptations in our vocation as well as to live exemplary Christian lives to the point of martyrdom. The Sacrament of the Anointing of the Sick helps us spiritually through the times of illness, surgery, and chronic health problems. At the moment of death it aids us in persevering in holiness to the end.

The Holy Eucharist spiritually nourishes you with the body

---

[4] *Catechism of the Catholic Church* #1211.

[5] 1 *Cor.* 11:26-32.

[6] Footnote in *The New Testament* cv (NY: Benziger Brothers, Inc., 1960) p. 479.

and blood of Jesus Christ so that the Holy Spirit can possess you while your thoughts, words, actions, and feelings become those of Jesus. (This can occur *only* if you cooperate totally with God's graces.)

The Sacrament of Reconciliation or Penance provides us with the spiritual medicine to heal our sinfulness while giving direction on how to get back on the path to holiness. The Sacrament of Holy Orders provides Christ a means to govern, teach, and sanctify us through the work of priests and bishops. In turn, the sacrament gives the priest the grace to fulfill his obligations properly. The Sacrament of Matrimony gives the laity graces to grow holy in marriage and to raise their children to be saints.

Pope John Paul II points out to parents: *Providence has made the family a community of communication with God. Therefore, prayer and the sacraments should find pride of place in family life.* The Holy Father adds, *In this area, good will, even love itself, is not sufficient. For parents it is an ongoing apprenticeship, where with the help of God's grace, they become stronger in their own moral and religious convictions, give good example, and at the same time reflect on, and share, their own experience with other parents, with experts in education, and with priests.*[7]

Why Is Baptism Necessary?

"I think more of the Church of Poissy where I was baptized than I do of the Cathedral of Rheims where I was crowned king. The latter I will lose at death but the former is my passport to eternal life."

St. Louis IX, King of France

Upon the birth of a baby the journey toward sanctity begins in earnest with the incredible gift from God, the Sacrament of Baptism. No other sacrament can be received without the prior reception of Baptism. This is the sacrament that makes your

[7] John Paul II, Address to the 3rd International Congress on the Family, October 30, 1978.

babies children of God by removing original sin and replacing it with God's life, sanctifying grace. Even more, according to Fr. John Hardon, S.J., *Baptism empowers us to believe everything God has revealed, gives the faith to confidently trust in God, and the will to love God above all things.*[8] Wow, please read that last sentence again. This sacrament not only forms the foundation for your faith but it gives you supernatural gifts, instincts and joys. The supernatural gifts are the infused virtues of faith, hope, and charity. Faith helps you to believe all that has been revealed by God. Hope keeps you persevering in the face of difficulties because of your belief in God's mercy. Charity moves you to love God above all, even yourself when you experience suffering. *The cross is the test of our love,* according to Fr. Hardon. *We either pay dearly for our love of God or we don't really love Him.* Charity motivates you to love others more than yourself. At Baptism a child also receives the four cardinal virtues and the gifts of the Holy Spirit. The gifts of the Holy Spirit give one supernatural instincts: *wisdom against folly, understanding against dullness, counsel against rashness, fortitude against fears, knowledge against ignorance, piety against hardness of heart, and fear of the Lord against pride.*[9] Your joy, and that of your children, comes from the twelve fruits of the Holy Spirit which are charity, joy, peace, patience, benignity, goodness, long-suffering, mildness, faith, modesty, continency and chastity. If you truly live a life in Christ you will possess these twelve qualities, since they are the fruit of one's union with Christ. In other words, you and your children will be unselfish, cheerful, relaxed and well-adjusted, even-tempered, kind, thoughtful, just and generous, hopeful, faith-filled, gentle, temperate, chaste and modest. These will be discussed in more depth in regard to the Sacrament of Confirmation.

John Paul II speaking to the youth of the world reminded them of the spiritual responsibilities they received at Baptism: **"You are the salt of the earth..."** *One of the main functions of*

---

[8] Paul Likoudis, *The Wanderer,* no date.

[9] John Hardon, S.J., *The Catholic Catechism* (Garden City: Doubleday & Company, Inc., 1975) p. 200.

salt is to season food, to give it taste and flavor. This image reminds us that, through Baptism, our whole being has been profoundly changed, because it has been "seasoned" with the new life that comes from Christ (cf. **Rom** 6:4). *Writing to the Christians of Rome, St. Paul urges them to show clearly that their way of living and thinking is different from that of their contemporaries:* **"Do not be conformed to this world, but be transformed by the renewal of your mind, that you may discern what is the will of God, what is good and pleasing and perfect** (**Rom**. 12:2).[10]

Since most Christians are baptized as infants they cannot explain the dramatic transformation that takes place but ask a convert. Adult converts have excitedly explained to me how baptism improved their personalities and changed their way of thinking. They could actually sense the infusion of the theological virtues of faith, hope, and charity and the cardinal virtues of prudence, justice, fortitude and temperance. They were aware of receiving the seven gifts of the Holy Spirit. St. Augustine saw this dramatic change in his dear friend who partook in his debauchery prior to his Baptism. Some in the early Church thought it better to have people baptized after adolescence or when in danger of death. The reasoning for this was that since the environment was pagan, young people tended to easily fall into serious sin. It was thought better for them to sin as a catechumen than as a Christian. Augustine later fought against this erroneous teaching. When Augustine's friend was near death, he was baptized. After his Baptism the young man seemed to recover. He was told of his Baptism and the obligations he was now obliged to live. Augustine, visiting the invalid, made jest of his Baptism. His friend stopped him in mid sentence. He told Augustine that if they were to remain fast friends than Augustine would have to respect the fact that he was now a practicing Christian. He would no longer be part of Augustine's sinful lifestyle. Furthermore, if Augustine continued to make fun of his faith, their friendship was over. Augustine laughed then left him. That night his friend died.

---

[10] Zenit, Aug. 2, 2001.

262 *Raise Happy Children...Raise Them Saints!*

Augustine never forgave himself for his conduct toward his dying friend.

Pope Paul VI explains: *Those who are baptized and by means of this sacrament are incorporated into the Mystical body of Christ, which is the Church,* **must give the greatest importance to this event.** *They must be very much aware of being raised to a higher condition, of being reborn to a supernatural life, there to experience the happiness of being adopted sons of God, the special dignity of being brothers of Christ, the blessedness, the grace and the joy of the indwelling of the Holy Spirit. They have truly been called to a new kind of life, but they have lost nothing of their own humanity except the unhappy state of original sin.*

Rather, whatever is human is now capable of the finest manifestations of perfection and of producing the most precious and holiest fruits. To be a Christian, to have received holy Baptism must not be looked upon as something indifferent or of little importance. It must be imprinted deeply and joyously on the conscience of every baptized person. He must look upon it, as did the early Christians, as an illumination which draws upon his soul the life-giving radiance of divine Truth, opens heaven to him, sheds light upon earthly life and enables him to walk as a child of the light towards the vision of God, the wellspring of eternal happiness.[11]

The Sacrament of Baptism incorporates a person into the Catholic Church including non-Catholic Christians although they do not belong in a visible way. All the graces of Christ's redemption are channeled through the Catholic Church. For a deeper understanding of this read **Dominus Iesus** by John Paul II.

When Should A Baby Be Baptized?

Louis Martin, the father of St. Thérèse, was baptized immediately upon his birth. Zélie Martin was baptized the day after her birth. Each of their children was baptized either on the day of birth or the day after, no later.

[11] Paul VI, *Encyclical Ecclesiam Suam*, n. 39.

St. John Vianney was baptized within hours of being born, as was St. Maximilian Kolbe, St. Teresa of Avila, and Bl. Pius Campidelli. St. Louis De Montfort was christened the day after his birth. St. Margaret Mary Alacoque was baptized three days after her birth. The Escrivás baptized St. Josemaría four days after his birth. Bl. Zeferino Agostini was also christened four days after his birth. Why was there such a sense of urgency in the parents of saints that their children were baptized immediately? These parents understood the incredible value of sanctifying grace, which is God's life within a soul. You see, there is an infinite difference between a person in the state of grace and a person not in the state of grace. For the sake of analogy the vast separation that exists between a person in grace and one who is not in grace is like the difference between a person and an ant.

The greatest gift you can give your children is to make them children of God within a week or so after their births. To delay baptism any longer is morally wrong besides being spiritually dangerous.

The **Catholic Catechism** #1250 notes *The Church and the parents would deny a child the priceless grace of becoming a child of God were they not to confer Baptism shortly after birth.* The **Code of Canon Law** is even more explicit:

#867: Parents are obliged to see to it that infants are baptized within the first weeks after birth; as soon as possible after the birth or even before it parents are to go to the pastor to request the sacrament for their child and to be properly prepared for it. An infant in danger of death is to be baptized without any delay.

God gives you nine months to prepare for the birth and Baptism of your baby. As soon as you learn you are expecting, call your parish to find out the requirements for Baptism. If classes are required take them immediately. Do not postponement them until after your baby's birth.

In the past it was the custom of not even permitting an unbaptized baby to leave home except for his Baptism for fear

264 *Raise Happy Children...Raise Them Saints!*

the child would be killed in an accident or die from catching an illness. What happens to an unbaptized baby who dies? The *Catechism of the Catholic Church* teaches:

> **#1261: As regards *children who have died without Baptism,* the Church can only entrust them to the mercy of God...Indeed, the great mercy of God who desires that all men should be saved, and Jesus' tenderness toward children which caused him to say: "Let the children come to me, do not hinder them," allow us to hope that there is a way of salvation for children who have died without Baptism. All the more urgent is the Church's call not to prevent little children coming to Christ through the gift of holy Baptism.**

Parents of the saints feared the possibility of a child dying without Baptism. Zélie Martin explained in a letter to her brother: *Whatever you say, we shall have another child...But if God wills once more to take this one from me, I pray that it may not die unbaptized, so that at least I may have the comfort of three little angels in Heaven."*

The question of infants dying without baptism troubled St. Thomas Aquinas. Where did the souls of these children go? *St. Thomas taught that limbo is a place of perfect natural happiness, but minus the supernatural vision of God to which, of course, no creature has a natural right,* according to Fr. John Hardon, S.J.[12] This is one of the reasons that abortion, as well as the modern contraception drugs such as "the pill" which cause chemical abortions and in vitro fertilization are so terribly wrong.

On a plane, I met a fallen away Catholic who was struggling to come back to the Church. As we discussed religion the woman explained how she was praying to understand grace. One Sunday she attended a Mass where a baby was baptized. She watched with keen interest trying to understand the ritual. At the moment the priest poured the water over the baby's head and said the words, *I baptize you in the name of the Father,*

---

[12] *The Catholic Catechism, Op. Cit.,* p. 510.

and of the Son, and of the Holy Spirit, this woman saw a shower of gold dust descend upon the baby. After asking others around her, she discovered that only she was privilege to see grace represented as gold.

Some Catholic couples have the mistaken idea that to baptize a child takes away the freedom of the child to decide in the future his own spiritual path. But let's face it, parents presume on the freedom of their children when they insist they eat and sleep, get medical check-ups, force them to wear coats and boots, and even go to school. This is all done for the good of the child. That is why God gave children parents. Children need someone to care for them until they are old enough to be able to care for themselves. It is the same in the matter of faith. By having your children baptized into a life of grace, you help your children to use their freedom to avoid sin and to reach their human and supernatural potential, which is the very purpose of freedom.

The Sacrament of Baptism is rich with meaning and symbolism. Unfortunately if the baby is fussy or if there are a lot of little toddlers among the guests the beautiful prayers and meanings may not be fully understood amid the confusion. For this reason I am summarizing them. Note what the priest asks the parents and the godparents:

You have come here to present this child for baptism. By water and the Holy Spirit he/she is to receive the gift of new life from God, who is love.

On your part, you must make it your constant care to bring him/her up in the practice of the faith. See that the divine life which God gives him/her is kept safe from the poison of sin, to grow always stronger in his/her heart.

If your faith makes you ready to accept this responsibility, renew now the vows of your own baptism. Reject sin; profess your faith in Christ Jesus. This is the faith of the Church. This is the faith in which this child is about to be baptized.

After the baby is baptized the priest anoints the child with sacred chrism saying ...*As Christ was anointed Priest, Prophet, and King, so may you live always as a member of His body, sharing everlasting life.* Next the child is clothed in a white garment: *See in this white garment the outward sign of your Christian dignity. With your family and friends to help you by work and example, bring that dignity unstained into the everlasting life of heaven.* A candle is lit from the Easter candle. This candle is given to the father or godfather with the priest exhorting *Parents and godparents, this light [which represents Christ] is entrusted to you to be kept burning brightly. This child of yours has been enlightened by Christ. He/she is to walk always as a child of the light. May he/she keep the flame of faith alive in his/her heart. When the Lord comes, may he/she go out to meet Him with all the saints in the heavenly kingdom.* The priest next touches the ears and mouth of the child: *The Lord Jesus made the deaf hear and the dumb speak. May He soon touch your ears to receive His word, and your mouth to proclaim His faith, to the praise and glory of God the Father. Amen.*

The Baptism ceremony underlines the task of the parents and the godparents to raise the child to be a saint. The Church teaches that the godparent *represents the family, forming a kind of spiritual extension of it, as well as representing Mother Church; when necessary the godparent helps the parents to ensure that the child comes to profess and live the faith.*[13]

Since this is such an awesome responsibility, choose the godparents carefully. The role of a godparent is not just a ceremonial one; it is an important spiritual role. It is not an honor to be bestowed as a "thank-you" or to charm a favorite relative or friend. Fr. Raoul Plus, S.J., warns: *Men and women who have held children at the baptismal font, I remind you that you will have to render an account of them before God.*[14]

The role of a godparent is to help *you* to raise your child a saint. Choose someone who loves the Catholic faith, practices it fervently, and who will be praying daily for your child. Select people who share your belief that the Catholic faith is your child's most treasured possession. Choose someone your child

[13] Congregation for Divine Worship, *Ordo initiationis Christianae, Praenotanda generalia,* no. 8.
[14] Raoul Plus, S.J., *Christ In The Home* (NY:Frederick Pustet Co., 1951) p. 340.

can go to with questions about the faith. Such a person was chosen for the godfather of St. Thérèse's grandfather, Pierre Martin. It was his uncle, Francois Bohard, who during the French Revolution hid the church bells in his home at the risk of his life. Blessed Pope John XXIII's godfather was his great-uncle Zaverio Roncalli. It was this godfather who influenced the future pope's spiritual formation.

If you are a godparent, pray daily for your godchild. Send gifts that reinforce the Catholic faith such as books on the lives of the saints, a crucifix, a statue of Our Lady, a rosary, a bible, a scapular or four-way medal. Keep in touch with them over the years with notes and special gifts for their First Communion, Confirmation and wedding. Let them know how important the faith is to you. If possible discuss the faith with them via letter, E-mail or phone if you live a distance away.

At the beginning of the Jubilee Year John Paul II baptized 18 babies from eight countries in the Sistine Chapel. He told the parents: *These little ones must find in you, as well as their godfathers and godmothers, support and guidance in the road of fidelity to Christ and the Gospel. Be an example of solid faith, profound prayer, and active commitment in ecclesial life to them.*[15]

The Next Step Is First Confession

When asked by her interrogators if she was in the state of grace, nineteen-year-old St. Joan of Arc replied: *"If I am not, may God put me there; and if I am, may God so keep me. I should be the saddest creature in the world if I knew I were not in His grace."*

Although Baptism restores the life of grace within our souls that original sin destroyed, we are left with four penalties: inordinate desires (concupiscence), sickness, bodily death, and a darkened intellect for knowing the truth about God and His Son. The irrational desires move us to offend God. These offenses are called sins. St. Teresa of Avila asks, *why can we*

---

[15] Zenit. Jan. 9, 2000.

not realize that sin is a pitched battle fought against God with all of the senses and faculties of the soul; the prouder the soul is, the more ways it invents to betray its King. Cardinal Joseph Ratzinger adds, *sin is by nature a departure from the truth of one's own nature and, by consequence, from the truth of the Creator God.*

When we sin we "feel" guilty. But guilt is not simply a "feeling." It is the objective loss of God's grace. This guilt causes anxiety, unhappiness, discouragement and sometimes despair. This feeling of guilt for offending God is programmed into our very nature. My sister-in-law, Mary, told her three-year-old daughter, Eileen, that she could not have any more cookies. But when Mary left the room, Eileen grabbed another cookie. Afterwards Eileen's conscience began to bother her. Before she went to bed she quietly took her father aside and whispered, *Mom told me "no more cookies" but I accidentally took one.* Just as telling her father about the cookie brought peace to her little soul, the Sacrament of Reconciliation removes that terrible feeling of guilt in our souls and replaces it with peace and joy. Eileen's brother, Patrick, when he was four was troubled by something. When his parents took their older children to confession he asked if he could go in and talk to the priest too. He came out of the confessional smiling. That's the great gift of peace that God has bequeathed to us. A priest related how he went through a fast food drive-in one day. As he pulled up to pay at the window, the young man saw that he was a priest and exclaimed, *Father, I need to go to confession. What with 9-11 and all that's happening in the world I want to make peace with God. I've done some terrible things in my life. Do you think God will forgive me?* There is a human need to confess one's sins as well as the need for reassurance that one is forgiven. This can only be given through the Sacrament of Penance.

Besides taking away guilt, confession is a means to grow holy, to become a saint. It trains us in self-knowledge, to know our vices. It motivates us to replace our vices with the corresponding virtues therefore making virtue easier to live. In fact, the virtues that God wants us to acquire are precisely the remedy to the vices (sins) we commit most frequently. The frequent reception of the sacrament also makes us humble. This helps us to conquer our pride. It teaches us to grow in patience. This helps us to bear the pain and contradictions of life. It leads us to become more prayerful because we realize that we need the assistance of God. We are more submissive to the inspirations of the Holy Spirit. The more we use the sacrament, not only do we become more sinless but we likewise become more Christ-like. The reverse is also true. There is no growth in sanctity if there is no growth in our sense of sinfulness. *Penance, the sacrament of Christ's peace—is a powerful channel of grace given to the Church by Jesus, and the more often an individual receives this sacrament, the more he experiences both inner peace and Christian joy,* according to Fr. John Hardon, S.J.[16]

All the Popes of the last century stressed the importance of frequent confession. Pope Pius XII insisted that frequent confession increased grace, strengthened the will, corrected bad habits, purified conscience, increased self-control, resisted spiritual neglect and tepidity, and increased genuine self-knowledge. Let's briefly consider these benefits. When you sin you lose some or all of God's grace depending on the gravity of the sin. Through the Sacrament of Reconciliation you restore and can even increase grace in your soul according to your disposition when you receive the sacrament. You become more Christ-like. Confession strengthens your will by giving you more courage to do God's will rather than your own will. On a purely natural level it can take years to correct the vices of your personality but with God's grace and your cooperation they can be corrected more swiftly. By purifying your conscience you can see clearly what should be done in a specific situation and then how to do it. Once your conscience is purified you can react almost without reflection because the gift of counsel is free to operate. As you grow in self-control you can more easily master your thoughts and actions so that they are in accord with the will of God. Remember, repeated actions lead to a habit. A good habit is a virtue. A bad habit is a vice. Each

---

[16] Paul Likoudis, *The Wanderer,* no date.

person needs self-knowledge because we are blind to our own failings. Only with self-knowledge can you determine what your vices are and how you have to work to overcome them. Self-knowledge is the ability to see yourself through the eyes of God. For self-knowledge you need the humility you develop through your preparation for confession. This preparation shows how weak and stupid one is in the face of temptation. It gives the Holy Spirit a chance to influence you. The Holy Spirit is constantly speaking to us but our minds are usually set on ourselves rather than on God so we miss these inspirations.

The Popes have all encouraged frequent confession. How often is "frequent confession"? For some people frequent confession is weekly, for others twice a month or monthly. Personally I find weekly confession beneficial not only for myself but for family harmony. When family members are "filled with grace" life runs smoother and everyone is happier.

Begin to prepare your child for the Sacrament of Reconciliation between the ages of five and six. With the use of reason, which means the understanding of right and wrong, moral life begins. This awakening of the moral life does not "happen" at a precise age but rather develops over time with physical maturity, along with the example of parents, siblings, neighbors and the child's schooling. Each child matures at his or her own pace.

As a parent, one of your most serious duties is to closely follow your children's development. What are their problems? How can you help them to find solutions to these problems? By carefully overseeing your children's development you can guide them in the formation of their consciences as to right and wrong, good and evil. Take advantage of the first lies, temper tantrums, jealousies, arguments and small thefts in the home to teach children the difference between good and evil. The daily events of family life are important opportunities to initiate children into the moral life.

The document, ***Gravissimun educationis,*** from Vatican II emphasizes that parents are to teach their children how *to make* *sound moral judgments based on a well-formed conscience and to put them into practice with a sense of personal commitment, and also how to know and love God more.* Teaching your children the Ten Commandments does this. Explain what each means along with the moral teachings of the Church. In the book of **Deuteronomy** (6:2-8) we are told that those who keep the commandments will have their days prolonged. God urges that we keep His law so *that all may be well with you, and you may be greatly multiplied* and brought to the land of milk and honey.

Sometimes children, particularly teens, view the commandments as God's means to curtail their personal freedom. Nothing can be further from the truth. Since original sin, our world has become a minefield of sin. The commandments and the moral teachings of the Church are maps that locate the "mines" that could destroy your soul and body. If you carefully follow the map God gives you out of love, you will avoid physically and spiritually destroying yourself. Sin may look appealing and fun. Yet when you sin, sooner or later you have to face the horrible consequences of your actions. This involves intense suffering—most likely on earth, other times in purgatory or in hell. If you follow God's map, and try to avoid the mines, you may also have to suffer, but this suffering is different. There is no remorse, nor regret. It's a suffering that brings interior joy and peace. St. Josemaría Escrivá wrote: *You need a heart which is in love, not an easy life, to achieve happiness.*[17]

Explain to your children that they are to conform their lives to God's law because it is given to them out of love...to save them from needless suffering and pain. Point out to them that they will never be happy if they violate God's law. Sin always brings sorrow in its wake, never happiness and joy. If your children do not live by the Ten Commandments not only will they become severely dysfunctional but also your family will become dysfunctional. An example of this is found in a "light" novel I selected to take on vacation. The book told the story of

[17] *Furrow, Op. Cit.,* #795.

four generations of wealthy women who spent their summers in a colony on the coast of Maine. Billed as a bestseller I found the book appalling. While the author indicated that her characters were everyday "lovely" people, there was not a single major character that had any morals. The people depicted were not simply immoral but amoral. There was no such thing as right or wrong except for keeping up appearances. The hero died after cursing out a Protestant minister for trying to save him through Baptism. His family and friends were thrilled he had not been cowed into "salvation." Yet these same characters led the most pitiful, dysfunctional, unhappy lives, which ended in miserable deaths...all because they refused to know God and follow His moral law. While the book could be taken as an example of *see what happens if you don't obey the Ten Commandments,* that was not the author's point. From her characters, story, tone and conclusion, she appears to have rejected God, along with all the goodness, truth, and joy morality brings.

John Paul II explained: ...*[T]he Ten commandments open before us the only authentically human future, because they are not the arbitrary imposition of a tyrannical God. Yahweh wrote them in stone, but He inscribed them above all in the human heart as the universal moral law, valid and current in every place and time. This law prevents egotism and hatred, lying and contempt, which destroy the human person. The Ten Commandments, with their constant recalling of the divine covenant, show that the Lord is our only God, and that every other divinity is false and ends up reducing the human being to slave, making him degrade his own dignity...*

...*[F]rom the time the Word of God took flesh and died on the cross for us, we hear the Ten Commandments through His voice. Jesus makes the Ten Commandments take root in the hearts of those who believe in Him by means of the new life of Grace. However, Jesus' disciples did not feel oppressed by a multitude of prescriptions, but, compelled by the force of love, they recognized God's Commandments as a law of freedom: freedom to love, thanks to the interior action of the Spirit.*[18]

---

[18] General Audience, March 1, 2000.

Discuss with your children what each commandment, work of mercy and the commandment of the Church means pertinent to their age. The book of **Deuteronomy** 6:7 counsels: **Talk about them when you sit at home and when you walk along the road, when you lie down and when you get up.**

As the children mature, deepen their understanding for each commandment. For instance the fifth commandment for five-year-olds would include killing, but it also includes anger, fighting, or hurting someone by hitting, pinching, slapping, spitting, or name-calling. By 5th grade the child should understand that this commandment forbids the peddling of drugs, the use of drugs or any other harmful substances such as glue sniffing, etc. 7th-8th graders should understand that this commandment forbids suicide, the underage use of alcohol, drunkenness, along with daring friends to do something dangerous. A person between the ages of 8th grade to adult needs to understand that this commandment forbids the use of contraceptives, the "morning after pill," RU-486, in vitro fertilization, willfully endangering another's life by passing on diseases such as HIV or other sexually transmitted diseases, procuring an abortion, helping someone procure an abortion, voting for abortion candidates or harming another in any manner. It also forbids endangering another's life by driving under the influence of alcohol or at excessive speeds. Maiming oneself or injuring another through premeditated activity such as gang initiation or witchcraft is also included under this commandment. Tattooing and body piercing, as mentioned before, disfigures the body, which is the temple of the Holy Spirit, along with exposing the person to the AIDS virus.

Our understanding of the Catholic Faith can never be stagnant. Develop a hunger in your children to learn more about the faith by showing them how you are continually learning more about the faith. Discuss the immorality of cloning, "designer babies," stem cell research on aborted babies.

Teach your children about sin, Satan and temptations. Give them advice not only on how to avoid temptations but how to fight temptations. Remind them that *demonic temptation can take place at various levels. The most elementary level is the sharp, one-time enticement which eventually passes, either because it is successfully resisted or eventually given in to,* writes Fr. Michael Scanlon, T.O.R. *...Evil spirits like to get involved in the little things of the day because they can lead to bigger things. Small irritations can escalate into anger and frustration. Disappointment can become envy and self-pity...Through them, evil spirits can keep Christians' lives off balance, stifle their relationships, and move them toward more opportunities to sin.*[19]

St. Peter Julian Eymard also warns that *he who aspires to holiness must expect to run into temptations and storms...[Y]ou say "But formerly I was not tempted in this way!" It is true. But the devil did not fear you then. Do not be frightened...if your temptations increase in direct proportion to your fervor in the service of God. If we were to look for something to glory about it should be this: that since the devil attacks us, we must be worth attacking.*[20]

Next teach your children the difference about a mortal and a venial sin. A *venial sin* is an offense against God that does not deprive your souls of sanctifying grace. Should you die with only venial sins on your soul you go to Purgatory. A sin can be venial when the evil done is not seriously wrong or when the evil done is seriously wrong, but the sinner sincerely believes it is only slightly wrong, or does not give full consent to it. A "white lie" is a venial sin because it is not seriously wrong. Refusing to forgive someone is seriously wrong but you may not realize the gravity of what you are doing.

People have the mistaken idea that venial sins are not something to avoid or to be concerned about, yet they hamper your spiritual growth. You give in more easily to temptations. You become spiritually lazy and lukewarm. The work of the Holy Spirit is obstructed in your soul. Not only that, venial sin weakens your wills. You become reluctant to do works of

---

[19] Fr. Michael Scanlon, TOR and Randall J. Cirner, *Deliverance From Evil Spirits* (Ann Arbor: Servant, 1980).

[20] St. Peter Julian Eymard, *In The Light Of The Monstrance* (Cleveland: Emmanuel Publications, 1947) pp. 7-8.

charity or works of service for family or neighbor. Your vices strengthen so that it is easier for you to fall into mortal sin. *Small sins pave the way for more serious ones....No one becomes wicked all at once.*[21] One becomes evil little by little. While venial sins may not be seen to "be a big deal" St. Peter Eymard writes how deadly they are to spiritual growth:

✓ Venial sin paralyzes God's power over our soul...God can do nothing with one whose conscience cherishes an affection for venial sin, for it is then impossible for Him to join His power to our power, His action to our action.

✓ Venial sin checks the flow of God's goodness...God simply cannot bestow His grace on someone who by his actions tells Him: "I do not want it."

✓ Venial sin thwarts actual grace, without which we cannot act supernaturally...Actual grace is a light...[which] repeatedly offers to enlighten our intelligence...But if we lock all the doors of our soul, the light of grace will not enter within. Actual grace is also a quickening warmth by which God means to soften our will and to move it gently in order to incline it to His wishes. But sin prevents the divine warmth from reaching our hearts. Actual grace is also the action of the Holy Ghost by which He renovates and maintains in us the life of Jesus Christ. He tells us: "With the help of my grace perform this or that good deed, make this or that sacrifice. Let us work together..." But sin rejects this love-inspired offer...Thus venial sin is the ruin of actual grace. It first hampers its action, then destroys it; it keeps Jesus Christ at the door of the soul; by degrees it ruins also habitual grace.[22]

Recall how St. Teresa of Avila was shown the place reserved for her in hell because of her indifference to venial sins! (These habitual venial sins would eventually have led her to commit mortal sins.)

Mortal sin, on the other hand, is a much graver offense against God. In **The Splendor Of Truth**, the Holy Father quoting

---

[21] *Christ Is Passing By, Op. Cit.,* #178.
[22] *In The Light Of The Monstrance, Op. Cit.,* pp. 16-20.

from the Council of Trent teaches that: *"...[M]ortal sin is sin whose object is grave matter and which is also committed with full knowledge and deliberate consent."*[23]

By committing a mortal sin a person loses sanctifying grace (God's life) within his soul. In other words, **mortal sin causes spiritual death.** We lose all supernatural merit for any good actions that we do while in the state of mortal sin. In addition, we allow ourselves to be manipulated by the tyrannical rule of Satan. Our natural inclination towards virtue is weakened. The sinner becomes more inclined to sin and less inclined to what is good. Passions become stronger and the power of the will weaker, debilitating even further the harmony that should exist between intellect, will and appetites. Mortal sin removes our interior peace. Suddenly there is inner conflict, remorse, unrest, discontentment, and turmoil. One cannot lose the life of God within and still maintain interior peace and joy. Eventually mortal sin can even cause mental and physical illnesses. The final effect of mortal sin is the separation of the sinner from his fellow Christians and mankind in general. Should we die in the state of mortal sin without asking God's forgiveness, we would spend eternity in Hell. To choose to commit a mortal sin is a **deadly** decision.

Impress upon your children the importance of saying a perfect act of contrition then going to confession *immediately* should they fall into mortal sin so as to restore sanctifying grace to their dead souls. Stress that death can come at any moment so why take a chance of spending eternity in hell? Sometimes a teen or child may delay going to confession thinking, "I'm not going to die soon." True, maybe he won't die soon, but if he is in the state of unrepentant mortal sin he is already spiritually dead. Bishop George Lucas observed that *God has willed the salvation of every person, in Jesus Christ, and so we might talk about a place reserved in heaven, knowing it is possible for any of us to give up the reservation.*

Only God knows the moment He will call us. The confession that is put off may be your child's last opportunity. Look at

---

[23] n. 70.

Tammy Wynette. She died in her mid-fifties taking a nap. Princess Diana died in her mid 30's while on a romantic date. Sony Bono and a Kennedy died on the ski slopes, John Kennedy, Jr. died in an airplane crash on his way to his cousin's wedding. John Denver also died flying his plane. Tornadoes, earthquakes, floods, storms, accidents, fires, terrorist attacks and gas explosions are killing people suddenly everyday. Right before Martin Luther died, he asked for a priest. Unfortunately, he died while the priest was bounding up the stairs to hear his confession.

We do not know the length of our lives nor the manner of our deaths so we must be prepared to meet God at all times. Each day we should live as though we were going to meet Him tonight. One pastor in Indiana is so concerned about his teens that he actually carries a beeper with him. A teen can beep him anytime day or night and he will come to hear his or her confession.

Likewise, teach your children that they cannot live in the state of mortal sin and still think that they can grow in holiness. It's impossible. Christ tells us in the Gospel that we cannot serve two masters.

Explain to your children that as they struggle to grow in holiness, each action should begin with the thought, does this please or offend God? What would Jesus do now? If they develop this habit, their conscience will quickly point out to them any sinful thoughts, words, actions and omissions. Do not permit your children to become cafeteria Catholics who pick and choose what they consider to be sins. Point out that when we read the Gospel passages during Holy Week, we recoil at Judas' betrayal of Jesus. Yet, don't we act like Judas when we pick certain commandments or teachings to accept and reject those that are more demanding of us? If we love God, we cannot put limits on our love. It's an all or nothing proposition with Him! St. Josemaría points out: ...[S]in is the fruit of selfishness, and selfishness is the root of sadness.[24]

During night prayers read or improvise an examination of

---

[24] *Christ Is Passing By, Op. Cit.,* #178.

conscience for your children. This acts as a reminder of how they should be behaving while helping to prepare them for their next confession.[25] One friend has twin daughters. Each night following prayers, she goes through a short examination of conscience. If she forgets, her daughters remind her. She asks such questions as: *Did I say my morning prayers? Did I talk in Church? Did I lie? Did I obey my parents? My teacher? Did I do what I was asked to do promptly or did I put it off? Did I fight with my brothers/sisters, parents, or friends? Did I use bad language? Did I do my homework well? Did I talk back to my parents?* Gear the questions to the children's personalities, ages and particular exams. Write down simple questions for their age level and then read them or let each of the children take a turn reading them while the other children silently reflect on each question. Encourage your children, before you begin, to use the examination of conscience to make a resolution to improve tomorrow. After the examination of conscience pray the *Act of Contrition* with the children.

One family has the custom of giving a gift to Our Lady every day. At the end of the day each child writes on a slip of paper what he or she had done for Mary and slips it under her statue. One day, one of the little boys was a terror yet at the end of the day he put a slip under the statue of Our Lady. His mother couldn't believe that he had the audacity to write something down as a gift for Our Lady so she pulled his slip out of the pile to see what he wrote. He had written, *Mary, I have nothing to give to you today but hopefully tomorrow I will.* This is the type of resolution we want to instill in our children.

By the particular exam I mean the area in which the child needs to devote particular attention. One child might have a fiery temper, another a moody disposition, the third could have a critical nature, the fourth a stubborn nature. Work individually with each child to help him discover his main defect. Then with the child's input devise a plan to help him overcome this defect. We all have one major passion that tends

---

[25] For more information on this and other aspects of confession read, *Looking for Peace? Try Confession!* by this author.

to rule our personalities. Uncertain how to approach this? Take each child and his spiritual concerns to your mental prayer. Ask the Holy Spirit to enlighten you in discerning how best to help each child to grow more pleasing to God. When praying in this manner, you will usually not get an immediate response during your prayer. But as you continue with your day, God will inspire you with His advice.

The purpose of the examination is to help them form a sound conscience,not to make them scrupulous. Instill in your children the idea that **they have to dare to be different.** They have to go against the prevailing culture and mores of the day. In a world that is drowning in sin, the humanists tell us that sin does not exist. Help your children to realize that personal sin does exist, teach them what it is, then how to avoid it. When they do fall they can get help through the Sacrament of Confession. If they learn this lesson when they are young, your children will develop the courage to stand up for the truth and the moral law as well as the fortitude to be different. This has to be fed to your children with as much determination as you put into feeding them dinner each night. If you start when your children are young by explaining why they cannot watch certain TV shows, movies or videos, or subscribe to some magazine, or listen to specific rock groups, you will be helping them to develop fortitude and courage. If you wait until they go away to college, your children may be lost.

Continually guide your children in the ways of God, like the mother of St. Martin De Porres. St. Martin, a mulatto, was the object of racist attacks. When he complained to his mother, she brushed off the incidents by saying, *Just keep your soul white and shining. That is all that matters.*

What Age For First Confession?

While seven years is the traditional age of reason, many children attain the age of reason much younger. If a child is ready at the age of six, take him to confession. St. Escrivá, who heard the first confessions of hundreds of children, felt that many children were mature enough to make their first confession at the age of six. One five-year-old little girl who accompanied her older sisters to confession was upset that she could not go. She told her mother, *I tell lies too!* This indicated to the mother the little girl was ready to make her first confession. St. Escrivá recalls: *[I went] for hours and hours all over the place, every day, on foot, from one area to another, among poor people ashamed of their poverty and poor people too miserable to be ashamed, who had nothing at all. Among children with runny noses—dirty, but children, which means souls pleasing to God. How indignant I feel in my priestly soul when they say that small children should not go to confession! That's not true! They should make their personal confession, speaking one on one to the priest in secret, just like everyone else. What good, what joy it brings them! I spent many hours in that work, and I'm only sorry that it was not more.*[26]

You do not have to wait until the traditional age of seven years or until the Catholic school prepares your child. When you feel that your child understands right and wrong, can pray the *Creed*, and the *Act of Contrition*, can recite the Ten Commandments and understand the concept of offending God (sin), the child is ready to make his first confession. Why delay the infusion of grace into the soul of your child? It was the Fourth Lateran Council that proclaimed that *all the faithful of both sexes, once they have reached the age of reason, should confess their sins faithfully to a priest at least once a year and strive to the best of their ability to fulfill the penance imposed on them.*[27] John Paul II adds: *In fact, apart from the question of the age necessary for committing a serious sin—and it should not be forgotten that the tendency to postpone this age for too long also implies an excessive lack of confidence in the capacity of good of the developing child—it remains true that even the lesser grades of moral evil have their importance, which is even more significant if considered within the educational perspective of a journey of human and Christian growth.*[28]

[26] *The Founder Of Opus Dei, Op. Cit.*, p. 209.

[27] Fourth Lateran Council, ch. 21, Dz 437 (812).

[28] John Paul II, Address to the plenary session of the Congregation for the Sacraments, April 17, 1986.

In some areas of the country there is confusion whether a child should make his first confession before or after First Communion. St. Pius X condemned *the practice that prevails in some places, of prohibiting from sacramental confession, or not giving absolution to, children who have not yet made their first communion. Thus it happens that they, perhaps having fallen into serious sin, remain in that very dangerous state for a long time.*[29] In 1973 the Holy See issued a reminder to parents and pastors that the rule decreed by St. Pius X was to be adhered to everywhere and by everyone.[30]

Explain to your children that they give Jesus joy when they express their sorrow for their sins in confession. Introduce your pre-schoolers to the priest in confession so that they can see that the priest is their friend and not someone to fear. I overheard one young mother telling her three-year-old, *Let's go into the confessional now because the priest is going to help Mommy.* When children begin at a young age to say "hello" to Father in the confessional and as they grow older chat with him, the first confession does not provoke any trauma. Rather than being a dreaded event for our daughters, they *loved* going to confession and talking things over with "Father." In fact, one day their zeal became downright embarrassing. As I left the confessional, I found Mary Kate and Marianne in hand-to-hand combat, wrestling on the ground in front of the confessional. The fight was over who got to go in next!

John Paul II reiterated: *The joyous and liberating nature of this sacrament, in which the victorious love of the risen Christ is expressed, is not always sufficiently perceived. The believer who goes to confession with the right dispositions does not experience a justice that condemns, but a Love that pardons. In the warm light of Christ's love, he learns to know better his own weaknesses, the deficiencies of his own temperament and the complex implications of his own shortcomings. Nor need one fear that this might lead to frustrations or traumas, since in the very act*

---

[29] St. Pius X, Decr. *Quam singulari,* August 8, 1910.

[30] Cf Congregation for the Sacraments and Congregation for the Clergy, Declaration, Mar. 24, 1973.

in which the penitent discovers the dimensions of his own culpability he is faced also with a renewed experience of the patient and powerful mercy of his Lord.

If this is the reality of the situation, who can fail to see the great help that even children can draw from an appropriate administration of this sacrament for a progressive and harmonious growth in self-knowledge and self-control, and in their ability to accept themselves with their own limitations, without however being passively resigned to them?[31]

In addition, when family members frequent confession together or individually there is more peace and harmony within the family. In my book ***Looking For Peace? Try Confession!*** I explain the "confession curve." My older daughters were five and six years old when I was introduced to the benefits of weekly confession. Since the eldest was very precocious, we spent our days locked in a perpetual battle of wills. After consulting with the priest, and preparation, Mary Kate made her first confession when she was six. After seeing the wonderful effects of confession on our relationship, this custom of age 6 for first confession became a family tradition.

Weekly confession caused such a radical change in our family life that my husband could tell which day we went the moment he walked in from work. His first comment would be, *You went to confession today, didn't you?* Frankly, I did find that a bit irritating but the changes in personalities, cooperation, peace, and kindness <u>were</u> noticeable. We could actually <u>see</u> the effects of sacramental and sanctifying grace; this is because the Sacrament of Penance not only forgives sins, it also gives us a specific grace to overcome the faults we confess. We even began discussing the "confession curve." The curve was at its peak the moment we left the church. As the days passed, the curve rapidly swung downward until it was time again for weekly confession. While I was tempted to skip a week for myself, I did not want to lose the family benefits by letting the girls skip a week. This custom of frequent confession is still practiced by

[31] John Paul II, Address to the plenary session of the Congregation for the Sacraments, April 17, 1986.

our daughters who are now adults. It simply became part of their lives.

When a person develops the habit of going to confession weekly as a child, it is natural to continue to receive the sacrament during the turbulent teen years and the "free at last" college years. Weekly confession is the greatest safeguard of your children's chastity. It also protects your youth against drug use, drunkenness, and suicide. Besides this, weekly confession helps parents and teens accept each other and work together more smoothly, thereby guaranteeing family harmony. Family controversies or problems can be resolved in the confessional. Several years ago, friends were having conflicts with their eldest daughter, who was in college. The young woman agreed to go to confession and discuss the situation with the priest. As she began her confession, there was a terrifying crash of thunder that shook the church. That was the moment of her conversion! The scare, combined with the priest's advice, restored peace in her family. John Paul II pointed out that *The celebration of this sacrament acquires special significance for family life. While they discover in faith that sin is contrary not only to the covenant with God, but also to the covenant between husband and wife and the communion of the family, the married couple and the other members of the family are led to an encounter with God, who is "rich in mercy" (**Eph** 2:4), who bestows on them His love which is more powerful than sin (cf **Enc. Dives in misericordia**,13), and who reconstructs and brings to perfection the marriage covenant and family communion.*[32]

The Sacrament of Confession enables our intellect to function more readily. St. John Bosco, in his training of young boys, insisted that each boy begin his education by first going to confession. Remember, sin dulls the intellect. So if your children are facing big tests or important examinations, take them to confession to sharpen their intellect!

Do children go joyfully to confession? Not always. Let's face it. Our pride makes going to confession distasteful. Children

---

[32] John Paul II, Apost. Exhort. *Familiaris Consortio*, November 22, 1981, 58.

may balk at going, but they also balk at going to the doctor or to school. Patiently take them anyway. While they may protest going to confession, they are always happy afterwards. My youngest daughter, Mary Terese, once went to confession and confessed that she threw a tantrum. The priest asked her, *was it because of a household chore you were asked to do? No,* she replied, *I did not want to go to confession!* She and the priest had a good laugh over that one.

It is <u>our</u> responsibility to get our children to confession at least monthly but wise parents will take their children more frequently. The effects of the grace of the sacrament are incredible. Wild kids become docile; moody kids become cheerful; ornery children become sweet after going to confession. Even more important, their conscience becomes more refined, more sensitive to the impulse of grace and the guidance of their guardian angels.

Be choosy as to whom you take your children to for frequent confession. Search out holy priests for confessors and spiritual directors. They can exert a powerful influence on the souls of your children. Holy confessors fashion saints. St. John of Avila was the spiritual director of St. Teresa of Avila, St. John of the Cross, St. Francis Borgia, and St. Peter of Alcantara. See what I mean?

St. Jerome was the spiritual director for St. Paula's family. Under his wise direction her family sprouted St. Pammachius, her son-in-law, and St. Eustochium, her daughter, as well as St. Paula, herself. These two women helped St. Jerome with the translation of the Bible when his eyesight failed.

What do the saints recall about their first confession? St. Thérèse writes: *Well instructed in all I had to say and do, I entered the confessional and knelt down. On opening the grating Father Ducellier saw no one. I was so little my head was below the arm-rest. He told me to stand up. Obeying instantly, I stood and faced him directly in order to see him perfectly, and I made my confession like a big girl and received his blessing with great devotion for you had told me that at the moment he gave me absolution the tears of Jesus were going to purify my soul. I remember the first exhortation directed to me. Father encouraged me to be devout to the Blessed Virgin and I promised myself to redouble my tenderness for her. Coming out of the confessional I was so happy and light-hearted that I had never felt so much joy in my soul. Since then I've gone to confession on all the great feasts, and it was truly a feast for me each time.*[33]

St. Escrivá recalls: *I was very happy after I made my First Confession—I was six or seven at the time—and I always look back on it with joy. My mother took me to her confessor, and...do you know what he gave me as a penance?...[Y]ou'll be very amused. Even now I still hear the chuckles of my father, who was devout but never sanctimonious. The good priest—could think of nothing else than to say: "Tell mama to give you a fried egg." When I told her this she exclaimed: "Good heavens! He could have told you to eat a sweet. But a fried egg!" Obviously he was very fond of fried eggs, that priest.*[34]

The Sacrament of Confession fills the soul with grace moving the heart to convert. After Sister Lucia Santos, the last living visionary of Fatima, made her First Confession she was moved to pray, *Make me a saint.*

In order to receive the sacrament of Penance worthily there are five steps you and your children should sincerely strive to fulfill. They are:

1.   Examine your conscience well.
2.   Be sorry for your sins.
3.   Have a firm purpose not to commit the sin again.
4.   Confess your sins to the priest.
5.   Be willing to do the penance the priest gives you.

Let's briefly consider each of these steps. Confession is the time to take off your rose colored glasses and view yourself as God sees you. Teach your children to pray to the Holy Spirit to enlighten them as to their sins. The daily examination of conscience helps to facilitate this. Review an examination of

---

[33] *St. Therese—Doctor of the Little Way*, Op. Cit., p. 34.
[34] *A Profile of Msgr. Escriva, Found of Opus Dei*, Op. Cit., p. 19.

conscience. Help your child to discern the main cause of his failings. Is he short of temper or irritable because he is tired? Maybe getting to bed earlier would help. If moodiness and sensitivity are the problem maybe pride is the root of unhappiness. If impure thoughts are a problem, avoiding TV, movies, and certain magazines may be the solution. For the vice of gossip, teach your children to avoid talking about others, change the subject, or find an excuse to leave the situation.

For your sins to be forgiven, you <u>must</u> be sorry for them. So many times we hear people justify their actions with this flippant comment, *Oh, I'll just go to confession later.* You cannot have the attitude that you can do whatever you please, as long as you eventually go to confession to be forgiven. To be forgiven, you have to be truly sorry that you committed the sin or sins. This sorrow comes from your heart and will rather than from the emotions. By meditating on the Agony, Suffering, and Death of our Lord, you and your children can develop a horror of sin and true sorrow when you sin.

To make a good confession, there must be a firm purpose of amendment in your will. In other words, you sincerely want to avoid committing the sin in the future. You cannot confess that you gossiped and then plan to continue gossiping. You cannot sincerely confess a lie without a willingness to work on being truthful and sincere. It would be a sham for a teen to confess that he saw a filthy movie or read a risqué book if he intends to go and see another such film or read the same type of book in the future. You have to be sincere with God. Granted, as a sinner you will probably commit the same sins again but at the time of confession, your will should be set to avoid these sins as much as humanly possible. To make a valid confession and to receive forgiveness, you need to confess *all* of your unconfessed mortal sins to a priest who represents God, no matter how many people may be waiting in line. *Nothing is more personal and intimate than this sacrament, in which the sinner stands alone before God with his sin, repentance and trust. No one can repent in his place or ask forgiveness of his sin. . . .Everything takes place between the individual alone and God* so states John Paul II in **Veritatis Splendor**, No. 21.

It is a confirmation of the availability of God's mercy in return for your sincerity. To complete the sacrament, you must be willing to perform the penance that the priest gives to you. The penance is a prayer or work given to you in order to make up for your sins. It helps to repair the harm caused by your fault. It should fulfill it as son as possible. In this way you show your prompt desire to make up for your sins. At the same time, remember that the small penance given nowadays usually just begins to make reparation for your sins. If you do not make atonement or reparation on earth, you will have to "do time" later in Purgatory. It is through your daily living, the acceptance of suffering and pain, through fasting, almsgiving, your Masses, and prayers that you make reparation for your sins on earth.

Sin, sadly, is part of our human condition. Look at the willful toddler, the defiant teenager, the promiscuous coed, the troubled marriages, and the countless problems in the world...all traceable to personal sin. Happiness, peace and joy come from the absence of sin. Dr. Karl Menninger, the founder of American psychiatry, knew well the effect of sin on peoples' psyches. He writes: *Is no one any longer guilty of anything? Guilty perhaps of a sin that could be repented and repaired or atoned for?...Anxiety and depression we all acknowledge, and even vague guilt feelings; but has no one committed any sins? Where, indeed, did sin go? What became of it?*[36]

In the last chapter we discussed how saintly parents and saintly grandparents usually form saints. The converse is also sadly true. William Murray, the son of Madalyn Murray O'Hair, recounted in an interview the effect of sin on his family that in turned resulted in the banning of prayer in schools. O'Hair's Supreme Court case started the destruction of religious rights in the U.S.A. Murray observed that *If my grandmother would not have practiced witchcraft, if my grandfather would not have run illegal stills during prohibition, they would not have been law-breakers, who made their money however they could,[and] the outlook for our family would have been quite a bit different.*

---

[36] Karl Menninger, *Whatever Became of Sin?* (New York: Hawthorn Books, 1973), p. 133.

Because of Madalyn's upbringing, *She was just somebody who could not stand God. She could not stand the rule of God. She could not function in a society with norms...*

...It was a matter of being a highly dysfunctional family— multigenerational. My mother was an atheist because of her lifestyle. Her personal conduct and the Bible and the Ten Commandments just didn't match up...

This was a family of sinners—serious, hard-core sinners. People who read tarot cards and practiced witchcraft...[37]

How you raise your children in regard to the moral law of God will have a huge consequence, not only for their souls, but also for the souls of others in our country and world.

The Importance of First Communion... And Every Communion Afterwards

The Blessed Sacrament is Jesus alive on earth, practicing the virtues He wants us to live, especially humility, obedience, patience, and charity, and the greatest challenge for faithful Catholics today is to convey the Church's truth about the Real Presence of Jesus in the Eucharist to their fellow Catholics points out Fr. John Hardon, S.J.[38]

Prepare your children well to receive their First Communion. Why? Because as Fr. John P. Grigus, OFM Conv. writes, *Holy Communion "augments our union with Christ" given at Baptism (CC 1391), "separates us from sin" (CC 1393) especially wiping away venial sin (CC 1394) while preserving us from future mortal sins (CC 1395), forms us to be the Church (CC 1396), "Commits us to the poor" (CC 1397), and finally becomes for us the "pledge of the glory to come" (CC 1402-5).*[38a] The best preparation is for your children to see your deep devotion to the Blessed

---

[37] Rich Rinaldi, "The Legacy of Madalyn Murray O'Hair," Register Radio News Correspondent. No date.

[38] Paul Likoudis, *The Wanderer*, no date.

[38a] Fr. John P. Grigus, OFM Conv., "Eucharist, God Among Us." *Call To Holiness*, Eastpointe, MI, Spring 2002, p. 9.

Sacrament. If you do not have a deep reverence, neither will your children. Let's face it, you cannot give to your children what you yourself do not have. How does one show reverence? By your reverent gestures, dress, visits to the Blessed Sacrament with your children and the manner in which you speak about the Eucharist. Fr. John Hardon, S.J., credits his vocation to the priesthood to his mother's devotion to the Blessed Sacrament. Fr. Hardon insists that a *Catholic must not only believe but act like a Eucharistic believer. It is one thing to claim to be a Catholic and another one to be one. Daily Mass and visits develop Eucharistic life. Teach also by word. The "whys" of children between the ages of three and seven are very important. How you answer their questions will shape their lives for time and eternity. It is impossible to overestimate the power of parents. Remember, the only reason children are brought into the world is to get to heaven...If your child does not understand the Eucharistic presence he cannot understand anything else in the faith. Explain to your child that the consecration is the moment of Jesus' death.*[39]

The proper reception and their cooperation with the graces of the sacrament *will* make them saints because when we receive the Eucharist, Jesus tells us that we have eternal life. Recall His words: **He who eats my flesh and drinks my blood has eternal life** (*John* 6:54). What a profound promise! Yet the more we receive Our Lord in the Eucharist, the more we yearn for Him: **Those who eat me will hunger for more, and those who drink me will thirst for more** (Sir. 24:21).

John Paul II reiterates: *Through communion with the Body and Blood of Christ, the faithful grow in the mysterious divinization that, thanks to the Holy Spirit, makes them dwell in the Son as children of the Father.*[40] Recall the words of Christ in **St. John's Gospel** (6:56): **He who eats my flesh and drinks my blood abides in me, and I in him.** Think about those

---

[39] Fr. John Hardon, S.J. ,"The Eucharist, Source and Summit of the Christian Life," audiotape from the series *The Sacraments and The Marian Catechist* (800) 842-2871.
[40] Zenit, September 27, 2000.

words and read them again. This is why the reception of daily Communion is so important. The Holy Father adds: *[P]articipation in the Eucharist...is the height of assimilation to Christ, source of eternal life, principle and strength of the total gift of self.*[41]

Participating in the sacrifice of the cross, the Christian communicates with the sacrificial love of Christ and is enabled and determined to live this same charity in all his attitudes and conduct of life. A moral life is revealed and practiced in royal Christian service. Such royal service has its roots in baptism and its flowering in eucharistic communion. The way of sanctity, love, truth is, therefore, the revelation to the world of our divine intimacy, brought about in the banquet of the Eucharist.[42]

St. Escrivá expresses it in this manner: *And precisely because He comes to us, everything is changed. Our being acquires new strength through the assistance of the Holy Spirit that fills our soul, affects all our actions, our way of thinking and feeling.*[43]

I believe that Holy Communion, received worthily, increases our union with the Lord, forgives venial sins and preserves us from grave sin, adds Fr. John A. Hardon, S.J. *The Sacrament also strengthens the bonds of charity between the communicant and Christ and reinforces the unity of the Church as the Mystical Body of Christ (CCC, 1416).*[44]

The preparation or lack of preparation you give to your children will dramatically influence their spiritual growth and future sanctity. When St. John Bosco made his First Communion his mother counseled him, *Keep yourself pure.* He did. When it came time for little Thérèse to make her First Communion her sister Pauline, then a Carmelite, asked Thérèse to prepare to receive Jesus by making little acts of sacrifices and love. Thérèse recorded 818 little acts of sacrifice and 2,773 aspirations of love. Upon making her First Communion, Thérèse told Jesus, *I love Thee, and I give myself to Thee forever.*

---

[41] *Veritatis Splendor,* No. 21.   [42] Zenit, October 18, 2000.
[43] *Christ Is Passing By, Op. Cit.,* #169.   [44] *Religious Life,* March, 2000, p. 8.

Why not have your children imitate the example of St. Thérèse in her preparation for First Communion?

Explain to your children the mystery of the Real Presence. Jesus is physically present but hidden under the appearances of bread (the large white host) and wine, the common food of the people of the Holy Land. Do not take it for granted that children understand this great mystery. Bl.Jacinta Marto begged to be in a Eucharistic procession because her cousin, Lucia, told her Jesus was to be there. She and Lucia were flower girls but Jacinta never scattered her flower petals during the procession because she kept waiting for Jesus to appear. No one had explained to her that Jesus was in the monstrance the priest was carrying behind her. Once it was explained, Jacinta, too young to receive Holy Communion, would ask to sit next to Lucia, when she received Holy Communion saying, *Come very close to me, because you have in your heart the Hidden Jesus.*

The first day that Jesus comes physically into the heart of one of your children should be the most memorable day of his or her life. Just think! Jesus, the Creator of Heaven and earth joyously comes to unite Himself with your child in the Holy Eucharist! This is a greater event than winning the lottery or the presidential election. Make this day special, not only with the external aspects of dress, but also with a festive celebration. Make the day so special that the date and event are engraved in your child's memory. I have no idea what today's date is but I do remember that my First Communion was on May 8th. My cousin's wife, Cindy, commissioned beautiful First Communion portraits for each of their three children. These hang in their front room. Not only is it a reminder to the children, but it also makes a powerful statement of the importance of the Eucharist to everyone who enters their home. What is even more beautiful is that Cindy is not even Catholic. In Poland, the celebration of a First Communion continues for weeks. The First Communicant and his family visit three Marian shrines in the following weeks wearing his First Communion outfit and carrying a lighted candle. Why not develop a similar custom in your family?

St. Pius X insists that a child's First Communion should simply be the beginning of a growing relationship with the Eucharistic Jesus. To parents he pointed out that it is the Church's desire that children *frequently approach the holy table, even daily if possible... and with a devotion becoming their age. [Parents] must also bear in mind that very serious duty which obliges them to have the children attend catechism classes; if this is not done then they must provide religious instruction in some other way.*[45]

Bl. Contardo Ferrini (1859-1902) was a layman who was a daily communicant from the age of fourteen. He was a brilliant law professor who authored over two hundred articles on law. Yet he had time to go to daily Mass from his teen years throughout his successful teaching career.

St. Maria Goretti, had to walk miles for each of her First Communion preparation classes. It was her priest instructor who counseled her during her classes, *Keep your soul pure! It is better to die a thousand times than to commit one mortal sin.*[46] She took his words to heart and became a martyr rather *than commit one mortal sin.*

St. John Bosco, in preparation for his First Communion, wrote four promises in a little book that he reviewed throughout his entire life. They were: *1) I will go often to confession and I will go to Holy Communion as often as I am allowed. 2) I will try to give Sundays and holy days completely to God. 3) My best friends will be Jesus and Mary. 4) Death but not sin.*[47] Encourage your children to make these same promises. They made St. John Bosco a saint!

Due to the persecution of the Church in France, St. John Vianney had to leave his home and move to another city in order to prepare for the reception of his First Holy Communion. He lived with an aunt for several months while two sisters of the order of St. Charles trained him and fifteen other children

---

[45] St. Pius X, Decr. *Quam singulari*, rule 6, August 8, 1910.

[46] Fr. Robert J. Fox, *Saints & Heroes Speak Vol Three* (Alexandria, SD, Fatima Family Apostolate, 1996) p. 72.

[47] Ann Ball, *Modern Saints, Their Lives and Faces, Book One* (Rockford, Tan Books, 1983) p. 19.

in secret. His final preparation was a retreat. *At an early hour the sixteen first communicants, in their ordinary clothes were conducted one by one into a large room, the shutters of which had been carefully closed, for it had been decided that each child was to carry the...lighted taper, the flames of which must remain invisible from without. By a refinement of caution carts laden with hay were placed in front of the windows, and were actually unloaded while the sacred ceremony was in progress. The mother of each child brought, carefully hidden under her cape, the white veil or armlet which was to be worn by the first communicant.*

"When we receive Holy Communion, we experience something extraordinary—a joy—a fragrance—a well-being that thrills the whole body and causes it to exult," exclaimed St. John Vianney.[48]

Closer to home, actor Ricardo Montalban recounts the preparation for his First Communion: *Just as I began to study the catechism, there came the Mexican government's persecution of the Church. In my fifth and sixth years of school, I would hide my books under my sweater or shirt, walk to a private home and go to the attic. There were three rows of chairs for each of the three grades of grammar school, and a French priest, Father Hajenele, who taught us all. He had a wonderful mind. When my preparation was done. I went to the basement of a house to receive my First Communion. Nuns were there, in hiding.*[49]

I spoke with a woman from Kansas who told me that she has been going to daily Mass since she was seven years old. *I had a wonderful second grade nun who instilled the value of receiving the Eucharist daily. How I wish I could thank her for this gift that changed my life!* She is the mother of a priest and the grandmother of a seminarian.

What sacrifices are you and your children willing to make to receive the sacraments frequently?

---

[48] *The Curé D'Ars, St. Jean-Marie-Baptiste Vianney, Op. Cit.,* p. 26.
[49] Ricardo Montalban, "In The Heart of Tinseltown, A Faith Lived Deeply," *BE,* March-April 2000, p. 4.

The Wonder Of It All...

Since Our Lord, in His humility, comes without fanfare or miraculous cosmic displays we tend to take Him so for granted in the Blessed Sacrament. Strive to avoid casualness toward the Eucharist. Teach your children to view their First Holy Communion and the Blessed Sacrament with awe. The awe and wonder at receiving Our Lord in Holy Communion should remain with your children the rest of their lives. This will only happen if they see your reverence and awe when you receive the Holy Eucharist as well as how you treat Our Lord in the Tabernacle.

When you pass a church, why not stop with your children to make a short visit to greet Our Lord? Jesus is present Body, Blood, Soul and Divinity just for you and for them. He is just as present in the tabernacle to you as He was to the people in the Holy Land during His thirty-three years on earth. Try this experiment. Visit a Protestant church then visit your parish church. Can you sense His absence in the Protestant church?

Jesus Christ is physically present in the nearest tabernacle to your home or apartment. He awaits your visit at your convenience. You never have to make an appointment to visit God. Rather impressive, don't you think, to have the Creator of Heaven and earth at your beck and call? *[T]he Master is here and he is calling you,* St. Escrivá reminds us. *The Tabernacle has to be a magnet for us.* As you kneel with your children before the King of Kings, teach them to make acts of adoration and reparation. Then teach your children to talk to Jesus as the Love of their lives, as a Friend, Teacher, Doctor, as God. Explain to your children how they are to confide in Him their cares, worries, joys and to ask Him for help in the difficulties of each day. Recall the words of Moses: ***What great nation is there that has a god so near to it as the Lord our God is to us, whenever we call upon him?*** (*Deut.*4:7).

One day I stopped to make an afternoon visit at St. Philip's parish in Northfield, Illinois. Parked outside the main door of the Church was a Big Wheel trike. Inside the dark church was a little boy, about six-years-old, kneeling at the altar railing praying his little heart out. When he got up to leave he fairly skipped down the aisle with the cutest smile on his little face. Introduce your children to the joy of knowing Jesus!

Should circumstances prevent a visit, teach your children to at least bow their heads then say an aspiration mentally or vocally to Jesus as they pass a Catholic church such as, *Jesus, I greet Thee.* When they say morning and evening prayers, unite your children with Our Lord in the tabernacle at your parish. Teach them to remain united during the day mentally to Our Lord in the Tabernacle. St. Escrivá encouraged people to *Go to the Tabernacle and offer our Lord that small vexation, that thing you find difficult. Offer that to Him and you will be happy...*

Introduce your children to Eucharistic Holy Hours. On Holy Thursday visit several churches, possibly one for each member of your family, to adore Our Lord who is waiting at the altar of repose.

Make clear to your children the distinction between praying to Jesus in the Blessed Sacrament and praying before statues. Catholics **do not** pray to statues but to the people the statues represent. This differentiation seems to confuse some people. In my local parish, we have a chapel with a beautiful statue of the Sacred Heart. In front are votive candles. Unfortunately, the location of this statue is at the back of the chapel. To pray in front of the statue one has to turn his back to the tabernacle. Several times I have been present at Eucharistic adoration in the chapel when people have come in, turned their back on Jesus in the Blessed Sacrament to pray to His statue. Why turn your back on Jesus physically present on the altar or in the tabernacle to pray to His statue?   This does not make sound theological or even common sense. An analogy of this would be for you to turn your back on your spouse to talk to his/her picture. Rather counter productive wouldn't you say?   When you speak to someone don't you want him to look you in the eye? So does our Lord.

What Age For First Communion?

St. Pius X, the Pope of the Holy Eucharist, explained why he disagreed with withholding the reception of the Blessed Sacrament from children who have reached the age of reason: *So it happened that children in their innocence were forced away from the embrace of Christ and deprived of the good of their interior life; and from this it also happened that in their youth, destitute of this powerful help, surrounded by so many temptations, they lost their innocence and fell into vicious habits even before tasting of the Sacred Mysteries.*[54]

St. Thomas Aquinas stated *as soon as children begin to have sufficient use of reason to feel devotion towards this sacrament, they can receive it.*[55]   When a child feels devotion toward the Blessed Sacrament and can distinguish between the Blessed Sacrament and ordinary bread, the child is ready to make his First Communion. *With regard to the age at which children should be given the holy mysteries, this the parents and confessor can best determine. To them it belongs to inquire and to ascertain from the children themselves whether they have some knowledge of this admirable sacrament and whether they desire to receive it.*[56]

A story is told of a mother who brought her young son with her to meet Pope Saint Pius X. The Holy Father was told the little boy was four-years-old and she hoped that in three or four years he could make his First Communion. At that Pius X quizzed the little one: *"Whom do you receive in Holy Communion?"* The boy piped up, *"Jesus Christ."* *"And who is Jesus Christ?"* Without hesitation, the boy replied, *"Jesus Christ is God."* Turning to the mother, the Pope told her, *"Bring him to me tomorrow and I will give him Holy Communion myself."*[57]

---

[54] St. Pius X, Decr. *Quam singulari*, August 8, 1910.

[55] St. Thomas Aquinas, *Summa theologiae, III,* q.80, a.9 ad 3.

[56] *Catechism of the Council of Trent* (McHugh and Callan, Marian Publications, 1972) Part II, p. 251. Cf St. Pius X, loc. Cit., rule 4.

[57] *Modern Saints, Their Lives and Faces, Book Two, Op. Cit.,* p. 174.

Although it was the custom for children to make their First Communion at the age of ten in Portugal, Sister Lucia Santos, the visionary of Fatima, was taught her faith so well by her mother that when examined by the parish priest, he gave permission for her to make her First Communion when she was just six-years-old. Bl. Jacinta and her brother, Bl. Francisco Marto, also visionaries of Fatima, received their First Communion from an angel. Jacinta was but six-years-old at the time. St. Dominic Savio received his First Communion at the age of seven, common today, but shockingly early in the mid 1800s. St. Anthony Mary Claret was able to receive his First Communion when he was ten, two years before it was normally given because he not only knew his faith well but attended daily Mass with his parents. Likewise Bl. Théodore-Anne-Guerin, who lived in the same century, made her first communion at the uncommon age of ten.

John Paul II reminds parents that *family catechesis precedes, accompanies, and enriches all other forms of catechesis.*[58] He continues: *[B]y preparing children for their first holy communion we introduce them to the principal mysteries of Christian life; we demonstrate how great is the dignity of man and his immortal soul, which can be transformed into a dwelling place of God; finally, we form in them a sensitivity of conscience when the preparation for first holy communion is accompanied by an examination of conscience and by repentance for sin and the sacrament of penance.*[59]

The reception of the Holy Eucharist works marvels of grace in souls, especially the souls of children properly taught Eucharistic devotion. Even the most incorrigible children can become saints when united with Jesus. Bl. Elizabeth of the Trinity is considered one of the modern age's greatest mystical writers. Her beginnings were not so promising. Her difficult, willful personality caused her to be nicknamed "a little devil." It was her First Holy Communion that transformed her.

---

[58] John Paul II, Apost. Exhort. *Catechesi tradendae*, October 16, 1979, 68.

[59] John Paul II, Address, May 13, 1979.

St. Bosco discovered that he became more obedient after receiving the Hidden Jesus. Bl. María Cardozo made a private vow of consecration to Christ on her First Communion. St. Gemma Galgani reminisced on her First Communion: *It is impossible for me to describe what passed between Jesus and myself in that moment. He made himself felt so strongly in my soul. I realized in that moment how the delights of Heaven are not like those of the earth, and I was seized by a desire to make that union with my God everlasting.*[60] Bl. Théodore-Anne-Guerin, after receiving Our Lord, announced to her family that she was going to become a nun. Sister Lucia Santos asked, when she received Jesus at the age of six, that He would make her a saint. Within her heart she heard the words, *The grace that I grant you today will remain living in your soul producing fruits of eternal life.*[61] Children have a tremendous capacity to utilize the Eucharistic graces if you train them in doctrine and devotion. These were ordinary children whom grace raised to extraordinary heights.

St. Escrivá made his First Communion on the feast of St. George, April 23, 1912: *I was then ten years old. At that time it was unheard of to make one's First Communion at such an early age, in spite of the dispositions laid down by Pius X. Now it is customary to make it even earlier than that. An old Piarist father, a good, simple and devout man, prepared me for it, and it was he who taught me the formula for the spiritual communion.*[62]

In St. Faustina's Diary (#1407) she noted when she received Holy Communion that the priest gave her a Living Host. She asked Our Lord in her prayer, *Why was one Host alive, since you are equally alive under each of the species?* Jesus replied, *This is true. I am the same under each of the species, but not every soul receives me with the same living faith as you do, my daughter, and therefore I cannot act in their souls as I do in*

---

[60] *Modern Saints, Their Lives and Faces, Book One, Op. Cit.* p. 174.

[61] *Saints & Heroes Speak, Vol. One, Op. Cit.*, p. 51.

[62] *A Profile of Msgr. Escriva, Founder of Opus Dei*, Op. Cit., p. 19.

yours. St. Elizabeth Ann Seton, a convert to the faith wrote after her First Communion, *At last, God is mine, and I am His! Let the things of the world go as they wish. I have received Him!*

Teach your children delicacy towards Jesus. If they receive Him in their hands, their hands must be clean. The Sacred Host must be consumed at the altar. Unfortunately communion in the hand has lead to abuses. Priests have told me of finding consecrated hosts in washrooms, in hymnals, and in other places. In view of these abuses, consider encouraging your children to receive communion on the tongue. Warn them never, ever to receive Jesus if they have committed a mortal sin. Don't encourage a child to go up to communion if the child appears reluctant. Honor the child's conscience. Don't ask embarrassing questions. Instead discreetly arrange to take the child to confession.

A teenager who comes homes drunk should be told to first go to confession before receiving communion. A college student who does not attend Mass while away at school should be advised to go to confession before receiving communion with the family so as not to scandalize the younger children. If you love Jesus and your children you will do everything possible to prevent your children from committing a sacrilege, which is receiving Jesus in the Eucharist in the state of mortal sin. The feelings of God come before the feelings of your children.

Teach your children to pray spiritual communions when they cannot get to daily Mass in addition to encouraging them to pray spiritual communions during the day even when they do get to Mass. This will deepen their Eucharistic love of Jesus.

Spiritual Communion

I wish, my Lord, to receive you with the purity, humility and devotion with which your most holy Mother received you, with the spirit and the fervor of the saints. Amen.

St. Rose of Lima insists *It is better to talk with God than about God.* Encourage your children to follow the example of St. Thérèse who said, *for me, prayer is an upward leap of the heart.*

The Sacrament of Confirmation

"Every saint knows how to overcome difficult situations with faith and confidence, relying on the Holy Spirit who helps us in our weaknesses and intercedes for us in our needs."   Archbishop Justin Rigali of St. Louis

Confirmation—the sacrament of spiritual strengthening—increases sanctifying grace received in Baptism in every way, but especially in the capacity to be spiritually alive, able to resist evil, bear suffering, and witness courageously to all the truths of the faith, according to Fr. John Hardon, S.J. He adds, *This sacrament gives us the power to resist spiritual dangers and to become more Christ-like with a supernatural strength against the world, the flesh, and the devil. It assimilates us to Jesus the priest, teacher, and king. This sacrament helps us to sacrifice ourselves for the faith. It gives us the strength to bear sufferings, which we unite to the sufferings of Christ because to be Christ-like one has to have the willingness to suffer with God, for God and in God. To suffer, to mortify oneself, to sacrifice for God assimilates us to Christ the priest.*

This sacrament assimilates us to Christ the teacher. It strengthens our will to adhere to the faith in spite of obstacles. It gives us a strong mind to never doubt the truths of the faith. It gives us true humility in professing the faith to others, and the wisdom to communicate the faith effectively.

This sacrament assimilates us to Christ the King through the quality of our leadership in the family, in society, and for priests and bishops along their path to Christ. It can give us strength to withstand bad example, control one's strong personality, help one to avoid the snares of worldly seduction and attract the enemies of Christ to the faith through one's example.[63]

The tremendously powerful Sacrament of Confirmation gives a strengthening grace by which the Holy Spirit helps you and <u>your children </u>mature so that you can be *soldiers of Christ*

[63] "Confirmation... ", *The Sacraments and The Marian Catechist, Op. Cit.*

(*II Tim*. 2:3), profess our Faith openly, overcome our spiritual enemies, and help extend the Faith in the world.[64] It can give you fearless apostolic zeal to witness and defend the faith. St. John Chrysostom points out that each of us will be judged on our charity of spreading the faith. Just think, you are responsible for strengthening the faith of every person your life touches but your ability to do so depends on the depth of your faith. Although it may feel uncomfortable having to defend the Catholic faith in your interaction with friends, family or business acquaintances the actual act of defending the faith has the effect of strengthening you also in your beliefs.

This sacrament, which leaves a character on the soul, as mentioned at the beginning of the chapter, can only be received once. When a person receives the sacrament he is infused with the gifts of the Holy Spirit which are seven in number: **wisdom, understanding, counsel, fortitude, knowledge, piety, and fear of the Lord.** Let's consider each of these gifts briefly.

*...**Wisdom** is the supreme gift. It enables us to be wholly committed to [God]. It makes us relish God above all else and whatever is concerned with the glory of God. Those who act in virtue of this gift are said to be able to do or suffer everything for God's greater glory.*

*The gift of **understanding** enables a person to penetrate in a wonderful way into a mystery of the Faith or into the meaning of words inspired by the Holy Spirit.*

*[The] gift of **counsel** makes us discern as by instinct what has to be done in every circumstance, whether it concerns our own conduct or the conduct of others.*

*...[T]he gift of strength or **fortitude**...prompts us to undertake very difficult things and bear sufferings when this is in accord with God's will and is seen to be for God's glory.*

*...[T]he gift of **knowledge**...enables you to judge things— for instance, events in this world, and particularly painful things—according to God's judgment about them.*

---

[64] *The Sacraments, Sources of Christian Life, Op. Cit.*, p. 3.

> *...The gift of **piety** prompts a person to imitate the Heavenly Father, the Son and the Holy Spirit in Their love for one another and in Their love for their creatures made after Their own image.*

> *...[A] child of God knows God's infinite goodness and mercy, and what such a child **fears** more than anything else is offending the parents even in the least manner.*[65]

If you cooperate with the plentitude of graces that the Holy Spirit lavishes upon your soul the **fruits of the Holy Spirit** become evident. According to Rev. Walter Van De Putte, CSSP, the fruits are *the Christian virtues which have reached their perfect development. We are told also that, besides such virtues, there are actions as well as states of sanctity...[T]he fruits of the Holy Spirit are those that have reached a high degree of perfection.*[66] These fruits number twelve: **love, joy, peace, patience, longanimity (long suffering), goodness, benignity, mildness, fidelity, modesty, continence, and chastity.** What exactly does each fruit mean? Fr. Van De Putte explains:

❏ **Love** (Charity) means the fruit found in those who are wholly committed and entirely delivered to the Holy Spirit's action. It consists in perfect love of God and neighbor.

❏ **Joy** means the intense and intimate satisfaction a person experiences when he realizes he is in possession of his Sovereign Good. He realizes he is infinitely loved by the God of Love and in turn he loves God with all the power of his free will.

❏ **Peace** is the quiet, perfect repose a person experiences when he is wholly and perfectly submissive to the Divine Will.

❏ **Patience** means lovingly and fully accepting the trials which the Divine Goodness sees fit to let a person undergo.

❏ **Longanimity** consists in knowing how to wait, feeling certain during trials that God's moment will come when He will fully aid the suffering person.

---

[65] Rev. Walter Van De Putte, C.S.SP., *Following the Holy Spirit* (NY: Catholic Publishing Co., 1978) pp. 97-101.
[66] *Ibid.*, pp. 113, 114.

❏ **Goodness** here means truly desiring the good of all our brothers and sisters in Christ and also that of all our friends and our enemies, making no exception of any kind. This is the love of perfect goodwill.

❏ **Benignity** means to procure for your brothers and sisters in Christ, without any distinction of persons, all the good you are able to give them. It is the love of beneficence.

❏ **Mildness** means bearing with gentleness and patience all the defects of others, without ever yielding to improper anger. It is lovingly accepting—always—such troublesome things.

❏ **Fidelity** means eagerly rendering to all people all that you owe them. It is the perfect virtue of justice.

❏ **Modesty** means always and in every circumstance keeping the just and golden mean, the proper measure, and never falling into contrary excesses.

❏ **Continence** means fully controlling the disorderly movements of one's sensible nature, in particular the movements contrary to chastity. This then is the laborious chastity of the soul which suffers such temptations.

❏ **Chastity** means perfect and unalterable purity when God, in His mercy, wants to preserve a person even from temptations against the virtue of chastity. Such certainly, was the chastity of Jesus and Mary.[67]

St. Padre Pio, writing to a spiritual daughter, explains what happens when one does not cooperate with the graces of confirmation: *The Christian who has forgotten his true vocation and is merely a Christian in name, a worldly Christian, judges things quite differently. His judgment is the exact opposite to that of the Christian worthy of the name who lives according to the spirit of Jesus Christ. The former judges things from the point of view of their capacity to satisfy his vanity and his passions. The latter, on the other hand, invariably judges them in relation to eternal things.*

Hence the one that is a Christian merely in name, the Christian in high society, sets a great value on honors, wealth, fleeting things, comforts and all that this wretched world has to offer. O

[67] *Ibid.,* pp. 114-118.

*foolish man, enter into yourself and remember that by your baptism you renounced the world and are dead to it. The Holy Spirit tells you so by the mouth of St. Paul: **"You have died, and your life is hid with Christ in God** (Col. 3:3)."*

*Remember, foolish one, that the life of those who live according to the spirit of Jesus will not always remain hidden and unknown. Remember what it will be in future in the Lord's day **"When Christ who is our life appears, then you also will appear with Him in glory** (Col. 3:4)"...*

Is the certainty of such boundless glory, O foolish one, not sufficient to make you enter into yourself and come to your senses, to live the rest of your life according to your vocation? [68]

The Power Of Confirmation

It was the Sacrament of Confirmation that turned the frightened eleven apostles into spiritual powerhouses on Pentecost. This is the sacrament that takes us, with all of our defects and failings, and turns us into potential martyrs for the faith as well as into potential canonized saints.

Huddled fearfully around Our Lady in the Cenacle, the apostles were at a loss as to what they were supposed to do. When the Holy Spirit descended upon each in the form of a flame, the Holy Spirit spiritually enflamed their souls. Immediately **Peter, standing up with the Eleven, lifted up his voice and spoke to the them** [the people gathered outside the Cenacle who were attracted by the sound of a violent wind]. **Now they who received his word were baptized, and there were added that day about three thousand souls** (Acts 2:14, 41). But that was just the beginning. The eleven apostles went out fearlessly preaching the Gospel throughout the world. All but St. John were martyred. We are Catholics today only because they cooperated with the graces of the Holy Spirit!

Throughout the **Book of Acts** the power of the Holy Spirit is manifested in mighty ways. The feats of the Holy Spirit even drew Simon, the sorcerer, who desired this power: **But when**

---

[68] St. Padre Pio "Letters To Raffaelina," *Voice of Padre Pio*, no date.

Simon saw that the Holy Spirit was given through the laying on of the apostles' hands, he offered them money, saying, "Give me also this power, so that anyone on whom I lay my hands may receive the Holy Spirit." But Peter said to him, "Thy money go to destruction with thee, because thou hast thought that the gift of God could be purchased with money. Thou has no part or lot in this matter; for thy heart is not right before God. Repent therefore of this wickedness (Acts 8:18-22).

As the apostles preached the Gospel in foreign countries, Gentiles asked to become Christians. This precipitated a heated controversy over whether Gentiles had to first become Jews (be circumcised) or if they could simply be baptized. This question threatened to split the young Church. Peter was called to resolve the problem when *the Holy Spirit came upon all who were listening to his message. And the faithful of the circumcision, who had come with Peter, were amazed, because on the Gentiles also the grace of the Holy Spirit had been poured forth...Then Peter answered, "Can anyone refuse the water to baptize these, seeing that they have received the Holy Spirit just as we did?" And he ordered them to be baptized in the name of Jesus Christ* (*Acts* 10:44-48).

Children need the strength of this powerful sacrament to protect their faith, grow in holiness and evangelize their peers. At what age can a child receive this sacrament? Actually, this sacrament has no rigid age requirements. In the Eastern rites children receive Confirmation along with Baptism. Many of the saints received the sacrament at Baptism, a few as pre-schoolers, and the rest at different ages. St. Vincent Mary Strambi of Italy was confirmed at the age of seven because of his knowledge of the faith. Due to the persecution of the Church in France, St. John Vianney did not receive the sacrament until he was twenty-one-years-old. The wise parent will see that his child receives the sacrament before or at the time of the awakening of the passions. In the U.S. children can be confirmed between *the age of discretion (about seven years old) and about 16 years of age.* Children, particularly teens need the graces of this sacrament to help them control their hormones and peer pressure. The sacrament will help them to avoid getting involved in gang activity, drinking, pre-marital sex, drugs, and even suicide. The Church states that *the sacrament of confirmation is to be conferred on the faithful about the age of discretion, unless the Episcopal Conference has decided on a different age, or there is a danger of death, or, in the judgment of the minister, a serious reason suggests otherwise.*[69, 69A]   To unduly delay this sacrament leaves your child with little defense.

Prepare your children by studying together the sacrament, the gifts and the fruits. Help them select a saint's name by providing lives of the saints in books and videos. Take time to discuss the lives of different saints and their outstanding virtue. Explain that by taking a saint's name, you are not simply honoring that saint, but asking the saint for guidance as well as help along the path of sanctity. Teach your child to develop a friendship with the saint through prayer. The saint's name becomes part of one's identity. St. Margaret Alacoque took Mary as her confirmation name. She is now known as St. Margaret Mary. Fr. John Hardon, S.J., points out: *Let's be honest. We cannot defend what we do not know. We have to know what we believe. We must learn how to cope with so much erroneous teaching that pervades society like the air we breathe. Heresy is pervasive. Error is the master of human thought...*

The ordinary Catholic cannot survive in our day and age. Only the extraordinary Catholic, with the grace of the Holy Spirit received in Confirmation, will survive. We have the power and strength needed to witness to Jesus. We need to use it. We cannot be slaves of human respect. We must profess our faith to everyone whose life we touch. We are to live this sacrament by following in the footsteps of the crucified Jesus.[70]

---

[69] Zenit, Sept. 4, 2001.

[69A] C.I.C., can. 891.

[70] Paul Likoudis, *The Wanderer, no date.*

Matrimony

"God finds His glory in our holiness."

Bl. Columba Marmion

The Sacrament of Matrimony, as discussed in **Raise Happy Children Through A Happier Marriage**, gives a dignifying and stabilizing grace, which enables the married couple to live in a stable and loving union, sanctifying themselves and their family, cooperating with God in the procreation and education of offspring. This grace helps married couples to live chastely and to fulfill their duties to each other and to their children.[71]

Christ, through this sacrament, restores marriage to its sublime state before the fall of Adam and Eve. Teach your children from little on that marriage is forever. Divorce is not to be considered as even a possibility. Marriage is a commitment of wholeheartedly pledging oneself to another person for life. Through the marriage covenant, a couple unites their bodies and souls. This union is only dissolved upon the death of one of the spouses. Recall how when Jesus expounded this truth his disciples protested saying: *If the case of a man with his wife is so, it is not expedient to marry (Matt.* 19:10). Jesus simply replied, *Not all can accept this teaching, but those to whom it has been given (Matt.* 19:11-12). The graces of this sacrament, instituted by Christ, provide the supernatural help needed to be faithful to the marriage covenant in good times but particularly in bad times or difficult situations.

Marriage is one of the most difficult of vocations to live well because it involves totally giving of one's time and self to another imperfect creature. But the graces of the sacrament are sufficient. John Paul II insists that *If marriage is not forever, it is not marriage, and without marriage the family, the very foundation of society, is undermined. The view of indissolubility as a limitation to the liberty of the partners and, consequently, as a weight that at times can become unbearable, must be surmounted.* Spouses must recognize *mutually that they are bound to one another forever, with a bond that calls for an ever-*

---

[71]*The Sacraments, Sources of Christian Life, Op. Cit.,* p. 3.

renewed and generous love that is disposed to sacrifice.
Furthermore, the Holy Father advised lawyers and judges that
they *must avoid being personally involved in anything that might
imply cooperation with divorce. In exercising a liberal
profession, lawyers can always decline to use their profession
for an end that is contrary to justice, such as divorce. [Judges]
must also find the effective means to favor marital unions,
especially through a wisely conducted effort at conciliation.*[72]

Marriage, an extremely important commitment for the souls
of the couple involved and for society in general, involves ideals,
personal relationships, and spiritual growth. Today there
seems to be two extremes in regard to entering into such an
extremely important commitment. People either enter
marriage without too much thought or preparation, or tend to
avoid marriage through fear of the demands the commitment
entails.

Children need to be taught the importance of marriage and
the seriousness of this relationship. Due to the seriousness of
the commitment, it should not be entered into without adequate
preparation. First, as parents you have the obligation to stress
the importance and seriousness of the marriage covenant. A
Catholic who marries without proper canonical form (before a
priest and two witness) does not receive the Sacrament even if
he marries a baptized person. Since marriage intimately
impacts the souls of the spouses the importance of religious
compatibility should be emphasized. Remember, only two
baptized spouses can receive the Sacrament of Matrimony. **If
one person is not validly baptized the marriage is valid
but it is not a sacrament.** Such a marriage will lack the
supernatural helps the sacrament gives. In other words, such
a marriage will be more difficult to live on a natural and
supernatural level. **In a mixed marriage, between a
Catholic and a baptized Christian, the marriage is a
sacrament** but religious differences will cause a strain between
the relationship of the couple and their children. In the *Gospel
of St. Mark* Jesus tells us, *If a household is divided
according to loyalties, that household will not survive* (3:26).

[72] Zenit Jan. 28, 2002.

Christ does not necessarily mean the marriage will falter. We all know mixed marriages that are stable and happy. What He means is that this division will make it more difficult to grow holy individually and as a family since there are two different belief systems at war against each other. Fr. John Hardon, S.J., reminds us that *only believers reproduce believers. Strong believers reproduce strong believers.*

Rev. Thomas J. Gerrard explains that young couples who are madly in love rarely see future problems in a mixed marriage. They believe that *where it is a question of so much love the faith must accommodate itself to circumstances. Yet, if they could only see the connection between faith and love, they would have to recognize that diversity of faith in the marriage union must eventually tell against love in the marriage union. Faith is the gift by which we believe in God and in His word. Without belief in God we cannot love Him. Without the full acceptance of His word we cannot follow His commands and ordinances. We cannot live in sympathy with that wonderful system of morality by which He adjusts and fosters the love between man and woman.*

Thus it is that the Protestant married to a Catholic cannot avail himself of the teaching and the Sacraments of the Catholic Church which might be so effectual in fostering love between man and wife. Real love is that only which has faith for its foundation. But in the mixed marriage the faith is all on one side. It does not flourish with that fecundity which would be present were the parties united in one and the same belief. Further, this absence of faith-informed love on the part of the non-Catholic partner must in a measure react on the Catholic partner. Grace is very powerful, but it needs a nature upon which to act. And if the faith-informed love of the Catholic partner finds no response in the non-Catholic partner, if it receives an inferior love in return, or if it discovers itself misunderstood and unappreciated, then, if it does not dwindle away, it at least fails in its possible measure of fruitfulness...

A mixed marriage [between a Catholic and a baptized non-Catholic] is a real Sacrament, and all the graces of the Sacrament are capable of being conveyed through it, though these graces may often fail in their effects through the want of disposition in the non-Catholic party. The Catholic party may do his or her best, as the case may be, but as human nature is so weak, there is naturally an ever-present danger of the Catholic losing the faith. Over and above the certainty of spoiling God's ideal, there is the disadvantage of risking the loss of faith altogether.

Foster a strong dislike for mixed marriages [in your children]. [Encourage them to] avoid company where they are likely to meet a partner of another religious persuasion. [Teach them to] reject the first overtures made by one who is not of your faith. Then, if circumstances have been too many or too strong for you, make up your mind at once that only by strict observance of the conditions laid down by the Church can your faith and your hope and your love be saved.[73]

Living immersed in a secular society it becomes very easy to grow lackadaisical about this important issue. When I was dating, my granduncle, a very holy Passionist priest, came to visit one evening. When he teasingly asked me about my "love life" I told him I was dating the boy next door. His next question was, *"Is he Catholic?" "No, he's not." "Don't you know that you are only to date Catholic boys?" "Well, I would if they asked me out but only Protestants are interested in dating me,"* I retorted a bit miffed. *"I will find you a good, Catholic husband and pray that you end your relationship with the Protestant."* His prayers were powerful. Within a matter of weeks my "romance" with the Protestant came to a crashing end precisely over the matter of religion. Invited to be his date at a military ball out of state, his mother, a fallen away Catholic, insisted that I attend Protestant church services with his family rather than a Catholic Mass on Sunday. The misery that I suffered over that experience is nothing compared to what I would have suffered if I had eventually married him. In the midst of this heartbreak, the prayers of my granduncle also brought my future husband, Bob, into my life. He did find me a perfect, Catholic husband.

---

[73] Rev. Thomas J. Gerrard, *Marriage and Parenthood, The Catholic Ideal* (NY: Joseph F. Wagner, 1911) pp. 61-65.

But before becoming engaged, I decided to check out several other options, both of whom were Southern Protestants. Easter weekend I attended a military ball in Alabama with an Episcopalian. Easter Mass was in a college classroom with six people present. Of those present only four of us were Catholics. It was such a depressing Easter. On my flight home I had a several hour layover in Atlanta where I was met by a boyfriend who was Presbyterian. His father was an elder of his church. He had met me at the airport over the objections of his parents who were scandalized that he was seeing a Catholic girl. The weekend had been a profound learning experience for me to see the differences in values, outlook and religious tolerance. More than anything else it taught me the importance of marrying within the faith.

One of the most beautiful love stories is that of famous Pre-Raphaelite artist, James Collinson and Christina Rossetti, a famous poet. Collinson was a Catholic and Christina was a devout Anglican. Although deeply in love and engaged for several years, the couple came to the realization that their religious differences would cause marital discord. As a final tribute to Christina, Collinson used her face for his famous painting of St. Elizabeth of Hungary. Fittingly the painting is entitled "The Renunciation." When the masterpiece was completed, Collinson left his vocation as an artist to enter the Jesuit novitiate. Christina never married.

Explain to your children that before they seriously consider becoming engaged to an individual they discuss deeply with their prospective spouses the issues of

- ✓ The primacy of living the Catholic faith;
- ✓ Indissolubility;
- ✓ Contraception;
- ✓ Self-giving and self-sacrifice in marriage.

Most difficulties in marriage arise in a misunderstanding of fidelity, primacy of spouse in each other's eyes (spouse comes before profession and children), spiritual compatibility, and the willingness to have and educate children along with the sharing of these responsibilities. Recall how Ted Turner's mother never

312 *Raise Happy Children...Raise Them Saints!*

addressed the religious differences with her prospective spouse prior to her wedding. She just "assumed" she would be allowed to practice the Catholic faith and raise her children as Catholics. It was immediately after her wedding that her husband informed her that she was never to step foot in a Catholic church again.

Highlight the fact that the primary purpose of marriage is to have children. It is not for legalized "lust." If the couple is not ready or interested in having children immediately, the marriage should be postponed until the couple is willing to accept children. Teach your children that natural family planning is not "Catholic birth control." It is to be used only when there is a serious reason for not having children at a particular time. This serious reason may be discussed with a priest in confession or in a pastoral counseling session. Bishop George Lucas of Springfield, Illinois, adds that a *couple could also rightly come to this decision on their own, after proper study, instruction and prayer.*

Obviously, those entering marriage will not have the experience necessary to bring sufficient depth to these discussions so they should seek qualified counsel from parents, relatives and older couples. Blind passion mistakenly called love is not adequate to insure a happy, lasting marriage.

On the other hand, young couples should not fear the commitment that marriage brings. Many young men today are delaying marriage until their late 30's or 40's. This situation has been on the rise since 1911 when Fr. Thomas Gerrard noted: *The number is growing of those young men who abstain from marriage in order that they may have the pleasure of trifling luxuries. They prefer to be free for the joys of cigarettes and billiards rather than undertake the burden of marriage with its greater joys. Such a choice is nothing but low, unworthy selfishness.*[74] By foregoing marriage for a mistaken notion of "freedom" a young man is missing the joys of fidelity that brings with it the comforting security of a spouse who is devoted to his best interests—a person on whom he can always depend.

---

[74] *Ibid.,* p. 37.

If a son seems to have a vocation to marriage but puts it off, it may be time to sit down and have a serious chat about the value and joys of marriage. Experience seems to indicate that the longer a young man or a young woman remains single the more self-centered and set in one's ways he or she becomes. Marriage then becomes a more difficult adjustment to make. In Moslem and Hindu families the parents decide when their children are mature enough to marry then help their children find spouses.

Another concern is long engagements lasting more than six months because they can become an occasion of serious sin for the young couple. If a couple dates for more than six months and there is no indication that the relationship is going to lead to marriage, the relationship should end so that each can pursue other marriage possibilities.

Once a couple is married, the marriage commitment has to be lived on a moment-to-moment basis. There are ups and downs in all marriages, but it is the commitment that cements the relationship and holds it together through good days and bad. It is a commitment based on true love. *True love means going out of oneself and giving oneself,* explains St. Josemaría Escrivá.

Teach your children that, once married, they have the obligation to strengthen and enrich their commitment to each other in marriage both individually and as a couple. Individually, each one should seek out spiritual formation and direction as well as intensify their frequent reception of the sacraments. As a couple, they should attend seminars, courses, and lectures on marriage, the family, and related topics. The Institute for Family Development has wonderful courses to enrich marriages and family life. Check it out on the Internet.

As parents you have an obligation to deeply instill in your children the permanence of marriage. Explain to your children that since divorce is not an option for them they must choose very carefully whom they marry. Once a child marries, you must do everything possible to keep the marriage together. In Moslem families, if there are marital difficulties, the parents come to live with the couple until the difficulties are resolved. The parents are willing to travel halfway around the world and stay for several months if that is what it takes to keep the couple married. As Catholic Christians we have an even greater responsibility to do the same because our marriages are sacraments. When Suzy comes home crying or John comes back home in a huff, your role is not to take her/him in, then call a divorce lawyer to settle the problem. Recall the words of Jesus, *If any man would come after me, let him deny himself and take up his cross and follow me* (*Mt.* 16:24). Your role is to help Suzy or John to live the marriage vows. Separation is permitted in the case of physical abuse or other grave dangers but be cautious about such an accusation. Young women tend to throw this term around loosely to gain sympathy. One bored young housewife decided to leave her husband for another man. Knowing that this would be unacceptable to her strong Catholic family, she accused her husband of physical abuse. Her parents, horrified by their daughter's claim, took her and her children in. She not only lied to her parents, but ruined her husband's fine reputation. In time the truth came out. In another case a young woman, with a volatile temper, left her husband accusing him of physical abuse. Her parents immediately took her in, hired a lawyer to file for divorce, and refused to work to bring about a reconciliation between the young couple. This young woman has a history of causing family problems with her parents and siblings verbally and physically because of her lack of self-control. Yet her parents refuse to even consider the possibility that their daughter might have precipitated the problems in her marriage. Reiterate to your children over and over again that wedding bells = commitment for better or for worse.

Teach your children how to evaluate people so they can select a good spouse. Train them to look for virtues in a prospective spouse rather than external beauty or handsomeness. Since marriage is a path to holiness, teach them to look for a spouse who has the same faith, morals, and spiritual ambitions. Develop friendships with families who are also seeking holiness so that your children have a support group from which to possibly choose a spouse. Ingrain the virtue of chastity in your children so that it will in the future protect fidelity in their marriages.

Parents, be very involved with your teens and young adults as they date. Insist on meeting your children's friends and dates. Invite them to your home for dinner and family activities. Watch how these prospective spouses interact with your child and family. Point out character flaws or lack of virtue in the beginning of a relationship, *before* your child's heart becomes too intertwined with the other. Once your child is madly in love it's too late to express concern. In considering a possible spouse, your child should take the following points into consideration:

- ✓ Is the person Catholic? Has the person made his First Communion, been confirmed? Is he/she practicing his/her faith now? Does he/she frequent the Sacrament of Confession? If the person is not practicing the faith is he/she sincerely willing to come back to the faith? (Review our earlier discussion on the importance of marrying a practicing Catholic.)

- ✓ What are the person's views on contraception and abortion?

- ✓ Is the person open to having as many children as God sends?

- ✓ Does this person believe in fidelity in marriage?

- ✓ Can this person make a commitment?

- ✓ Does this person believe that marriage is forever? Even when the going gets tough?

- ✓ Is the family background of the boyfriend or girlfriend compatible to yours?

- ✓ What type of family background does the person come from? If from a divorced family, what are his/her views on divorce?

- ✓ Which virtues does this person possess? Is he/she honest, sober, trustworthy, and chaste? Is the person moral, truthful, and sincere?

- ✓ Which vices does this person possess? Is he or she aware of them and willing to work on them?

- ✓ Can the boyfriend make a decent living so his wife can stay home with the children? Is the girl willing to give up her career to care for a family?

- ✓ How does the person treat his/her parents and siblings? Treat your child? Are there indications of thoughtfulness, spirit of service, kindness, and self-sacrifice?

- ✓ Do the couple quarrel constantly, complain about each other, show unrestrained rage or exhibit jealousy? These are dangerous symptoms that only grow worse in marriage.

- ✓ Does the person have or exhibit indications of mental illness? This can cause serious marital problems.

- ✓ Has the person suffered from some abuse as a young person or teen? If so the prognosis for a happy marriage is slim.

- ✓ Does the person take drugs or drink alcohol excessively? Such a person is a bad marriage risk.

- ✓ Is the person willing to participate in your family activities and share holidays with your family? If not this will cause future marital problems.

At the closing Mass of World Youth Day in Rome, John Paul II addressed the topic of selecting a spouse. Here is what he told the young adults gathered: *You are thinking about love and the choices it entails, and I imagine that you agree: what is really important in life is the choice of the person who will share it with you. But be careful! Every human person has inevitable limits: even in the most successful marriages there is always a certain amount of disappointment...Every human being finds himself sooner or later saying what [the Apostle Peter] said: "To whom shall we go?"*

...[T]he answer regarding the path to follow is already given. It is the path that leads to Christ. The Eucharist is the sacrament of the presence of Christ, who gives Himself to us because He loves us. He loves each one of us in a unique and personal way in our practical daily lives: in our families, among our friends,

at study and work, in rest and relaxation. *He loves us when He fills our days with freshness, and also when, in times of suffering, He allows trials to weigh upon us: even in the most severe trials, He lets us hear His voice. Yes, dear friends, Christ loves us and He loves us forever! He loves us even when we disappoint Him, when we fail to meet His expectations for us. He never fails to embrace us in His mercy. How can we not be grateful to this God who has redeemed us, going so far as to accept the foolishness of the Cross? To God who has come to be at our side and has stayed with us to the end?*

To celebrate the Eucharist, "to eat His flesh and drink His blood," means to accept the wisdom of the Cross-and the path of service. It means that we signal our willingness to sacrifice ourselves for others, as Christ has done.

Our society desperately needs this sign, and young people need it even more so, tempted as they often are by the illusion of an easy and comfortable life, by drugs and pleasure-seeking, only to find themselves in a spiral of despair, meaninglessness and violence. It is urgent to change direction and to turn to Christ. This is the way of justice, solidarity and commitment to building a society and a future worthy of the human person...

Jesus is no lover of half measures, and He does not hesitate to pursue us with the question: "Will you also go away?" In the presence of Christ, the Bread of Life, we too want to say today with Peter: **"Lord, to whom shall we go? You have the words of eternal life"** *(Jn.* 6:68).[75]

See how each of the sacraments intertwines with the others to help your children to grow holy?

The Question Of Vocations

"We who work for God should be lighthearted."
St. Leonard of Port Maurice

Before discussing the Sacrament of Holy Orders, let's first consider the concept of vocation. A vocation is simply one of

[75] Zenit, August 20, 2000.

several possible paths that God calls us to chose in order to grow holy...to become saints. People are called to select a vocational path from among marriage, holy orders, the religious life, and the celibate single life. It is in this vocation that we will find peace, happiness and holiness because it is the specific path chosen for us by God.

During your children's night prayers have them pray for their future vocation whether it be to marriage, the priesthood, religious life or the celibate single life. Encourage your children to offer their lives to God in the manner He has planned for them. Only when your children follow the vocation that God has chosen for them will they be happy, at peace. My Passionist priest uncle, whom I mentioned earlier, told me about a married couple he knew who were utterly miserable in their marriage. *The reason they are so unhappy is that the husband had a vocation to the priesthood and his wife had a vocation to the religious life. They refused to heed the call of God so now they spend their lives making each other miserable.* In another family, a couple had just one child, a daughter. After high school she asked to enter the convent. Her parents refused to even consider such a vocation for her. As a result of their objections the young woman not only never found her niche in life but eventually turned to witchcraft then to a satanic cult to quench her desire for the "spiritual." God's grace is always available to help reverse the bad decisions you and your children make but many times one's will is so set that even this help of God is rejected. Such was the case in the above examples.

While we fret about the lack of vocations, could society's obsession with and our acceptance of the quest for fame, power, and money be another one of the reasons we have so few priestly vocations? Recall the story of the rich young man in the gospel. He could have been one of our first priests, one of our first great saints. He was a good, moral young man. He was doing everything right until God asked more of him, as He asks more of our children and us. This young man could not give up his riches to follow Christ. Sadly, he turned away and never came back. His name is not even recorded in the two gospels in which his story is mentioned...only his rejection of God's will. Since his soul exists for all eternity, how embarrassed he must be to have every Christian who ever existed read about him saying "no" to God. His money is long gone but his "no" resonates down through the centuries. Do you want a similar legacy for your children? *The principal cause for the decrease in the number of priests is due not so much to defections as to the lack of young men responding to God's call,* according to John Paul II.[76] *[M]ay the young be attentive to the call of the Lord who invites them to follow him, and may they respond with generosity by committing themselves to him in the priesthood or the active or contemplative consecrated life!* [77]

How do we encourage vocations in our families? For the most part, vocations depend on the spiritual fervor of families. I was chatting with a friend who lives in Kansas who has four sons. The parents prayed daily that their sons would become priests. From the four sons, one did become a priest a year ago. In addition, one of their grandsons, who was home schooled, is a seminarian. As I prodded her to find out more about how she raised her sons, she told me that besides personally going to daily Mass, her family said the daily rosary. *Daily I ask God to guide all of us to do what He wants us to do. We pray 24 Glory Be's a day to the Little Flower for our spiritual and physical well-being. This custom prevented my son from being on a military plane that crashed, as well as saving another son's eye from being destroyed by a golf ball that knocked him out. I could tell by the time my priest-son was eight or nine that he had a vocation to the priesthood but I did not push.*

The parents of St. Thérèse, the Martins, realized that each of their children was a child of God, a temporary gift He had given them to form in faith and virtue. They did not dream of earthly success for their children. Instead, the Martins focused on sanctity for them. While they prayed for their sons to become priests, none lived to fulfill their dream. But how they reacted to the religious vocations of their surviving daughters is telling.

---

[76] Zenit, Jan. 30, 2000.

[77] Zenit, Feb. 25, 2000

While Zélie did not live long enough to see her dream realized, Louis knew the joy and pain of offering all his daughters as Brides of Christ. Marie explains his reaction when she asked permission to join Pauline in the Carmelites: *He stifled a sob and said brokenly: 'Ah!...Ah!..But...without you!...The good God could not have asked a greater sacrifice of me! I thought that you would never leave me!*

When her younger sister, St. Thérèse, asked to join the Carmel by her 15th birthday, her father not only took her to the Bishop so that she could personally ask for early admittance but then took her to church saying: *Come, let us go together to the Blessed Sacrament to thank the Lord for the graces he bestowed on our family, and for the honor He gave me of choosing His spouses in my home. Yes, if I possessed anything better, I would hasten to offer it to Him.*

St. John Bosco was gifted with dreams. When he was about nine-years-old he received his call to the priesthood. He dreamt that he was wrestling with young boys. *Our Lord said to me: "Stop fighting. You must win them over with love." I answered: "What you tell me is impossible. Who will teach me this love?" Our Lord replied: "My Mother will be your teacher." Our Lady then appeared and said: "You did not know it, but you were fighting with wolves. Go among them with courage, and they will change into lambs. This will be your vocation later on."* [78] When John told his family about his dream, his mother interpreted that the dream meant he would become a priest.

When St. Josemaría Escrivá was fifteen he decided to become an architect. But God had already decided that he would become an architect of souls. Seeing one day the barefoot prints of a discalced Carmelite in the snow, he began to think, *If that Carmelite was able to offer up that sacrifice out of love for God, then what can I do for God myself?* Josemaría began to go to daily Mass and Communion. He went to confession more frequently along with developing the custom of making daily sacrifices. He then began to feel that God was asking something

---

[78] *Saints & Heroes Speak Vol. Three, Op. Cit.* p. 11.

of him and felt that he could better fulfill "that something" if he became a priest. When he confided his change of plans to his father, his father cried then said, *My son, priests have to be very holy. I will not stop you, but I want you to think about it some more.*" Several days later Don José took his son to see a priest friend who could guide the young boy in his decision. The support of parents is critical.

During the final Mass at World Youth Day 2000 in Italy, John Paul II asked, *If any of you dear young men and women hear the Lord's inner call to give yourselves completely to Him in order to love Him "with an undivided heart," do not be held back by doubts or fears. Say "yes" with courage and without reservation, trusting Him who is faithful to His promises.*" Five thousand youth came forward to give their lives to God. Among this number 3,000 young men indicated a desire to enter the seminary while 2,000 young women indicated interest in the religious life. This came after John Paul II reminisced about his vocation: *My priestly vocation came to its full maturity during the Second World War, during the occupation of Poland. The tragedy of the War gave a particular coloring to the gradual maturing of my vocation in life. In these circumstances, I perceived a light shining ever more brightly within me: the Lord wanted me to be a priest! I remember with feeling that moment in my life when, on the morning of 1 November 1946, I was ordained a priest...Spend time in prayer, letting the Spirit speak to your hearts. To pray means to give some of your time to Christ, to entrust yourselves to Him, to listen in silence to His word, to make it echo in your hearts...*

Ask the Holy Spirit to enlighten your minds, ask Him for the gift of a living faith which will forever give meaning to your lives...[79]

The **Wall Street Journal** ran an interesting article written by Gil Troy, a history professor at McGill University in Montreal concerning the ordination of his college roommate to the priesthood. He writes: *Recently, my college roommate became a priest. Even though he was the only Catholic among*

---
[79] Zenit, Aug. 15, 2000.

us...all of his senior year roommates attended the ordination...

While in college days Justin had been...a Greek god seeking glory for Harvard and football, now, as a Jesuit, he was going to apply his discipline and intelligence seeking glory for God—and salvation for humanity. As his friends blazed career paths, he embarked on what the presiding bishop called "a faith journey." As we worked on securing professorships and partnerships, he was trying to save souls. Our vocabulary was one of promotions and raises, of successes and failures; his was a language of love, of holiness, of mysteries...

Watching the clerics welcome new colleagues into this venerable fraternity of spiritual leadership, I felt ashamed by our crass culture, a culture so self-indulgent that we mock the priest's self-discipline, a culture so negative that it demonizes all priests because of the sins of the few, a culture so cynical that many of us seem relieved to find that God's supposed emissaries have feet of clay...

These days it is fashionable to harp on all the cultural toxins in the modern world. But if our society still leaves room for a journey like Justin's maybe, just maybe, there is hope for us all.[80]

Remember, for your children to be truly happy, you have to help them discern their true vocation, then accept it with a cheerful heart rather than throwing up obstacles to dissuade them from the path selected for them by God. In the late 1800's the parents of Bl. Enrico Rebuschini opposed the priestly vocation of their son although he had felt a personal attraction to it from his childhood. It was only after he attended college, served in the military, then worked in his brother-in-law's silk factory that they realized how unhappy he was following their will rather than God's will. Eventually he was ordained by the future Pope St. Pius X.

How does a parent help a child to discern his vocational path? First discover what the child loves. Love rests in the will rather than in the passions. *I may have a love for the religious life...without having any affection for it. I may see that only by*

[80] Gil Troy, "His New Fraternity," *The Wall Street Journal*, June 15, 2000.

entering religion shall I be able to do the greatest good to my fellow men. Even though I have an aversion for common life and loss of liberty, yet I may see in those things my best chance of salvation and love them accordingly, writes Fr. Gerrard.[81] If you reread page 37 under the heading *Spiritual Struggles,* you will see that this was the case in the vocations of the Martin sisters.

Discuss with your children the various vocational choices. Ask them the following questions: *Which state of life do you really love? Do you want to be married? Do you want to live singly in the world and devote yourself to a special profession? Do you want to be a priest? Do you want to be a nun? Above all, is your desire constant, or do you waver between one thing and another, never knowing your own mind?* [82]

Marriage is the most common vocation and is indicated when a couple falls responsibly in love. *It is the state for which they are by nature fitted, and for them the highest and most perfect life which they can live.*[83]

Rev. Gerrard explains: *Vocations to the celibate life usually begin to show themselves before the age adapted to marriage.* My research indicates the first two years of high school seems to be a key period for discerning a vocation to the priesthood. Parents should take care to discuss vocations more deeply at this time in a very positive manner. Also realize that some children mature earlier. Be especially alert to the indications given by your teens. Saint Elizabeth of Schonau entered the convent at the age of twelve.

Parents need to know that such a vocation is a special gift of God. Its chief sign is a spontaneous and constant desire. Two dangers are to be avoided. Parents must not force the idea of the priesthood or of the cloister on their children. Nor on the other hands must they suppress it when it appears. Indeed, they will be on the lookout for the signs of zeal and piety which accompany the desire, so that the vocation may have every chance of coming

---

[81] *Marriage and Parenthood, The Catholic Ideal, Op. Cit,* p. 34.
[82] *Ibid.,* pp. 34-35.   [83] *Ibid.,* p. 35.

to maturity. It is a great privilege to be able to offer a child for the special service of God. St. Tigridia, the daughter of a Spanish count who lived in the 11th century, had such signs of a religious vocation. Despite the grandeur of her surroundings she was pious, preferring to spend her time before the Blessed Sacrament and in prayer rather than in attending balls. Her father not only gave his consent to her religious vocation but encouraged her by founding a monastery and church for her.

There are four chief signs of a religious vocation, namely: constant desire; fitness for the order as to health, ability, and character; acceptance by the order; the absence of any obligation of supporting parents in need.[84] In cases of uncertainty it is best to consult a spiritual director.

Fr. C. John McCloskey III, STD, makes an interesting observation: *St. John Bosco was reported as saying that one out of every ten Catholic men has a vocation. We could say that he employed the word "men" in the inclusive sense and say that one out of every ten persons has a specific supernatural calling from God...Nowadays, it is more and more recognized that the vocation to apostolic celibacy for the kingdom of God is also a viable choice for the lay person. Indeed, the Church has made it quite clear through its enthusiastic endorsement of the need and the efficacy of specific vocations to the various movements and institutions of the Church that are lay-oriented.*[85]

As to the single life, Fr. Gerrard notes that some women are *obviously intended to be free from the cares of a family so as to be able to take a more active and independent part in the social and spiritual regeneration of the community....Single blessedness, thus sanctified by the Church, has a social as well as an individual value. The restraint practiced in the single life re-acts generally on the whole social organism. It re-acts particularly on the marriage state, strengthening it and keeping it pure. We are all members one of another. The power of self-conquest which virginity implies is bound to tell in greater or*

---

[84] *Ibid.,* p. 134

[85] Fr. C. John McCloskey III, STD, "The Family: Seedbed of Vocations," *Religious Life,* Oct. 2000, p. 2.

less degree on every member of society...What is meant, however, is that the life shall be lived at least in a state of grace and that effort shall be made towards spiritual perfection.[86]

How can you, as a parent, foster a supernatural vocation in your children? Fr. McCloskey has five tips:

1. Parents must be their children's best friends...Speak positively about the Church and a life dedicated to God. Never speak negatively about persons who have dedicated their lives to God...Your children should know that you pray...everyday that they be holy and happy and generous to whatever God calls them...

2. Foster a simple life of piety in the home adjusted to the conditions and ages of the children.

3. Teach them to value poverty and detachment. Keep them short on money. Do not let them...measure people by the amount of their possessions. Teach them to make things last and how to go without happily. Teach them to share cheerfully. Make sure they spend their summers productively. That often times will mean they work and/or spend time in generously serving others less fortunate then themselves.

4. Expose them, according to their age, and ability to "take it", to misery. Soup kitchens, nursing homes, and hospitals for incurables—including for children—should be places where, over time, they feel comfortable. One of the most effective ways to assure this quality of generosity is simply to have a large family and to treasure the children God has sent to you. This will help them to place the person and not the pleasure or object at the heart of their moral universe...Thus...they will never see another person as a means or an object but rather as another Christ whom it is their privilege to serve.

5. Instill an appreciation of beauty; whether it be in nature, literature, music, or art. Take special care with their formation outside the house. Encourage them to have a wide variety of friends with whom they can share the joy of your own family life. By the time they graduate from high school they simply must have an excellent grasp of Catholic doctrinal and moral teaching and be able to give an account to others of the hope that is within them. This is your primary responsibility.[87]

---

[86] *Marriage and Parenthood, The Catholic Ideal, Op. Cit,* pp. 41, 40.
[87] "The Family: Seedbed of Vocations," *Op. Cit.,* p. 4-5.

Fr. McCloskey concludes by noting: *Vocations are a supply-side phenomenon. Supply creates demand. If you supply (offer) your children to God through your prayer and careful preparation, He will match you by taking them through His grace and their collaboration. Don't forget the shortcut of entrusting them to Mary...If Our Lady takes a special liking to them, her Son will form them into the new evangelizers of the third millennium...And if your children don't receive a divine vocation which is unlikely if you follow the advice given above? Don't worry, your grandchildren will. You cannot outdo God in generosity.*[88]

Two families in New York bear out Fr. McCloskey's advice. Arnold and Marcia Pilsner have four sons of which three are priests. Fr. James Pilsner recalls that *my parents are religious people. They didn't talk about the priesthood much, but they did make sure that we were practicing the faith.* His brother, Fr. Peter Pilsner adds, *my parents never pushed priesthood but placed a high value on spiritual life and faith.* Mary, their only sister, died at the age of 25 from bone cancer. *Her suffering through the years was an example of selfless love and a source of grace for her brothers' vocations.* "*I sincerely believe that the primary message my family has to offer is that we can never overestimate the supernatural value of suffering united to that of Jesus,*" Marcia Pilsner explained.

John and Bernadette Higgins have only two sons both of whom are priests. Fr. Vincent Higgins recalls that his parents never pushed them to become priests but *their example of their faith encouraged us. Their love of the Church and the Eucharist, and their reverence for the liturgy were passed on to us.* His brother, Fr. John Higgins, notes, *In some ways, it's a mystery to me how my brother and I both ended up as priests. It's the mystery of vocation, God's call, which is a gift given not only to an individual but also to a family...When a man places his life in the hands of God and follows His call a whole new world of possibilities opens up.* His mother, Bernadette, insists that *one's home should always be a sacred place, and the Church should*

---

[88] *Ibid.*, p. 5.

be the center of your lives. As for her husband, John, *he has no regrets that his sons will not have children and will not pass on the Higgins name to them. "As priests, they will have many spiritual children, and I will be in that sense a spiritual grandfather."* Both families frequently invited priests over for dinner,expressed a positive attitude toward religious life, and encouraged their sons to be altar boys.[89]

Since each person's vocation impacts the soul in a profound manner, Satan is every ready to tempt us away from our lawful vocation. The day before St. Thérèse was to make her vows she writes: *My vocation suddenly appeared to me as unreal as a dream. The devil—for it was he—assured me that I was wholly unsuited for the Carmelite life...the darkness became so intense that one fact alone stood out clear—I had no vocation and must return to the world. I cannot describe all I went through.*[90]

Pauline, Thérèse' older sister, had always felt called to be a religious. In fact, she planned to join the Visitation Convent where she had attended school and where her aunt, Sister Marie-Dosithee, was a religious. Only twenty when she asked for admittance, the prioress told Pauline that she could not enter until she was twenty-two. Attending Mass with her sister, Marie, and her father on Feb. 16, 1882, in the chapel of Our Lady of Mount Carmel, Pauline knew God was calling her to become a Carmelite instead. She later recounted, *I had never before thought of Carmel.* Marie tried to dissuade her thinking that the austere life would be too difficult for Pauline's health. In the evening, after speaking several times with her father about this, Louis took her aside and told her: *You mustn't think, dear Pauline, that because I am happy to give to God I shall not suffer at your leaving me, for I love you dearly.*[91]

Thérèse was devastated when she learned of Pauline's leaving. *In a flash, I realized what life was like. Until then it had not seemed too miserable a business, but then I saw what it*

[89] "Two families with five priests, reflect on God's gift", *Catholic Times,* May 27, 2001, p. 16.

[90] *Storm of Glory, Op. Cit.,* p. 81.

[91] *Saint Therese, The Little Flower (The Making of a Saint), Op. Cit.,* p. 76.

really was—nothing but suffering and continual partings. I wept bitterly, for then I didn't understand the joy of sacrifice. I was weak, so weak that I thought it a great grace to be able to endure a trial which seemed far beyond my strength. If the news of Pauline's departure had been broken to me gently I shouldn't have suffered anything like as much, but coming on me as a complete surprise, it was like having a sword plunged into my heart.[92]

Holy Orders

"The priest is above all a man of charity, destined to the greatest possible good, to sanctify others by word and example, with holiness and knowledge."

BI. Joseph Allamano

Fr. John Hardon, S.J., explains that the Sacrament of Holy Orders makes the priest a partner *in the* Savior's *work of redemption, to save a sinful world from its follies and bring sinful men to Heaven.*[93] Fr. Hans Urs Von Balthasar gets more specific: *The humble priest will not be tempted to offer me anything other than the Word of God for me; the zealous priest will not tolerate my attempts to slide away from this Word. He will make me stick to my last, and I can easily accuse him of intruding and interfering; but what intrudes and interferes in truth is only the Word of God itself...[W]here there is a genuine transparency of self-giving [in a priest]stemming from prayer in union with God, from humility which is itself a readiness to pass on what it has received, then the miracle can occur that in the Holy Spirit within the Church I receive true instruction from God, in such a way that, however uncomfortable it may be, I cannot afford to neglect it.*[94]

Holy Orders gives a sacred power and a consecrating grace which enables deacons, priests, and bishops to act in the <u>Name</u> and in the <u>Person</u> of Christ, and helps them to sanctify the other members of the Church by aiding them to carry out the duties of their sacred ministry faithfully.[95]

---

[92] *Ibid.,* p. 70.
[93] "Holy Orders..." *The Sacraments and the Marian Catechist, Op. Cit.*
[94] John Riches, *Elucidations* (San Francisco, St. Ignatius Press, 1975).
[95] *The Sacraments, Sources of Christian Life, Op. Cit.* p. 3.

Do you realize that the most powerful person on earth is a priest? <u>Only</u> a priest has the power to bring Jesus down from heaven so that we can physically receive Him, Body, Blood, Soul, and Divinity. <u>Only</u> a priest can say Mass, which is the perpetual sacrifice of Calvary. <u>Only</u> a priest can say the words of absolution to forgive you your sins. <u>Only</u> a priest can give the anointing of the sick to help those who are ailing or near death. <u>Only</u> a bishop, who is a priest, can infuse you with the Holy Spirit at Confirmation and perpetuate the priesthood through Holy Orders. To put it simply, the priest holds the powers of heaven within his consecrated hands.

Teach your children the great dignity of the priesthood. Explain to them that the priesthood is a vocation, not a profession, career, or job. In this vocation there are neither days off nor retirement. Neither advancement nor promotion should be goals. Ambitions should center on saving as many souls as possible for the Kingdom of God. Such examples of selfless dedication are the many "retired" priests who fill their days saying Mass, hearing confessions, giving spiritual direction, visiting the sick, and teaching doctrine. Fr. John Hardon, S.J., who up to his death at the age of 86, was busily writing various books at the same time, giving Marian catechist lessons, lecturing, giving retreats, advising the Holy See, and working on various projects that took him all over the world. Three elderly priests, Fr. Tom Davenport, Fr. John Sheahan and Fr. Frank Corrigan, who live at our diocesan retirement center, are also diligent examples of priests consumed with the desire to bring people closer to God. They are available to hear confessions at anytime. Fr. Davenport, 84, and Fr. Sheahan say daily Mass in the late morning for those of us who can't make early Masses. Fr. Corrigan, 90, gave weekly classes on the ***Catechism of the Catholic Church*** and the Holy Eucharist until he became ill and had to be moved to an infirmary. Visiting him at the infirmary I found that Fr. Corrigan is still a fisher of souls although he's now hooked up to oxygen. He told me of two of his nurses that he is evangelizing. One has five children, none of whom is baptized. Another has three children but none know anything about the faith. He organized classes in his room on the nurses' days off to teach them the faith. He's working to get the children baptized. On the nurses' breaks, he teaches them the rosary. By phone he purchased rosary explanation booklets and found a man who will make rosaries for him. As I left, he gave me his blessing then told me that he says daily Mass in his room so if I ever need to attend a Mass at a certain time to just give him a call and he'll say his Mass at my convenience. Fr. Frank O'Hara, at 85, ran a parish, without any assistant. On his "free days" he worked as a chaplain at St. John's Hospital walking the corridors saving many souls near death. Recently he suffered several strokes. During the last stroke it looked as though he would not survive. One of his concerned visitors was a young Protestant minister, who also makes pastoral visits to the sick at St. John's. During their final chat, Fr. O'Hara told the minister that it was now time for him to come into the Catholic faith. The minister agreed to pray about this possibility and to begin reading and studying the teachings of the Church beginning with the *Catechism of the Catholic Church.* The minister told my friend, who was present at the time, that when he first met Fr. O'Hara he decided "to put him in his place" by calling him "Frank" rather than "Father." Within several weeks of working with the elderly priest, the minister found himself affectionately calling him "Fr. O'Hara." *I think of him as a spiritual father.* This minister is now attending daily Mass at the hospital. Each of these priests is filled with the zeal of Christ. They are the real heroes of our culture. One of the most touching stories involves Fr. Don Roberts of the Springfield Illinois diocese. The priest who brought Fr. Roberts into the Church through baptism was prepared to meet God through the last sacraments administered by Fr. Roberts on his deathbed. Four months after the priest's death, Fr. Roberts was given his antique chalice.

If a son is called to the priesthood stress the fact that he **must** be a holy priest since only holy priests can produce holy laity. This is called "spiritual reproduction." A priest who does not strive for holiness causes tremendous spiritual damage to souls. It was a Catholic priest who began every heresy in the Catholic

Church. Unholy priests caused every major break in Catholic unity. Fr. John Hardon, S.J., reminds those thinking of a priestly vocation that Christ ordains them *for others, not for oneself.* **You must be a holy priest or do not be ordained.**

The Sacrament Of The Sick

"God is occupied with each soul as though there were no others like it."
St. Thérèse

The Anointing of the sick (Extreme Unction) gives an alleviating grace to the seriously ill to lighten their sufferings, forgive their sins, and bring them to eternal salvation. It also comforts them in their last agony and helps them overcome final temptations.[96] The *Catechism of the Catholic Church* teaches:

> **#1501 Illness can lead to anguish, self-absorption, sometimes even despair and revolt against God. It can also make a person more mature, helping him discern in his life what is not essential so that he can turn toward that which is. Very often illness provokes a search for God and a return to him.**

How wonderfully God cares for us in all the stages of our lives, from birth to death. It is in the *Epistle* to *St. James* (5:14-15) that we find the basis of this comforting sacrament: *Is any among you sick? Let him call for the presbyters [priests] of the Church, and let them pray over him, anointing him with oil in the name of the Lord; and the prayer of faith will save the sick man, and the Lord will raise him up; and if he has committed sins, he will be forgiven.*

The *Catechism of the Catholic Church* instructs :

> **#1515 The Anointing of the Sick "is not a sacrament for those only who are at the point of death. Hence, as soon as anyone of the faithful begins to be in danger of death from sickness or old age, the fitting time for him to receive this sacrament has certainly already arrived."**

> **#1516 If a sick person who received this anointing recovers his health, he can in the case of another grave illness receive this sacrament again. If during the same illness the person's**

---

[96] *"The Sacraments, Sources of Christian Life," Op.Cit.,* p. 3.

condition becomes more serious, the sacrament may be repeated. It is fitting to receive the Anointing of the Sick just prior to a serious operation. The same holds for the elderly whose frailty becomes more pronounced.

Only a priest/bishop can minister this sacrament, not the pastoral minister or Eucharistic minister of a hospital.

#1531 The celebration of the Anointing of the Sick consists essentially in the anointing of the forehead and hands of the sick person (in the Roman Rite) or of other parts of the body (in the Eastern rite), and the anointing being accompanied by the liturgical prayer of the celebrant asking for the special grace of this sacrament.

#1532 The special grace of the sacrament of the Anointing of the Sick has as its effects:
—The uniting of the sick person to the passion of Christ, for his own good and that of the whole Church;
—the strengthening, peace, and courage to endure in a Christian manner the sufferings or illness of old age;
—the forgiveness of sins, if the sick person was not able to obtain it through the sacrament of Penance;
—the restoration of health, if it is conducive to the salvation of his soul;
—the preparation for passing over to eternal life.

#1524 In addition to the Anointing of the Sick, the Church offers those who are about to leave this life the Eucharist as viaticum. Communion in the body and blood of Christ, received at this moment of "passing over" to the Father, has a particular significance and importance. It is the seed of eternal life and the power of resurrection, according to the words of the Lord: *"He who eats my flesh and drinks my blood has eternal life, and I will raise him up at the last day."* [97] The sacrament of Christ once dead and now risen, the Eucharist is here the sacrament of passing over from death to life, from this world to the Father.

Instill in your children the importance of this sacrament when they, or someone they know, are seriously ill, or

---

[97] *Jn.* 6:54.

undergoing surgery. Explain to them clearly and repeatedly that should you be seriously injured or near death you expect them to contact a priest for you. Although the physical welfare of a person is important, the spiritual welfare should be topmost in our minds. Sometimes in the flurry of sudden shock we forget the spiritual. As an example of this, two priests hurried to the bedside of a fellow priest who was near death. After their visit, as they were leaving the hospital, they ran into some friends of the priest coming to visit. After talking a bit, one asked if the dying priest had been anointed. *I was dumbfounded that I had never thought to anoint the priest,*one of the priests related. *It was embarrassing that a lay person had to remind me of this serious obligation.* Take nothing for granted. The greatest gift you can give a person who is seriously ill, facing surgery or dying is to arrange for them to be anointed by a priest. Engrave this in your children's minds! St. Thérèse's father, Louis Martin, made sure that anyone dying in his neighborhood had a priest present to give the last sacraments. Imitate his example.

Prior to Vatican II, all of the senses were anointed rather than just the forehead and hands, as is the custom now. (This was because the sacrament forgives all sins committed by our senses.) Only a person capable of sinning can validly receive this sacrament. Children who have reached the age of reason can be anointed, but a baptized infant, who is dying, would not receive the Sacrament since the child is already in the state of grace and incapable of sinning.

To receive this sacrament, the person must be baptized, as well as, have a sincere repentance for past sins. God's mercy is so great that even if a person has been out of the Church for numerous years but nevertheless regrets his past sins even though he is unconscious and cannot make a confession, the anointing will remove his sins. A person who is conscious but has been away from the sacraments does not even need to make an act of perfect sorrow. He only needs to cooperate by fearing God's just punishments to have the right disposition for forgiveness. **The open (conscious) reception of the**

334 Raise Happy Children...Raise Them Saints!

sacrament assures salvation. Bring a priest to all Catholic relatives, friends or acquaintances who are dying, **even** if they have not been practicing Catholics for years. Don't allow a false sense of human respect, or the fear of "interfering," prevent you from saving their souls. Teach this to your children.

As is mentioned in the *Catechism* #1532 this sacrament confers supernatural courage, patience, and the loving acceptance of death. It also gives the person the power to resist the final temptations of Satan who tries to tempt us to discouragement and despair. It gives peace: peace of mind because one is assured of God's mercy. It gives peace of heart because one is confident of being in God's grace. It can also restore body benefits accordingly. It can speed one's healing. But the physical effects are dependent on the will of God. A person will be healed if the healing will be of spiritual benefit to the person's soul. Remember, the healing of the body is not the main reason for the anointing.

Permit me to digress just a moment here. Along with the sacrament of anointing, when a person is seriously ill or has suffered some physical trauma, consider placing a Miraculous Medal on the person. The medal, originally called the Medal of the Immaculate Conception, is nicknamed the Miraculous Medal because of all the miracles attributed to it. Fr. John Hardon, S.J., was a strong proponent of the medal but he wasn't always. In fact, in the beginning of his priestly ministry he did not give the medal much credence until one day he was called to a hospital to anoint a patient. As he was leaving the hospital, a nun stopped him and asked, *would you please take this Miraculous Medal and place it around the neck of the young man in the next room. He has been in a coma for six weeks and there is little hope of his recovery.* To please the nun, Fr. Hardon did what she asked, then prayed over the young man. Immediately the young man's eyes opened and he began speaking. *After that experience, I became a promoter of the medal,* explained Fr. Hardon.

Another benefit of being anointed involves the lessening of one's stay in Purgatory. Although our sins are forgiven through the Sacrament of Reconciliation or through the Anointing of the Sick, we still have to make reparation for all the sins we committed. If this reparation is not completed on earth it must be completed in Purgatory. The more sins one has to make reparation for in Purgatory the more one will suffer there. But this sacrament can lessen or remove altogether one's Purgatory depending on the degree of a person's resignation to the will of God and the depths of his love for God.

In emergency situations a priest gives conditional Baptism and absolution then anoints. If a person apparently has just died the person can still be anointed because we do not know exactly when the soul leaves the body. While the Bishop blesses the normal oil used for anointing, in an emergency a priest can bless and use any type of vegetable oil.

Along with teaching your children about this powerful sacrament, prepare your children for death. Life is simply our testing ground. Death gives us our test results. The saints never feared death because death was the door that brought them to the eternal vision of God. They grieved when those they loved died, yet they had a supernatural outlook at all times. St. Elizabeth Ann Seton lost her oldest daughter, Anna, a novice in her new order, before she was eighteen as well as her other daughters, Elizabeth and Rebecca. In her sorrow she prayed: *Oh Lord, my beloved is with you; she will no longer be in danger of offending You. I give her to You with all my heart.* Elizabeth herself died when she was only forty-seven-years-old.

For twelve years, St. Thérèse's mother, Mrs. Martin, suffered from breast cancer. When medication and other treatments failed to arrest the cancer, she and her three oldest daughters made a pilgrimage to Lourdes to beg Our Lady for a cure. When she was not cured she wrote, *what do you want? If the Holy Virgin does not cure me, it is because my time is done and the good Lord wants me to rest someplace other than on earth.*

Each person is a temporary gift from God. As such we have to strive to have a supernatural outlook when God calls someone we love, or ourselves, to Him. I was told of an elderly woman who was dying but she was resentful over her pending death. Her mother had lived well into her nineties and this woman felt she was being robbed by dying only in her early eighties. Despite her bitterness, she continued to say her daily rosary, as she had done all her life. One day her daughter was surprised to hear her mother talking to someone but she could not see anyone in the room. After the conversation, her mother turned to the daughter to ask who the visitor was. Rather than agitating her mother by saying that no one was there, she just let the old woman talk. Later that evening, she and her sister went in to check on their mother. This time they noticed a radiant smile on her face. She was talking to someone they could not see. Then turning to her daughters she explained, *I now know who it is...I asked Our Lady to take me with her but she said "no" I'm not yet ready. I realize now that it's my pride that keeps me here.* Later that night the woman did die a peaceful death. The daughter told me that was the start of her conversion back to the Church.

When someone is dying, lavish the person with spiritual attention. The time prior to death is Satan's last stand. He spiritually attacks the dying person with a vengeance. Make sure that the person is receiving the sacraments. If the patient cannot swallow a fragment of the Sacred Host, ask if he can receive a drop of the Precious Blood. Has the patient been to confession lately? If not, call a priest. The Sacrament of the Anointing of the Sick will calm agitated patients. Periodically bless the patient with holy water. I have observed numerous cases where this sacramental brings instant calm to the patient. Pray the rosary and the Chapel of Divine Mercy at the bedside along with the prayer to St. Michael the Archangel. Remember, he is the Patron of the Dying. Read spiritual books to the patient even if the patient is comatose. Make sure that the patient is wearing a Scapular of Our Lady of Mt. Carmel. Our Lady promises a special protection for those who wear the scapular and have led good Christian lives.

See if you can procure an indulgence for the dying. This is a way for the person to avoid Purgatory. To receive the indulgence, one must be in the state of grace, and want the indulgence. There are various ways to receive such an indulgence. Research this for your own circumstances. For instance, members of Opus Dei and cooperators of Opus Dei receive a plenary indulgence at the moment of death. Fr. John Hardon, S.J., had the faculties to grant this indulgence to crucifixes that he blessed. If a person dies holding one of these blessed crucifixes, is in the state of grace, and wants the indulgence, the soul can avoid Purgatory. Numerous friends and acquaintances have died holding one of his crucifixes. Maybe there is a priest in your area that also has this faculty and he can bless crucifixes for you. To better understand "indulgences" read the **Catechism of the Catholic Church** numbers 1471-1479.

The corporal work of mercy tells us to *bury the dead.* Teach your children that once a person dies, their next responsibility to that person is to ensure a Catholic funeral Mass and burial in blessed ground, preferably a Catholic cemetery. Attendance at wakes and funerals is also part of this corporal work of mercy. These actions also serve as acts of charity. Teach your children the importance of having at least one Mass said for the repose of each soul who is departed.

In Conclusion...

"If man does not accept inwardly the grace of God, if he does not pray, if he does not approach the Sacraments frequently, if he does not strive for personal holiness, he loses the very meaning of his earthly pilgrimage. "
John Paul II

St. John Vianney sums up the importance of the seven sacraments: *[W]e must frequently receive the holy Sacraments so as to preserve sanctifying grace. A Christian who makes use of prayer and the Sacraments is to the devil what a soldier on horseback, equipped with weapons, is to a defenseless enemy, who flees at the very sight of him. Should he, however, get off his horse and lay aside his weapons, the enemy will fall upon him, throw him to the ground and overpower him. While he was*

338 *Raise Happy Children...Raise Them Saints!*

armed, the sight of him alone seemed to crush his enemy.

The devil said to St. Teresa that on account of her great love of God, her frequent reception of the Sacraments, he could not breathe in the places where she had been. Why? Because the Sacraments gave her strength to persevere in the grace of God. There has never been a saint who kept away from the sacraments and still preserved the friendship of God. In the Sacraments they gained the necessary strength to resist the devil and not to be overpowered by him. The reason is this: when we pray to God He lavishes innumerable graces upon us, to fortify us and to give us courage. He Himself comes to destroy our enemy. As soon as the devil is aware of His presence, he casts himself in despair into the abyss. This is the principal reason why the devil strives his utmost to prevent us from receiving the Sacraments, and incites us to profane them...[W]hen any one receives the Sacraments frequently the devil loses his power over him.

However, we must make a distinction. I am speaking of those who receive the Sacraments with the right dispositions, who have a real horror of sin, who gladly avail themselves of all the means which God offers them to avoid a relapse into sin. Christians who go to confession one day, and the next day fall again into the same sins, I do not include them, nor those who confess their sins without contrition and without detestation, who repeat them every time as if they were telling a story, who make not the slightest preparations; who without examining their conscience, tell just of what sins they happen to think; who approach the Lord's table without having examined into the recesses of the heart, without having obtained the grace to recognize their sins, without feeling the proper repentance, and without any resolution of not sinning again. All these persons work out their own perdition. Instead of fighting against the devil, they range themselves on his side, and bury themselves in hell.

*What are we, then, to conclude from all this? That we should promptly obey the incentives of grace, never fail in our prayers, and with proper dispositions receive the Sacraments. If...we carry out this resolution, if we remain faithful to it to the end, there shall be fulfilled in us the words of Christ: "**He that shall*** *persevere unto the end, he shall be saved."* *This I wish you all. Amen*[98]

The Sacraments are powerful sources of grace to help you raise your children saints. As Fr. Hans Von Balthasar illustrates, children *are to be dedicated to God, so that they maybe called, if He wills it, to the religious state...Without in any way turning the family into a monastery, the truly Christian family will allow the light of God to permeate every natural event and attachment so that they all become symbolic of Christ and the Church; thus the effect of the sacraments, their transforming power, is felt in the smallest, everyday incidents. The Christian family must be a reflection of the Holy Family, which is itself the type of the supernatural Christian family:* **"For whosoever shall do the will of my Father that is in heaven, he is my brother and sister, and mother"** *(**Matt.** 12:50) so true is it that the Christian family has to be a form of sanctity that the child who is born into it and grows up there should be so impressed by the sacramental, symbolic reality of the family that it learns to pass naturally through fleshly images to the sanctity of God and the Church. At the same time it is reminded that these images, no matter how wonderful, are no more than images whose molding lies in the hands of Christ.*[99]

Additional Helps

✓ Read the section on the Sacraments in the *Catechism of the Catholic Church* #1210-1679.

---

[98] St. John Vianney, "We Must Persevere," *Sermons of the Cure D'Ars* (MN:The Neumann Press, 1901) pp. 147-148.

[99] *Therese of Lisieux, The Story of a Mission, Op. Cit.,* pp. 70-71.

- ✓ After reading #1669 begin the custom of blessing your children whenever they leave the house.
- ✓ Consider purchasing the 12-tape series, "The Seven Sacraments of the Roman Catholic Church" by Fr. John Hardon, S.J., from Eternal Life, P.O. Box 787, Bardstown, KY 40004, or by calling 800-842-2871.
- ✓ Read the **Screwtape Letters** by C. S. Lewis with your children in 5th-6th grade. Let your older children read the book themselves then discuss it with them.
- ✓ Read **Dominus Iesus** by John Paul II.
- ✓ Have your preteens and teens read **The Meaning of Vocation** by John Paul II from Scepter (800-322-8773).

CHAPTER 5

WHICH METHOD OF EDUCATION IS BEST FOR YOUR CHILD?

"[E]ducation is to form people into what they ought to be and to show them how to conduct themselves in this life in order to achieve the sublime objective wherefore they have been created by God."   Pius XI

What precisely do we mean when we talk about education? Is it simply acquiring knowledge? Pope Pius XI, in the quote above, seems to reject that definition. Education is actually the formation of habits in your children. *The formation of good habits is good education. The formation of bad habits is bad education. [So] education is not merely the acquisition of knowledge,* explains Fr. Gerrard.[1] In **Raise Happy Children...Teach Them Virtues!**, the next book in the **Raise Happy Children** series, we will discuss these habits in depth but for now we want to consider the best method of education for your children.

Education is more than simply teaching one's children the

[1] *Marriage and Parenthood, The Catholic Ideal, Op. Cit.* p. 153.

"three Rs" so that an Ivy League university accepts them. Its purpose is to raise your children to become intellectually developed saints. St. Thomas Aquinas highlights this importance by insisting that *Nature intends not only the begetting of children, but also their education and development until reaching the perfect state of man as man, the state of virtue.*[2] This is not an easy task. *If the bringing of children into the world is attended with great pain and labor, the bringing of their souls to perfection is attended with still greater pain and labor. It requires nothing else than the united life and love of both parents,* advises Fr. Thomas J. Gerrard.[3]

Through education the will is taught what is good; the memory is exercised; the intellect is taught how to perceive the truth through reason; the senses are educated to desire what is beautiful; and the body is taught how to care for itself. The child's *bodily health, his habits of memory, feeling, taste, intellect, and will must be so trained and directed as to bring forth the best possible fruits in the spiritual life. The supernatural is that which is built on the natural, not that which is built up in mid-air...The two merge, one into the other, in such a way that the natural becomes supernaturalized, the psychic becomes spiritualized.*[4] A child who is well educated can more easily become a saint than a child who is not well educated. When the faith is excluded from the educational process the child does not receive a complete education.

Pope Pius XI emphasizes that *the family has been directly instituted by God with its own proper end, the procreation and education of children. Therefore parents have the right to educate their children, a right that is inalienable since it is inseparably united to a strict obligation. It comes before any other right of civil society or of the State, and is thus inviolable by any earthly power.*[5]

---

[2] St. Thomas Aquinas, Suppl., q. 41, a.1.

[3] *Marriage and Parenthood, The Catholic Ideal, Op. Cit.* p. 18.

[4] *Ibid.*, pp. 154-155.

[5] Enc. *Divini illius Magistri,* December 31, 1929, 9.

For this reason the saints and the parents of most of the saints put heroic efforts into the education of their children. Why? In addition to developing good habits, the role of education is to form sound judgment and an upright conscience along with excellent academics in the child. ***Proverbs*** (22:6) teaches, ***Train a child in the way he should go, and when he is old he will not depart from it.*** St. Edith Stein, besides a martyr of the 20th century was a great scholar. She *describes the image of God planted as a seed in the human soul: the seed comes to development by the supernatural aid of grace and the natural help of education—plus, of course, the student's own inner dedication. And this full development of personality implies a wholeness of the person because it is the whole person that is needed for God's service. This requires a balanced development of all physical and psychical powers.*[6]

Pius XI reminds us that *it is very important not to err in matters of education, just as it is important not to err in one's direction towards the last end, to which the whole task of education is necessarily and intimately linked.*[7]

St. Thomas More knew he could not delegate his responsibility as the primary educator of his children but he could share it with tutors who agreed with his faith, morals and values. So More educated his three daughters and son in Latin, Greek, Logic, Philosophy, Theology, Mathematics and Astronomy. This was unusual in a time when women were not given classical educations. His daughters were so well educated that King Henry VIII invited them to debate Philosophy before him. But in the mind of St. Thomas, education was connected to the development of the Christian virtues. In a letter to one of his children's tutors, William Gunnell, More writes: *warn my children to avoid the precipices of pride and haughtiness, and to walk in the pleasant meadows of modesty; not to be dazzled by the sight of gold; not to lament that they do not possess what they erroneously admire in others; not to think more of themselves for gaudy trappings, nor less for the want of them; neither to deform the beauty that nature has given them by neglect, nor to*

---

[6] *Edith Stein, Scholar, Feminist, Saint, Op. Cit.,* pp. 21-22.

[7] Enc. *Divini illius Magistri,* December 31, 1929, 5.

try to heighten it by artifice; to put virtue in the first place, learning in the second; and in their studies to esteem most whatever may teach them piety towards God, charity to all, and Christian humility in themselves.

By such means they will receive from God the reward of an innocent life, and in the assured expectation of it will view death without dread, and meanwhile possessing solid joy will neither be puffed up by the empty praise of men, nor dejected by evil tongues.

These I consider the real and genuine fruits of learning, and I would maintain that those who give themselves to study with such intent will easily attain their end and become perfect.[8]

Explain to your children the purpose of education. School is not simply something one <u>has</u> to attend but it has a specific purpose, the formation of the whole person. In a letter to his oldest son, John Quincy Adams, President John Adams did just this: *You will ever remember that all the end of study is to make you a good man and a useful citizen. This will ever be the sum total of the advice of your affectionate father.*[9] His wife, Abigail, urged their son, Charles, to excel at his studies by doing his work well. She stressed that a person did not become educated without effort. She insisted that learning *must be sought for with ardor.*

The graces of matrimony are sufficient to guide you and your spouse in your task as the primary educators of your children. Remember, the method of education or school you choose will mold the character of your children; therefore you are morally obligated to check out the curriculum, the teachers, and the tone of the school <u>before</u> you enroll your children. Will the school supplement what you are teaching the children at home? Is the goal of the school to lead your children to sanctity, to teach virtues? Are the academics excellent? St. Elizabeth Seton, like St. Thomas More, was prudent in the matter of her

[8] Thomas J. McGovern, "Sir Thomas More: The Making Of A Saint," Scepter Booklets (Scepter, New Rochelle, 1981) p. 10.

[9] David McCullough, *John Adams* (NY: Simon & Schuster, 2001) p. 260.

children's education. As a widow, she felt that her sons, Richard (seven) and William (nine) needed male influence. When her Italian friend, Antonio Filicchi, offered to pay their school tuition she gratefully accepted his offer. A wise woman, Elizabeth sought advice as to where to send her sons to school. Several schools were considered and Father Tisserant, a friend and advisor, suggested the Sulpician Seminary and College in Montreal, Canada. After checking out the school for Elizabeth, Antonio agreed upon Montreal but advised her to prepare her sons to *appear well-bred* and to *know how to write and read well, at least.*[10] Elizabeth, reluctant to send her sons so far away, asked Antonio to visit Georgetown and the Sulpician School in Maryland. Antonio checked out both schools for her. He was not impressed with either despite his meeting with Bishop Carroll, the founder of Georgetown, and Bishop Neal, the President of Georgetown. In the end it was Bishop Carroll who finally persuaded Elizabeth to send her sons to Georgetown. When William completed his schooling he joined the Navy. Elizabeth feared the Navy would corrupt him. In her concern she wrote: *Be not my dear one so unhappy as to break willfully any command of our God, or to omit your prayers on any account...You cannot ever guess the incessant cry of my soul to them [Jesus and Mary] for you. Don't say Mother has the rest to comfort her. No, no, my dear William, from the first moment I received you in my arms and to my breast you have been consecrated to God by me; and I have never ceased to beg him to take you from this world rather than you should offend him or dishonor your dear soul; and as you know my stroke of death would be to know that you have quitted that path of virtue which alone can reunite us for ever. Separation, everything else I can bear—but that never. You mother's heart must break if that blow falls on it.*[11]

The school you send your children to becomes an extension of your home. For that reason nothing contrary to what you are teaching your children should be taught in their school. St. Escrivá explained to parents, *I prefer to see things*

---

[10] Joseph I. Dirvin, C.M., *Mrs. Seton* (NY: Farrar, Straus and Cudahy, 1962) p. 183.

[11] *Mothers of the Saints, Op. Cit.,* pp. 184-185.

distinguished by their results and not by their names. A school is truly Christian when it strives for excellence, and gives a complete education—which includes Christian ideals—at the same time respecting personal freedom and earnestly furthering social justice. If this is accomplished then the name is of little importance.[12]

Remember, it is at school where peer pressure, teachers and curriculum will negatively or positively influence your child. Besides the neighborhood and the mall, it is also at school that children pick up filthy language, undesirable friends, drugs, materialism, gang involvement, and pressure to become sexually promiscuous.

Once a school is selected, parents are called to diligently follow the progress of their children, not only as to grades but as to subject content, as well as to moral and religious teachings. Attend all parent-teacher conferences, assemblies, and parents' meetings. Play an active part on the school board and other parent groups within the school so that **your** values and morals influence decisions. Encourage your friends to imitate your example of involvement.

Even from a secular point of view, parental involvement is considered crucial. *You have got to have parents understand that they do make a difference, and you've got to get the teachers and the principals to understand the importance of parental involvement,* according to Christopher Cross, the Education Department's assistant secretary for research. Mr. Cross blames the lackadaisical attitude of U.S. students on *the disengagement of parents from the schools and from their children's performance.*[13]

If you notice or are informed by your child or other parents of a moral or spiritual problem within the school, you have a serious moral obligation to go with your spouse to protest to the teacher. If nothing is resolved with the teacher, go to the principal, and finally to the board of

[12] *Conversations With Mgr. Escrivá.* (Scepter: Dublin, 1969) *n.* 81.
[13] Kenneth H. Bacon, "Many Educators View Involved Parents As Key To Children's Success in School," *Wall Street Journal,* August 2, 1990.

directors. To not do so would be a sin of omission. Get into the fray even if it means organizing other parents. If you find yourself in a difficult situation, don't just wring your hands. You have the graces of the Sacraments of Confirmation and of Matrimony to help you to be courageous and persevering. You have the virtue of infused fortitude to keep you going in the face of hardship. Remember, you also have the legal right to remove your child from any objectionable class. Likewise, you can organize parents to work to get rid of an objectionable class or problem. Unfortunately, trying to get a group of school parents to support you, even though they may be equally concerned, is difficult. Human respect prevents many people from "getting involved." If the situation cannot be resolved, the parents, by necessity, must remove the child from the class or school if the child's faith or morals are endangered. To not do so would be a sin of omission. When we relocated from a Chicago suburb to Springfield, we sent our youngest daughter to the local parish school that was quite good...until they put in a diocesan mandated sex education program in fifth grade. My husband and I spoke with the principal and she agreed to release our daughter from the class. Withdrawing our daughter from the class was embarrassing for her, but it gave us a chance to discuss with Mary Terese how Christians must stand-up for what is right, even when it hurts. If you are striving to raise your children saints you cannot accept something that you know is evil. Our daughter was young to have to stand up and be different from her peers, but sooner or later all our children will have to suffer in defense of their faith and morals. For her it just came sooner. Rather than being a terrible thing, it began the development of the virtue of fortitude (courage) in her and in us. This experience evoked our family motto: "Dare to be Different!"

With this in mind, one of the most critical choices you make as a parent is the manner in which your children are educated. The decision should not be made hastily nor be primarily based on reasons of convenience or finance. As parents, you have the obligation to make sacrifices, financial and otherwise, to choose a school where sound doctrine is taught, where your values are respected and promoted at the same time that a challenging, academic education is given. If this is not possible home schooling or starting your own private school may be your only options.

The problem of quality education is not unique to our century. St. John Chrysostom, a Father of the early Church, found early Christian parents lax in this regard as well. He writes, *We are more careful of our mules and our horses than of our children. The man who owns a mule makes sure to hire a good herdsman, who will not be a fool, nor a robber nor a drunkard, but a man who knows his job well. On the other hand, when it is a question of looking for a teacher for the soul of child, we hire the first one we meet. And yet there is no art superior to this one. What is there to compare with the art of forming a soul, of shaping the intelligence and the spirit of a young person? He who professes this task must proceed with more care than a painter or a sculptor when carrying out his work.*[14]

Demand high educational standards for your children. A futuristic science lab or a state of the art computer lab or TV's in every classroom may not necessarily indicate academic and moral excellence. Many of our geniuses and great historical figures, such as Thomas Edison and Abraham Lincoln, were educated in one-room schoolhouses or at home. Remember, it's not equipment or furnishings that educate. In the U.S. there are state-of-the-art schools that are turning out illiterate graduates who cannot read, do simple math or spell. If you have not already read *John Adams* by David McCullough I urge you to do so. John Adams is one of the founding fathers of the United States and our second President. He was also George Washington's Vice President. His son, John Quincy Adams, was the sixth U.S. president. It is startling to read the educational program that the educated Colonists considered basic for their children. Compare the education their children received to the education your children are exposed to. It made me realize that our education system is shockingly deficient when compared to theirs. For instance, by the time John Adam's

---

[14] St. John Chrysostom, *Homilies on St. Matthew,* 59, 7.

oldest son, John Quincy, was fourteen-years-old he had studied geography, literature (in French and English), philosophy, Latin, Greek, French, math, history (Thucydides' history of the Pelaponesian War in Greek), Scripture, natural history, science, arts, commerce, law, medicine, chemistry, poetry, and the arts.

John Adams felt that extensive travel was part of the educational process so he took his son to France when he was posted there on a diplomatic mission. While in Europe, John Quincy attended a University where his lectures were in Latin. When his father learned that his studies did not include Cicero and Demosthenes he was irate insisting that he must begin to study them immediately: *I absolutely insist upon it.*[15] At fourteen, John Quincy was so well educated that he was chosen to act as the interpreter for the American delegation to the Russian court of Catherine the Great. The purpose of the trip was to seek recognition of the United States from the Russians. The journey to Russia was not only dangerous but it took months of arduous travel. When John Quincy completed his assignment, although still in his early teens, he was mature and responsible enough to make the dangerous and lengthy trip of several months back to France alone through Russia, Finland, Sweden, Denmark, and Germany. His father did not drop him off and his mother did not pick him up.

John Adams writes: *I must study politics and war that my sons may have liberty to study mathematics and philosophy. My sons ought to study mathematics and philosophy, geography, natural history, naval architecture, navigation, commerce, and agriculture in order to give their children a right to study paintings, poetry, music, architecture, statuary, tapestry, and porcelain.*[16] He did not mean that each generation should drop the subjects of the previous generation but rather that each generation should add subjects to the educational curriculum. Instead of studying Greek, Latin, geography, great literature, foreign languages etc. in grade school, our children are being taught basket weaving, sex ed, drug education, alternative life styles, inclusive language, political correctness, values

[15] *John Adams, Op. Cit.,* p. 259.
[16] *Ibid.,* pp. 236-237.

clarification, etc.

To be well educated, so that they can become saints, your children must not only be educated in the Catholic faith but also in the use of their reason because the Catholic faith appeals to reason rather than emotion. John Paul II addresses this truth in his encyclical, **Faith and Reason**. To educate a child in the faith, the child's ability to think and reason need to be developed. This is why Euclid, Latin and classical subjects were standard courses in the past.

[T]he Catholic religion is the religion of the highest morality. It is the religion which is marked out above all others by its fruitfulness in moral goodness, its production of saints. It must, therefore, appeal to that faculty which has goodness for its object. It must appeal to the will as affording it the widest arena for its exercise and satisfaction, nothing less than the striving for the perfect imitation of Jesus Christ. It must appeal to the will also, as affording it the strength to arrive at moral perfection, the strength which comes through the grace of the seven sacraments.

The stronger, then, a man's will is, the more perfectly it is exercised in the natural virtues, so much the more fitted it is to avail itself of the helps to supernatural action...[T]he Catholic religion is a beautiful religion. It must, therefore, appeal to the faculty which has beauty for its object, the esthetic sense. All sound training in the fine arts, therefore, whether in music, painting, or literature, may be used for the development of the finest and most difficult of all arts, the art of saintliness, the art which absorbs at once all the power of intellect, will, and feeling, the art which expresses the greatest inspirations of truth, goodness and beauty.[17]

Education also impacts on how people are governed. Michael Novak, in his book **On Two Wings,** points out that the United States was founded on the two wings of faith and reason. *The Founders also believed that religious faith keeps liberty from degenerating into license and tyranny, because self-government*

---

[17] *Marriage and Parenthood, The Catholic Ideal, Op. Cit.,* pp. 156-157.

requires citizens who can first govern themselves,[18] writes Lee Bockhorn. John Adams, one of these notable founders, knew that a high level of education was necessary for self-government to survive. As a young man of twenty-five he asked, *how can I judge, how can any man judge, unless his mind has been opened and enlarged by reading?* As the author of the Massachusetts Constitution he inserted his views on education in Section II of Chapter 6: *Wisdom and knowledge, as well as virtue, diffused generally among the body of the people being necessary for the preservation of their rights and liberties; and as these depend on spreading the opportunities and advantages of education in various parts of the country, and among the different orders of the people, it shall be the duty of legislators and magistrates in all future periods of this commonwealth to cherish the interests of literature and the sciences...especially the university at Cambridge, public schools, and grammar schools in the towns; to encourage private societies and public institutions, rewards and immunities, for the promotion of agriculture, arts, sciences, commerce, trades, manufactures, and a natural history of the country; to countenance and inculcate the principles of humanity and general benevolence, public and private charity, industry and frugality, honesty and punctuality in their dealings, sincerity, good humor, and all social affections, and generous sentiments among the people.*[19]

With many new programs being introduced into the school curriculum, such as sex education, secular humanism, socialism and values clarification, parents can no longer send "Johnny" off to school and feel reassured that he is going to be taught the "three Rs" and positive moral values. Parents need to continually check public, private and parochial school textbooks, and curriculum. Schools should welcome your interest. If they do not, something is wrong with them. John Paul II, while in New Orleans, told Catholic educators: *Permit me...to mention briefly something that is of special concern to the Church. I refer to the rights and duties of parents in the*

---

[18] Lee Bockhorn, "A Republic on the Rise, With Powerful Minds and Earnest Prayers," *The Wall Street Journal*, Feb. 4, 2002.

[19] *John Adams, Op. Cit.,* p. 223.

*education of their children...In comparison with the educational role of all others, their role is primary; it is also irreplaceable and inalienable. It would be wrong for anyone to attempt to usurp that unique responsibility (cf. **Familiaris Consortio**, n. 36). Nor should parents in any way be penalized for choosing for their children an education according to their beliefs.*[20]

Under federal law, parents and children must be informed regarding the nature and content of any course and/or test the child is being asked to take, and of its *relevant circumstances and likely consequences.* This means parents must be told the purpose of the course or test being given, and what the school administration intends to do with the information. Under the law, your child has the constitutional right to refuse to participate in any test, class program, project or questionnaire that he feels is a violation of his right to privacy. In other words, students do not have to participate in any values clarification activities, sensitivity group sessions, or classes that offend his/her moral standards or are personally offensive to him. This includes sex education. In California, two new laws took effect January 1, 2001 in which all public school children from K through high school will be taught homosexuality to develop "tolerance." An additional law funds field trips to teach this perversion.[21]

Many schools rent textbooks. To insure the longevity of the texts, students are discouraged from taking them home. This prevents parents from being able to review them. To overcome this problem, contact the school and ask to borrow a set of books. Try to review the curriculum before school begins. If there is a sex education program or values clarification course, **insist** on reading **all** materials and seeing **all** films and exhibits before deciding whether to let your children participate. Inquire about the identity of **all** guest speakers. One local Catholic high school invited a homosexual activist to give a class on homosexuality. Check out the philosophy of the organizations behind the

[20] John Paul II's address to religious education leaders-Superdome, New Orleans, Sept. 12, 1987.

[21] California parents wishing to "opt out" of these programs can contact the Pacific Justice Institute 888-305-9129.

speakers. Are they connected to Planned Parenthood or other objectionable groups?

Each day after school, encourage your children to speak about their day. Dinnertime is an ideal opportunity to find out what the children are learning, what the teacher said, etc. Insist on checking over homework. For parents serious about the responsibility of educating their children, ignorance is not bliss, it endangers the souls of your children. Do you know what your children are being taught?

St. Thomas More, concerned about the education of his children, wrote to his daughter while abroad on a diplomatic mission: *Please Margaret, let me know how your studies are getting on, for I assure you that if, through my neglect, my children and family were not to be properly cared for, I am capable of spending all my fortune and saying goodbye to business and occupations in order to devote myself entirely to you.*

Once children leave grade school and high school, parents must be equally diligent in the choice of a college or university. Prof. Paul Vitz, of New York, contends that most colleges today destroy the character of their students. *The atmosphere on most campuses is less honest and sexually promiscuous. College dorms are sexual zoos.* He further believes that colleges graduate spoiled, disillusioned young people unwilling to accept jobs *beneath them.*[22] **The Wall Street Journal** reports another disturbing trend: *The Chronicle of Higher Education reports that the hottest trend on campus is a growing movement back to one of the oldest forms of worship—paganism, whose "most significant influence" is witchcraft...[T]here are chapters on 113 college campuses—38 of which were added last month alone.*[23] This is really nothing new. Bl. Bartolo Longo, who died in 1926, became so involved with a satanic sect while studying law at the University of Naples, that he was ordained a satanic priest. It took him a long time and a complex spiritual battle to return to the Catholic Church. The wrong school choice can cost your child his soul. Pope Pius XI wrote about this in 1922: *If God*

[22] Audiotape, "Catholic Manhood." Available from R.B. Media, Inc.
[23] "Tony & Tacky," *The Wall Street Journal,* October 20, 2000.

and His law are uprooted from education, it is impossible to see how young people can be educated so as to flee evil, and to lead an honest and virtuous life, nor how men of good habits, lovers of order and peace, capable of contributing to public prosperity can be prepared for the family and for society.[24]

What a prophet Pope Pius XI was! With God and His commandments prohibited in our public schools, policemen patrol the hallways in an attempt to prevent rapes, murders, and drug sales. Yet students are still gunned downed by fellow students. Politicians muddy reality with their diatribes about guns. It's not guns that kill people but people without God who pull triggers.

Enrolling your child in the best preschool, and later on, the most prestigious university does not make a virtuous person, the main reason for education. Programming children from sun-up to sundown in various activities is not an answer either. In fact, it can actually deform the character of the child as was mentioned in an earlier chapter. Such programmed children have seven strikes against them:

- ✓ Parents have less contact with their children. While parents chauffer, other people are instilling their values in your children.
- ✓ Constant activity prevents the development of the children's imagination.
- ✓ Constant activity negatively influences your children's reading ability.
- ✓ Your children will not be able to develop friendships by themselves.
- ✓ Children do not learn how to program their own free time.
- ✓ Children develop a need for constant activity and hunger to be on "the go." They grow to be discontented adults if not kept constantly active.
- ✓ The children do not develop interior peace.

In Minneapolis, Ann and Greg Baufield along with other families formed Family Life 1st. *Among other things, the*

---

[24] Pius XI, Enc. *Ubi arcano,* February 23, 1922, 14.

organization urges parents to think more carefully about signing up their youngsters for one activity after another. It is also offering its seal of approval to activity groups that sign a pledge to cut kids some slack for family events and refuse to schedule practices on holidays... "We are trying to help parents strike a balance." [25] This organization was born when the Baufields realized that in ten days they only had one meal together.

Besides forming children intellectually to live a life of virtue, children need to be taught how to be helpful, considerate, sensitive individuals who think of the needs of others first. This is instilled through lessons in courtesy, spirit of service and social manners along with responsibilities in the home. This was discussed in **Raise Happy Children Through A Happier Marriage** and will be discussed in more depth in **Raise Happy Children...Teach Them Virtues**.

The Influence Of Teachers On Children
"Give me the children of England and I will make England Catholic." Cardinal Manning

Be aware that next to you, the greatest influence on your child is his teacher. Your child's teacher not only instills his/her values but will influence your child's conscience as well. The saints, and the parents of saints, recognized the tremendous power teachers have with their pupils. For this reason royalty usually had saints tutor their children. St. Henry II, elected to be the Holy Roman Emperor in 1002, not only married a saint but was also educated by one, St. Wolfgang, Bishop of Ratisbon. St. Leopold became the ruling prince of Austria in the eleventh century. He was educated by St. Altman. The King of Naples asked St. Elzear, the Count of Ariano, to tutor his son. St. Mechtilde became the teacher to five-year-old St. Gertrude the Great in 1261. The parents of the future St. Stephen of Hungary, concerned for the spiritual and intellectual formation of their son, asked St. Adalbert, the Bishop of Prague, to educate Stephen.

---

[25] Chris Williams, "Parents organizing to get days off for busy kids," *Houston Chronicle*, Aug. 16, 2000 p. 9A.

Not just royalty wanted the best for their children. In the sixth century St. Placidus' parents sent him to be educated by St. Benedict. In the seventh century St. Aidan, a missionary, was asked to educate St. Eata, a young man who later became an English bishop. St. Eata in turned educated St. Cuthbert. St. Finian, the abbot of Clonard in Ireland, is called the "teacher of the saints of Ireland." One of his students, St. Ruadan, is known as one of the "twelve apostles of Ireland." St. Ita, also of Ireland, was asked to educate young boys.When two of her students, the future Sts. Brendan and Mochoemoc, asked her what three things God loved and what three things God abhorred, she told them, *True faith in God with a pure heart, a simple life with a religious spirit, and an open hand inspired by charity.* God detests, *a scowling face, obstinacy in wrongdoing, and arrogant trust in the power of money.*[26]

Blessed Jordan of Saxony tutored St. Albert the Great, a Doctor of the church. He in turn was the teacher of St. Thomas Aquinas: *St. Albert the Great was a man of immense knowledge and erudition. His works are voluminous in bulk and encyclopedic in scope: they include—besides biblical and theological works and sermons—treatises on logic, metaphysics, ethics, and the physical sciences. His interests extended to physics, astronomy, chemistry, and biology, to human and animal physiology, to geography, geology and botany. This "Universal Teacher" stands out for his recognition of the autonomy of human reason in its own sphere and the validity of knowledge gained from sense-experience. Yet he never ceased to regard the Scriptures as the fount of man's spirituality of true wisdom.*[27]

Since the teachers of your children have a profound effect on their point of view, moral development, faith and conscience you, as a parent, must check out the teachers to whom you entrust your children's souls. How does the teacher's background and moral values compare with your own? This is a difficult and time consuming task, but then, no one ever said that parenthood is easy! There is no such thing as a "value

[26] *Lives of the Saints Illustrated Part I, Op. Cit.,* p. 33.
[27] *Lives of the Saints For Every Day Of The Year, Op. Cit.,* p. 474.

neutral school" nor a "value neutral teacher." The teacher either supports the values of your home or substitutes his/her own personal values of secular humanism and personal morals. Consider the sad case of Catholic parents who sent their children to Catholic grade and high schools only to have their sons and daughters graduate as fallen away Catholics. Was it the curriculum, the anti-Catholic values of the teachers or both that caused the loss of faith?

St. Padre Pio's parents were not prudent in this regard. Francesco (Padre Pio) began his junior high studies with Dominic Tizzano, but he did poorly. When his father, who was working in the U.S., learned of the situation he sent a telegram telling his wife to find another teacher for their son. *If my son wants to become a friar, what can he learn from one who has left the priesthood?* Later he admitted, *Our choice of a teacher for our son was poor. Sending him to a former priest who had left the Church and married was an error on our part.*

Returning to the story of sex education in our parish school, by the time our daughter reached 8th grade, I was able to convince the principal to change the curriculum to an abstinence program. Mary Terese was back with her class and I was confident that all was well...that was until she came home one day to tell me that not only did her Catholic teacher tell the class that she disagreed with the abstinence program but she spent the class time extolling the benefits of contraceptives. This experience taught me that not only must we be concerned about the programs our children are being taught, but also to be aware of the influence of our child's teacher. If the teacher does not share your faith or values your child will be caught in the middle of conflicting value systems.

Another situation that is causing serious problems in schools is the lack of parental support for good teachers. Many parents, rather than supporting the work of their children's teachers, help their children to resist the teacher's efforts by belittling the teacher, undermining the teacher's authority, and excusing their children from the educational demands of the curriculum by labeling it "too difficult," "too demanding," or "too unreasonable." In other instances parents refuse to accept the disciplinary actions of the teacher making the teacher's job almost impossible to carry out. Rather than instilling in their children the idea that the teacher must be respected and obeyed, parents take the side of "Dennis the Menace" or "chatty Kathy" who disrupt the classroom thereby preventing the other students from learning. When a child receives a correction or punishment from a teacher, support the actions of the teacher rather than protesting them. Presume your child is guilty unless he can prove himself innocent. It's the vice of pride that says, *My child did not do that*. When a teacher reprimands your child, teach your child to apologize to the teacher either verbally or in a written note. This may help to curtail future disciplinary problems. *To be ever taking the child's part against the teacher is simply to ruin the child's character.*[28]

Then there are the problem parents who protest when a teacher teaches their children the truth that they themselves have rejected. Case in point, a parish priest taught a class on modesty and chastity to eighth graders. Some parents violently objected to the high standards the priest presented to the students. They demanded that the priest be censored, that he apologize for his remarks, that he be barred from teaching the students further classes. The priest did nothing wrong. He simply was presenting to the students the moral teachings of the Catholic Church. The parents were the ones in need of disciplinary action. Fr. Thomas J. Gerrard explains: *The schoolmaster, the [teachers] have in their own measure a claim on the love, reverence, and obedience of the children committed to their care. The teacher stands in place of the parent or pastor. It is his duty to recognize in himself an instrument in the hand of God, for the education and improvement of those committed to his care. On this account, therefore, he is entitled to his share of love, reverence, and obedience. True, the love cannot equal the love of a parent. Still, in proportion as the schoolmaster takes upon himself the responsibility of training a child, he may lawfully expect from the child corresponding duties. The*

---

[28] *Marriage and Parenthood, The Catholic Ideal, Op. Cit.,* p.166.

principle involved is the same. The teacher is doing the work of God. The child, therefore, in honoring the teacher thereby acknowledges its submission to God; and in doing so it does honor to himself, for it makes profession of its right place in the order of the world.

In these days there is a strong tendency among men to exaggerate their rights and to undervalue the rights of their superiors. In the family, and in the State and in religion, there is a strong force of opposition to law. It is well, then, for children to realize early the dignity of dutifulness to parents, spiritual pastors, and temporal masters. From a merely natural point of view such dutifulness can only lead to the good of the children. But from a supernatural point of view the thought is noble in the highest degree. We see that in serving our parents and those in authority for the sake of God, we are serving our own best interests; for we are thereby doing our best to place ourselves in that adjustment of the universe which God has ordained as the most perfect.[29] Fr. Gerrard then cites the example of St. Thomas More who showed great reverence and respect toward his parents and tutors. This led him in later life to have great respect for the Church and his government. Yet once he became Lord Chancellor, the highest position in the government under the King, he still maintained his respect and affection for his parents going each day to see his father who held a position in a lower court. *[H]e used to be seen every morning to go and kneel and ask for the old man's blessing.*[30]

Fr. John McCloskey of the Catholic Information Center in Washington, D.C. writes: *I like to speak of three particularly strong influences on young people today: first, the general culture; second, the educational system; third, the family environment. At least two out of three of these should be positive influences working to create a favorable environment for young men and women to commit themselves totally to God. Unfortunately this is not the case. The secular education system, from top to bottom...represents the ideology of secular humanism as the*

---

[29] *Ibid.,* pp. 136-137.
[30] *Ibid.,* p. 138.

norm. The general culture appears almost to have been designed by a demonic intellect to destroy any notion of beauty or truth in a young mind or heart. This leaves the family, which is under unprecedented attack by the aforementioned forces and others, apparently alone to fend for itself.[31]

Educational Choices

"Few people seem to recognize the supreme importance of education in early childhood, when growth is so fast and impressions leave a lasting mark. The waste of this period can never be compensated."

Dr. Alexis Carrel, Nobel Prize Winner

Today parents have a variety of educational choices. Unfortunately in the U.S. parents are not permitted the financial freedom to select a school for their children. Archbishop Edward Egan of New York raised his concern on this point: *To suggest for a moment that morals or ethics are not being taught in government-controlled schools is ridiculous. A definite point of view from a definite culture is being imposed...So, all I'm asking for is school choice. Parents are the first educators. Who in the world says that all taxpapers' money, all parents' money, must be for only a specific type of schooling with a specific type of culture being taught? This is outrageous. It's very much a problem in the United States of America, but not elsewhere. The parent is the one who has the right to decide how the child is going to be formed, intellectually, spiritually, and humanly...*[32]

Parents who do not choose to send their children to the public school are financially penalized by being forced to pay for public education through their taxes as well as tuition for a private school, a Catholic school, or home schooling materials for their children. In Canada and in many European countries this is not the case. Parents have the freedom to indicate where they

[31] "The Family: Seedbed of Vocations," *Op. Cit.,*

[32] Henry V. King, "Archbishop Egan Pushes For School Vouchers," *The Wanderer,* July 13, 2000, p. 1.

want their educational tax money to go. When John Paul II made his first trip to Poland after his election to the papacy he told world governments, *The Church does not want special privileges. It only wants these governments to honor in practice the principle of religious freedom promised in their constitutions.* Vatican II reiterates that: *The public authority, therefore, whose duty it is to protect and defend the liberty of citizens, is bound, according to the principles of distributive justice, to ensure that public subsidies to schools are so allocated that parents are truly free to select schools for their children in accordance with their conscience.*[33]

The Congregation for the Doctrine of the Faith adds: *The State cannot, without committing injustice, limit itself to toleration of the so-called private schools. These schools offer a public service, and they have, as a consequence, the right to financial assistance.*[34]

In New Orleans in 1987, John Paul II noted the financial sacrifices of Catholics families in the U.S. who value Catholic education: *At this point I cannot fail to praise the financial sacrifices of American Catholics...to Catholic education in the United States. The heroic sacrifices of generations of Catholic parents in building up and supporting parochial and diocesan schools must never be forgotten.*[35]

Secretary of Education William J. Bennett, addressing the National Catholic Educational Association in 1988 told Catholics, *You can't wait around for tax credits or tuition vouchers or other forms of new government funding. Rather on the political level, you have to press for the principle that a free people are entitled to choice in education...*

If you are timid about making your case, you will lose this fight. For the sake of your children, I urge you to be more aggressive in this area.[36]

---

[33] *Gravissimum educationis,* 6.   [34] *Libertatis conscientia,* March 22, 1986, 94.
[35] John Paul II to Catholic Educators in New Orleans, Sept. 12, 1987.
[36] Virgil C. Blum, SJ, "Secretary Bennett's Last Challenge," *Catholic League Newsletter,* Aug., 1988 p. 8.

That great champion of educational freedom, founder of the Catholic League and my former professor, Fr. Virgil Blum, S.J., urged parents to: *Organize, organize, organize, for unless you organize with Protestant and Jewish school educators and parents—unless you become less "timid" and "more aggressive" in making your case—you will "lose this fight" to one of the most powerful interest groups in American politics—the National Education Association."*[37]

This is an area in which Catholic activism is urgently needed in the U.S. Write your congressmen. Send letters to the media pointing out this grave injustice. Pressure political candidates to take a stand on this issue. *Organize, organize, organize!* Become involved in the issue of educational freedom but be prudent in accepting or presenting proposals. Remember the goal is freedom of choice in education, not government control of Catholic, private and home schools.

What are your educational choices? Parents can home school or select a private, public or Catholic school for their children to attend. Parents can even start their own schools. Let's consider the pros and cons of each. Choose carefully because all schools are *not* equal in the same category.

Let's begin with public schools. After being home schooled in the basics by his mother, St. John Vianney attended a public school. His parents had no other option.

Public schools by their very nature should not be the first choice for education. Pope Leo XIII was quite firm in this regard: *To separate religious formation from general instruction is, in fact, to want children to remain "neutral" in their duties towards God. This educational method is false and very pernicious, particularly during the early years, because what it does is to open the path to atheism, and close it to religion. Conscientious parents have a serious obligation to watch over their children, and make sure that, as soon as their studies begin, they start to receive religious instruction, and that there is nothing in the school which offends the integrity of the faith or morals.*

---
[37] *Ibid.*

The obligation to exercise this care and watchfulness in the education of their children is imposed on parents by natural law and divine law, and they cannot excuse themselves from it for any reason whatever.[38]

Academically, U.S. public schools rank poorly. The U.S. Department of Education's National Center for Education Statistics, gave math and science tests to 8th graders around the world. U.S. students ranked 19th in math and 18th in science. South Korea, Taiwan, Japan, Hungary, Finland and Canada ranked in the top ten. In math our students came in after Latvia. In science our students ranked behind Bulgaria. School violence, which is unknown in other countries, ranked high in the U.S. We spend more money on education than most countries and our class size is smaller.[39] Unfortunately public school academics have taken a backseat to a politically correct curriculum that dumbs down our student population.[40] Rather than academics our children are being taught humanism, evolution, one-world government, individual autonomy, anti-free enterprise, situation ethics, moral relativism, distorted realism, anti-biblical bias and death education which is fueling the rising suicide rate among teens.[41] Textbooks are often inaccurate. *North Carolina State University physics professor John Hubisz says 12 of the most popular science textbooks used at middle schools...are riddled with errors...According to Hubisz, the errors range from maps depicting the equator passing through the southern United States to a photo of singer Linda Ronstadt labeled as a silicon crystal...Among the books included in the study was a multi-volume Prentice Hall series called* **Science**...*Errors in some editions of their series, according to Hubisz, include an incorrect depiction of what happens to light when it passes through a prism...He said that one textbook even misstates Newton's first law of physics, which has been a staple*

---

[38] Leo XIII, *Enc. Nobilissima Gallorum gens,* February 8, 1884, 4.

[39] John J. Metzler, "American Students Get Average Grades On Global Report Card," *The Wanderer*, Dec. 21, 2000.

[40] Read *Dumbing Us Down* by John Taylor Gatto.

[41] "Humanism in Textbooks (Secular Religion In The Classroom)," The Mel Gablers, 1983.

of physical science for centuries.[42]

This destruction of our public educational system has been ongoing for decades. In fact, in a novel written in 1957 Taylor Caldwell has two characters, a Protestant minister and a Catholic priest discussing this problem:

> *"Lots of churches go in for athletics and dancing and juke boxes in the parish halls," he said, "But the kids get all that in their new schools. What they don't get, in some of our public schools, is a full education. They get group integration and life-adjustment stuff instead, and a smattering of mechanical trades in the vocational schools. Not in yours, though, Father...*
>
> *"No," replied the priest thoughtfully. "We still believe in education, in the liberal arts, in religion, in languages, and Latin, in the humanities. ' The whole child,' the educationists say. But the brain, and the disciplined learning, are part of the 'the whole child' too. They forget that. Or," he added sternly, "maybe they know only too well, and they don't really want 'a whole child' at all. Just robots."*[43]

Outcome Based Education (OBE) emphasizes emotions and feelings over academic content, and Goals 2000 seeks to restructure our educational system along with the restructuring of our country. Kenneth C. Jones explains the dangers of Parents as Teachers Program (PAT) that is part of Goals 2000: *The goal of PAT is nothing less than complete governmental control over the raising of children. In his address to the PAT National conference, Dr. Ernest L. Boyer, President of the Carnegie Foundation, stated, "[P]arents cannot do the job alone. It is simply unrealistic to expect mothers and fathers, acting on their own, to be heroically self-sufficient...[W]e seek to...define a ready-to-learn agenda for the nation, one that reaches into every neighborhood and touches every aspect of children's lives." Such a statement expresses in summary the basic premise*

---

[42] P. Samuel Foner, "U.S. Middle School Textbooks Riddled With Errors," *Spotlight*, Jan. 29, 2001, p. 5.

[43] Taylor Caldwell, *Tender Victory* (NY: Warner Books, 1957) p. 299.

of PAT and all government social programs...ordinary men and women are incapable of raising their families...[44]

Many of the people pushing these programs also promote abortion. Dr. C. Arden Miller, from the University of North Carolina addressed the National Parents as Teachers Conference. He *blamed the large number of unwanted pregnancies here on cutbacks in federal family-planning funds and restrictions on legal abortions.*[45]

If this isn't bad enough, read this excerpt from *The Humanist Magazine*: *...If God has failed in his role as cosmic policeman and if Christianity has failed to uphold the dignity of humankind...and who can argue with either hypothesis—then a viable alternative to both must be sought. That alternative is humanism.*

I am convinced that the battle for humankind's future must be waged and won in the public school classroom by teachers who correctly perceive their role as the proselytizers of a new faith: a religion of humanity that recognizes and respects the spark of what theologians call divinity in every human being...The classroom must and will become an arena of conflict between the old and the new—the rotting corpse of Christianity, together with all its adjacent evils and misery, and the new faith of humanism...[46]

While academic excellence has plunged, immorality has risen to new heights or shall I say, new lows? The Department of Justice distributed in 1999 a program entitled "Healing the Hate: A National Bias Crime Prevention Curriculum For Middle Schools." The curriculum teaches that people opposed to homosexuality are "hateful bigots." Not to be outdone, the Department of Education put together another national curriculum called "Dealing with Our Differences." Aimed again

---

[44] Kenneth C. Jones, "Suffer the Children to Come unto Me: Parents as Teachers," *St. Louis Observer*, July 1994, p. 3.

[45] Martha Shirk, "Expert: Families Need Aid," *St. Louis Post-Dispatch*, June 20, 1992.

[46] *The Humanist*, Jan.-Feb., 1983, pp. 25-26.

at middle schools. It teaches acceptance of homosexuality.[47] But such propaganda has filtered down even to the lower grades. An acquaintance told me that her granddaughter was being taught, through role-playing, the acceptance of the homosexual life-style in second grade. This teaching of the "gay lifestyle" has led to the formation of high school homosexual clubs. In Massachusetts public schools have "Gay Appreciation Day."[48]

Other objectionable programs include the three curricula provided by the Center for Disease Control entitled, "Programs That Work" for public schools. These programs teach students how to use and shop for condoms along with other subjects I cannot discuss in a family book.[49]

California public schools teach Islam in seventh grade social studies. The book that is used is entitled *Across the Centuries* and is published by Houghton-Mifflin of Boston. *There are many verses in the Koran that must be memorized in this Public School course and students are taught to pray, "in the name of Allah, the compassionate, the Merciful" and to chant, "Praise to Allah, Lord of Creation." There are 25 Islamic terms that must be memorized, six Islamic (Arabic) phrases, 20 Islamic Proverbs to learn along with the Five Pillars of Faith and 10 key Islamic prophets and disciples to be studied...Even more disturbing; students are to pretend that they are Muslims, wear Muslim clothing to school, stage their own Jihad via a dice game, and pick out a Muslim name (to replace their own) from a list of thirty.*[50]

In other schools both parochial and public, sex education, which is really the orchestrated destruction of your child's morals, begins as early as kindergarten. When I refer to "sex education" I am not referring to the excellent chastity and

[47] *Mission: America,* "News On Homosexual Issues," Fall, 1999,p. 12.

[48] Ingri Cassel, "Homosexuality A Required School Topic?" *Spotlight,*July 17, 2000.

[49] Linda P. Harvey, *Choice 4 Truth,* "Ohio Officials Say 'No' To Dollars from CDC," May, 2000.

[50] Austin Miles, "Public Schools Embrace Islam—A Shocker," ASSIST News Service, Jan. 9, 2002.

abstinence programs that some schools use to promote sound moral values. If the high school has a school-based clinic your teen will have access to contraceptives and pro-abortion advice. *France's National Assembly voted...to allow public school nurses to distribute an abortifacient "morning-after" pill in junior and senior high schools...*[51] In 1987 when he worked as vicar of education, Archbishop Edward Egan appeared before the New York City Council to protest the distribution of contraceptives in public schools. He told Council members, *Try decency. Try chastity. Try Western civilization.*[52] Equally objectionable is the restructuring of the basic family unit found in various courses.

In a positive development, Paul Vallas, the former CEO of the Chicago Public Schools, permitted a religious group to hand out Ten Commandment book covers to public school students as long as it was done off school property and the students wanted the covers. In commenting on the book covers, Vallas said, *I am enthusiastically supportive. I view the Ten Commandments as history's value statements. They're certainly universally accepted.* Alderman Jesse Granato, in whose district two teens were killed last summer, was also enthusiastic: *People talk about separating church and state, but separating these two—it's not working.*[53]

In high school and college your children will encounter teachers who will attack their Catholic faith and morals. Should you accept this situation you will be teaching your child cowardliness. Meet with the teacher, then the principal, and if they will not rectify the situation, remove your child from the school. You have no other moral choice.

At other times, a simple call to the right person can resolve the problem. One Catholic teen attending the local public school had a history teacher who was blatantly anti-Catholic. When she objected to his attacks against the faith in class, he verbally attacked her in front of the other students. Along with this he made off color jokes and comments that were embarrassing to

[51] "French Assembly Votes For Abortifacient Pill For Schools," Zenit, Oct. 6, 2000.
[52] Zenit, Mary 11, 2000   [53] Zenit August 17, 2000.

the girls in class. Her mother only had to make one phone call to the principal outlining the teacher's attacks on the Catholic faith and the sexually suggestive jokes for the principal to immediately put a stop to this teacher's conduct. Maybe it was the mother's charge of "sexual harassment" that focused the principal's attention on the problem of a potential lawsuit. The mother, in voicing her concerns, also told the principal that she did not expect to see her daughter's history grade negatively influenced by her call. At any rate, the teacher apologized to the student, watched himself in her class, and did not tamper with her grade. Remember, *the only way that evil can triumph is if good people do nothing.*

What type of financial and personal sacrifices are you willing to make to insure the best moral, spiritual and intellectual education for your children?

A Better Choice...Catholic Schools

"The bishops' primary concern is to see how it is possible to transmit the faith in today's culture, and how it is possible to overcome the religious illiteracy of the members of the Church." Cardinal Schotte

St. Elizabeth Seton (1774-1821) and St. John Neumann (1811-1860) are considered the co-founders of the Catholic school system in the U.S. St. Elizabeth converted to the Catholic faith after seeing the faith lived by friends in Italy. Facing financial reverses upon her husband's death, Elizabeth began a school to support herself and her five children. With the blessings of Archbishop John Carroll of Baltimore, she founded the American Sisters of Charity and the first free Catholic day school in the early 1800's. It was the foundation of Catholic parochial schools in the U.S.

St. John Neumann, a native of Bohemia, decided as a young man to be a missionary to the United States. On his own he studied English and French since no classes were available to him. He was ordained in the U.S. and later joined the Redemptorist order. As Bishop of Philadelphia, he built up the

Catholic School system by mandating a Catholic school in each parish in his diocese. Student enrollment rose from 500 students to 10,000 by the time of his death. Since Catholic schools were founded to teach the faith, St. John authored two catechisms besides publishing a German Bible history for the students.

The rise of Catholic schools was accelerated by the growth of a publicly funded school system that was rooted in Protestantism. Robert P. Lockwood, in a fascinating article entitled "Anti-Catholicism and the History of Catholic School Funding," describes how it all began: ...[I]n New York City...in 1840...the Public School Society dominated city schools by controlling the allocation of the common school fund from the state. Ascribing to its definition of "sectarian," the Public School Society funded schools that were generically "Christian." These were "common" schools sharing in the "common" understanding of Protestant Christianity, rather than those operated by a specific Protestant congregation.

Within the common schools in New York City—and elsewhere— daily scripture readings from the King James Version of the Bible were required. Anti-Catholic sentiments extended through the curriculum with references to deceitful Catholics, murderous inquisitions, vile popery, Church corruption, conniving Jesuits and the pope as the anti-Christ of Revelation were common place.

The firestorm began in 1840. Catholic schools in New York City petitioned the Common Council for a share of the state school fund distributed through the Public School Society. The Society answered with a message that resonates with today's rhetoric. It argued that by funding Catholic schools, money would be dissipated and that "sectarian" Catholic education would replace the common schools. The common council agreed and the Catholic petition was denied.

It was then that Bishop John Hughes of New York stepped into the picture. Blasting the Public School Society for corrupting Catholic children, Hughes submitted a renewed petition demanding Catholics be given a portion of the state funds for schooling. In response, the Common Council scheduled a debate *on the issue...At the debate, Hughes represented the Catholic schools and spoke for three hours. The Protestant response covered two days and dealt primarily in anti-Catholic vitriol rather than the issues at hand.*[54]

You can read the complete political history of Catholic schools by logging on to www.catholicleague.org and searching under "Research Papers."

Not only in the U.S. but around the world many men and women earned their crown of sanctity by either educating youth themselves or founding orders to educate the young in faith, morals, and intellectual subjects. Just a small sampling of these men and women includes St. John Bosco, St. Madeleine Sophie Barat, St. Mary Mazzarello, St. Paula Frassinetti, St. Mary-Magdalen Postel, St. Francis Cabrini, Bl. Mary De Matthias, Bl. Edmund Rice, Bl. Maria Theresa of Jesus Gerhardinger, Bl. Théodore-Anne Guerin, Bl. Pauline Von Mallinckrodt.

When St. Ignatius of Loyola developed his famous educational methodology he insisted on three points:

1. Students should attend daily Holy Mass.
2. They should go to confession at least monthly.
3. Prayer should precede class work.[55]

In 1691 in France, St. John Baptist De La Salle, the founder of the Institute of the Brothers of the Christian Schools trained his followers to not only dispel ignorance but to save the students from evil.

Bl. Placida Viel of Normandy opened free elementary schools for girls in the 19th century. She hoped to accomplish for young girls what St. John De La Salle did for young boys.

In the 18th century in Tuscany, St. Lucy Filippini devoted her life to Catholic education working to open schools throughout Italy.

---

[54] Robert P. Lockwood, "Anti-Catholicism and the History of Catholic School Funding," Catalyst, March 2000, p.8.

[55] *Saints & Heroes Speak Vol. Three, Op. Cit.* p.107

St. Joseph Calasanz, a Spaniard, was born in 1556. While working in Rome as a theologian for a Roman Cardinal he became convinced of the importance of teaching young children the faith. He rented some rooms in Trastevere and opened a school where he taught reading, writing, math and the faith. In time his efforts lead to a religious community known as the Clerics Regular of the Poor Schools of the Mother of God.

The Importance of Catholic Education

"In our schools, the Catholic community forms a strong partnership with parents to help our children become responsible Catholics, in love with God and with the Church." Bishop George J. Lucas

Professor James D. Hunter of the University of Virginia writes that the purpose of a Catholic school is not only to teach faith and morals but to serve an even greater goal: *to preserve the religious identity of the group—to maintain the purity of the traditions for succeeding generations.*[56] Unfortunately Catholic schools are diminishing in number as evangelical schools are multiplying. Between 1965 and 1985 Catholic schools decreased by 28% (4,000) along with an enrollment decline of 54% while the Catholic population has grown from 25% to 29% as of 1987.[57] Mr. Hunter contends that the decline is due to two factors— the upward mobility of Catholics from the city to suburbia and *the liberalization of the Catholic religious experience...The consequence of both trends is that the thought, behavior and values of ordinary Catholics have come increasingly to resemble those shared by other Americans...[A] pluralistic and secular America therefore has become a more comfortable place to live for the majority of Catholics. For most Evangelicals, however, it has become significantly more hostile. The private schools of each community reflect these changing realities.*[58]

Besides the two factors that Professor Hunter found

[56] James Davison Hunter, "Evangelical Schools in Growth, Catholic Schools in Decline," *Wall Street Journal*, Sept. 8, 1988.
[57] *Ibid.*   [58] *Ibid.*

responsible for the shrinking of our Catholic School System, there is a third problem, the absence of orthodoxy in some Catholic schools. This is the result of the liberalization of the Catholic schools. Parents who would normally support Catholic schools have in many cases removed their children. They either send them to the public schools, private schools, home school or found their own private Catholic schools. Pope Pius XI warned: *The mere fact that religious instruction is given in a school (and often very little of it) is not enough to make that school one which conforms to the rights of the Church and the Christian family, and thus worthy of being attended by Catholic pupils. To achieve this, all the teaching and all the organization of the school, teachers, curriculum and books in each subject, must be imbued with a Christian spirit.*[59]

This concern is being addressed in various dioceses. Bishop George J. Lucas of Springfield, Illinois writes: *The big challenge beyond keeping our schools open is making them Catholic in the richest sense of the term. It is not enough for us to be good people and to operate good schools. Our schools have a mission that is part of the saving mission of Jesus Himself. We have to develop a clearer understanding all the time of what distinguishes those who follow Jesus Christ in the Catholic Church, in the United States, in the 21*[st]* century. We have to be able to articulate for ourselves the age-old wisdom of the Church. Then, we have to teach our children to both articulate and internalize that same revealed wisdom.*

A great deal is expected of young Catholics in today's world. And they have a great deal to offer. Catholic schools can help prepare them for a life of discipleship.[60]

John Paul II quoting from his document **Familiaris Consortio**, no. 40 told the Nigerian bishops: *The rights of parents to choose an education in conformity with their religious faith must be absolutely guaranteed. The state and Church have the obligation to give families all possible aid to enable them to*

[59] *Divinillius magistri,* 49.

[60] Bishop George J. Lucas, "Our Catholic schools are integral part of Church's mission," *Catholic Times,* Jan. 27, 2002, p. 2.

perform their educational role properly...Those in society who are in charge of schools must never forget that the parents have been appointed by God Himself as the first and principle educators of their children and that their right is completely inalienable.

Professor Hunter disclosed that *the number of Catholics attending college, for example, has more than doubled since World War II to the point that exceeds the national average.*[61] Why are more Catholics attending college? Setting aside the problem of the lack of doctrinal fidelity in many Catholic schools, traditionally our schools provide a first class education. In 1988, Secretary of Education William J. Bennett pointed out that Catholic students are as much as two grade levels higher than their counterparts in public schools. The dropout rate in Catholic high schools is only 3% compared to 14% in public schools.[62] Likewise in England, Catholic school students and other denominational students boast higher achievement than their public school contemporaries. *Psychologists maintain...in good religious schools, students have a peaceful, disciplined and serious environment from the perspective of the quality of the teaching offered and the proof of student achievement, where there are no drug problems or "bullying"...which affects many government-run schools...There is an additional element that affects education at a deeper level. Over the last year, the collection of primary and secondary school textbooks of Christian inspiration has had an unexpected success. The collection includes books on different subjects like English, history, mathematics, etc. that are based on Christian values, which can be transmitted in any field of learning. For example, a traditional math textbook...asks the student to calculate, given the requirements of his/her own family, how much of their salary could be allocated to the needy. These books are being used especially in Christian schools, but also in a considerable number of non-denominational schools, which is seen as a sign of an ever-increasing need for stronger values, both on the part of students as well as teachers and families.*[63]

[61] "Evangelical Schools in Growth, Catholic Schools in Decline," *Op. Cit.*

[62] "Secretary Bennett's Last Challenge," *Op. Cit.* p. 8.   [63] Zenit, May 15, 2000.

In New Orleans, Pope John Paul II explained to Catholic educators his vision of what a Catholic school should encompass: *The content of the individual courses in Catholic education is important both in religious teaching and in all the other subjects that go to make up the total instruction of the human person and to prepare them for their life's work and their eternal destiny. It is fitting that teachers should be constantly challenged by high professional standards in preparing and teaching their courses. In regard to the content of religion courses, the <u>essential criterion is fidelity to the teaching of the Church.</u>*

Educators are likewise in a splendid position to inculcate into young people right ethical attitudes. These include attitudes toward material things and their proper use. The whole life style of students will reflect the attitudes that they form during their years of formal education.

*The ultimate goal of all Catholic education is salvation in Jesus Christ. Catholic educators effectively work for the coming of Christ's kingdom; this work includes transmitting clearly and in full the message of salvation which elicits the response of faith. In faith we know God and the hidden purpose of his will (cf. **Eph** 1:9). In faith we truly come to know ourselves. By sharing our faith we communicate a complete vision of the whole of reality and a commitment to truth and goodness...By enriching your students' lives with the fullness of Christ's message and by inviting them to accept with all their hearts Christ's work, which is the Church, you promote most effectively their integral human development, and you help them to build a community of faith, hope and love.*

While in England Christianity is seeping into government run schools through texts and curriculum, in the U.S. secular humanism is contaminating our Catholic schools through state textbook loan programs. As a "gift" from the government, Catholic students are using the same books as the public school students. This same problem is also happening in Ireland where there is a movement for the government to control all schools. If government control is not overtly successful, plan B is to implement government mandated programs that violate Catholic morality.

Our first choice for educating children should be a Catholic school. But all Catholic schools are not equal owing to the curriculum, teachers, textbooks and sex education or chastity programs used. Check out your parish school. Many times by becoming involved on the school board, as a volunteer, or coach, you can influence the choice of textbooks and curriculum, and introduce abstinence rather than sex education courses. If the situation is impossible to correct, check out the other area Catholic schools.

Many times problems in Catholic schools are due to ignorance rather than bad will. Get a copy of the document, ***The Religious Dimension of Education in a Catholic School***,[64] put out by the Congregation for Catholic Education. Share it with your pastor and principal. This document contains guidelines for bishops, religious orders, and officials of Catholic primary and secondary schools. The document expresses concern that some youths leave Catholic schools without being touched by God or the faith. It calls for teachers to witness what they teach. Furthermore, it asks teachers to frequently refer to God and to encourage prayer in the classroom. It states that each classroom should have a crucifix on the wall. Religious texts are to be based on the ***Catechism of the Catholic Church*** and teach the students Scripture based on the life of Jesus [i.e. the Gospels], Christian anthropology, ecclesiology, the sacraments, the Creed as well as Christian ethics presented in a systematic manner. Religious formation is to be given to teachers because *an unprepared teacher can do a great deal of harm.* The document sadly comments that *for some of today's youth, the years spent in a Catholic school seem to have scarcely any effect. They seem to have a negative attitude toward all the various ways in which a Christian life is expressed—prayer, participation in the Mass, or frequenting of the sacraments.*

Purchase a copy of ***The Truth and Meaning of Human***

---

[64] Browse the website for the Vatican document, try Catholic News Service (202)541-3290 or The Catholic Information Center (202)783-2062.

Sexuality (1996) promulgated by the Pontifical Council for the Family for yourself, your pastor, and the principal. This is compulsory reading for all parents.

Besides checking out Catholic grade schools, check out curriculum, text, and teachers at the Catholic high school level. Many Catholic high schools are excellent while others leave much to be desired. Roseanna Hatke, a freshman theology teacher at Central Catholic High School in Lafayette, Indiana, sends out a newsletter to all the parents of her students outlining exactly what she is teaching their children. To ensure that parents read the newsletter it must be signed by the parent and returned to school. What impressed me so about her letter was the fact that she was evangelizing the parents in addition to teaching their children. Here's just a glimpse of one of her monthly letters:

Dear Parents:

During the month of November, we will begin an introduction to the New Testament and discuss the Gospels, the Acts of the Apostles, the Epistles, and the Book of Revelation. We will go into greater detail with the New Testament during the second semester.

We will also study the roles of Scripture and Tradition in the Church. We will discuss doctrine and dogma, especially the central doctrine of our faith, the Trinity. We will go over the Nicene Creed in great detail. We will begin our study of the Sacraments and the Liturgical Year. The prayer for this month is the "Memorare."

November is the month traditionally dedicated to the Sacred Heart of Jesus and we will be talking about that and about First Friday devotions and Eucharistic Adoration. November is also the month in which we remember the saints in Heaven (All Saints Day, Nov. 1), and the souls in Purgatory (All Souls Day, Nov. 2). We have talked about these special days and about the fact that the Church is an ongoing body which continues beyond earthly time in the Church Militant, the Church Suffering and the Church

Triumphant. Several other saints we will study this month are: St. Martin of Tours, St. Charles Borromeo, St. Elisabeth of Hungary, St. Albert the Great, St. Cecilia, and St. John of the Cross. The lives of the saints should be an inspiration for all of us, but studying them will also help the students pick a special patron saint for their Confirmation name.

We continue to study the Ten Commandments in detail. We are currently on the Fifth Commandment, "Thou Shall Not Kill."

In this month when we give thanks to God for all of our blessings, I thank God for the opportunity to share the faith with your children and teach in a school where Jesus is present in every classroom. As always, let's pray for one another.

In addition, her newsletter contained short articles on the Sacred Heart of Jesus, an explanation of the poor souls, the communion of saints, and purgatory. Roseanna deserves the Catholic Teacher of the Year award!

Unfortunately all Catholic high schools are not as faithful to the Catholic faith and morals. When we relocated to Central Illinois we sent our older daughters to the "top" Catholic high school in town, the school where past governors sent their daughters. The school was rated so highly by people we respected that we naively did not check into the curriculum nor the textbooks. When our freshman daughter, Marianne, announced that she was going to have to flunk her religion test because to study the material would be sinful, I sat down and spent the evening reading the text. All the sins that St. Paul insisted that we should never mention were part of her assignment. Marianne was required by her teacher to be able to spell and define each perversion. Past experience taught us that for "mom" to protest is pointless but if both parents go to the school to discuss a problem the matter is taken more seriously by the administration. Bob and I met with the theology teacher and the principal. They gave us the standard canned speech: *If all parents were like you, we would not have to have sex education in the religion program but since they aren't we do.* Since the school was caught off guard by our protest, they permitted our daughter to pursue an independent religious course of my choice. As more parents began protesting, the school contracted with a religious order to use their correspondence religious course. That option is no longer available. After two years at this school, my husband and I felt morally obligated to remove our daughters from the school. Our only acceptable option was to send them away to a private school that teaches the fullness of the Catholic faith. We personally knew all the teachers and their backgrounds. The administration was approachable and accommodating if we ran into any problems. Mary Kate and Marianne boarded with family and friends. It was a difficult, painful decision but the right one. Upon her graduation from grade school, our youngest daughter, Mary Terese, was also sent to this school. Not only were their faith and morals protected but they were enriched. The girls had the opportunity to attend daily Mass, and weekly confession was available. As a result, each of our daughters still has a vibrant, living Catholic faith. Not so their friends who graduated from that local Catholic high school. Few, if any practice their faith.

The situation at that Catholic school has deteriorated further. A freshman mother called with shocking documentation on the orchestrated destruction of faith and morals at the school. Prominent in our community, this valiant mother tried to rally her friends with children in the school to protest. Some refused to read the material, others were afraid that if they protested the teachers would dock their children's grades. Others did not want to complicate their lives by getting involved. She met with the religion teacher, the head of the theology department, the principal. She and her husband addressed the board, went to our former bishop and even took her case to Rome. She worked for a year on this without the support or help of a single parent. Finally, she sold her beautiful, newly custom built home to moved into another school district so she could send her daughter to a "safe" public school. Unfortunately, her experience soured her on Catholic education. Her brilliant daughter is now attending a Protestant College. Will she graduate from that Protestant school still a Catholic?

The administration of this school has become so bold as to actually tell parents who inquire about their theology program, *You will not be happy here. We do not teach doctrine. We present all options and respect the students' freedom to choose what they want to believe.* The administration does not seem to understand that if a student is not presented the truth he is no longer free to choose an option. They have forgotten that Christ told us that the truth will make us free!

The protection of your children's faith today could mean that you have to take heroic measures. One important point that was learned from these battles is that it must be fought locally by winning the support of other parents. Parent-power can turn schools around or force their closure. The Vatican has its hands full fighting the big battles; we have to take care of the skirmishes in our sphere of influence.

The Question of Catholic Universities...

"[W]hat is important is that we judge everything that we do, every college that we run, every grade school and high school...by how it contributes to the holiness of God's people."[65] Cardinal Francis George

The Church and the university are the greatest instruments of influence. It is through them that ideas are spread to form or mold our culture. As the Church goes, so goes the university. As the university goes so goes society. *The purpose of a Catholic university is to form professionals and scientists capable of "living a synthesis between the Gospel and culture,"* explained John Paul II. *"Intelligence certainly has its laws and paths, but it gains everything when the person who seeks it is holy. In fact, sanctity places the scholar in a condition of greater interior liberty, with effort charged with meaning, which sustains his exhaustion with the contribution of those moral virtues that forge authentic and mature men."*[66]

[65] Zenit, July 16, 2001.   [66] Zenit, Nov. 10, 2000.

When you tour college campuses seriously consider Catholic colleges and universities such as Ave Maria University, Christendom College, Franciscan University at Steubenville, Thomas Aquinas College, and Magdalen College. From personal research these schools seem to be turning out well-educated, articulate, rock solid Catholics who are on fire with the love of God. They are also the ideal place to find a Catholic spouse for your child. Looking for a law school? Check out Ave Maria University. Give your children the best educationally. If these schools do not have the majors your children wish to pursue, at least start them out in one of these schools to give them a solid foundation before switching them to another university in their junior year.

Other Catholic colleges and universities have prestigious names but go beyond the name to check out the tone, the orthodoxy, and the dorm rules before turning your child's immortal soul over to one of them. Dorm life on Catholic campuses, sadly, is no different from secular schools. If your child attends a secular school consider the Newman dorm or a student residence that is run by Opus Dei or other Catholic organizations. Insist on placing your child into either an all-male dorm or an all-female dorm. Check into visiting hours and rules. Either insist on a private room or make arrangements for your child to room with a friend whose morals you trust. Our eldest daughter attended a large Catholic university where she was placed with a professor's daughter who was promiscuous and on drugs. It took us months, threats and finally a trip to the university to get her out of that mess. Before you send your son or daughter away to school look up the report entitled "Hooking Up, Hanging Out and Looking for Mr. Right." This report is put out by the Institute for American Values for the Independent Women's Forum.[67] It is chilling.

The Holy See promulgated ***Ex Corde Ecclesiae*** which requires all professors of Catholic theology and morality to have a mandatum from the local bishop attesting to their fidelity to the Magisterium of the Catholic Church before they can teach

---

[67] "Girl Meets Boy," *The Wall Street Journal*, Aug. 3, 2001.

theology and morality in a Catholic college or university. It is up to the ordinary (bishop) of the diocese in which the university is located to determine the conditions and fulfillment of the oath of fidelity to the Holy See, after which the theologian can receive the mandatum. An example of one draft of the signed statement would be: *I am committed to teach authentic Catholic doctrine and to refrain from putting forth as Catholic teaching anything contrary to the Church's Magisterium.*[68] Bishops began granting "canonical mission" to teach in the name of the Church in 1931 but it was done in an informal manner that made it difficult to remove unorthodox professors. *Ex Corde Ecclesiae* includes a detailed procedure for the granting or the retraction of a mandatum.

Many Catholic colleges and universities are either ignoring this decree or fighting it. Check with the Catholic university administration about this matter <u>before</u> you enroll your child. Why financially support an institution that is not faithful to the Holy See? Why entrust your child's soul to such a school? Again, while in New Orleans in 1987, John Paul II told leaders of Catholic universities and colleges: *Undoubtedly, the greatest challenge is, and will remain, that of preserving and strengthening the Catholic character of your colleges and universities—that institutional commitment to the Word of God as proclaimed by the Catholic Church. This commitment is both an expression of spiritual consistency and a specific contribution to the cultural dialogue proper to American life. As you strive to make the presence of the Church in the world of modern culture more luminous, may you listen once again to Christ's prayer to his Father for his disciples:* **"Consecrate them by means of truth—Your word is truth"** *(Jn 17:17).* In a November 14th, 2001 Zenit article, Cardinal Avery Dulles noted that, *In the United States, Catholic universities have been very apologetic, almost embarrassed, by their obligation to adhere to the faith of the Church. The time has come for them to regain their confidence and proudly proclaim the faith that animates them. Shifting the burden of proof to the secular institutions, they should challenge the other universities to defend themselves and to show how it is possible to find and transmit the fullness of truth if they neglect* *or marginalize the word of God.*

Consider Private Schools...

"Parents must educate their children according to the will of God."   Fr. Thomas J. Gerrard

Private schools are another educational option. Henry Ford, concerned about the education of his employees' children, founded a private school for them in Greenfield Village, Michigan. His school utilized the famous **McGuffey Readers** that are still popular today. These textbooks not only teach the "three Rs" but patriotic and moral values.

The paternal grandfather of St. Thérèse, Pierre Martin, moved his family to Alencon rather than to Normandy which he so loved, because he believed his children would receive a better education in Alencon, France. The Guérins, the maternal grandparents of St. Thérèse, sent their two daughters to be educated as day-boarders by the Sisters of the Sacred Heart. The foundress of this school is in the process of beatification. The education the two Guérin sisters received from the nuns reinforced the faith they received from their parents at home. The Martins themselves educated their five daughters in private schools either as day students or as boarders.

St. Mildred was sent from her home in England to study at such a school in Paris in the 7th century. St. Angadrisma was educated at Thérouanne by St. Omer. St. Vincent Pallotti and St. Escrivá were educated by the Piarist Fathers.

Today, as in the past, private Catholic schools are springing up all over the world to answer the need for authentic Catholic education. The force behind most of these schools is concerned parents willing to make heroic sacrifices to educate their children. In London, eight families decided to found a private school that teaches the Catholic faith. The building they were able to rent for the school was not conveniently located for any of the families so all eight families sold their homes and moved to Surrey, England to begin the school. They began with 6th grade and added another level each year until the school included high school. Now the families are working to found a grade school.

In the U.S. there are private Catholic grade and high schools founded either by parents, Catholic organizations, religious orders or individuals. The following are some schools that sound excellent. You probably know of others. Parents founded several academies in Wisconsin, and the Embers[69] and Kingswood Academies in the Chicago area. The Heights Academy for Boys[70] in Potomac, Maryland is a corporate work of Opus Dei. The Willows Academy for Girls[71] and Northridge Prep for Boys[72] in the Chicago area, Oakcrest for Girls[73] in DC, and Montrose[74] in Natick, Massachusetts are parent-run schools with the spiritual formation of the students under the direction of Opus Dei. The private schools under the spiritual direction of Opus Dei have daily Mass and weekly confessions available. The Mission statement of The Willows Academy, which is similar to the other schools inspired by the spirituality of Opus Dei, summarizes why we selected this school for our three daughters:

The Willows Academy is an independent school for young women grades six through twelve. Through the cooperative efforts of educators and parents, students receive the necessary means to grow in knowledge, virtue and responsibility. The Willows is committed to providing a college preparatory academic program of the highest caliber, a moral atmosphere within the school complementary to that of the home, and character formation to instill lifelong values. The Willows Academy is inspired by the teachings of the Catholic Church and the spirituality of the Prelature of Opus Dei.

---

[68] Zenit, Nov. 19, 2000.

[69] The Embers Elementary School, Park Ridge, IL (847-518-1185).

[70] The Heights Academy for Boys, Washington, DC area (301-365-4300).

[71] The Willows Academy for Girls, Des Plaines, IL (847-824-6900).

[72] Northridge Prep for Boys, Niles, IL (847-375-0600).

[73] Oakcrest Academy for Girls, Washington, DC (202-686-9736).

[74] Montrose Academy for Girls, Natick, MA (508-650-6925).

National Consultants for Education (NCE) provides another excellent private Catholic school option. NCE is a support organization for private, independent Catholic schools in the United States and Canada. This organization assists private schools across the country to implement the Integral Formation philosophy of education developed by the Legionaries of Christ. Integral Formation is the formation of the whole person: intellectual, character, spiritual and apostolic. NCE assists schools by providing curriculum that supports this philosophy of education as well as by providing ongoing training for the teachers and staff. It also provides assistance in the areas of school operations and development. To locate NCE schools in your area you can call (301) 767-6940 or write to them.[75]

In Chapter 2, I discussed how Thomas Monaghan, a concerned parent and founder of Domino's Pizza, founded the chain of Spiritus Sanctus Schools in Ann Arbor, Michigan. These schools are administered by the Sisters of Mary, Mother of the Eucharist, a new religious community. The Mission Statement of the Spiritus Sanctus Academies explains:

Designed intentionally to be small, family-oriented schools, it is the mission of the Spiritus Sanctus Academies to create a unique, multi-age educational environment in which learning and practicing the truths of the Catholic faith are central to the development of each child. While providing for the primacy of faith development, the Academies simultaneously furnish superior academic instruction tailored to the needs of each student. In partnership with its families, the Academies strive to produce well-rounded individuals rooted in the truths of the faith and the educational scholarship needed to prosper in the worldwide community of the third millennium.

Spiritus Sanctus Academies exist primarily for the purpose of assisting families with the education of their children regarding the truths of the Catholic Faith, and to nourish both families and students in the Eucharistic life and Marian

---

[75] National Consultants for Education, PO Box 34515, Bethesda, MD 20827.

spirituality of the Church...All involved in SSA are to be committed to the Magisterium of the Church while applying and living out the Catholic Faith regarding its sacraments, prayers, and devotions and, in particular, to the Eucharist and Consecration to Mary.

In order to make disciples of all children that pass through the doors of every Spiritus Sanctus Academy, we have committed ourselves to building a Catholic culture within these walls, which permeates every moment of every day and which, with God's help, flows out into the world.

In order to build a Catholic culture within a school, four major areas of formation need to be considered: doctrinal, liturgical, moral and spiritual. Each of these areas touches on the life of the school as a whole and on life in each individual classroom. There is not a moment of the day or place within the school building that is not touched by these four areas of formation...[76]

In addition to the above, the children who attend the Spiritus Sanctus Academies attend daily Mass, participate in Eucharistic adoration and have the opportunity to go to confession on a regular basis. This is just a sampling of some private Catholic schools available in the U.S. Check out the private schools in your area. What is their mission statement? How is the faith taught? Are daily Mass and frequent confession available to the students?

Many academically challenging, spiritually sound parent-founded schools close due to the lack of cooperation among the parents. Infighting, a desire for control by one faction of parents over another faction, disagreements over teachers, the headmaster or texts has resulted in the senseless destruction of excellent schools. Remember, no academic situation will be completely perfect. If you become involved with a parent-founded school, you have a moral obligation to work together with all the other parents for the good of all. Sometimes your point of view will be accepted, at other times it will be rejected.

---

[76] Admissions Office, 2600 Via Sacra, Ann Arbor, MI 48105 (734-995-0917).

Cooperate with everyone involved with the school. If the theology is sound and moral values are correct you can correct any perceived academic deficiencies by tutoring your child in the subject at home or hiring a tutor. Recall the words of Sister Lucia on page 220:*Where God is, the devil appears stirring up conflicts, battles and contradictions. All these things are a sign of the presence of God. If they did not come from God, the devil would have nothing to fear as he would not be in danger of losing his domain.*

Home Schooling

If local schools are objectionable and good private Catholic schools are unavailable then the only option is to home school your children. Mothers who home school are heroic. With the wonderful programs that are available, as Bl. Peter Casani would say, *Patience and prayer are enough.*

Home schooling is nothing new. The saints have been doing it for centuries. In the 4th century, St. Emmelia trained her daughter St. Macrina to read the Book of Wisdom and the Psalms when she was about four years old. At the age of twelve St. Macrina in turn taught her younger brothers, St. Basil the Great, St. Peter of Sebaste, and St. Gregory of Nyssa. In the 5th century St. Pulcheria, the daughter of the Byzantine Emperor Arcadius, became regent upon the death of her father. She was fifteen-years-old. Besides this responsibility, she was also put in charge of the education of her brother, Emperor Theodosius. Alice of Montbar, who lived in the 11th century, home schooled her seven children—all of whom are saints. Alice was not only proficient in Latin but she was schooled in Cicero and Virgil. When she found that her son Bernard excelled in his studies she sent him away to a private school for advanced education.

The maternal grandmother of St. Maximilian Kolbe, unable to afford schooling for her five children, home schooled her little ones in reading and writing while at the same time she taught them how to weave. Once the older siblings became weavers and were able to contribute to the family income, the two younger daughters were sent to the local elementary school. The parents of St. Maximilian, Marianna and Julius Kolbe home schooled their sons not only in the faith but also in reading, writing, math, Polish history, culture, and language since it was suppressed by the Russian government. In 1834 in Portugal a Masonic government came to power which suppressed the Catholic Church. In 1910 the situation grew worse forcing Catholic parents to home school their children. Sister Lucia of Fatima was one of these children who was home schooled. Her mother taught her the faith so well that by the age of nine, Lucia was named a catechist by her pastor. She was assigned to teach children her age and older the faith.

Others hired tutors such as St. Thomas More, who was mentioned before. In Ireland St. Colman educated St. Columba. St. Alphonsus Liguori, Doctor of the Church, was raised near Naples, Italy in the early 1700's. His parents insisted on the best education for their son. His mother schooled him in piety and his father found the best tutors for the secular subjects. This combined with his keen intellect found him admitted to the Neapolitan bar as a lawyer at the age of 16. As a lawyer he was brilliant. For eleven years he won every case he tried. Then at the age of 27 he lost a case. It was then that he decided to become a priest.

Many of the tutors of the saints were saints themselves such as St. Jarlath who tutored St. Brendan and St. Colman. A bishop tutored Bl. Theresa of Jesus Gerhardinger, the founder of the School Sisters of Notre Dame.

In Italy in the late 15th century, St. Angela Merici, the foundress of the Ursuline Order, educated young girls by sending her sisters into the homes of the girls rather than founding schools. She felt strongly that *disorder in society is the result of disorder in the family.*[77] By educating the girls at home, the sister could positively influence the atmosphere in the home.

Some parent may be concerned that home schooling provides

[77] *Lives of the Saints Illustrated Part I*, *Op. Cit.* p. 49.

only a mediocre education. This simply is not true. One of the greatest creative geniuses of all time, Thomas Edison, received only three months of formal education. His schoolteacher informed his parents that he was dumb, that he was "learning disabled." Mrs. Edison did not accept the teacher's verdict. She decided to home school her son herself. Her efforts were further complicated by the problem of Tom's growing deafness. She could only communicate with him through notes, shouting into his ear and when he was much older through Morse Code. But by personally working with her son, Mrs. Edison found that he not only had a photographic memory but also could read at an astonishing rate of speed. She was able to educate him to develop all of his God given talents, which he in turned used to help mankind in very diverse ways.

Some Modern Day Examples...

Ange and Peter Popovich of Springfield, Illinois, have home schooled for the past eight years. They are the parents of six children: Peter (12), Nicholas (10), Alexandra (8), John Isaac (5), Lilli (4) and Christina (one month). Their children are featured on the cover of *Raise Happy Children...Teach Them Virtues!*, book three of this series.

Ange from Shawnee Mission, Kansas, majored in business administration at the University of Kansas. Pete from Youngstown, Ohio, majored at the University of Kansas in biology, where he met Ange. He is an emergency room physician at Memorial Hospital in Springfield, Illinois. Pete is a convert to the Catholic faith. While the Popoviches plan to home school their children throughout grammar school they are unsure about high school.

Ange explains, *We had home schooled Peter from kindergarten through first grade. When we moved to Springfield we put him into a Catholic school for 2nd grade because I had just given birth to our fourth child and was overwhelmed. While we put Peter into school, we decided that my husband would home school Nicholas who was starting kindergarten. For Peter the year was a repeat. Home schooling had put him far ahead of his class. We also noticed a gradual change in him. He was losing his personality. We found that he became closed toward us. He wouldn't share his day. There was a quiet sadness about him when he came home from school. His family situation was so different from his classmates. Peter found it difficult to understand. It was an eye opening experience.*

Pete adds, *One benefit of home schooling is learning about your child's soul. It's a great blessing to know the intimacies of your child's soul.*

When asked why the couple chose to home school, Ange replies, *We felt God was calling us to home school all the kids after seeing Peter's exposure to the culture and how it had affected him. We begin home schooling our children at the age of five.*

Pete's emergency room schedule is flexible enough to allow him to home school along with his wife. Ange teaches spelling and vocabulary while Pete teaches grammar, and science. Both teach religion, math, writing, reading, art, history and a cooking class. *We both are flexible and keep close track of what each is doing so we can step in and take over any of the subjects.*

The Popoviches selected their home schooling materials by *trial and error. We started off with a Catholic home schooling program but found that the program was dry and boring. Catholic programs in the beginning were too rigid and restrictive. They have changed in the last five years and are getting better. Next we used a secular program and supplemented Ignatius Press' **Image of God** series for religion. Protestant programs are more colorful with pictures and drawings. Now we use much of Laura Berquist's material, **Designing Your Own Classic Curriculum.** This book lists all the resources home schoolers need. This book can be purchased through a Catholic bookstore. Our home schooling group also shares and exchanges materials.*

As to the benefits of home schooling Pete observes, *Our children are developing a love of learning. They have a genuine inquisitiveness. We have found that home schooled children are better at socialization than other children. They can carry on conversations in an adult manner. They are thinkers, not sheep.*

But the spiritual benefits far outweigh everything else. The children realize that our faith and our family are two of the greatest gifts and they see this lived daily. Home schooling helps family unity tremendously because the children spend each day with each other. They understand that it is ok to play with your little brother or younger sister. It fosters family love and loyalty. The children learn to forgive each other and work things out. Since you are constantly present to your children they know they have to obey you. Parents, on the other hand, realize that they must be kind and charitable to the children. This knowledge helps you all to get along much better.

As to the drawbacks Ange finds *the biggest drawback is the tremendous sacrifice of time and energy. A home schooling parent has to give everything one has. It's actually an additional vocation to parenthood. Home schooling can become stressful. When a person first begins to home school it seems that there is just too much to do. It's hard to figure out the core of what you should be doing when there are so many subjects to teach, so many different ages, housework, dinner, etc. Yet the more you home school, the more confidence you develop. The father has to be involved in the home schooling otherwise the wife can feel overburdened.* Pete believes, *if a person is not disciplined the person cannot home school. I work with single mothers at work, nurses, who are having discipline problems with their children. It would not be a good idea for these mothers to home school.*

Besides the help of the father, we found a tutor for two subjects one year, explained Ange. *That was very helpful but the tutor must have the same beliefs as the parents for the parents to trust the tutor.*

Dr. and Mrs. Popovich find that home schooling parents need spiritual help to persevere. The Popoviches try to attend daily Mass, pray the rosary together as a couple, *and use lots of holy water with the children. By this I mean, when the children are quarreling or uncooperative I bless them with holy water. When I feel that I'm starting to lose my temper, I bless myself with holy water. This sacramental restores peace.* While the couple says a decade of rosary with the children each day they find praying more than that difficult because of the wide age span of the children. They prefer to say the rosary as a couple: *Us saying the rosary together has sustained our marriage and vocation to home schooling. Home schooling is a stress on marriage so we have also implemented a weekly family holy hour each Wednesday afternoon.* Before moving to Springfield, Pete and Ange help start Eucharistic adoration at their former parish. In Springfield they were instrumental in also starting Eucharistic adoration in their new parish. *Primarily the holy hour has taught the children to be still. It's difficult for all of us to be quiet but it is a prerequisite for praying. This holy hour has deepened the children's devotion toward the Eucharist. Some of their revelations are truly inspired after we leave Adoration,* remarks Pete. Ange recalls how when someone called her to cancel the holy hour on Christmas because it would interfere with the person's dinner, their older son, Peter, observed to his father, *They want to celebrate Christmas but they are leaving the Infant Jesus alone by not wanting to keep their adoration time.* Ange also explains *there are cards in the chapel that can be sent to people telling them that an hour of adoration was offered for them. This teaches the children that prayer is a way to help others. They see that prayer is a priority in our lives and so they know the importance of it. Actions speak louder then words.*

When asked about the socialization of home schooled children, Peter replies, *We allow them to play selectively with children in the neighborhood.* Ange adds, *We also get together at least once a week with our home schooling group for a co-op class on Friday afternoons for a couple of hours. We have 12 families in our home schooling group with children ranging in ages from high school down to babies. We go on field trips together to visit the weather station, museums, or a neighboring city. We take the children bowling and have our own Girl Scout troop. In addition to this, each of our children plays an instrument. Their teachers are associated with the Springfield Symphony. On Fridays Peter and Nicholas serve Mass at the Priests' Retirement Center, while the other children in the family attend Mass there with one or both parents.* The Popoviches develop friendships with priests and religious so as to expose their children to these vocations.

Ange explained their family is part of the "Adopt-A-Nun" program. *Each family has a sister as part of their family. We visit monthly and share our lives and faith. It has been a great experience for us!*

Ange finds the home schooling support group necessary. *Our members are a great support group for the mothers. Unfortunately some home schooling groups can become divisive. The same individualism that prompts parents to home school can intrude to make cooperation difficult.*

The Popoviches home school nine months out of the year. They begin the last week or two weeks in August and usually quit the third week in May. They use vacations to enrich their children by visiting historic sites and cultural events.

A typical day begins at 8:30am. *We say our morning offering, read the gospel, sing, and discuss the reading of the day. We always begin with religion or it can get lost. Then we do grammar, math and reading in the morning. After lunch we tend to do lighter subjects such as history, science, and memorize poetry, vocabulary and spelling. The children become very independent and can jump ahead if they complete their assignments ahead of time. We are usually done between 2-3pm if we are organized and work hard. There is no homework because it's completed during the day. Art and a cooking class are sandwiched in at least once a week.*

Having such a large span of age groups is difficult. Half the week Pete teaches together with me. The pre-schoolers are the most difficult because they want your time. This means that your interests are divided. A friend, who home schools, Kim Reardon, assigns an older child to work with the younger child for half an hour to an hour. This works well for me also because it gives me time to privately teach the other children. The schedule cannot be too rigid or the children will dread it. When school becomes too intense, we take field trips. We have found we can turn anything into a field trip, even a vacation.

Initial cost can be expensive but the cost varies with each

program. *The total cost for our children is about $2,000 per year but that is high,* Ange admits. *Some parents get away with $100 a year. Parents can reuse the materials for younger children.*

Before a parent decides to home school Ange recommends that the *couple pray together to see if they have the vocation to home school. Then they both have to agree on the value of home schooling before they begin. Dr. Mary Kay Clark of Seton Study School*[78] *wrote a book about how to start your own home school. Get the book and read it. Visit someone who is home schooling. Review their materials. Get in touch with home school support groups. You can find these online, by word of mouth, through your parish, newsletter, or where you buy your curriculum. Ask to review the different curriculums that others are using before you decide on one.*

People home school for different reasons. For Jane Aldrich, of Arlington Heights, Illinois, home schooling is an important educational option for families. Although her husband was the principal of an excellent Catholic school, rather than sending her oldest daughter to the school, *I home schooled Molly solely from an academic perspective. Molly was reading before kindergarten so she was way ahead of the class. In Springfield I thought it would be better to go at her own pace and own level.* When her husband became the principal of Morgan Park, an exclusive day school in the Chicago area, Molly and Meg attended that school for two years. When Kevin Aldrich was appointed headmaster of Embers Academy, a private Catholic school, *the children were home schooled for a year as a transition. This year they attend the Embers. We find the character and social setting superior. The children are very social, always meeting people so although their educational situation has changed from year to year whether they attend school or are home schooled they are happy.*

For parents interested in home schooling, Jane recommends Kimberly Hahn's book, ***Catholic Education Homeward Bound***, by Ignatius Press.

---

[78] 1350 Progress Drive, Front Royal, VA 22630 (540-636-2141).

Criteria for choosing an education option consist of two main priorities: the Catholic faith and excellent academics. Note that the sports program is not a factor. Dr. David Isaacs maintains that if a parent has to choose between the Catholic faith and excellent academics, choose the academics and home school religious education. But you cannot send a child to a school with excellent academics if the child's faith and morals will be harmed.

The Education Of Free Time...

The education of your children does not stop when they leave school. It's at home that the most important education is given. You need to spend time with your children so that you can initiate deep conversations on all the important areas and aspects of life, to discover their problems, their worries.

Charles Lindbergh, who changed the world of aviation, although a busy professional, made time to educate his children in the task of daily living. He also made an effort to guide their interests. He taught them to *do the toughest thing first.* He insisted on obedience because until his children learned how to obey they could not practice self-control. Lindbergh challenged his children but at the same time he clearly explain what his expectations were. He wanted them to *learn how to handle difficult situations.*[79] Through his relationship with his children he learned what areas interested them and where their talents lay. Then he encouraged them to focus on those interests. His son, Jon, loved to fish so Charles paid him three cents a pound for the fish he caught. Jon's catch was then frozen for family meals. This led Jon to eventually *pioneer the field of deep-sea diving and [to] develop salmon farms in the Pacific Northwest.*[80] His son, Land, loved the great outdoors, farming, and ranching. So his parents sent him to spend his summers out West on ranches. In time he learned to run the family ranch in Montana. Their daughter, Anne, loved dolls. Their encouragement of her interest led to her becoming the author

[79] James Newton, *Uncommon Friends* (NY: Harcourt, Inc. 1987) p. 288.
[80] *Ibid.*, p. 289.

of children's books. Son Scott loved animals. His parents encouraged his acquisition of various pets along with insisting that he care for them. He grew to be an authority *on wild monkeys and their habitats.*[81] The youngest Lindbergh daughter, Reeve, became an author like her mother and older sister.

Find time to talk to each child individually. If it's too chaotic at home, invite individual children to accompany you on errands, or take each one out periodically for a treat. With all the demands on your time, this takes fortitude, which means interior strength. Pray about ways to help your children to open up. People are more inclined to chat when involved in some activity. Invite your children to help you fold laundry, do yard work or just go for a walk together. Don't give up at the first rejection or rebuff. Keep trying. Reactions of anger are usually "cries for help." Children need lots of help to grow up these days so stay close to them even when they seem unlovable. The longer you ignore a problem the more difficult it becomes to resolve it.

As children grow older, letters can have a powerful impact. Often you can say things in letters that you would be too intimidated to say in person. Make your letters to your children at college or away from home deep and as formative as you can manage.

In addition to individual time with each child, it's important to spend time together as a family. Avoid outside commitments that destroy family mealtime. The average family today has 2.2 meals a week together out of a possible 21 meals. Conversation around the dinner table can be animated and fun, besides a time to impart your values and standards. It is over the dinner table that social virtues are instilled. It is a time to develop closeness with the family between parents and children, children and siblings. Through dinner time conversation the family shares daily experiences. Make sure that the TV does not intrude on meals and conversation. When the family says "grace" before meals it is a time to pray together as a family, to thank God for His bountiful gifts.

---

[81] *Ibid.*

Encourage your children to develop hobbies, play an instrument, and participate in cultural activities. These activities require effort, endurance, and a sense of responsibility. Little by little give your children freedom as they prove to be responsible.

Sport activities are fun, and can even be formative (teamwork, fortitude, effort) unless they become all consuming. The American Academy of Pediatrics reports that children who specialize in a single sport before adolescence can suffer physical and psychological damage such as fractures, burnout, stress, and delayed menstruation.[82]

The Spiritual & Corporal Works of Mercy

Living the Spiritual and Corporal Works of Mercy is one of the most important areas in which to educate your children.

The Works Of Mercy	
Spiritual	Corporal
To admonish the sinner.	To feed the hungry.
To instruct the ignorant.	To give drink to the thirsty.
To counsel the doubtful.	To clothe the naked.
To comfort the sorrowful.	To visit the imprisoned.
To bear wrongs patiently.	To shelter the homeless.
To forgive all injuries.	To visit the sick.
To pray for the living and the dead.	To bury the dead.

Teaching the Works of Mercy will encourage your children to become sensitive to the needs of others and to develop a spirit of service. How can your children live the works? Let's begin with the Spiritual Works of Mercy.

To admonish the sinner: Once your child is grounded in the faith he becomes a junior evangelizer. When his friends discuss their activities, plan entertainment, or use bad language, your child can raise the tone. He can suggest alternatives to drinking or drugs for a high. He can invite his

[82] Lindsey Tanner, "Academy: Youngsters Should Not Specialize," *The State Journal-Register,* July 4, 2000, p. 27.

friends to attend Sunday Mass or take them to confession. He can bluntly tell them to cut out using bad language or taking the name of God or Jesus in vain. Teach your child that he cannot accept or remain silent in the face of evil. He must speak out.

Teach your child how to use conversation, dress and example to help his friends live in a manner pleasing to God. When kids discuss abortion, euthanasia, or other moral problems, educate your child how to interject the Christian point of view. Give examples how your child can tactfully change the subject when friends begin to gossip or tell "dirty jokes" You may even find your children correcting you. On the evening when one of my favorite movies, *Gigi*, was going to be on TV I had to attend a meeting. I asked my daughter, who was in 8th grade, to video tape it for me. As I came home I could see that the movie was still on but just then the tape ran out. Mary Terese, exasperated, announced *that's the fourth end of a tape I used!* Furious with her that she had used the tail end of tapes rather than a blank tape for the film, she looked me in the eye and pointedly told me, *I should not have even video taped that movie because the subject matter is immoral!* Gigi did triumph over evil in the end, but my daughter was right. The premise of the film is not moral.

To instruct the ignorant: When friends do not have well formed consciences your child can lend books, bring them to a catechism class, take them on retreat, or bring them to a priest to discuss concerns or problems. Have your older children work with the younger children on their catechism and the memorization of prayers. They can also read Bible stories and the lives of the saints to the little ones.

Suggest that your children invite their friends to pro-life rallies or marches. Teach them how to write letters to newspapers and networks to complain about objectionable material appearing in the media or attacks on the Catholic Church.

To counsel the doubtful: When your child senses that his friends are distancing themselves from the faith, he can give them sound advice, good criteria for morality, and encouragement to dig deeper into the Catholic faith. Explain to your child that if he doesn't know the answer to his friend's question on faith or morals, to tell the friend he will find out the answer, then get back to him.

To comfort the sorrowful: Life is filled with sorrows—sickness, death, rejection, disappointment, and fear. During such times a person, especially a teen, can feel abandoned. Teach your child to be there to listen and to console sorrowing friends. Your child's concern for another may even prevent a suicide. Help your child to understand the purpose of suffering so he can reassure his friend. Many times kids think suffering is a punishment from God. God uses suffering to bring a person closer to Him, not to punish.

To bear wrongs patiently: The only person who will never disappoint us is God. Everyone else will let us down at sometime in our life. Life is neither fair nor just. Help your child to understand this fact of life so that he can help his friends to bear up cheerfully and forgive when they are wronged. By bearing these wrongs patiently we unite ourselves more intimately with the sufferings of Christ. If accepted in the spirit of patience, these injustices can lead us to great spiritual heights. When we lash out at those who wrong us we stunt our spiritual growth. We can offer these personal hurts to our Lord in reparation for all the injustices in the world.

To forgive all injuries: This spiritual work of mercy is actually related to the last one. Just as Christ forgave His executioners we, as Christians, must forgive those who hurt us in some manner. This is difficult because it goes against nature but with the grace of God, we can do it. Holding grudges hurts us spiritually, emotionally and even physically. It makes our blood boil, our stomach twist into knots, and can even impair our sleep. It can lead a person to murder or injure another. It hinders our spiritual growth and if prolonged can kill our souls through bitterness.

We had a situation on our block where two teenage girls were vying for the same guy. When "Amy" lost her boyfriend to the other girl, "Amy," the daughter of a doctor, went after her rival with a hatchet. Fortunately she was stopped before physical harm was done. The vice of pride is usually the culprit in our reluctance to forgive. By imitating the humility of Christ, we can stifle our pride and learn to forgive. Teach your child to offer all injuries to the Sacred Heart of Jesus for the conversion of sinners. He in turn can then help his friends to the do the same. Only then will we have peace in our hearts, in our homes, and in the world.

To pray for the living and the dead: This work of mercy has a twofold purpose. We are counseled to offer prayers for those passing through life and for those who have passed on to another life. During Mass, through our rosary intentions, in our personal mental prayer, we can pray for our families, friends, teachers, for those who asked for our prayers, and for the souls of our loved ones in purgatory. We can also extend our prayers to those most in need of God's mercy, whether living or dead. We can pray for the living and the dead by offering our work for them or having Masses said for them. Explain, then show your children how to have Masses said for the repose of souls and for the living who are sick or suffering.

The Corporal Works of Mercy are likewise necessary for our children to practice:

To feed the hungry: Prepare food baskets at Christmas and Easter for the poor and deliver them with your children. If your parish collects food for a food pantry, have them help you purchase and carry the food to the drop off point. Consider volunteering at a soup kitchen or breadline with your children. Older teens can volunteer to drive for Meals-On-Wheels.

Teach your children to be sensitive to the needs of others. A friend teaches Confirmation CCD. Her class, for service hours, is helping out on Saturdays at a Food Pantry. Carol mentioned to her class that while people donate food, they don't think to donate candy and poor people like candy too. One of her students, taking what she said to heart, wrote to a candy company asking for donations for the poor. The company shipped the boy four cases of candy.

Another aspect of this corporal work of mercy is our own approach to food. Teach your children to never take seconds at home or in social situations until they are sure everyone has been served first. Sometimes people become so gluttonous in the face of food that charity is tossed out the window. In situations in which food must be shared take only small amounts of each item so that everyone will have a chance to eat. Also, teach your children to take only what they will consume at that meal. By taking more than one can eat, others may be denied food. Recently I spoke at a seminar held at a retreat center. At lunch we shared the dining room with another group. As another woman and I were the last to go through the buffet line there were only two servings left. As I approached the main serving dish, an elderly woman cut in ahead of me with her dirty plate and scooped up a second serving for herself, telling me how delicious it was. She then gave the last serving to her husband who was right on her heels looking for his seconds. It was such a startling example of selfishness. Cookies were the dessert but those were also gone. Some of the people at lunch had taken a stack of them but were too full to eat them. So the people either threw them away or left the dining room with a stack of them to snack on later. It never occurred to these adults that by being so greedy they denied others dessert.

Another way to help is to participate in the "Adopt-a-Father" program publicly endorsed by Pope John Paul II. Families can "adopt" the father of a family in a third world country for $25 per week. This is the average weekly wage in these countries. For information on this program, which is headquartered in Milan, Italy, you can e-mail: microproject@microproject.org. The website is http://www.microproject.org/Dad.htm[83]

To give drink to the thirsty: In a large family every child

---

[83] The address is: Committee of Catholics United for a Civilization of Love at Via Mosè Bianchi 94, 20149 Milan, Italy or phone 011-0039-2-48.01.78.14. Fax: 011-0039-2-48.00.88.56.

can help with this work of mercy by getting water for the little ones who can't reach the faucet themselves. When parents and siblings are sick, a pitcher of water and a glass can be placed on a nightstand next to the bed. Friends who stop by should be offered something to drink. This work is simply an exercise in thoughtfulness. Teach your children to think, *What does the person I'm with need and how can I satisfy that need?*

To clothe the naked: If children care for their clothing, it can be passed down to siblings, on to relatives or given to the poor. Suggest your children throw a shower with their friends for a pro-life center. This helps single moms who have little means to clothe their babies. Instruct your children to look for quality clothing that will last. Teach them not to judge clothing by labels. That's simply vanity. Famous labels simply up the price, not always the quality. By buying good, classic, durable clothing, money saved by not having to replacing clothing can be donated to the poor.

To visit the imprisoned: The "imprisoned" are not all in jails. Sometimes a young mom needs a babysitter. Recommend that your child volunteer his/her time to sit so that the mom can get out to shop, have lunch with a friend or attend a Day of Recollection. Elderly people can be housebound by snow. Suggest your child shovel the snow without pay. Your children can visit the elderly in nursing homes, or friends who have no transportation. Letters can be written to elderly relatives who live a distance away. Have the children make regular phone calls to out-of-town grandparents or to shut-ins. Prison chaplains are always in need of Catholic books, videos, magazines, rosaries, and medals. This spirit of service keeps a child from becoming self-centered or developing a disordered desire for independence.

To shelter the homeless: With so many natural disasters occurring around the world, children can help by collecting items and money for Catholic Relief Services. Organize a group of teens or college students to help rebuild an area that has been hit by a disaster or encourage your child to join an already organized group on spring or summer break. Volunteering at a halfway house or homeless shelter is another possibility. To shelter the homeless may mean taking in an aging parent or relative.

To visit the sick: Suggest your child call to see how his sick friend is doing. Maybe your child could drop by homework assignments, send a card, or even visit the ailing friend. When friends or relatives are in the hospital bring your child along to visit with you. Explain to your children the importance of the last rites and the Sacrament of the Anointing of the Sick. Teach your children to call a priest if any Catholic is in danger of death, especially you!

To bury the dead: Explain the importance of attending wakes and funerals by taking your children along with you when you attend. At these services we pray for the soul of the deceased while comforting the family members left behind.

The Importance of Reading...

Teach your children to treasure books. Small children love to be read to. Use bedtime to read the lives of the saints, fairy tales and the classics. As your children grow, share favorite books, then discuss them over dinner or after dinner rather than watching TV. As a child, St. Catherine of Siena's father would read the **Lives of the Saints** out loud to her. It was those stories that her father read that fired her zeal for holiness. A.A. Milne, the author of **Winnie-the-Pooh,** drew on all the stories his father read to him for his own adventure stories. He in turn read to his son, Christopher, the model for Christopher Robin. Christopher Milne, a bookshop proprietor reminisced, *I was read to until I was 14 or 15, and I believe that reading aloud to children is essential. It was almost a tradition in our house to have our daily chapter of Wodehouse. In fact, my mother read Wodehouse to myself and my father, and we also had Lewis Carroll and lots and lots of Lear.*[84]

Dr. Jeanne S. Chall of Harvard finds *Reading to children can enhance their language development, can expand their vocabularies and give them a more advanced understanding of*

[84] Glenn Collins, "Reading To Children: It Runs In Families," *New York Times,* 1982.

grammatical forms. *Not only does it give young children a* *background for formal reading instruction, but also it imparts* *the whole ritual of the book—of looking at it, puzzling it out and* *turning the pages.*[85]

The curriculum guide for Spiritus Sanctus Academies recommends reading books that *illustrate virtue and struggles.* The books should have truth, goodness and beauty:

- ❏ TRUTH—Is the story truthful? (Does sin have consequences? Is the character better after struggle? Are the "good guys" really good?)

- ❏ GOODNESS—Does the book have a message and what is it? (Look for agendas, subtle messages) How are parents, teachers and other authorities portrayed? Are the characters better people at the end? Why or why not?

- ❏ BEAUTY—Is it beautiful? (Good writing is like good art...should excite the imagination, move the heart towards the beautiful— God) Does it lead the listener to want more like it?[86]

The academy also recommends specific types of books:

- ❏ *Fairy Tales:* good and evil are very clear; even though it is an imaginary world—it should work the way the real world does (as in the **Chronicles of Narnia**).

- ❏ *Biographies:* important to know real heroes like Abraham Lincoln, Helen Keller, George Washington, Fr. Damien (missionary to the lepers) and, of course, the Saints. Older children (teens) can learn from the biographies of infamous people: Hitler, Stalin, etc.

- ❏ *Literary Fiction:* the reader takes the story into themselves and experiences events and characters out of the scope of their daily life; they can try on for size the experience of a difficult virtuous act (**The Yearling**—having to shoot the pet deer to protect the family).[87]

- ✓ Presenting Books: Some books are better read aloud: read aloud to all age groups (even adults!).

---

[85] *Ibid.*

[86] Spiritus Sanctus Academy, Ann Arbor, Michigan

[87] *Ibid.*

✓ Discuss the victories and failures of the characters. Ask "How?" "Why?" and "What if?"

✓ Identify virtues and vices in characters.

✓ Identify right actions and wrong actions and their consequences.[88]

During the school year read assigned books together. Encourage your children to read during their summer vacation. Dr. Madonna M. Murphy in her book, ***Character Education In America's Blue Ribbon Schools,*** lists in Appendix C recommended books for children for general character development. The list is broken down under the headings of various virtues such as courage, courtesy, culture, discipline/dependability, honesty, human worth and dignity, justice, patriotism, respect for authority, personal obligation for public good, respect for self and others, responsibility, and tolerance. Do consult her book and consider using her recommendations for a summer reading program.[89] This can be a pleasant change of pace from the swimming pool and sports. Summer is a great time to teach your children selectivity in their choice of books. They need your guidance initially in choosing books that help the mind and spirit to grow. Here are some more criteria for choosing books:

❑ Is it a topic I am interested in?

❑ Is the author one I have heard of, enjoyed before, or seen on a recommended reading list?

❑ Are the characters depicted ones I would like to emulate?

❑ Is the language such as will improve my own speech, vocabulary and writing skills?

❑ Is the moral tone of the book positive?

These concepts may seem self-evident but parents should carefully instruct their children in prudence before allowing them freedom in the stacks. Take your children to the library to help them select books or take time to skim the books the

---

[88] *Ibid.*

[89] Technomic Publishing Co., Inc. (800) 233-9936 or (717) 291-5609 or www.techpub.com

children select before they read them. Check out Appendix B for book recommendations for various ages.

Some of the current "children's books" glorify immorality and seek to have the reader become accustomed to irregular situations as the norm. Many books that purport to help children from broken families adjust to their difficult situations in fact do this by glorifying the one-parent home. In order not to have these children upset, the authors almost proselytize for divorce. The good author helps one cope with upsets but does not attempt to justify or praise these aberrations.

I especially caution parents about the Judy Blume and Norma Klein books. Blume's first books that paved the way for her popularity are harmless. But her later books are offensive to parents promoting positive family values. Norma Klein's books are suggested for grade 5 and up. The material is that found in "adult" books that most adults would be shocked to read. Another problematic series of books is Harry Potter. These books are so popular that in 1999 one out of every ten books sold was a Potter book. Today this is the top selling series for children. Space does not permit me to discuss the Potter books in depth although I have a thick file on the dangers of this series. I do know good people, including Catholics, who enjoy the Potter books and see nothing wrong with them. But I disagree with them because I feel these books glorify the occult making it seem humorous, acceptable, **attractive** and **inviting**. The theme seriously distorts the moral order as well as opposes the first commandment, *I am the Lord your God. You shall not have other gods besides Me,* since part of the first commandment pertains to superstition. Let's consider for a moment what this means. *Superstition: The attribution of divine powers to created things is another sin against God. This includes spiritism, fortune-telling, horoscopes, astrology, psychics, tarot cards, interpretation of omens, sorcery (even to restore health), charms, palmistry, clairvoyance, mediums, and the ouija board. As Catholics, we have to be very wary of being pulled into any of the above. Dabbling in the occult is dangerous. Fr. Gabrielle Amorth, the official exorcist for the diocese of Rome revealed that there was a "great rise in occult practices in Italy* *and this was leading to the possession of many people, especially women.*[90,91]

Zenit News Service in Rome recently released three disturbing press stories. The first noted a meeting of 150 exorcists who met in Rome to discuss the rise of the *phenomena of esotericism and Satanism* in regard to youth. They were addressing the concerns raised by bishops at the Italian bishops' conference who had released this statement: *We are currently witnessing a rebirth of divination, sorcery, witchcraft and magic often mixed with a superstitious use of religion...All this offends the dignity of the person and his freedom, as man becomes subjected to dark, impersonal forces, psychological dependencies and moral degradation.*[92] The second report indicates that *Christians in former Communist countries are facing a new crisis: an influx of sects and a rise in astrology..." Astrology is so popular that even 'mediums' are on the TV screen...and several non-Christian groups have registered as churches, including the Church of the Hungarian Witches and the Church of the New Fresh Wind," said Father Lukacs. "It is an attack against God himself."*[93] The final story said that *experts estimate that 7,000 people, the majority adolescents, engage in Satanic rituals in Germany.*[93a] Murders have been linked to these practices.

In J.R.R. Tolkien's **Hobbit** and **Lord of the Rings** as well as in C. S. Lewis' **Chronicles of Narnia** magic is considered dangerous. Not so in the Potter books. In fact, the books glamorize the world of wizards and sorcery rejecting anyone opposed to magic. Another troubling aspect of the series is its negative portrayal of family life. His adopted parents are bad (not into magic) but the wizard and his Hogwart School of Witchcraft and Wizardry are good. In Appendix C there are resources and references for you to check out in regard to the Potter books. Please take the time to do so. Why take a chance

---

[90] *Inside the Vatican,* (January 1994) quoted in the book *Call of the Ages* by Thomas W. Petrisko (Santa Barbara: Queenship Publishing Co., 1995) p.145.
[91] Mary Ann Budnik, *Looking For Peace? Try Confession!* (Springfield, IL: R.B. Media, Inc., 1997), p. 71.
[92] Zenit, Oct. 2, 2001.   [93] Zenit, Oct. 22, 2001.   [93a] Zenit, Jan.17, 2002

on endangering your children's soul through this series of books?

Most schools contract with a company to put on a yearly book fair for the school. The school has only to supply the personnel and space. The company selects the books then ships them to the school. Unless someone knowledgeable checks through the books and removes the objectionable ones, unsuspecting parents and children alike can purchase offensive books with attractive, innocent-looking covers. This is happening in public and parochial schools alike, so go to these book fairs when they first open, examine the books and point out those that should not be sold. Better yet, volunteer to coordinate it so you have the opportunity to tell the company which books not to ship and then remove objectionable books and authors that slipped through.

Negative Outside Influences...

Control computer and Internet use. Children and adults can become addicted to the Internet to the exclusion of family, friends, and responsibilities. Put a screen on your Internet to limit access and prevent pornography from invading your child's mind and home. Check into E-Kids Internet. Since its inauguration, over 3 million U.S. families are part of this service founded by El St. John and her husband. Their program impedes strangers from entering the new domains protected by their servers. *On our site, a family registers its request and we send them a CD-ROM with the cryptographic software. One can only connect to our server, via modem, through that program. A child can then navigate with no problem to "E-Kids" services and games, but also to his favorite sites, verified daily, to which he can ask us to add others he tells us about. We take a look at them and then decide. However, there are enterprises that already provide us every day with versions from their sites that are adequate for children.*[94] To use the service children are expected to avoid bad language, inappropriate e-mails and to give a name of a friend, once every six months, who might enjoy the service.

Watch what is being sent to your child in e-mails. Forbid your

---

[94] Zenit, ZE00112804

child to use chat rooms. They are breeding grounds for trouble. Katherine Tarbox wrote about her dangerous experience in the book, **Katie.com**. I recently received an e-mail invitation to plug into a program on how I could learn to utilize the magic and sorcery of Harry Potter.

Screen movies, videos, TV, and music. The eyes are the windows to the soul. What goes in through the eyes sticks to your memory and imagination. Fr. John Hardon, S.J., went as far as to say that what you see and read *literally becomes part of your brain.* That is why the media exerts such a powerful influence on your children through TV, videos, movies, radio, magazines and newspapers. James Stenson, an authority on how to raise successful children, writes: *[Successful] parents do not permit television or the other entertainment media to act as rivals for their children's respect and affection. They monitor and control what the children watch at home. This is not done merely to shield the children (impossible, in any event) but rather to express the lessons of disapproval. Children see that the home is not open to persons and activities that offend the parents' principles—period. Moreover, successful parents seem to realize that the children's time is too valuable to waste on mindless entertainment. Children need time for conversation and reading, the age-old means by which children have learned about adult life in the world outside the family. Television does not reflect this life realistically. How often do you see anyone on television reading a book, doing productive work, or praying?*

An easy way to monitor TV is to have only one set that is shared by all family members. Position it in a place where you can keep track of the programs your children are watching. Limit TV to weekends during the school year. Allow them to watch only programs that you know are in keeping with your values. Don't be afraid to say "no" when they want to go to the show with friends or view an objectionable video. Check all the films out. PG films do have sex scenes and terrible language.

Fr. Peter Armenio,[95] who has worked with youth the past

---

[95] This section is taken from "The Effects of Music, TV, and Movies On Youth," audiotape by Frs. Peter Armenio and Frank Hoffman. Available from R.B. Media.

twenty years, finds that movies create moral confusion in regard to sexual morality. Along with screening this material, explain why this screening is necessary to your children. This way you will be teaching them how to protect their chastity while at the same time developing the virtue of prudence. It also teaches them how to develop the moral criteria to judge correctly what can be seen and what should be avoided. Crudity in language and subject matter is degradation of the human person. Art, literature and music should be a reflection of God. It should bring out human virtues, not destroy them. The criteria for viewing films are:

- ❑ Does the movie promote human dignity or does it destroy it?

- ❑ Does the film have a Christian message?

- ❑ Does it teach sound moral principles? Remember, moral relativism teaches immorality. When the emotions take over they not only contradict truth but also craft one's own version of truth.

- ❑ In respect to sex, does the film depict sex in a respectful manner as sacred?

If sex is demeaned, made fun of or portrayed as a "good" outside of marriage, the film is not one your children or you should see. Sex loses its mystery while at the same time it develops a sexual obsession in the viewer. It strains friendships between girls and guys. It makes praying and a relationship with God almost impossible. The *Catechism of the Catholic Church* (#2351) teaches that lust, the pursuit of sexual pleasure outside of its correct exercise within marriage, is morally wrong. Any conversation, actions, or images that excite sexual pleasure outside of marriage are gravely wrong. When you are not specifically clear on sexual moral guidelines with your children they will become confused in our sex-saturated culture. TV and films brainwash your children into thinking that all friendships, dates and relationships end up in bed. This damages the conscience of the viewer. In addition, the viewer is lead to believe that in the real world it is impossible to be chaste. Rather than just telling your children what they cannot see, lead by example by avoiding such films and TV shows yourself. When adults watch objectionable material it makes it acceptable.

Wondering if a film is good or not? Check out www.screenit.com. Add your own wisdom and prudence to the critique in deciding whether the film is one you or your children should see. Remember, each time a person watches TV or a film that projects immorality or false values, the viewer loses sensitivity toward the good while at the same time the will accepts evil. Eventually people begin to expect to live in this sinful manner or accept such lifestyles in others.

Music is another area in which you need to educate your children. Learning an instrument introduces a child to classical music as well as music appreciation. Fr. Frank Hoffman recommends parents read the book ***Music and Morals*** by Alan Bloom and Richard Weaver. Fr. Hoffman, a musician himself, warns parents that music does have an effect on behavior: *Your children can live in a subculture you aren't aware of. As Christians you have to draw the line, set standards. Why allow your kids to go to the concerts of Judas Priest, WASP, the Spice Girls, and listen to those people? Other groups are Satanic or drug based. Why permit your children to watch them?*

Music can inspire different emotions and promote desire. Choose good music that has words of truth, that makes one think. Music can move us to actions. Good music can move us to valiant deeds while evil music can move us to violence, lust, and drugs. Music can energize, or make people nervous or erotic. As with TV and films, train your children as to what is good and what is not acceptable music. Pay attention to lyrics. They act in the same manner as brainwashing. Rock has an ideological strain to it. It promotes violence, drug abuse and a sexual way of life. The tone is anti-Christian. It can corrupt morals and the conscience. Remember, bad companions corrupt good people. Listen to the message of the songs your children are listening to. Point out the message and how it conflicts with Christianity. Teach your children to enjoy classical music and musicals. Moderation is the key in all things. If they are to be happy, they need to pray. To pray, one needs silence. If the mind is always distracted with music and noise, the mind cannot pray nor hear the inspirations of God.

Katie Brown, while a sophomore in high school in Springfield, Illinois, wrote a paper on "Singing Violence." I would like to share part of her paper with you:

> As if television and movies were not enough, violence is now spread throughout the nation in song...One such genre that is particularly known for its graphic displays of violence is gangster rap...Many of the songs involved lyrics that glorify such things as gangs, misogyny, and even murder...Gangster rap is also being blamed for many other suicides and deaths...
>
> Rock musicians have taken the violence one step further. They have brought the violence with them to concerts and they gruesomely depict grotesque scenes of violence and sex while performing on stage. Music groups such as Limp Bizkit, Eminem, and Kid Rock are capable of stirring up crowds with loud songs and displays of violence. Some groups have been known for not only attacking each other on stage but some have gone as far as to attack members of the audience. Another thing that can lead to violence is dancing. Moshing and pogo are two forms of dance that are popular at many rock concerts...About 5,711 people were injured at rock concerts in 1998; and eleven fans were killed at a WHO concert in 1979.
>
> Music video channels...can be very violent in nature. "Stabbing, kicking, and hitting were in 14.7% of videos observed over a period of one month with an average of six violent acts per video." [96] Black males were the usual aggressors in the videos, taking out their anger on women with violent acts. Females in the videos are most likely represented as whores or servants. This definitely creates negative images for their viewers to see...
>
> "Seventh and tenth graders who watched an hour of rock videos were more likely to approve of premarital sex than

---

[96] Lisa M. Krieger, "Study of Violence on Music Videos." *World Africa Network* Apr. 8, 1998.

those who did not watch."[97]

"The American medical association concluded in a 1989 report that music is a greater influence on teenagers than TV."[98] *Lyrics such as, "If I had a shot gun, I'd blow myself to hell"*[99] *are putting ideas of death and murder into teenagers' heads...*

"Out of 470 adolescents who participated in violent acts, 59% listened to heavy metal. Of those 59%, 74% were involved in violence, 50% in stealing, and 71% in sexual activity...[100] *A police chief estimated that heavy metal indicators, or things that relate to rock bands, were found at 35% to 40% of the crime investigations involving satanic worship."*[101]

Katie concludes her paper by noting several more disgusting facts about popular music:

"In 1995, only 25% of the forty most popular CDs were free of profanity, drugs, sex and violence."[102]

There are at least thirteen bands named after the male genitals, six after female genitals, eight after abortion, and one after a vaginal infection. At least ten bands are named after various sex acts, eight including the f-word and twenty-four referring unflatteringly to blacks, the disabled, or homosexuals...

Katie Brown wrote this paper because she sees the impact of music on her peers. Parents take heed!

Foods Can Influence Your Child...

Despite the best efforts of parents to educate their children,

---

[97] Scott Barbour, "Violence in the Media," San Diego: Greenhaven Press, Inc., 1995

[98] Thomas L. Jipping, "Youth Violence Parallels Violent Music." NLJ ONLINE, June, 1999.

[99] Ann Powers, "The Stresses of Youth, the Strains of the Music," *New York Times,* April 25, 1999, p.18.

[100] "Violence in the Media," *Op. Cit.*   [101] *Ibid.*

[102] "Youth Violence Parallels Violent Music," *Op. Cit.*

sugar, food coloring, caffeine and food allergies can dramatically impact your efforts. It took until our middle daughter, Marianne, was in 8th grade to discover that she had an allergy to corn that caused mental confusion in school. Once we took her off all foods made with corn products her grades shot up. When I'm writing I have to refrain from corn, tomatoes and chocolate. If I don't I transpose the letters in the words. These foods also intensify my stuttering. For this reason I eliminate them from my diet for five days before I give a lecture. If your child is having trouble in school or at home, consider food allergies or diet.

My husband. Bob, and I had the opportunity to watch four of our grandchildren ages 1½, 2½, 4½ and six-years-old for a week. The children, while precious, are extremely active. During the week we watched them I decided to take the children off all sugar, food coloring and caffeine. Since the children are allergic to dairy products their usual beverage is an orange drink (with red dyes). I substituted water for the "juice." Within 24 hours of taking the children off everything the change in their personalities was dramatic. They were obedient, helpful, and enjoyable to be with. Toward the end of the week we took them out to celebrate our oldest grandson's birthday. Not thinking we ordered kiddie cocktails for them. By the time we began the trip home in the van they were beginning to wind-up. By the time we arrived home the children were out of control. They were laughing over nothing. They were either hitting each other or throwing a tantrum. No matter what we did we could not get them to obey nor go to bed. The next day they woke up earlier than usual. The sugar and the red dye had created a disaster! The next day, not thinking, I gave them cupcakes for an after school snack. The two older boys had vanilla ones. The two younger girls had chocolate ones. Within 15 minutes of eating the cupcakes the little girls were "wild." They experienced mood swings, were throwing tantrums, and would not obey. Many times we blame children for being disobedient, poor students, or unruly when it is really the sugar, food coloring, and caffeine in soda, candy and Kool-Aid that is playing havoc with their little bodies. Substitute instead healthier snacks such as fruit, nuts, pretzels, graham crackers, and natural fruit juices.

Saintly Children Are Happy Children

"We must serve our Lord according to His liking, not according to our own."
                                                      St. Jane Frances de Chantal

The great Catholic philosopher, Dr. Dietrich Von Hildebrand, was a convert to the Catholic faith. Strangely enough it was a fallen away Catholic philosophy colleague, Dr. Schuler, who triggered his conversion when he told Von Hildebrand that the Catholic Church possessed the truth. When Von Hildebrand protested, *How can this be?* Schuler replied, *It makes saints.*

If you want happy children, raise them saints! Saints are the happiest people in this world, as well as in the next. How can a person not be happy when he knows God, who is Love, intimately? As a faithful son or daughter of God your son or daughter is the object of God's intense, all-consuming personal love. How can that not infuse one with joy and happiness? *A man convinced that he is the object of so much love ought to be filled with joy. He ought to live love and be consumed by it,* insists St. Peter Julian Eymard. When your children know God personally, love Him deeply, serve Him enthusiastically, they will experience great joy, happiness, peace and a sense of purpose in their lives.

As a parent you have a limited block of time in which to teach your children how to achieve happiness in this world and glory in the next...to raise them saints. Your training must begin at birth then continue with **intensity** and **constancy** until they leave for college. You have only eighteen <u>short</u> years. If you are a new parent, that time may seem long but as the parent of three grown daughters I know how fast the time flies. If you concentrate on teaching your children the spiritual basics from birth to age seven, your most important work will be accomplished. From age eight until college you will only have to deepen your children's understanding of the Catholic faith and moral teachings while reinforcing what has already been taught. You will also have the added benefit of your older children helping you by teaching their younger siblings what you have taught them.

If your children are older and the material in this book is new to you, you simply have to play catch-up, understanding at the same time that you will need to practice the virtues of fortitude and perseverance when dealing with difficult pre-teens and teens. God **will** reward your efforts.

God has entrusted the souls of your children to you because He has great confidence that **you can raise them saints**. As Dr. Von Hildebrand wavered whether to convert or not to convert to Catholicism, his sister told him, *Grace is knocking at your door. If you don't answer it, you will lose it.* Use now the grace God has given you through the Sacrament of Matrimony as well as the other sacraments to raise your children saints! There is no other demand on your time more important than this one.

The next two books in the *Raise Happy Children* series, *Raise Happy Children...Teach Them Virtues!* and *Raise Happy Children...Teach Them Joy!* will explore how you can teach your children the natural virtues as well as at what age the development of each virtue should begin. Without developing the natural virtues (good habits), the supernatural life has no foundation. The infused virtues your children receive in the various sacraments need the corresponding natural virtues as a foundation for spiritual growth. Without this foundation, teaching prayers and doctrine will only raise mediocre Catholics at best, certainly not saints.

In J.R.R. Tolkien's book, *Lord of the Rings*, the reader wades through over 1,100 pages to see if the "ring-bearer," Frodo, will be faithful and successful in his mission to destroy the evil that is consuming the world. By virtue of the Sacrament of Baptism, God has entrusted your children with a similar mission. Rather than being a "ring-bearer" each of your children is called to be a "Christ-bearer" whose sole mission in life is to destroy evil in the world by bringing about the reign of God. It is up to you to see that your children fulfill their mission!

Additional Helps

- ✓ Read John Paul II's Encyclical, *Faith And Reason.*
- ✓ Read *The Religious Dimension of Education in a Catholic School* by the Congregation for Catholic Education.
- ✓ Read *The Truth and Meaning of Human Sexuality* by the Pontifical Council for The Family.
- ✓ Check over all your children's textbooks carefully.
- ✓ Investigate what specifically your children are being taught each year in religion class. If the books are only "love and fluff", lobby the school for catechism books that have substance.
- ✓ Invite your children's teachers for dinner or lunch to get to know them, their values and moral standards.
- ✓ Talk to your children about respecting authority such as you, their parents, your pastor and all priests, religious, teachers, and civil authorities.
- ✓ Invite the parents of your children's classmates over for an informal gathering to get to know them and their standards. Encourage the group to meet monthly to discuss any concerns and to develop friendships.
- ✓ Develop friendships with the parents of your children's closest friends so that you can share your values, beliefs and standards with them.
- ✓ Plan activities with other families who have your faith and values. This will give you and your children a support group.

Book Three
Raise Happy Children...
Teach Them Virtues!

Book Four
Raise Happy Children...
Teach Them Joy!

CHAPTER 1
HOW TO TEACH THE VIRTUES OF TEMPERANCE, MODERATION, MODESTY, CHASTITY, SOCIABILITY, FRIENDSHIP, RESPECT FOR OTHERS, SIMPLICTY, AND PATRIOTISM

What's in store during the rebellious teen years? This chapter studies ages 13 to 15. Why do teens rebel? Learn what the awakening of intimacy means and how to deal with it. Discover how to exercise authority through consistency, flexibility and personal prestige with your teens. Why do teens crave independence, uniqueness and attention? Why is there a generation gap? Why are these specific virtues so important for teens? How are they taught? What can you do when your teen falls in love? These questions, along with others are addressed in this chapter.

CHAPTER 2
HOW TO TEACH THE VIRTUES OF PRUDENCE, FLEXIBILITY, AUDACITY, UNDERSTANDING, LOYALTY, HUMILITY, AND OPTIMISM TO TEENS

The final stage of adolescence, 16 to 18 years, is considered along with how to develop the critical virtues of prudence, flexibility, understanding, loyalty, audacity, humility and optimism that teens need for holy, productive and happy lives.

CHAPTER 3
HAPPINESS & JOY

What is happiness? How is it related to hope? How does one develop the virtue of cheerfulness? What is joy and how can you and your children possess it? These are the topics covered in the concluding chapter of the series.

Book One

Raise Happy Children Through A Happier Marriage!

Chapter 1 So Why Is Holiness Important?

We are all called to be saints. Discover how you can become a saint through your vocation to marriage. Personal holiness requires generosity but how does one live this generosity in the vocation of marriage?

Chapter 2 Marriage Creates Future Saints!

What is a Catholic marriage? The mystery of marriage, the powerful graces of the sacrament are explored as well as how to utilize these graces for a happier marriage.

Chapter 3 What's So Important About Virtues?

How does one obtain the virtues necessary for a happy marriage and for raising responsible, happy children? How does one cope with the defects in one's spouse?

Chapter 4 Life In The Married Lane

"I Do" is simply the beginning. Discover the secret of a happy marriage and how it can be achieved by developing the characteristics of empathy, appreciation, congruence, and character. Learn how to improve communication in your marriage. Have fun as you grow in married love...and holiness. Study how to resolve problems. The stages of marriage are explained as well as mid-life "crisis."

Chapter 5 Why Is The Family So Important?

What are the duties of each parent? How does one raise a child? Issues of upbringing are explored, such as bonding, the role of parent/leader, and the setting of family goals. Learn how to teach your children the value of suffering.

Chapter 6 Mom & Dad, You Are Important!

Why are a male and a female necessary as parents? What can single parents do to parent successfully? The secret to successful parenting is explained through the example of the saints as well as the example of the parents of saints.

Appendix A

Explaining The Mass...

Try to first purchase these items through your local Catholic bookstore so as to encourage them to carry these excellent items. If this is not possible, call the numbers listed after the items or the number footnoted at the bottom of the page.

For toddlers I suggest *We Go To Mass* by George Brundage. For ages three to seven consider *The Mass for Children* by Rev. Judge Winkler, OFM Con. or *My Picture Missal* by Rev. Lawrence G. Lovasik, SVD. I was extremely impressed with the beautiful artwork produced by Catholic Book Publishing Co. It lifts one's spirit besides being appropriate for the sacred material the books cover. The only artwork that I did not care for was Rev. Basil Senger, O.S.B.'s, book entitled the *New Children's Mass Book*. His artwork is more primitive and child-like but the Mass book itself is well done. These books can be purchased from Catholic Book Publishing Co.[1]

Our Sunday Visitor sells a little workbook for children in English and in Spanish on the Mass entitled *Joy, Joy The Mass* by Jeannine Timko Leichner. The book looks like a coloring book on the inside with blanks to fill in and dots to connect. While I did not care for the artwork, my two-year-old granddaughter, Emma, snatched it up and carries it around the house each day. The back pages, for parents and teachers, explain how to teach each lesson. While this book is useful in helping children ages six to eight to deepen their understanding of the Mass, the consecration was viewed solely in relation to the Last Supper but not to Christ's sacrifice on Calvary. This is a serious omission, which must be corrected by you if you choose to use this workbook. In the section on receiving Jesus in the Holy Eucharist it did

---

[1] Catholic Resource Center (800-874-8453).

not explain how our souls must be free from mortal sin in order to receive Jesus. This is another serious omission. On the plus side the book does help the child to understand each part of the Mass so as to better participate. Our Sunday Visitor (800-348-2440) also publishes *Teach Me About The Mass*. This book gives a simple explanation for everything in church, plus each action within the Mass. It is an informative discussion and activity workbook on the Mass. My favorite for older children is *The Mass Explained to Children* by Maria Montessori. Although written prior to Vatican II, it inspires awe and love of the Mass. Roman Catholic Books, PO Box 2286, Fort Collins, CO 80522.

Our Father's House (www.ourfathershouse.com) offers a miniature Mass Kit for Children. This was successfully used at the St. Louis Eucharist Congress to help children learn about the Mass. It can be used for First Communion preparation, to teach altar servers, and for little boys to play "saying Mass." The kit includes a small chalice, paten, crucifix, 2 candles, bell, 2 cruets, fingerbowl, snuffer, censer, sanctuary lamp, and match receptacle. To order, check out the website or call (206-725-0461) You can also purchase separate pieces rather than a whole kit from them. Since most of the items in the set are imported it may take several months to get it once it is ordered so plan ahead if you plan to give it as a gift. I waited almost two months to get a kit for my grandsons.

To teach children about Eucharistic Adoration contact Fr. Antoine Thomas, CSJ. He has a wonderful video on Eucharistic Adoration for Children (Community of St. John, 116 W. College, Peoria, IL 61606).

Prayer Books...

Suggestions for prayer books...George Brundage has a book for toddlers entitled *Daily Prayers*. Fr. Lovasik, SVD has written a variety of different prayer books to teach children how to pray prayers to the Trinity, the saints and angels as well as prayers of thanksgiving and petition: *Book of Prayers for Children* (ages 5-7); *My Picture Prayer Book* (ages 6-8) has prayers for all occasions; *Picture Book of Prayers* (ages 6-9) with prayers for major feast days, name day, birthday, First Communion and Confirmation; ***Our Father and Hail Mary*** (ages 4-8) beautifully explains each prayer in words and pictures; ***The Holy Rosary*** (ages 4-8) teaches how to say the rosary besides explaining each of the fifteen mysteries. These are available from the Catholic Resource Center (800-874-8453).

Besides books there are wonderful CDs, audiotapes and videos to teach your children to pray produced by Catholic parents concerned about the spiritual formation of their own children. From Australia comes the powerful CD or audiotape of ***The Rosary For Children***. The tape is the complete rosary with meditations, music and lyrics by children. Email: http:www.iinet.net.au/~sbunter/rosaryforchildren.html or sbunter@opera.iinet.net.au.

Children love videos. Hartwick, Inc. produces ***The Rosary For Little Children*** and ***Prayers For Little Children***. Children will watch these videos over and over again. You can obtain them from CCC of America (800-935-2222). It makes praying so natural for your children.

Children love music and stories. Rose of Sharon Media (309) 383-2898) produces ***Bread of Life, Bread of Heaven*** on the Eucharist. Children tell the story of the Eucharist in word and song. It's charming. This same company recently produced ***My Spirit Rejoices: Story of Mary, Model of Love.*** You can order either a CD or an audiotape. This has been turned into a a great music video also entitled, **My Spirit Rejoices.** It was co-produced with EWTN.

Teaching the faith...

The Catholic Book Publishing Company (800) 874-8453 carries ***Our Blessed Mother*** by George Brundage for ages 1-3; ***The Story of Jesus*** by Rev. Lovaskik, SVD, ages 3-10 and ***Our Lady of Fatima*** by Rev. Lovaski, SVD, ages 3-10. This company also carries Fr. Lovasik's wonderful explanation of the ***Ten Commandments*** in hard or soft covers. It explains each commandment in a clear, concise way to children. ***The Seven Sacraments*** are equally well treated in a book for toddlers and for children a little older. Fr. Lovasik, SVD, has also written *The Stations of the Cross, The Works of Mercy, The Eight Beatitudes, The Miracles of Jesus, Mary, My Mother, and My Life With God.* This same company has wonderful coloring books and puzzles on the sacraments, the Mass, the commandments, the holy days, angels, etc.

Catechism Suggestions...

Check out Cynthia Blum's website for resources such as the *Little Saints Preschool Program* and reading lists at www.catholicpreschool.com

Order a catalog from Catholic Heritage Curricula (800)490-7713 or www.catholichomeschooling.com.

An excellent series for grade school is the *Faith And Life Series* produced by Catholics United for the Faith. We used this series along with the *Batimore Catechisms* for our daughters. You can purchase this series from Emmaus Road Publishing (800-693-2484). Some other catechetical options that are available include the *New American Catechism Series* by Fr.Lovaskik, SVD. The four books cover grades one through twelve. There is also a teacher's guide. You can also purchase the *St. Joseph Catechisms* that are the revised *Baltimore Catechisms*. These are available from Catholic Book Publishing (800) 874-8453.

Ignatius Press has a great series entitled *The Image of God.* This series starts in pre-school and goes through 8th grade. This or their *Children's Catechism* on CD-ROM can be ordered by calling (800-651-1531).

For high school students, C.R.Publications produces a wonderful four volume set with discussion manuals. The series is entitled *Catholicism & Reason* (Creed and apologetics) *Catholicism & Life* (commandments and sacraments), *Catholicism & Society* (marriage, family, and social justice) and *Catholicism & Ethics* (medical/moral issues). We used this series with our two youngest daughters in junior high and high school. It is excellent and can be ordered by phone (877)

730-8877 or through their website: www.crpublications.com.

Fun Ways To Teach The Faith...

Toys are another area to consider. Action figures are popular today so why not purchase Biblical action figures? Christian Soldiers is a company founded by a mother and grandmother to produce quality toys, books, and tapes to make learning about the Bible fun. Their series of actions toys is called *Footsteps To Follow*™. Each set comes with either a hardcover spiral bound book or a soft cover book, a color coordinated audiotape and 6-12 action figures depending on the set purchased. The inside book covers are play scenes for the action figures. There are three sets: David, Daniel, and Baby Jesus. If you cannot get this locally, you can order by calling (888) 442-8697.

Leaflet Missal Company www.leafletmissal.org or (800)328-9582 has a large variety of fun games and toys for children. Just some of the toys and games include: Noah's Ark miniature play set, Catholic Trivia, Catholic Doctrine Playing cards, Bibleopoly, Catholic Scattergories, prayer charts, saints trading cards, Catholic flash cards on the sacraments, catechism, prayers, and saints. Order their catalog.

Matthew Pinto developed "The Friendly Defenders Catholic Flash Cards." The cards consist of 50 full-color cards with short explanations of "why" the Church teaches as it does (800-376-0520). Check out his Friendly Defenders Web site at www.friendlydefenders.com/index-flash.htm

Grace Publications is more Christian based than Catholic (800)421-5565), although they sell to Catholic retail stores and are part of the Catholic Marketing Network. It has fun games, activity books, puzzle games, sequencing cards, bible sorting and matching game, memory match, Christian dominoes, crafts and various charts. For example they have *The Story of Joseph* that is a multiplication and division game for grades 2-4. *Noah's Ark* is addition and subtraction. Activity books are inexpensive and can be copied. They include dot-to-dot, word puzzles, word searches, mazes, hidden pictures, math, reading, and cursive books from pre-school through fifth grade. This company also carries a series of books called **Shining Star.** I only reviewed one book called **The Armor of God** for children grades 4-6. This book, based on Ephesians 6:13-17, is written by a children's minister. It is cleverly done with plays and other activities to explain St. Paul's passage. Since it is written from a Christian perspective rather than a Catholic perspective the numbering of the Ten Commandments is off and needs to be corrected. Diligently check the books you use to teach your children the faith. Just because the books are published by a Catholic publishing house or are sold in a Catholic retail store does not guarantee they teach solid Catholic faith and morals.

Biblical Helps...

My personal favorite children's bible is **The Children's Bible** by Golden Press. Scepter (800) 322-8773 also has **The Children's Bible** by J.M. Surinach.

The Catholic Book Publishing Company has great biblical helps (800) 874-8453. St. Joseph Bible Story books: **Abraham, Joseph, Joshua, Moses, Ruth, Isaac** and **Jacob** for ages 3-10 are inexpensive besides being very well done. Others include **St. Joseph Beginner's Bible** for ages 3-8. Rev. Lovaski, SVD, has also written: **First Children's Bible** (ages 3-8); and **New Catholic Picture Bible** (ages 9-12); Rev. Jude Winkler, OFM Conv., wrote the **Illustrated Children's Bible** for ages 4-10.

CCC of America (800) 935-2222 has the animated Bible, 25 tapes, on video. You can sample a clip online at www.cccoffamerica.com. Pauline Press Books & media produces a fun Bible for little ones entitled the **Read & Do Bible** by Robin Currie.

Angels...

CCC of America (800) 929-0608 has a darling video entitled **My Secret Friend, A Guardian Angel Story.** While children two years old love it and ask for more, children four and older will understand it better. Wonderful books for children include **Our Guardian Angels** by George Brundage for ages 1-3; **My**

Guardian Angel by Rev. Thomas J. Donaghy for ages 2-5 and *The Angels, God's Messengers* by Rev. Lovaski, SVD, ages 3-10 which my grandchildren loved. These are available from the Catholic Resource Center (800) 874-8453.

The Lives Of The Saints

Catholic Children's Treasure Box edited by the Maryknoll Sisters and published by Tan Books was originally written in 1957. Each book tells part of a story about how a child lived so as to become a saint, as well as poems, games, things to do, and fun things to make. This series is powerful.

Interested in wonderful resources for learning about saints? Catholic Resource Center (800)874-8453 has a fascinating two-set series entitled *Lives of the Saints Book* I and *Lives of the Saints Book II* for every day of the year by Rev. Hugo Hoever, SO Cist.,Ph. D. and Rev. Thomas J. Donaghy, ages 9 to adult. It can be purchased as a boxed set. Each volume has a different saint for each day of the year. After the short biography, there is a prayer to the saint. *Volume II* also includes a couple of sentences on how one can imitate the saint of the day. Consider getting this set then reading the saint of the day before or after dinner or at the start of the day. The inspiring artwork makes the saints look like "normal" people. This would be a perfect First Communion or Confirmation gift.

Other great books are *St. Joseph's Beginner's Books of Saints* by Rev. Lovaskik, SVD, (ages 3-10); *The First Book of Saints* (different saints) by Rev. Lovaskik, SVD, (ages 3-10); *Picture Book of Saints* (different saints) by Rev. Lovaskik, SVD, (ages 3-10); *Good Saint Joseph* by Rev. Lovaski, SVD, (ages 3-10); *Picture Books of the Saints* by Rev. Lovaski, SVD, (ages 3-10) or a boxed gift set of 26 saints or 12 saints from the Catholic Resource Center (800) 874-8453.

Scepter Publishers, Inc. (800) 322-8773 or www.scepterpub.org publishes *Yes! The Life of Blessed Josemaría for Young Readers* for preschoolers-grade school. It's a charming book.

Regina Press (800) 625-4263 or www.malhame.com offers a variety of beautiful books that can be purchased at your local Catholic bookstore. They publish the Catholic Classics lives of the saints and coordinating coloring books. The coloring books are every inexpensive. *The Lives of the Saints for Girls* by Louis M. Savary, ages 3-8 and *The Lives of the Saints for Boys* by Louis M. Savary, ages 3-8 are also very inexpensive.

The Daughters of St. Paul have a series of beautiful books on the saints called **Encounter Books** for ages 9-90. These are among my favorite books. Each book is interesting and gives practical details on how the man, woman, or child became a saint. The story either starts at the birth of the saint or during the saint's childhood. These books skillfully encourage the reader to imitate the saints in living virtue along with doing simple mortifications in order to grow holy.

Fr. Robert J. Fox (Fatima Family Apostolate, PO Box 55, Redfield, SD 57469) has written a four volume set entitled *Saints & Heroes Speak* with discussion questions and activities after the biography of each saint. The stories are written in the first person. One feels that you are reading the saint's diary. Fr. Fox's style is powerful. This set can be used from second grade through high school.

Additional videos that are excellent are the series from Edumundo Productions put together by Lyrick Studios geared to ages 2-9. Kim Redington of Springfield, IL, finds that these films truly teach the love of God. Some of the titles include "Francesco's Friendly World" and "The Gift of Christmas." Each video is a musical with catching songs that children love. Your Catholic bookstore carry these videos. Another set of videos from Focus On the Family (1-800-A-Family) is the "JJ, The Airplane series." These, while not as good as the Edumundo Productions, are better than the Veggie Tales because the virtues that are taught are more specific.

CCC of America (800) 929-0608 has delightful cartoon videos on various saints. It inspires the viewer to shoot for holiness. All of the above books and videos make wonderful gifts.

Also check out   www.TotallyCatholic.com

Appendix B

Recommended Reading Lists...
Grade School...

There are so many wonderful books for children of all ages that it would be impossible to include them all. Please consider the following lists as simply a sampling. As I was going through them I noticed that so many of our family favorites were omitted. There are probably many of your favorites not on this list either. On the other hand books were recommended which I have read and not enjoyed. Reading, like everything else, depends on one's personal taste.

Dr. Russell Kirk recommends beginning your children on historical novels when they are young since so much of literature has historical background. Try to find *Story of Mankind* and the *Story of America* by Hendrik Willem Van Loon.

Fairy tales stimulate the child's imagination such as those by the brothers Grimm, Hans Christian Andersen and Andrew Lang while *Aesop's Fables* teach a moral. *Pinocchio,* by Collodi, introduces children to evil and temptation through the characters of the Fox and the Cat. For pure enjoyment your daughters will enjoy the delightful series *Anne of Green Gables* by L.M. Montogomery and *Daddy—Longlegs* and its sequel by Jean Webster as well as *Little Women* and the sequels by Louisa May Alcott. Other books that are favorites but not listed are: *Friendly Persuasion* by Jessamyn West and the books of Elizabeth Goudge such as *Green Dolphin Street.*

Alexander, Lloyd	*Prydain Chronicles* (five volumes)
Baum, Frank L.	*The Wizard of Oz* (many volumes)
Boyd, James	*Drums*

	The Princes and Curdie
	The Golden Key
Maeterlinch, Maurice	*Blue Bird*
Marryat, Captain	*Children of the New Forest*
Masefield, John	*Martin Hyde, Duke's Messenger*
Nisbet, E.	*Book of Dragons*
Norton, Mary	*The Borrowers* (4 volumes)
Pearce, A. Philippa	*Tom's Midnight Garden*
Pyle, Howard	*Book of Pirates*
	Jack Ballister's Fortunes
Quiller-Couche, A.	*Spur*
Sampson, Emma	*Miss Minerva*
	William Green Hill
Seton, Thompson	*Two Little Savages*
Stafford, Jean	*Elephi, The Cat With The High I.Q.*
Stevenson, R. L.	*Black Arrow*
Stover, Jo Ann	*Mr. Widdel and the Sea Breeze*
Tarkington, Booth	*Penrod and Sam*
	Penrod Jashber
	Arabian Nights
Taylor, Sydney	*All-of-A-Kind Family*
	McGuffie Readers
Traylor, Sarah	*The Red Wind*
Von Stockum, Hilda	*Canadian Summer*
	Friendly Gables
	Cottage on Bantry Bay
	Pegeen
	Winged Watchman
	The Borrowed House
Wallace, Lew	*Ben Hur*
	The Fair God
White, E. B.	*Charlotte's Web*
White, T. H.	*Mistress Masham's Repose*
Wilder, Laura I.	*The Little House series*

For Girls 7ᵗʰ Grade And Up...

The Willows Academy for girls in Des Plaines, Illinois recommends the following books as enjoyable and worthwhile reading for girls in grades 7 through 12. Most of the titles are available in paperback editions.

Adamson, Joy	*Born Free*
Alcott, Louisa	*LittleWomen*
Aldrich, B.	*A Lantern in Her Hand*
Barrett, Wm.E.	*The Lilies of the Field*
Barrie, J.M.	*The Little Minister*
Benary-Isbet, Margot	*The Ark*
Bishop, J.	*The Day Lincoln Was Shot*
Bruckberger, R.	*The Seven Miracles of Gubbio and the Eighth*
Burnford, Sheila	*The Incredible Journey*
Caldwell, Taylor	*Dear and Glorious Physician*
Carroll, Lewis	*Alice in Wonderland*
Chesterton, G. K.	*The Amazing Adventures of Father Brown*
Christie, Agatha	*A Murder is Announced*
Ciardi, John	*How Does a Poem Mean?*
Cleaver, Vera	*Where the Lilies Bloom*
Cole, William	*Poems from Ireland*
Connolly, Myles	*Mr. Blue*
Copeland, Aaron	*What to Listen for in Music*
Cronin, A.J.	*Hatter's Castle*
	The Spanish Garden
Curie, E.	*Madame Curie*
Daugherty, James	*Abraham Lincoln*
Day, Clarence	*Life with Mother*
DeFare, Penny	*With All My Love*
DeFoe, Daniel	*Robinson Crusoe*
DeKruif, P.	*Microbe Hunters*
Dooley, Tom	*The Night They Burned the Mountain*
	The Edge of Tomorrow
	Deliver Us from Evil

Doss, Helen	*The Family Nobody Wanted*
Doyle, A.C	*Famous Tales of Sherlock Holmes*
Ferber, Edna	*So Big*
	Cimarron
Fitzhugh, Louise	*Harriet the Spy*
Forbes, E.	*Johnny Tremain*
	Paul Revere and the World He Lived In
Forbes, K.	*Mama's Bank Account*
Frank, Ann	*The Diary of A Young Girl*
Gallico, Paul	*The Snow Goose*
	Mrs. Arris Goes To Paris
Gilbreth, Frank	*Cheaper By the Dozen*
Gladstone, M.J.	*A Carrot for A Nose*
Godden, Rumer	*A Candle for St. Jude*
Guareschi, G.	*Don Camillo's Dilemma*
	The Little World of Don Camillo
	Don Camillo and His Flock
Gunther, John	*Death Be Not Proud*
Hemingway, Ernest	*The Old Man and the Sea*
Henry, O.	*The Best Short Stories of O. Henry*
	Sixes and Sevens
	The Trimmed Lamp
	Heart of the West
Heyerdahl, Thor	*Kon-Tiki*
	Aku-Aku
Hickok, L.A.	*The Story of Helen Keller*
Hilton, James	*Goodbye Mr. Chips*
	Lost Horizon
Hunt, Irene	*Across Five Aprils*
Ince, Elizabeth	*Thomas More*
Irving, W.	*The Legend of Sleepy Hollow*
Keller, Helen	*The Story of My Life*
Kennedy, J. F.	*Profiles in Courage*
Kielty, B.	*Marie Antoinette*
Kipling, R.	*Captains Courageous*
	Kim
Landon, M.	*Anna and the King of Siam*

Lee, Harper	*To Kill a Mockingbird*
L' Engle, M.	*A Wrinkle in Time* series
Lerner, A.J.	*My Fair Lady*
Lewis, C.S	*The Lion, the Witch and the Wardrobe* series
Llewellyn, R.	*How Green Was My Valley*
London, Jack	*The Call of the Wild*
Lynn, Janet	*Peace and Love*
Macauley, David	*Cathedral: the Story of Its Construction*
Kaufman, B.	*Up the Down Staircase*
McGinley, Phyllis	*Sixpence in Her Shoe*
Medearis, Mary	*Big Doc's Girl*
Morris, Jeannie	*Brian Piccolo: A Short Season*
Morth, Sterling	*Rascal*
O'Dell, Scott	*Island of the Blue Dolphins*
Oursler, Fulton	*The Greatest Story Ever Told*
Petry, Ann	*Harriet Tubman*
Pyle, Howard	*Men of Iron*
Rawlings, Marjorie	*The Yearling*
Rose, Anna	*Perrot Room for One More*
Saint Exupery, Antoine de	*The Little Prince*
Sanchez-Silva, Jose M.	*The Miracle of Marcelino*
Sarnoff, Jane	*What? A Riddle Book*
Saroyan, W.	*My Name is Aram*
Scott, Sir Walter	*Ivanhoe*
Shakespeare, William	*As You Like It*
	The Tempest
	The Merchant of Venice
	Hamlet
	Julius Caesar
	King Lear
	Twelfth Night
	Romeo and Juliet
Speare, E.	*The Witch of Blackbird Pond*
Spellman, Francis	*The Foundling*
Steinbeck, John	*The Pearl*

	Travels with Charley
Stevenson, R.L.	*Kidnapped*
	Treasure Island
Stewart, Mary	*Nine Coaches Waiting*
Swift, Jonathan	*Gulliver's Travels*
Tarkington, Booth	*Alice Adams*
	The Gentleman from Indiana
Thoreau, Henry	*David Walden*
Thurber, James	*The White Deer*
Tolkien, J.R.R.	*The Hobbit*
	The Lord of the Rings
Trapp, Maria A.	*The Story of the Trapp Family Singers*
Twain, Mark	*The Prince and the Pauper*
	The Adventures of Huckleberry Finn
Washington, Booker T.	*Up From Slavery*
White, T.	*The Once and Future King*
Wibberly, Leonard	*The Mouse that Roared*
Wyss, Johan	*The Swiss Family Robinson*

Girls 9ᵗʰ Grade and Up...

Abbott, J.	*Mary Queen of Scots*
Adams, Richard	*Watership Down*
Anthony, K.	*Catherine the Great*
	Queen Elizabeth
Austin, Jane	*Emma*
	Pride and Prejudice
Bernanos, George	*The Diary of a Country Priest*
Bjorn, Thyra	*Papa's Wife*
Boulle, Pi ere	*The Bridge Over the River Kwai*
Bowen, Catherine	*Yankee from Olympus*
Braithwaite, E.R.	*To Sir, With Love*
Bronte, Emily	*Jane Eyre*
Brown, Dee	*Bury My Heart at Wounded Knee*
Browning, Robert	*Famous Poems*

Bunyan, J.	*Pilgrim's Progress*
Burdick, E.	*Fail-Safe*
Cather, Willa	*My Antonia*
	Death Comes for the Archbishop
Cervantes	*Don Quixote*
Chaucer	*The Canterbury Tales*
Chesterton, G.K.	*The Everlasting Man*
Churchill, Winston	*The Crisis*
Cooper, James F.	*The Spy*
	The Last of the Mohicans
Costain, T.	*The Tontine*
	The Silver Chalice
	The Three Edwards
	The Last Plantagenets
	The Conquering Family
	The Magnificent Century
	The Black Rose
Craven, M.	*I Heard the Owl Call My Name*
Dickens, Charles	*A Tale of Two Cities*
	Great Expectations
	David Copperfield
Dickinson, Emily	*Love Poems*
DuMaurier, D.	*Rebecca*
Eliot, Charles W.	*Virgil's Aeneid*
Eliot, George	*Silas Marner*
Ferber, Edna	*Show Boat*
Freedman, Benedict	*Mrs. Mike; the Story of Katherine*
	Mary Flannigan
Griffin, James	*Black Like Me*
Hemingway, Ernest	*The Snows of Kilimanjaro*
Hemon, Louis	*Maria Chapdelaine*
Hersey, J.	*Hiroshima*
	A Single Pebble
Lewis, C.S.	*Narnia Chronicles*
Massie, R.K.	*Nicholas and Alexandria*
Maxwell, G.	*Ring of Bright Water*
Melville, H.	*Billy Budd*

	Moby Dick
Monsarrat, Nicholas	*The Cruel Sea*
Morris, Edita	*The Flowers of Hiroshima*
Nathan, Robert	*Portrait of Jennie*
Orczy, Baroness	*The Scarlet Pimpernal*
Orwell, George	*Animal Farm*
Paton, Alan	*Cry the Beloved Country*
Renault, Mary	*The King Must Die*
	The Bull from the Sea
Richter, Conrad	*The Trees*
	The Fields
	The Town
	The Lady
Robinson, H.M.	*The Cardinal*
Shaw, Bernard	*Pygmalion*
Sienkiewicz, R.	*Quo Vadis*
Sinclair, Upton	*The Jungle*
Stevenson, R.L	*Dr. Jekyll and Mr. Hyde*
Taylor, Joshua C.	*Learning to Look: A Handbook for the Visual Arts*
Thackeray, W.	*Monsieur Beaucaire*
	The Beautiful Lady
	Vanity Fair
Van Dyke, Henry	*The Other Wiseman*
Wallace, Lew	*Ben Hur*
Wilder, Thornton	*Our Town*

Boys 7th Grade and Up...

Northridge Preparatory School For Boys in Niles, Illinois recommends the following books as enjoyable and worthwhile reading for boys in grades 7, 8, 9,and 10. Most of the titles are available in paperback editions.

Adamson, Joy	*Born Free*
Aldrich,T. B.	*The Story of a Bad Boy*

Armstrong, William H.	*Sounder*
Arnold, Elliott	*Broken Arrow*
Bartos-Hoppner, B.	*The Cossacks*
Boyd, James	*Drums*
Braymer, Marjorie	*The Walls of Windy*
Troy Carson, Rachel	*The Edge of the Sea*
	The Sea Around Us
Catton, Bruce	*Banners at Shenandoah*
	A Stillness at Appomattox
Childers, Erskine	*The Riddle of the Sands*
Clark, Walter	*The Ox-Bow Incident*
Cooper, James Fenimore	*Last of the Mohicans*
Corbett, Jim	*Man-Eaters of Kumoan*
Cousey, Robert	*Basketball Is MY Life*
Dana, Richard Henry	*Two Years Before the Mast*
Daugherty, James	*Daniel Boone*
Day, Clarence	*Life With Father*
de Kruif, Paul	*Microbe Hunters*
Diaz, Bernal	*The Conquest of Mexico*
Dickens, Charles	*Oliver Twist*
	A Tale of Two Cities
Dooley, Dr. Thomas A.	*Night They Burned the Mountain*
Doyle, Arthur Conan	*Adventures of Sherlock Holmes*
	Hound of the Baskervilles
Edmonds, Walter D.	*Drums Along the Mohawk*
Ellsburg, Edward	*"I Have Just Begun to Fight"—*
	The Story of John Paul Jones
	Men Under the Sea
Forbes, Esther	*Paul Revere and the World He Lived In*
Forester, C. S.	*Captain Horatio Hornblower*

Gipson, Fred	*Old Yeller*
Golding, Morton Jo	*Mystery of the Vikings in America*
Grahame, Kenneth	*Wind in the Willows*
Haggard, Ho Rider	*King Solomon's Mines*
Heyerdahl, Thor	*Kon-Tiki*
	The Ra Expeditions
Hillary, Sir Edmund (ed.)	*Challenge of the Unknown*
Hough, Clara	*Leif the Lucky*
Hunt, Sir John	*Conquest of Everest*
Innes, Hammond	*Wreck of the Mary Deare*
Lamb, Harold	*Alexander the Great*
Lindbergh, Charles	*Spirit of St. Louis*
London, Jack	*Call of the Wild*
Nordhoff and Hall	*Mutiny on the Bounty*
	Men Against the Sea
Parkman, Francis	*The Oregon Trail*
Rawlings, Marjorie	*The Yearling*
Rayner, D. A.	*The Enemy Below*
Rice, Grantland	*The Tumult and the Shouting*
Roberts, Kenneth	*Northwest Passage*
	Oliver Wiswell
	Rabble in Arms
Ryan, Cornelius	*The Longest Day*
Sandburg, Carl	*Abe Lincoln Grows Up*
Schaefer, Jack	*Shane*
Scott, Sir Walter	*Ivanhoe*
Shipper, K. B.	*Men, Microscopes, and Living Things*
Sperry, Armstrong	*Danger to Windward*
	Frozen Fire
Stevenson, Robert Louis	*Black Arrow*
	Dr. Jekyl and Mr. Hyde
	Kidnapped
	Treasure Island
Sutcliff, R.	*Robin Hood*
Tarkington, Booth	*Monsieur Beaucaire*

	Penrod
Tolkien, J. R. R.	*The Hobbit /Lord of the Rings*
Trumbull, Robert	*The Raft*
Twain, Mark	*Adventures of Huckleberry Finn*
	Adventures of Tom Sawyer
Ullman, James Ramsey	*Banner in the Sky*
Verne, Jules	*Journey to the Center of the Earth*
	20,000 Leagues Under the Sea
	Mysterious Island
White, T. H.	*The Sword in the Stone*
Wibberly, Leonard	*The Epics of Everest*
Wister, Owen	*The Virginian*
Wren, Percival	*Beau Geste*
Wodehouse, P. G.	*All About Jeeves*
	Blandings Castle
Wyss, Johann	*Swiss Family Robinson*

Boys 9ᵗʰ Grade And Up...

Agee, James	*A Death in the Family*
Beston, Henry	*The Outermost House*
Carson, Rachel	*The Sea Around Us*
Cather, Willa	*My Antonia*
	0 Pioneers
	Shadows on the Rocks
Catton, Bruce	*The Coming Fury*
Collins, Wilkie	*The Moonstone*
Conrad, Joseph	*Typhoon*
	Youth
Cooper, James Fenimore	*The Deerslayer*
	The Spy
Costain,Thomas B.	*The Conquering Family*
	William the Conqueror
DeFoe, Daniel	*Robinson Crusoe*
Dickens, Charles	*Great Expectations*
	David Copperfield
Forester, C. S.	*Last Nine Days of the Bismarck*

Galsworthy, John	*The Forsythe Saga*
Greene, Graham	*The Power and the Glory*
Hardy, Thomas	*Far From the Madding Crowd*
Hemingway, Ernest	*The Old Man and the Sea*
Heyerdahl, Thor	*Aku-Aku*
Homer	*The Iliad*
	The Odyssey
Howells, W. D.	*The Rise of Silas Lapham*
James, Henry	*The Turn of the Screw*
Kantor, Mackinlay	*Andersonville*
Lee, Harper	*To Kill a Mockingbird*
Lord, Walter	*Day of Infamy*
	A Night to Remember
Miller, William	*A Canticle for Liebowitz*
Morehead, Alan	*The Blue Nile*
	The White Nile
Morison, Samuel Eliot	*Admiral of the Ocean Sea*
	John Paul Jones
	European Discovery of America
	Vol. I — Northern Voyages
	Vol. II - Southern Voyages
O'Connor, Edwin	*The Edge of Sadness*
	The Last Hurrah
Paton, Alan	*Cry, the Beloved Country*
Philbrick, Herbert	*I Led Three Lives*
Remarque, Erich	*All Quiet on the Western Front*
Roberts, Kenneth	*Arundel*
	Northwest Passage
	Rabble in Arms
Ryan, Cornelius	*The Longest Day*
Sayers, Dorothy	*Murder Must Advertise*
	The Nine Tailors
	Unpleasantness at the Bollona Club
Steinbeck, John	*The Grapes of Wrath*
	Of Mice and Men
	The Pearl
	The Zimmerman Telegram

Tregaskis, Richard	*Guadalcanal Diary*
Tuchman, Barbara	*The Guns of August*
Waugh, Evelyn	*Brideshead Revisited*
	End of the Battle
	A Handful of Dust
	Scoop
Wodehouse. P. G.	*Laughing Gas*
	Louder and Funnier
Wouk. Herman	*The Caine Mutiny*

Advance Reading List...

For teens interested in political science and philosophy here is a proposed reading list put together by a professor of political philosophy, Dr. John Gueguen.

Prologues:

Mortimer Adler, *How to Read a Book* (1940)
Christopher Derrick, *Escape from Skepticism: Liberal Education as If Truth Mattered* (1977)

A Text:

John Wild, *Introduction to Realistic Philosophy* (1948)

Context:

José Ortega y Gasset, *Revolt of the Masses* (1929)
Nikolai Berdyaev, *The Fate of Man in the Modern World* (1935)
Romano Guardini, *The End of the Modern World* (1956)

Interesting Political Lives:

St. Thomas More: William Roper, *Life of Sir Thomas More* (1584)
St. Louis IX: Jean de Joinville, *The Life of St. Louis* (1309)
St. Catherine of Siena: *The Letters* (1380)
For contrast: Jacques Maritain, *Three Reformers: Descartes, Luther, Rousseau* (1928)

Classical lives:

Plato, *The Apology of Socrates*; *The Crito* (c 375 B.C.)
Plutarch, *Lives of Eminent Greeks and Romans* (110 A.D.)

American Lives:

The Correspondence of John Adams and Thomas Jefferson (1780-1826) [ed., Lester Cappon]
Richard Hofstadter, *The American Political Tradition and the Men Who Made It* (1951) [esp. Lincoln]

Fictional lives: [the context of all three is war]

Herman Melville, *Billy Budd, Sailor* (1891)
Stephen Crane, *The Red Badge of Courage* (1895)
Antoine de St.-Exupéry, *The Little Prince* (1943)

Thoughts on our political system:

Alexis de Tocqueville, *Democracy in America* (1835-1840)
Walter Lippmann, *Essays on the Public Philosophy* (1955)
Aleksandr Solzhenitsyn, *A World Split Apart* (1978) [the Harvard speech]
Jean-Francois Revel, *How Democracies Perish* (1984)

For contrast:

Thomas More, *Utopia* (1516)
Fyodor Dostoevsky, *The Possessed* [or The Devils] (1871)
Frank Sheed, *Society and Sanity* (1953)
William Miller, *A Canticle for Leibowitz* (1959)
Aleksandr Solzhenitsyn, *The First: Circle* (1968)

Concluding and always timely advice:

Cicero, *On Duties* [or *On the Offices*] (45 B.C.)

Appendix C

Resources on Harry Potter

Articles:

Michael D. O'Brien, "Harry Potter and the Paganization of Children's Culture," *Catholic World Report*, April 2001.

USA TODAY editorial by Ken McCormick (no date).

Audio tapes:

Michael O'Brien's critique of the Potter series is available on audio tape at www.surprisedbytruth.com

Faith and Family Live presents "Parental Concerns About Harry Potter," #F186. This tape features Steve Wood, O'Brien, Fr. Scott and Mrs. Dudro. Can be purchased at www.dads.org or write to Faith and Family Center, P.O. Box 660, Port Charlotte, FL 33949.

St. Joseph's Communications presents a three-tape set entitled "The Trouble with Harry," with Matthew Arnold. It can be purchased from www.stjoe.com or by calling (800) 526-2151 or (661) 822-2050 or writing St. Joseph's Communications at P.O. Box 1911 St., Tekachapi, CA 93581.

Books:

Michael D. O'Brien, *A Landscape With Dragons: The Battle for Your Child's Mind* (Ignatius Press, 1998).

Fr. Gabriel Amorth, *An Exorcist Tells His Story* (Ignatius Press, 1999). This book does not address the Harry Potter books but rather the rise and problems of witchcraft and sorcery in our culture.

Video tapes:

Frightening Fantasies: Harry Potter and the Paganization of Our Children's Culture by Living His

Life Abundantly, Int'l, Inc. Two-60 minute videos. ID # FF-ALBUM. These can be purchased by calling (800) 558-5452 or through www.lhla.org

Websites:

Check out the Zenit Web site. Search the archives for the December 6, 18 and December 20, 2001 interviews with Michael D. O'Brien (ZE1121820 and ZE011122021). Two other sources: www.catholiceducation.org and www.studiobrien.com

Check out the CANA Web site of Marcia Montenegro who was a former occult practitioner. As a former practitioner of the occult, she describes the dangers readers of the series can encounter.

EWTN Online Services: Go to the "Faith" menu at the bottom of their home page and click on "Catholic Q & A," then "Frequently Asked Questions." Harry Potter is on the list.

www.crossroad.to/text/articles/Harry_&_Witchcraft.htm

www.letusreason.org (search under current trends)

www.crossroad.to/News/Harry.html

Family Friendly Libraries at www.fflibraries.org

www.worthynews.com/news-features/harry-potter-3.html

World On The Web: www.worldmag.com/world/issue/10-30-99/cover_1.asp

Check out the Web sites of Focus on the Family and the American Family Association for updates on this series of books.
www.cwnews.com/news/viewrec.cfm?refnum=13581

BIBLIOGRAPHY

Aquinas, St. Thomas. *Summa theologiae.*

Armenio, Fr. Peter and Hoffman, Fr. Frank. "The Effects of Music, TV, and Movies On Youth." Springfield, IL.

Ball, Ann . *Modern Saints, Their Lives and Faces, Book One.* Rockford, 1983.
Modern Saints, Their Lives and Faces, Book Two.

Barbour, Scott "Violence in the Media." San Diego, 1995.

Baudouin-Croix, Marie. *Léonie Martin, A Difficult Life.* Dublin, 1993.

Beevers, John. *Saint Therese, The Little Flower (The Making of a Saint).* Garden City, 1955.
Storm of Glory. Garden City, 1955.
Abandonment to Divine Providence. NY, 1975.

Bernal, Salvador. *A Profile of Msgr. Escrivá, Founder of Opus Dei.* NY, 1977.

Blum, S.J., Virgil C. "Secretary Bennett's Last Challenge," *Catholic League Newsletter*, Aug., 1988.

Bockhorn, Lee. "A Republic on the Rise, With Powerful Minds and Earnest Prayers," *The Wall Street Journal*, Feb. 4, 2002.

Brown, Katie. "Singing Violence," Springfield, 2000.

Budnik, Mary Ann. "How The Forgiones Raised A Saint," *Padre Pio The Wonder Worker.* New Bedford, 1999.
"Heroic Parents—Models For Our Times," *St. Thérèse— Doctor of the Little Way.* New Bedford, 1997.
Looking for Peace? Try Confession!, Springfield, IL, 2000
"The La Salette Seers—Faithful to Their Mission," *Marian Shrines of France.* New Bedford, 1998.
You Can Become A Saint! Springfield, IL, 2000.

Caldwell, Taylor. *Tender Victory.* NY, 1957.

Cappasso, Tony. "Jacob, Emily most popular names," *State-Journal Register,* Jan. 18, 2001.

Cassel, Ingri "Homosexuality A Required School Topic?" *Spotlight*, July 17, 2000.

Catechism of the Catholic Church. Boston, 1994.

Catechism of the Council of Trent. 1972 edition.

Catholic Times. "In naming kids, Catholic parents pick Jennifer over Mary." Oct. 28, 2001.
"Downpour greets day of prayer for rain in parched West Texas," Sept. 9, 2001.
"Two families with five priests, reflect on God's gift," *May* 27, 2001.

Castillo, Professor Gerardo. "Educating In the Faith," Instituto de Ciencias de la Educación, University of Navarre, 1987.

Chrysostom, St. John. *Homilies on St. Matthew.*

Ciszek, SJ,Walter J. *With God In Russia.* NY, 1966.

Clarke, O.C.D., John. *Story of a Soul.* Washington, D.C., 1972.

Collins, Glenn . "Reading To Children: It Runs In Families," *New York Times,* 1982.

Congregation for Divine Worship, *Ordo initiationis Christianae, Praenotanda generalia.*

Congregation for the Doctrine of the Faith, *Libertatis conscientia.* 1986

Congregation for the Sacraments and Congregation for the Clergy, Declaration, Mar. 24, 1973.

Day, Dorothy. *Therese.* Springfield, IL.

DiMucci, Dion. "The Wanderer Comes Home," *Envoy.* May-June 1999.

Dirvin, C.M., Joseph I. *Mrs. Seton.* NY, 1962.

Ducrocq, Marie-Pascale. *Therese of Lisieux, (A Vocation of Love).* New York, 1982.

Eymard, St. Peter Julian. *In The Light Of The Monstrance.* Cleveland, 1947.

Escrivá, St. Josemaría. *Furrow.* New York, 1987.

    Christ Is Passing By. New York, 1982.

    Conversations With Mgr. Escrivá De Balaguer. Dublin,1969.

Foner, P. Samuel. "U.S. Middle School Textbooks Riddled With Errors," *Spotlight*, Jan. 29, 2001.

Fourth Lateran Council.

Fox, Fr. Robert J. *Saints & Heroes Speak Vol. One.* Alexandria, SD, 1996.

    Saints & Heroes Speak Vol. Three. Alexandria, SD, 1996.

Gablers, The Mel . "Humanism in Textbooks (Secular Religion In The Classroom)," 1983.

Gerrard, Rev. Thomas J. *Marriage and Parenthood, The Catholic Ideal.* NY, 1911.

Grigus, OFM Conv., Fr. John P. "Eucharist, God Among Us." *Call To Holiness,* Eastpointe, MI, Spring 2002.

Haffert, John. *A Letter from Lisieux.* Sea Isle City, 1942.

Hardon, S.J., John. *50th Anniversary Homily.*

    "Sacrifice and Vocations," *Call to Holiness News,* Vol. 5, No.1, Winter 2001.

    The Catholic Catechism. Garden City, 1975.

    The Sacraments and The Marian Catechist. Bardstown, 1998.

Harvard Women's Healthy Watch. "At the Heart of Recovery, Personal Resilience," Nov. 2001, Volume IX, #4.

Harvey, Linda P. *Choice 4 Truth*, "Ohio Officials Say 'No' To Dollars from CDC," May, 2000.

Hatke, Roseanna. "November Newsletter." Indiana, 2000.

H. Daniel-Rops. *The Church Of Apostles And Martyrs,* New York, 1960.
          The Church In The Dark Ages. New York, 1959.

Helming, Dennis M. *Footprints In The Snow.* NY, 1985.

Hoever, SO, Cist., Ph.D., Rev. Hugo. *Lives of the Saints Vol. I and Vol. II.* NY, 1999.

Hunter, James Davison. "Evangelical Schools in Growth, Catholic Schools in Decline," *Wall Street Journal,* Sept. 8, 1988.

Inside the Vatican. January, 1994. Quoted in the book *Call of the Ages* by Thomas W. Petrisko. Santa Barbara, 1995.

Jipping, Thomas L. "Youth Violence Parallels Violent Music." NLJ ONLINE, June, 1999.

John Paul I. *Illustrissimi,* Letters from Pope John Paul I. Boston, 1978.

John Paul II. Address to the 3rd International Congress on the Family, 1978.
          Address, May 13, 1979.
          Address to religious education leaders-Superdome, New Orleans, Sept. 12, 1987.
          Address to the plenary session of the Congregation for the Sacraments, April 17, 1986.
          Address, Aug. 20, 2000.
          Audience. March 1, 2000.
          Apost. Exhort. *Familiaris Consortio.* 1981.
          Apost. Exhort. *Catechesi tradendae. 1979.*
          Gravissimum educationis.
          Novo Millennio Ineunte. 2000.
          Veritatis Splendor.

Jones, Kenneth C. "Suffer the Children to Come unto Me: Parents as Teachers," *St. Louis Observer,* July 1994.

King, Henry V. "Archbishop Egan Pushes For School Vouchers," *The Wanderer,* July 13, 2000.

Knox, Ronald. Translation of *Autobiography of St. Therese.* New York, 1958.

Kreeft, Peter. "Being Catholic," *Talking To Your Children About Being Catholic.* IN, 1995.

Krieger, Lisa M. "Study of Violence on Music Videos." *World Africa Network* Apr. 8, 1998.

Leifeld, Wendy. *Mothers of the Saints.* Ann Arbor, 1991.

Leo XIII. *Enc. Nobilissima Gallorum gens.* 1884.

Lucas, Bishop George J. "Our Catholics schools are integral part of Church's mission," *Catholic Times,* Jan. 27, 2002.

Lockwood, Robert P. "Anti-Catholicism and the History of Catholic School Funding," *Catalyst,* March 2000.

Lucia, Sr. Maria. *Fatima In Lucia's Own Words II-5th and 6th Memoirs,* Edited by

Fr. Louis Kondor, SVD. Fatima, 1999.

Matthew, Margaret and Bunson, Stephen. *John Paul II's Book Of Saints.* Huntington, 1999.

Martin, Malachi. *The Keys Of This Blood.* NY, 1990.

McCloskey, C. John. *Catholic Position Papers,* "The Family: Seedbed of Vocations." Princeton, NJ, 1998.

McCullough, David. *John Adams.* NY, 2001.

McGovern, Thomas J. *Sir Thomas More: The Making of a Saint.* New Rochelle, 1986.

Menninger, Karl. *Whatever Became of Sin?* New York, 1973.

Metzler, John J. "American Students Get Average Grades On Global Report Card," *The Wanderer,* Dec. 21, 2000.

Miles, Austin. "Public Schools Embrace Islam—A Shocker," ASSIST News Service, Jan. 9, 2002.

Mission: America, "News On Homosexual Issues," Fall, 1999.

Molinié, O.P., Fr. M. D. *The Struggle of Jacob.* NJ, 1977.

Monaghan, Mr. Thomas. Interview, 2000.

Monforte, Josemaria. G*etting To Know The Bible.* New Jersey, 1998.

Montalban, Ricardo. "In The Heart of Tinseltown, A Faith Lived Deeply," *BE.* March-April 2000.

Morice, Henri. *The Apostolate of Moral Beauty.* St .Louis, 1961.

Murphy, Dr. Madonna M. *Character education In America's Blue Ribbon Schools.* Lancaster, 1998.

Murphy, Sr. M. Veronica. *Catholic Society of Evangelists Newsletter.* August, 1999.

Newton, James. *Uncommon Friends.* NY, 1987.

Oben, Ph.D., Freda Mary. *Edith Stein, Scholar, Feminist, Saint.* NY, 1988.

Parker-Pope, Tara. "More Physicians Make Spiritual Well-Being Part of Health Profiles," The *Wall Street Journal,* (no date) Fall, 2001.

Paul VI, *Encyclical Ecclesiam Suam.*

Piat, O.F.M., Stephane-Joseph. *Celine, Sister Genevieve of the Holy Face.* San Francisco, 1997.

     The Story of a Family (The Home of the Little Flower). New York, 1948.

Pio, St. Padre. "Letters To Raffaelina," *Voice of Padre Pio,* no date.

Pius X, St. *Decr. Quam singular.* August 8, 1910.

Pius XI, *Enc. Divini illius Magistri.* 1929.

     Enc. Ubi arcano. 1922.

Plus, SJ, Raoul. *Christ In The Home.* NY, 1951.

Powers, Ann. "The Stresses of Youth, the Strains of the Music," *New York Times,* April 25, 1999.

Rause, Vince. "Searching for the Divine," *Reader's Digest,* December 2001.

Religious Life, March, 2000.

Riches, John. *Elucidations.* San Francisco, 1975.

Rinaldi, Rich . "The Legacy of Madalyn Murray O'Hair," Register Radio News Correspondent. No date.

Rohrbach, O.C.D., Peter-Thomas. *The Search for Saint Therese.* Garden City, 1961.   *Saint Therese of Lisieux: Her Life, Times and Teaching.*

Scanlon, TOR, Fr. Michael and Cirner, Randall J. *Deliverance From Evil Spirits.* Ann Arbor, 1980.

Scepter Notes. *The Sacraments,Sources of Christian Life.*

Schicker, Maryann. "Epiphany is feast rich in church, family traditions," *Catholic Times*, Jan. 6, 2002.

Shirk, Martha. "Expert: Families Need Aid," *St. Louis Post-Dispatch*, June 20, 1992.

Smith, Dr. Janet E. "The Sacraments and the Moral Life," *Magnificat,* Vol. 3, No. 8, Oct. 2001.

Smith, Fr. Robert D. "The Mark of Faith," *The Wanderer*, no date.

Strohl, Lydia. "Faith Heals", *Reader's Digest,* May, 2001.

Suso, Bl. Henry. *The Exemplar, Volume Two.* Dubuque, Iowa, 1962.

Tanner, Lindsey. "Academy: Youngsters Should Not Specialize," *The State Journal-Register,* July 4, 2000.

The Atlanta-Journal-Constitution , "Mother Teresa expressed doubts." Sept. 15, 2001.

The Humanist, Jan.-Feb., 1983.

Thein, Reverend Edward J. Homily notes, Aug. 2001.

The New Testament (Confraternity of Christian Doctrine). New York, 1960.

The Wall Street Journal. "Sons of Liberty," Dec. 7, 2001.
                          "Tony & Tacky," Oct. 20, 2000.
                          "Girl Meets Boy," Aug. 3, 2001.

The Wanderer. "Thousands Attend Fatima Family Congress," June 25, 1998.

Trochu, Abbe Francis. *The Curé D'Ars.* Rockford, 1977.

Troy, Gil. "His New Fraternity," *The Wall Street Journal*, June 15, 2000.

Van De Putte, C.S.SP., Rev. Walter. *Following the Holy Spirit.* NY, 1978.

Vatican Council II, *Apostolicam Actuositatem*, no. 11.

Vianney, St. John. "We Must Persevere," *Sermons of the Cure D'Ars*. MN, 1901.

Vitz, Prof. Paul. "Catholic Manhood." Springfield, IL.

The Vatican II Weekday Missal. Boston, 1975.

Vaudouin-Croix, Marie. *Léonie Martin, A Difficult Life.* Dublin. 1993.

Vázquez de Prada, Andrés. *The Founder of Opus Dei, The Life of Josemaría Escrivá ,* Vol. 1. NJ, 2001.

Von Balthasar, Hans Urs. *Therese Of Lisieux (The Story of a Mission).* New York, 1954.

Williams, Chris. "Parents organizing to get days off for busy kids," *Houston Chronicle*, Aug. 16, 2000.

Zdrojewski, CSSF, Mary Felicita. *To Weave A Garment.* Connecticut, 1989.

Zenit. Jan. 9, 2000.

      Jan. 30, 2000.

      Feb. 25, 2000.

      May 11, 2000.

      May 15, 2000

      Aug. 15, 2000.

      Aug. 17, 2000.

      Sept. 14, 2000

      Sept. 27, 2000.

      Oct. 6, 2000.

      Oct. 18, 2000.

      Nov. 10, 2000.

      Nov. 19, 2000.

      July 15, 2001.

      July 16, 2001.

      July 30, 2001.

      Aug. 1, 2001.

      Aug. 2, 2001.

      Oct. 2, 2001.

      Oct. 21, 2001.

      Oct. 22, 2001.

      Oct. 30, 2001.

      Nov. 4, 2001.

      Jan. 28, 2002.

Index

YOU CAN BECOME A SAINT!

by
Mary Ann Budnik

"The best kept secret in the world is that God created you to be a saint! Since your vocation is your path to holiness, learn how to use it to become a saint!"

You Are Called To Be A Saint!

Sainthood isn't optional. We are all called to holiness by virtue of our baptism. Pope John Paul II told us New Orleans in 1987: "The world needs...saints. Holiness is not the privilege of a few; it is a gift offered to all."

But Aren't Saints Special People?

No! Robert Louis Stevenson writes: *The saints are the sinners who keep on trying.* Saints are people like you and like me. *No one* is born a saint. Saints become saints by the way they live their lives. Our sanctity depends on how we use our free will to cooperate with God's grace. With the grace of God, our determination, and applying what the experts consider the A B C's of becoming a saint, we can all grow in holiness. Mary Ann Budnik writes in a simple to understand, conversational tone...as though the author was chatting one on one with you over a cup of coffee.

What Topics Are Covered?

Topics include the universal call to sanctity; the various types of graces and how they effect our souls; the theological virtues, moral virtues and natural virtues and how we can obtain them; a plan for growing in holiness; how to sanctify daily work; how to order your life; the role of your guardian angel; mental prayer and its necessity; the importance of daily spiritual reading and scripture reading; what to read to grow in holiness; the problem of sin, the commandments, and the sacrament of penance; the power of Holy Mass and the Blessed Sacrament and why we need them; how to develop devotion to Our Lady and her rosary; why suffer?; how to perseverance in striving for holiness; along with fascinating examples from the lives of the saints.

"To read this book is to change your life." **St. Louis**
"This book has made such an impact on my life." **Wichita**